Country Life at Peeper Pond Farm

By David A. Umling

With a contribution from Barbara A. Umling

© 2019 by David A. Umling

U.S. Copyright Office Registration - TXu 2-145-952

All Rights Reserved

All pictures by David and Barbara Umling

Reproduction or reuse in any form of any portions of this book or the images contained therein without advance written permission from the author is expressly prohibited.

Printed by Kindle Direct Publishing – Seattle, WA

Library of Congress Control Number – 2020909044

A special thank you to my wife, Barbara, for her writing contribution (*Post 118: Sew Many Pieces*) and her gracious assistance in editing this book.

This book is dedicated to our remaining small family dairy farms and the farmers who desperately struggle against all odds to keep them operating.

About this book and its author:

My life has taken me many places within this country that most people have never seen or experienced. That observation is also the point of my book. I want to tell you stories of true farm living—both funny and sad. I want to explain the core values that farmers live by and that govern how they view life. But, most of all, I want to teach you how to understand farmers and farming issues from *their* perspective. After all, these are the people who raised me. Even though I left farming for 37 years to live life in the modern, outside world, I was drawn back to it in my retirement. Farmers are my people, and I have come to understand them well. I want to teach you how they are different from the average urban-dweller of today. I also want you to understand how you need to broaden your perspective to truly respect and embrace them. True enlightenment is gained by broadening your understanding, not by casually ignoring or selectively dismissing what you don't wish to consider.

As for the farmers I represent, I want my book to inspire and empower you. I want you to feel gratified that someone truly understands and puts into words things you wish you could have said many times before. I want to make you feel proud of being a farmer and of the sacrifices you have made for others—many of whom simply fail to appreciate them. I want you to know that someone will support you and how you think. It's easy for farmers to feel overlooked and marginalized today, and I want to assure you that some people can see it differently. I want you to be secure in the knowledge that you are not wrong simply because your basic values and perspective on life are very different from those living in the modern outside world.

I hope my book is all these things to all my readers. But, in the final analysis, it's the true story of a farmer and a farm life lived as fully and traditionally as possible—within the economic constraints imposed by modern society. I hope I can persuade all of you to cherish our traditional rural folkways and lifestyles as much as I do. That was our mission for Peeper Pond Farm, and it remains my underlying goal in life. I hope in writing about it, I can help you see and understand life for what it really is and for what it can be.

David lives with his wife of 28 years, Barbara, on Peeper Pond Farm in the northern Pendleton County community of Brushy Run, WV. Having lived the first eighteen years of his life on a small family dairy farm, David has been an outspoken advocate for rural communities and their special needs throughout his 30-year professional planning career, from which he retired in 2017. David is the author of two previous books, Lifestyle Lost (2012, Xlibris) and Reflections on My Lives: An Adoptee's Story (2014, Amazon Kindle).

Contents

Introduction 1
   My Dairy Farm Upbringing 1
   Understanding A Farmer's Way of Life 3
   The Evolution of Peeper Pond Farm 6
   The Purpose of This Book 13

Post 1: Welcome to Peeper Pond Farm 15
Post 2: A Lifestyle Lost 17
Post 3: Why Would I Want to Do All That Farm Work? 20
Post 4: Final Arrangements 23
Post 5: The Fine Art of Fencing 26
Post 6: A Three Season Weekend 29
Post 7: A New Day Dawns 31
Post 8: Early Signs of Spring 33
Post 9: Angel's Breath 35
Post 10: Our First Goat Kids Are Born! 37
Post 11: Sugarin' Time 38
Post 12: Winter's Snowy Reprieve 39
Post 13: Essie & Gertie Come Home 41
Post 14: Introducing Essie & Gertie To the Great Outdoors 43
Post 15: Preparing the Garden for Spring Planting 44
Post 16: Peeper Pond Farm Comes to Life 46
Post 17: Dignity 49
Post 18: Welcoming Cara 52
Post 19: Forty Shades of Green 54
Post 20: Blackwater 55
Post 21: A Year of Goat Experience in One Day 57
Post 22: Presenting Our Dancing Lady 62
Post 23: Goats & Tractors Are People Too 64
Post 24: Memories 67

Post 25: Thank You PPF Website Patrons 70
Post 26: Legendary Pendleton County 73
Post 27: Goat Milking Basics 77
Post 28: Trout Fishing in Smoke Hole Canyon 81
Post 29: Swarm! 83
Post 30: Bear Rocks 85
Post 31: Ferguson Is Back on the Job 87
Post 32: Spruce Knob 90
Post 33: Our Canaan Valley Escape 92
Post 34: Our Garden of Plenty 94
Post 35: Livestock Fugitives 97
Post 36: Bye, Bye Billie 99
Post 37: Remembering Ninny 100
Post 38: The Great Pumpkins Are Coming! 103
Post 39: Deluge 105
Post 40: And Then There Were Four 107
Post 41: Tri-County Fair 110
Post 42: The Old Ways 112
Post 43: Fox Hunt 116
Post 44: Kaput 118
Post 45: As the Seasons Turn 121
Post 46: The State Fair of West Virginia 123
Post 47: The Total Solar Eclipse of 2017 125
Post 48: Brandywine Lake 129
Post 49: Harvesting the Bounty of the Land 131
Post 50: Treasure Mountain Festival 133
Post 51: The Peeper Pond Farm Story 135
Post 52: Peeper Pond Farm Goes Leaf Peeping 137
Post 53: To Market, To Market 139
Post 54: Putting the Garden to Bed 141

Post 55: Making Cider – A Pressing Issue 143
Post 56: Anyone Want Some Fresh Honey Cornbread?... 145
Post 57: A Peeper Pond Farm Ghost Story? 146
Post 58: As Fall Fades Away 150
Post 59: Reunions 152
Post 60: Christmas Spirit 155
Post 61: Meet Our New Kitten, Calli 157
Post 62: Caring for the Carroll Farm 159
Post 63: The Pit of Winter 161
Post 64: What the Reaper Sowed 163
Post 65: Spring Returns to Peeper Pond Farm 165
Post 66: Essie's First Doe Kid 166
Post 67: The Lion Roars 167
Post 68: A Lackluster Snowfall Season 169
Post 69: "Udder" Disappointment 173
Post 70: Spring Fever 177
Post 71: The Demise of a Legacy 178
Post 72: Sacred Places 179
Post 73: How's the garden doing, Mary? 182
Post 74: Waterworld 185
Post 75: Man, I Lived It, Too 187
Post 76: Calli's Catch 193
Post 77: All Washed Up 196
Post 78: Practicing Hydroponics 199
Post 79: Sinks of Gandy 201
Post 80: WHSV Tells Our Story 204
Post 81: Reaping Wheat – A Shocking Experience 211
Post 82: Farmer's market 2018 & Our Trash Bandit 216
Post 83: Coalwood 220
Post 84: Bringing in the Sheaves 223

- Post 85: Extracting Liquid Gold from the Hives 225
- Post 86: Our Deer Hunter 228
- Post 87: 2018 Tri-County Fair 232
- Post 88: The Romaine Tenney Legacy 235
- Post 89: Winnowing It All Down 241
- Post 90: Our Abandoned Doe Returns 243
- Post 91: A Dairy Kind of Day 247
- Post 92: Family Gathering 251
- Post 93: An Ode to Fall 254
- Post 94: Smithsonian 256
- Post 95: A Mist Opportunity 259
- Post 96: The Siege of Fort Seybert 261
- Post 97: Emerging from the Fog 264
- Post 98: Passing on the Tradition 266
- Post 99: Grinding Wheat 269
- Post 100: Baking Homemade Wheat Bread 273
- Post 101: Our Diminishing Farmlands 276
- Post 102: Early Winter Snow Cover 282
- Post 103: Natural Bridge 284
- Post 104: Meet Our New Official Peeper Pond Farm Meteorologist 287
- Post 105: Another Good Drenching 290
- Post 106: Happy New Year 292
- Post 107: Defending Sales of Farm Fresh Raw Milk 294
- Post 108: Our Dairy Bill Has Been Introduced! 304
- Post 109: Calli's Pink Leg 306
- Post 110: Shanksville 308
- Post 111: Imagine 312
- Post 112: Shame 315
- Post 113: Mountain Music 319
- Post 114: It's Snow Quiet Outside 323

Post 115: Turn, Turn, Turn 325
Post 116: Missing the Mark 327
Post 117: Indian Spring 329
Post 118: Sew Many Pieces 331
Post 119: Preparing Garden Soil - Back to the Basics 335
Post 120: Making Goat Milk Soap 339
Post 121: A Glimmer of Hope 342
Post 122: Whippoorwills 346
Post 123: Spring Rebirth in Smoke Hole 348
Post 124: Our Son Becomes a Homeowner 350
Post 125: Crickets 354
Post 126: Weeds 356
Post 127: Marketing Our Wares 358
Post 128: They're Baaa-ck: Essie Comes Home 360
Post 129: Catchin' Up 363
Post 130: Another Fair Showing 366
Post 131: Our Mischievous Goats 368
Post 132: Haying Season 370
Post 133: Adversity 372
Post 134: Can-Do 376
Post 135: Fall In 380
Post 136: How to Identify A Native West Virginian 382
Post 137: Autumn Glory 386
Post 138: Apple Butter Season 387
Post 139: Allegheny Gnats 389
Post 140: The Denigration of Rural America 391
Post 141: Windstorm 395
Post 142: Our Raw Milk Dairy Bill – Round 2 398
Post 143: Christmas Frost 400
Epilogue 403

A Brief History of Farming 403
What It All Means to Us 407
Appendix 411

A distant view of Peeper Pond Farm and the eastern flank of Cave Mountain as viewed from the south along Jake Hill Road (2016).

Introduction

My Dairy Farm Upbringing

I WAS RAISED on a small, family dairy farm that stretched more than 3,000 feet along the banks of the Connecticut River in North Charlestown, New Hampshire. We milked between 30 and 32 head of cows, most of which were Holsteins. We also kept one or two Jersey cows to raise the butterfat levels of the milk we produced. Our farm specialized in milk production, but we also maintained a very large vegetable garden, and we obtained most of the meat we needed from our slaughtered cows and calves.

We tried to make maple syrup for a few years when I was very young. I can barely remember tapping our maple trees and hanging sap buckets. We boiled the sap we collected in a large metal tub (we didn't have, nor could we afford, an evaporator), but we were never able to produce any syrup worth keeping. It was either too thick (overboiled) or just not very tasty (perhaps compromised by too many contaminants). After several disappointing attempts, we simply abandoned our syrup-making aspirations. Although we weren't beekeepers, we did allow one from Maryland to place six or more bee hives on our property for a number of years in exchange for a five-gallon tin of honey.

Our farm, which encompassed between 80 and 120 acres over the years, was both family-owned and operated. Except for the earliest years, when we kids were too young to work on the farm, we had no hired hands. We couldn't have afforded hired help even if we needed it. We did all of the work ourselves or with the periodic help of extended family members, primarily our maternal grandparents and one of my cousins who had an interest in farming when he was young.

During the early spring planting season, we all worked together picking rocks out of the freshly plowed fields and planting the garden. In the summer months, we loaded and unloaded what seemed like an endless number of square hay bales. I would help load the bales on a flat wagon and, as they were unloaded, receive them at the top of the hay elevator and stack them neatly in the hayloft in the top of our barn. It was dreadfully hot work, and the air was so thick with dust and chaff that we nearly suffocated as we privately prayed for each bale that marched up the elevator to be the last. We would be so covered in sweat, dust and chaff after each load was stacked that we often looked like more like miners than farmers when we emerged from the barn. Then, we would drink a large pitcher of Kool-Aid and return to the field to pick up another load. At the end of the day, we would trudge across the road to our pond and dive in to cool off. With all the accumulated chaff we wore, it was a wonder why the pond wasn't covered with a thin layer of hay after we had finished swimming.

When I was six years old, I was given my first regular farm chores. I would break up and distribute bales of hay to feed the cows before each milking, mix up milk formula and feed the calves, carry water buckets to the heifers, carry firewood from the cellar to the kitchen to fuel our antique Home Comfort wood cookstove and help my father carry milk buckets into the milk room during the twice daily milkings. I always carried the partially full buckets of milk and referred to the work as "building my muscles." I followed my father around the farm like a loyal puppy-dog whenever and wherever I could and often rode on the back of the tractor, standing with one foot on the tow bar and the other on one of the bottom three-point hitch arms, while he drove it around the barnyard. That was in the days before farm safety practices were invented. I guess I was lucky to have survived.

Over the years, my farm chores evolved to include heavier work, such as: cleaning manure out of the gutters in the barn and spreading sawdust (which we used for bedding); cutting, splitting and stacking firewood; driving the tractor to rake hay or to collect and deliver loads of hay bales to the barn; riding and operating the corn planter (which was designed to be pulled by a horse rather than our tractor); hand-milking the cows when we lost power; mowing our acre-plus of lawns (which I often tried to do with bare feet), and the obligatory "other miscellaneous farm duties as assigned." My father had very good farm work delegation skills.

I remember one time when our old sickle bar mower had broken down, I was told to mow a three-acre (more or less) field using a scythe. I had never done that before, but it needed to be done to harvest the hay before the coming rains. I spent the *full* day (from sunrise to supper time) mowing that field—stopping only to eat my lunch and as necessary to sharpen the blade as best I could with a whet stone. By the time I finished mowing, I could feel sore muscles that I didn't even know I had. I then spent the next day raking it along with two other larger fields we had mowed before the mower broke.

I also once assumed sole responsibility for operating the farm over two days (three consecutive milkings), so that my father could attend an Agway Cooperative conference in Springfield, Massachusetts. He was hoping to land a part-time sales job to supplement our meager income during the Arab Oil Embargo of the early 1970s. Finally, I remember one time following a brutal winter blizzard that we lost power for four consecutive days, and I helped my father hand-milk all the cows eight consecutive times before the power was restored. Thank heaven that occurred during the winter so that we could spend the extra time required to milk all of those cows without falling behind on other essential chores. However, it was frustrating work because we had to dump all of the milk that we couldn't drink ourselves, as we couldn't store it in our bulk tank without power to ensure the temperature of the milk was consistently maintained.

Understanding A Farmer's Way of Life

Although farming is hard and tedious work, it is not very profitable (especially family-scale dairy farming). I've heard it said many times that farming is the best way to take two million dollars and turn it into one million. We were always poor by the prevailing standards of my childhood (1962-1980), but we were never hungry. We always found a way to make do, and we never felt as poor as we appeared to be. We used outdated technology and did things by hand when it was necessary. We did without anything we could not afford to buy. Buying goods on credit was synonymous with economic slavery to us, because it would make us slaves to debt that we couldn't afford to repay.

We were so fiscally austere that we would find clever ways to avoid paying cash for the things we needed. We actually engaged in an early form of recycling. This activity my mother would not support. She routinely refused to ride with us on our infrequent trips to the town dump. As she often said, she was not going to be seen by our friends and neighbors riding in a vehicle that might leave the dump with more than it delivered. Of course, she was exaggerating about our situation, but we were not the only people who occasionally "dump-picked" over the years in Charlestown—despite all the posted signs prohibiting it. In fact, I recently learned that, in 2016, the town's voters approved funding for a new building to be built at what is now known as a "transfer station" so that waste items that remain in good (and presumably sanitary) condition could be reused by those who are less fortunate. I was told that the town already had a list of volunteers to man the station before the warrant was approved. I imagine some of the volunteers were eager to have the first pick of the recycled goods.

I also remember many times when my father would tell us to get into the car because we were going for a ride. When asked where we were going, he would only reply, "to see a man about a horse." When he told us that, we instantly knew we were going to see another farmer to barter or dicker for some item or service we needed. Whatever that was to be, we never returned with a horse. Bartering and support networks like that are one of the defining cornerstones of a traditional farming community. It empowers people to satisfy their basic needs without exchanging money.

Over time, we gradually acquired some modern technology when we could afford to buy a used item or a relative passed away leaving us with things we couldn't afford. For instance, my father eventually inherited an electric clothes dryer from his mother, which reduced our dependency on an outdoor clothesline and indoor drying racks to dry our laundry. However, the stories I can tell of our self-reliant living during my early childhood set me apart from most people who grew up during my generation. Many of the peers I have met since leaving home actually refused to believe that we lived that way during that time. Eventually, I got tired of trying to convince them. When they asked about my childhood on our farm, I would simply say that I "lived through the Great Depression during the 1960s and '70s." After all, my experiences living simply and self-reliantly during my childhood were not going to help me get ahead in the modern world.

Farm work can be unexpectedly difficult and unpleasant. It tries your determination as much as it does your physical abilities. It is not something you merely persevere; it is something you constantly struggle to accomplish. Therefore, you must be self-motivated, determined and disciplined to do the necessary work. You can't succeed in farming if you believe that society owes you a life. Farmers know and accept that success in life is never guaranteed—no matter how hard you work for it—but they also understand that you can't succeed if you don't work hard for it. They value honesty and personal integrity because they face reality on its own terms. You can't effectively overcome the adversities that life may throw at you, if you expect it to conform to your perceptions of it. The harsh realities of life are never limited or governed by our understanding of them, and adversity is not something you can simply allow to control your life without a struggle. There is always something more we don't know or expect that can interfere with our best laid plans. Farmers understand this because they face those unexpected adversities in life, so they tend to be humble and, by consequence, less pretentious or ego-driven than most other people.

Perhaps that's also why farmers internalize and live by fundamentally conservative values. Small farmers may not possess advanced college degrees, but they are far wiser than you might think. They may not be wealthy, but they are staunchly independent. Farming remains one of the few lines of work I know that can give you such a strong sense of personal freedom and independence for so little pay. It may also explain why farming is considered a way of living, rather than just another job. I was raised to internalize and respect those values throughout my childhood, and I struggled throughout my adult life to decide how to reconcile them with, and function within, the vastly different lifestyle, attitudes and values of modern society.

At this point, I feel it is important to explain what I mean when I talk about self-reliant living within the context of a rural community and why that is very different from the way most people live in the modern outside world. When I use the term self-reliance, I'm sure many people form a picture in their minds of a frontier pioneer living independently in the wilderness. That is the way the earliest settlers in our country were forced to live by their circumstances because they didn't have convenient access to manufactured goods and professional labor. However, I see that as an overly narrow perception of self-reliant living.

There are many different degrees of self-reliance, most of which can and do occur within the context of rural communities. The Amish and Native Americans prior to European settlement are prime examples. I believe that a person *can* live self-reliantly without having to live in complete isolation in the same way that we can live in a free society without having the right to do anything we want whenever we want to do it. I ask you to consider thinking about the term self-reliance as a spectrum of living experiences, rather than as a single inflexible image of pioneer living. If you can't do that, it will be difficult to understand how living in a rural community is fundamentally different from living in a modern urban society, where people are far more dependent on money to purchase goods and services from others that they lack the time or determination to do for themselves.

Those people who *aspire* to live as independently as they can, even though they can't do it all for themselves, should be considered to be *pursuing* a self-reliant lifestyle. This way of living, which is far more prevalent in rural areas, fosters very different attitudes and perspectives towards life, based on different core values than the lifestyle of conveniences and social interdependencies that is so prevalent and accepted as normal in modern urban society. That distinction is why city-dwellers have such a difficult time understanding some of the different needs and aspirations of rural people. If you try to explain that to young urban planners, who dominate the professional ranks today, you will quickly understand why I ultimately became so frustrated with the planning field in later years of my career. I simply couldn't convince them of the need to view rural issues and needs from a different sociological and ideological perspective. That is, assuming they were even willing to listen.

The Evolution of Peeper Pond Farm

Although we were not the only dairy farmers in Charlestown and surrounding areas during my childhood, they were clearly in decline. We watched several of them cease operation as I was growing up, either because they couldn't earn enough from the milk they produced to survive or the owner became too old to continue milking and the children weren't willing to farm. Our parents always told us we weren't to aspire to live as we did, and we could not expect to inherit the farm. My father suffered from emphysema and farmer's lung from years of smoking and working on the farm, and he needed to sell our farmland and operation, piece by piece, to afford the mounting medical bills. By the time he passed away in April 1984, only about 55 acres of the original farm remained. Our future, so we were told, was in the outside world, where we would go on to college and find a career that would provide us with a better living. That was what I did. It was their subtle epitaph for a traditional farming lifestyle that was coming to a sad and undignified end.

I would be lying if I said I always enjoyed farming, but it was the only life I knew and accepted. I did enjoy the rural environment in which we lived, especially the quiet nights and dark, starry skies and the changing patterns of the daytime sky and landscape. I fondly recall the reassuring sounds of wildlife that drifted through the air and changed with the ebb and flow of the seasons. It was the natural "sound of quiet" reminding us that we are never truly alone— even when there are no other people in sight. I sincerely enjoyed our rural lifestyle, even though my adoptive father and I grew apart over the years, and our family was divided and frequently quarrelsome.

I honestly can't tell you if the animosity that drove a wedge between my father and me was caused by our differences or if our differences arose from the animosity that grew between us, but it clearly became self-reinforcing over time. In many ways, our relationship ultimately resembled the father-son relationship that Kevin Costner portrayed in the 1989 movie, "Field of Dreams." I always remember Kevin Costner's remarks in the closing scenes of that movie. Upon realizing that his father was one of the players for whom he was driven to build the ballfield, Costner laments that he came to know his father only after he was old and had been "worn down by life." Farming can do that to you, especially the haunting regrets of successive failures. That mounting anxiety is perhaps the biggest cause of depression among farmers. Personal dignity is very important to self-reliant people.

I, too, experienced that kind of stormy relationship with my adoptive father, even though I obviously respected and internalized the values and virtues for which he stood. By the time I left home for college, the distance between us was too great to bridge before he died. That failed relationship, combined with other conflicts, jealousies and resentments that arose from a family bitterly divided between adoptive and natural children ultimately became another motivation for me to leave my childhood life behind and face the uncertainties of my compelled transition into the outside world. The ultimate downfall of my adoptive family is detailed in my 2014 book, Reflections on My Lives: An Adoptee's Story, which can be purchased through Amazon.com.

It took many years for me to distinguish and disconnect the frustrations and resentment I felt about our failed family relationships from the genuine affection I embraced for the rural, mountain setting in which I was raised. However, as I moved up and down the eastern U.S. throughout my adult professional life, I was always drawn back to rural areas and specifically, the Appalachian Mountains. I always feel exposed and disoriented living in flatlands. I simply lose my sense of direction. It is more reassuring than confining for me to see the landscape rise up before me in full display of its natural beauty like a peacock proudly displaying its brilliant feathers. Mountains, especially the gentle and graceful forested ridgelines of the Appalachians, feel as familiar, reassuring and comforting to me as a soft, warm blanket on a bitterly cold winter's night. When we finally decided to make West Virginia our final home, my wife (Barb) would say that my desire to live here made sense. West Virginia allows me to enjoy the setting and lifestyle that I truly appreciated from my childhood without all the excess baggage. I couldn't say it any better or more simply myself.

As I became increasingly frustrated and disenchanted with modern society over the course of my 30-year professional planning career, I eventually decided that I wanted to pursue a more self-reliant lifestyle in my retirement. The great recession of 2007-2009, the effects of which lingered on for years, taught me that there *is* inherent value in the simple, traditional, self-reliant lifestyle we led during my childhood. Homestead farming may not be a good way to make money, but t can be a fine way to lead a healthy lifestyle while minimizing your basic cost of living. I also wanted to enjoy living in an authentic, working rural environment like the one I remembered from my childhood. Over time, that desire became the inspiration for Peeper Pond Farm.

Barb and I had already been looking for retirement property in the central Appalachian Mountains for nearly a year when we stumbled across our initial 6.13-acre property in Pendleton County. We purchased it in October/November of 2006 and immediately began making plans to build our own home and establish an agricultural use there. In the early years, our idea was to plant as much of the three to four-acre open field as we could with grapes and operate a home-based wine making operation. At that time, home based wine operations were becoming very profitable, and it seemed to be a good way to supplement our meager retirement income.

However, the economic recession delayed our construction plans, and we didn't begin building our house and shed until late in 2009. Although we both worked demanding professional jobs (with often conflicting work schedules) in the Cumberland/Keyser area more than 50 miles away from our Pendleton County retirement land, we spent as much time as we could on weekends, holidays and vacations to build our own house within our financial constraints. We wanted to retire in our Pendleton home without a mortgage and remain as close to completely debt-free as we could. I felt that was necessary to afford our agricultural business venture on our meager retirement income.

I always told my colleagues and employees there really are only two ways you can expect to retire in today's society. The first is to keep striving for that next higher-paying job in a frantic effort to achieve an income and savings that will exceed the cost of your increasingly expensive and often excessively extravagant, lifestyle. The second, and the approach I pursued, is to acquire the basic possessions you truly need early in life, then strategically reduce your cost of living and any accumulated debt you incurred until you can afford what you truly need to live on your retirement income. Which approach do you feel best serves the practical lifestyle constraints of the vast and growing number of Americans who can barely afford to live from paycheck to paycheck?

Despite our best efforts to manage our time and do the lion's share (at least 75%) of the work ourselves, the house took much longer for us to build than I anticipated. By August 2013, we had completed enough work to make it possible for us to camp in it over the weekends, but we had no electricity, running water, or septic system. Our bathroom was a cedar tree near the ravine behind our house. Our water supply was obtained from a nearby spring or water we brought with us. We used a Coleman camping stove to cook our meals, and we listened to a battery-operated radio for entertainment. All the while, we continued working on our house. In mid-November 2013, we installed electric power service to the house. For the first time, we had lights to work by and electric space heaters to keep us warm at night. Running water from our well was activated in June 2014, which allowed us to use indoor bathrooms for the first time in the five-plus years we had been building our home. We finally declared the interior finished for furnishing and permanent living in May 2015.

With all our work and financial resources committed to the construction of the house, we realized by 2012 that our wine-making business aspirations were becoming unrealistic. It would eventually cost us $15,000 to $30,000 to plant our field in grapes (depending on whether or not an irrigation system was included). Once planted (sometime after our work on the house was to be completed in 2015), we would have to wait at least five years for the plants to mature, then at least one additional year to produce properly aged wine from the grapes they produced. That would delay any income from our operation until 2021 or later, depending on when we could afford to begin planting the grapes. It seemed unreasonable to expect a favorable return on our initial investment because, based on my conversations with other established wineries, the local cottage wine market was becoming saturated. Furthermore, we had spent so much money on building materials, we would need to incur debt to finance the planting of the grapes.

After some careful thinking and considerable research regarding our options, we decided that it would be more affordable—or so it seemed—for us to pursue a homestead dairy goat farm and to rent our spare bedrooms to people who would be interested in gaining hands-on experience learning to live more self-reliantly. The changes that had ultimately transformed my childhood home were driver by the gradual influx of wealthier people from Massachusetts who had very different and often conflicting values and lifestyles. Over time, they bid up the price of land and took it out of production. What historic farms they bought were preserved as museum pieces to validate their wealth and image, rather than function as useful tools to serve the traditional lifestyle they had been designed to support. Even the most loving acts of historic preservation cannot restore economic vitality to a traditional lifestyle that has heaved its final breath.

As a professional planner, I worked closely with rural communities for over 30 years, with only marginal success, to plan for such changes so that they could manage the impacts and preserve at least some of their traditional agricultural bases. Eventually, I determined that I might have a better chance of managing that change in my retirement by teaching rural newcomers to appreciate that lifestyle and keep their land in agriculture—even if it was conducted at a smaller scale. It's harder for people to disrespect and casually destroy something that they learn to understand and appreciate. At least, that was my operating theory.

Since I knew there was a growing demand for home-grown food and interest in learning simple, self-reliant skills to live more affordably, I felt that an in-home, on-the-farm training program might give us the additional income we would need to finance our planned homestead farm operation. These practices, and the basic lifestyle values they engender, represent the core of West Virginia's cherished heritage, which is an essential element of the state's image and tourism marketing. It also seemed to us to be a better, simpler and more appropriate way to finance our retirement life.

Between the two of us, we knew or relearned many of the traditional self-reliant skills I was exposed to during my childhood, such as milking, raising livestock, gardening, canning and food preservation, quilting, sewing, cooking scratch recipes and wood-working. Although Barb was raised in Schenectady, NY, she had a lifelong interest in traditional skills and had practiced many of them throughout our married life. Over time, we learned additional skills. Barb and I took an adult education course in wine-making at Potomac State College in 2009. We also read books and learned beekeeping and how to process milk into cheese, butter, soap, ice cream and other useful household products. Most working-age people in today's modern society are two to three generations removed from these traditional practices, but all of them and more are still being practiced by multi-generational natives living in our region today. That is, in a nutshell, how Peeper Pond Farm was conceived.

As we approached the scheduled date of our retirement—on or before March 1, 2017 – we scrambled to sharpen our new skills and purchase the equipment, supplies, livestock and feed necessary to support our homestead farm operation. We had established a small fruit orchard in 2007, but we still needed to create, fence and plant a small herb garden (July 2015), establish our large vegetable garden (March-April 2016), build a garage designed to include a workshop, milking parlor and a goat birthing pen (April-May 2016), establish two bee hives (June 2016), build a small goat barn (July 2016), purchase a tractor and cultivating equipment (July 2016), create a website to support and market our farm operation (August-September 2016), build fencing around our garden, orchard and goat pens (November 2016) and purchase all the remaining equipment and supplies we needed to raise our goats, milk them and process the milk we produced (October 2016-April 2017). We were barely able to keep up with it all before our first goats arrived in early March 2017.

Our farm began full operation in mid-March 2017. By that time, we had been working our fruit orchard for a decade, our herb garden for over one-and-a-half years and our beekeeping operation for nine months. Our garden, which was plowed and amended in 2016, was being planted, and we began feeding and raising our first two goat kids. We had to wait until early May to obtain our milking adults, but all elements of our farm operation had been initiated. We had some initial problems when we began milking our goats, primarily because they had difficulties adjusting to their new home and a different milking process, and I was struggling to hand milk a goat with very small teats. After some early adjustments, we settled into a very comfortable milking and farming routine and produced a steady supply of good quality goat milk. Barb was able to learn and refine our milk processing practices during the first month and soon we were successfully producing soap, yogurt, butter, ice-cream and a variety of cheeses from our goat milk. The vegetables we planted in our garden were growing rapidly, and we were harvesting fresh vegetables by early June 2017.

While we had successfully initiated all elements of our homestead farm operation, some of them were disappointing. Our fruit orchard was only marginally productive and the quality of the fruit we produced was not good. We struggled to combat an apple-red cedar rust problem that repeatedly damaged the leaves of our apple trees and impaired their fruit production. Most of the fruit our trees managed to produce were undersized with blistered and cracked skins. Some of the fruit would fall prematurely or were eaten by deer. We applied a variety of sprays to protect the leaves, but none of them were effective. We simply couldn't afford to seek the professional treatment services that commercial orchards use. We managed to harvest enough apples one year to make an apple pie, but the trees never produced more than a handful of fruit.

We also tried replacing our most damaged or dead trees with other varieties said to be blight resistant, but we never found one that could successfully overcome the aggressive scourge. We eventually began replacing and augmenting the apple trees with other fruits, including peach trees, blueberries, elderberries and grapes. Unfortunately, our fencing has not kept all of the deer out of our orchard, and we battled with them to protect our blueberries and grapes. One of our Red Haven peach trees was producing a fine crop of peaches in early 2017 until the deer got to it. Barb managed to pick only about a dozen peaches that they couldn't reach. I guess I can't call our orchard a complete failure, but it has been the least successful and most disappointing element of our farm operation.

Our beekeeping operation has also been disappointing. We had been able to maintain our hives for more than a year, and they were very helpful in pollinating our flowering trees, plants and vegetables. However, we weren't able to harvest any honey. Our bees were just getting established during the 2016 season when one of our hives swarmed in 2017, eliminating any chance to harvest honey from that hive. I discovered that I had difficulties finding the queens in our hives, which posed a potential long-term management problem. I found it almost impossible to focus on individual bees to locate the queen when there is so much active movement on each frame. Our colonies eventually died out in December 2017 due to an aggressive varroa mite infestation, and we have been reluctant to make the investment to rebuild them.

We were very successful with all of our other farm operations. Our herb and vegetable gardens have produced far beyond our wildest expectations as well as our ability to make use of our entire bounty. We have been frequent vendors at the Grant County Farmer's Market in Petersburg ever since our initial harvest in 2017. Likewise, our goats produced all the milk we expected and needed for our home use. I have often said that working to pursue my childhood dairy farm lifestyle in my retirement was my penitence. Maybe it also gave me a sense of redemption. Perhaps that explains why I was so motivated and determined to do it. I got far enough along to actually prove I could do what it takes to successfully operate my own dairy farm, virtually on my own. That was something my adoptive father insisted throughout my childhood that I could never do--just as his own step-father had told him during his own childhood.

However, we decided after three months of milking that we couldn't continue our milking operation. It wasn't because we couldn't do the work or produce the milk we needed. Rather, it was because we were unable to establish the lifestyle training business operation that we needed to offset the ongoing operating expenses of our dairy goat operation. Our monthly costs for feed and essential supplies became the most significant cost of our entire homesteading operation, and our retirement income was not enough to cover those costs and our basic living expenses—especially whenever we incurred unexpected and unavoidable major expenses. Without a supplemental business income, we were forced to reduce our operating expenses accordingly. After a careful assessment of our expenses, it was clear our dairy operation was and would continue to be our biggest ongoing expense. Sadly, we decided to sell all of our goats after only four and a half months of raising them and three months after we began milking them.

The primary reasons that we could not get our homesteading skills training operation started were that the insurance coverage and start-up costs for the operation were so expensive that it became obvious it would not create the income stream we needed to supplement our retirement income. The cost of permitting the operation, the anticipated additional costs to cover insurance and the estimated annual increase in our local property taxes we would incur to operate a business use from our house were substantially more than the income it would generate for us. We also realized that we could not satisfy the regulatory requirements and standards necessary to sell any of the milk products we could produce for human consumption without significant and costly upgrades. The combination of these financial and regulatory impediments was too great for us to bear, despite all the work we did and sacrifices we made to get it going. It appeared that my parents had been correct about it all along. There is simply no future for small-scale (homestead) farming unless you can afford a substantial cost subsidy to support it.

The loss of my dairy goat operation was very difficult for me to accept—especially considering all the work I did to build it and the success I was having with it. The more time I spent thinking about it, the less sense it made to me. As I thought about all the standards and requirements that I had to satisfy to make use of the milk we produced, I realized that exaggerated public health fears appeared to be the driving factor in both the permitting requirements and liability insurance costs. West Virginia has adopted a perspective that fresh, unprocessed milk (whether from goats or cows) is an "elixir of death." Our state (like some, but not all others) has adopted strict and inflexible prohibitions on the sale or distribution of milk for human consumption, the compliance costs for which can only be assumed by a large or industrial scale of operation. The prevailing public health fear induced by this attitude is a driving force in the cost of liability insurance for dairy operations, which represented the highest single cost to our farm.

However, I have great difficulty understanding how the actual threat can be as great as public health officials fear. I and three of my four sisters were raised on unprocessed milk throughout our school years, and we never experienced any sickness from the milk we consumed. In fact, we had better school attendance records than most other students. I also drank our goat milk exclusively for the three months we milked our goats and never once experienced any illness—not even a cold. I have to wonder if the prevailing public health fears regarding unprocessed milk consumption are commensurate with the actual threat. The overwhelming magnitude of our current health regulations has had the practical effect of promoting industrial scale dairy farming to the detriment of small homestead and family farms, thereby forcing a fundamental lifestyle choice to the brink of extinction. It is for these reasons that I have embarked on a legislative effort to end the state's current prohibition on unprocessed milk sales.

The Purpose of This Book

Now that our traditional lifestyle skills training aspirations are in limbo, at least until the outcome of our legislative effort is known, I decided that the work we have done to date, as documented on our farm website, www.peeperpondfarm.com, could be a beneficial training tool to many prospective homestead farmers in the form of a book. Therefore, I have compiled all the farming posts I placed on our website since I created it in September 2016. They serve as a diary or compendium of sorts, documenting all our efforts over the past three-plus years to get the farm operation going and our adventures since then, including the successes and failures we have faced, as well as the lessons we have learned from them along the way. In reality, this book was built from my unpublished 2017 manuscript for <u>The Peeper Pond Farm Story: Where Did All the Small Family Dairy Farms Go?</u> which focused more specifically on the painful loss of our dairy goat operation. I eventually decided I had more to say and teach about traditional rural farm living than the more limited focus of that prior book allowed.

My website posts consist of instructional essays on various traditional farming and homesteading practices, whimsical musings on rural farm life from a farmer's perspective, as well as descriptions of the scenic natural resources in our area and the legends surrounding them. Our website posts included many colorful pictures that I could not include in this book because they would significantly increase the publishing cost and ultimately impact its marketability. Although I removed most of the references to pictures within the posts, a few of them may remain. To view all the original pictures, you should access the posts on our farm website.

Barb and I have worked hard to establish our retirement homestead farm, and we would like to preserve some meaningful aspect of our lifestyle skills instructional program. This book is the best we can do at this point in time. However, our journey will continue, and we encourage all of our loyal readers, both website visitors and purchasers of this book, to accompany us on this ongoing adventure. We hope you will discover what we already know—that the many intangible rewards of farm life can be truly worth the work, and our remaining rural areas are treasures to enjoy and actively live within. Additionally, we hope you will learn to value the traditional folkways and lifestyle skills that make true rural living possible. Our success or failure to live them should in no way be the yardstick by which their value is measured. That is the perspective my adoptive family overlooked. They are important elements of our shared heritage and should be preserved because they still have value and meaning in our lives. Don't assume that we can live without out them or you may find yourself quite hungry in the next economic collapse to come. We hope you will enjoy reading the story of our life at Peeper Pond Farm that we have to tell you in the following website posts.

Post 1: Welcome to Peeper Pond Farm

September 7, 2016

After twelve years of planning and hard work, we have finally realized our retirement dream. Peeper Pond Farm is ready to begin operation. It has taken so long to get to this point, it's hard to believe that we made it. As a child, growing up on a small family-operated dairy farm in the mountains of rural New Hampshire, my parents taught us there was no future in farming, and we shouldn't aspire to live the way we did. *Our* future was in the outside world, and we were advised to attend college and get an education that would give us a *real* job. That's what I did. It took me at least twenty years to realize that I didn't fit into the modern world. Life in the outside world never felt "real" to me. The core values I learned from my rural upbringing and tried to follow as an adult weren't always respected or followed by others. Now, after completing more than thirty-year professional careers in the outside world, my wife and I can retire to a simpler lifestyle in our adopted home of Pendleton County, WV.

Peeper Pond Farm is now our future. Some may feel that we are simply running away from the outside world and hiding in the past. That way of living is too outdated to be relevant today. After all, we've "progressed" so far from that. If that's the way people *choose* to view it, they're welcome to think that way. As a child, I was always told that there was no future in farming, and small family farms have been in steady decline since then. However, the way I see it, that's not a very respectful or optimistic perspective to take. Maybe it's that way of thinking that makes our modern society so unpopular in other cultures.

Why should our technology-driven, wealth-based modern society be the only proper lifestyle choice we should make? From what I see today, most people say they desire "inclusion" and support "alternative lifestyles," except, perhaps, for those aspects of the past they don't like and seek to stereotype away. Fortunately, our retirement plans mean something different to me. As I see it, we are finally transitioning away from doing what we *have* to do for someone else to *buy* our life to living as we *choose* to *make* a better life for ourselves. If doing so gives us a healthy, simple and peaceful retirement lifestyle we can afford, who can say that's a bad choice no matter how you *choose* to view it? Why *plan* for a retirement if that's not ultimately what you hope to achieve? Perhaps the way others view our retirement lifestyle choices actually says more about them than it does about us.

Our farm is intended to be a not-for-profit homestead venture. While we are not a commercial farm, we will still offer some of our products for sale. We also hope to teach interested people what we do and how we do it so that future generations will carry on those traditions. We may be nearing the end of our lives, but the lifestyle we cherish does not have to perish with us. We hope it will endure in you; those who have a sincere interest in our traditional folkways and desire to live a less consumptive, less complicated and less pretentious life. These lessons are the real value we have to offer. We hope you will follow us as we undertake this journey. We hope you will support us and discover the reward in a simpler life. Hopefully, we can help you discover what I didn't question critically enough as a child--that there truly *is* value to living as we do. I look forward to telling you all about it in future journal posts on our website. Thank you in advance for your interest and for keeping an open mind to other lifestyle choices!

Post 2: A Lifestyle Lost

October 11, 2016

    I took some extra time off from work this Columbus Day weekend to entertain my biological aunt and uncle from Willoughby, OH, who came to see the retirement house we built and our emerging homestead farm operation. Although Uncle Walter did not grow up on a farm, he talked about his experiences working on a neighbor's farm during his childhood. Unlike some of my other immediate relatives, he understands the lifestyle we are working to establish here on Peeper Pond Farm, and he was eager to see what we have done. Unfortunately, we still don't have our dairy goats and we still have more prep work we have to finish before we retire and begin farming full-time, but we explained our plans for the future operation. They both understood and supported our plans and determination, as we work to bring meaning to a lifestyle that is gradually being lost to history.

    As I explained the reasons for our lifestyle change, we were able to share farming and life experiences. The pace and degree of change over the past two generations has been faster and more dramatic than in any generations before them. The lifestyle I lived growing up on a small dairy farm in rural New Hampshire may have been remarkably similar to farm life in West Virginia and Western Pennsylvania (where Uncle Walter was raised), but those experiences are completely alien to anyone my age who was raised in an urban or suburban environment and even more alien to those younger than me today.

    I am amazed to realize how many people I meet have no concept of how our food is grown or produced, much less what fresh food really looks like. For example, my wife and I bought some fresh vegetables at the Harrisonburg, VA Wal-Mart the day before my aunt and uncle arrived, and the cashier had to ask us if the onion we placed on the counter was a yellow or sweet onion. I told him, "Son, if that was a sweet onion it would be white and a lot bigger. This is a yellow onion. You know, you really should spend more time in a garden." He grinned and thanked me for the advice. I still don't know if he was convinced or just embarrassed. While little experiences like this are increasingly common today, it strikes me as more troubling because he lives and works in Harrisonburg, the economic heart of the Shenandoah Valley, which is historically known as the "breadbasket of Virginia" for the breadth and diversity of its agricultural production!

When I left home 36 years ago for college and a professional career in the modern, outside world, I discovered quite quickly that most of the young people I met from the cities found it hard to accept the stories I told of how we lived. None of them had any experience heating soap stones in a wood stove to warm up a bed in an unheated bedroom before going to sleep at night. None of them raked fall leaves into lawn and garden bags to pack them around the house foundation for added winter insulation. None of them had split or stacked firewood, milked a cow, canned vegetables, driven a tractor, picked rocks from a freshly plowed field or garden, or mowed hay with a scythe. It wasn't just that they hadn't done them and I had, it was their utter refusal to believe that I *did* do them that surprised me the most. I quickly stopped talking about them because I realized that my farm experiences would not help me earn the respect of my peers and transition successfully into the modern outside world. My resume was not enhanced by my prior work experiences as a backwoods hick from the farm. That knowledge only reinforced my parents' persistent lectures that we were not to aspire to live the way we did because there was no future in farming.

I must admit that my childhood on our farm did not leave me with a great appreciation for that lifestyle. It took me many years of reflection and alternative life experience to understand that my rejection of farm life had more to do with our failed family relationships and society's casual disrespect for traditional rural lifestyles than to any sincere distaste I had for rural living. In fact, I was always drawn to rural areas for my professional work and my weekend activities. I've always felt more relaxed and satisfied in rural Appalachian Mountain settings than I ever did living in urban communities. Modern urban and suburban life never felt "real" to me. It is only now that I understand why enough to realize that there *is* value to living more self-reliantly and simply.

Simply stated, that's why I'm retiring to rural Pendleton County, West Virginia. Although I've lived and worked in the modern, outside world for more than thirty years, I finally found what I missed most in life here in Pendleton County. As my wife correctly says, "My desire to live in Pendleton County makes sense because it allows me to revive those aspects from my childhood that I cherish most without all the excess baggage." To me, I have found the home I never had. Perhaps it is my absolution for not appreciating as much of my upbringing as I should have. Whatever the truth may be, there can be no question that this life is right for me, even if it continues to become extinct elsewhere. I sincerely hope that is the understanding that Aunt Betty and Uncle

Walter left with when they returned to Ohio this morning. I also hope it will make sense to and inspire you as we embark on this new adventure.

Post 3: Why Would I Want to Do All That Farm Work?

October 23, 2016

After five warm Indian summer days, fall has returned with a vengeance at Peeper Pond Farm. A strong cold front moved through our area over the weekend accompanied by rain and snow showers, brutal winds gusting up to 50 miles per hour and heavy dark clouds. I scrambled to get down to our farm on Friday afternoon, so I could install the plywood wind screens that we built and painted last weekend to protect our beehives from fierce winter winds. The weather was fine when I arrived, so I went straight to work. As luck would have it, the cold front arrived just as I was beginning to install the wind screens and I was thoroughly drenched with heavy rain and wind. Of course, the squall departed as I rushed to retreat from the deluge, but not before it had completed its work. It had turned a simple 45-minute task into a miserable experience and then fled swiftly and glibly, satisfied that it had completed its mischievous work. Such can be the nature of farm work.

The incident reminded me of a recent conversation I had with a professional colleague about my previous (October 11) post. In it, I had talked about some of the typical farming tasks I had done during my childhood that my college peers had never done and wouldn't even believe that I had. My friend had read that post and, while he accepted that I had done them, he couldn't believe that I would want to go back to that lifestyle in retirement when I didn't need to. He insisted I could earn an adequate supplemental income by doing part-time consulting work and have more leisure time to enjoy my retirement. He understood that farm work would help keep me healthy, but he felt it was too demanding and could be as hazardous as it is healthy. He simply couldn't understand what would be so attractive about such unnecessary hard work that I would choose to do that instead of extending my career and making use of the professional skills I had learned.

From his perspective, that reasoning is perfectly sound. He had never lived on a farm and was following my web postings to try to understand why I wanted to abandon my professional career for a farm lifestyle. In his mind, there was no good reason for me to do that. I must admit, after struggling in cold, soaking wet clothes to protect my beehives from the brutal squall on Friday afternoon, I understood the point he was trying to make. There's no doubt about it; many farming chores are hard, frustrating, hazardous tasks even in good weather. I have spent a lot of time "picking rocks" out of our future garden plot, which is one of the tasks I dislike most. It's not easy and it certainly isn't any fun. But, as I tried to explain to my friend, no line of work I have ever done in my life protects me from difficult or unpleasant tasks. Can anyone really tell me there are no aspects of the work they do for a living that they don't like or find difficult to do?

    I think the real pleasure of any job you do is in the balance of the work versus the outcome. It wouldn't be a "job" if it didn't require "work." Is the work you do for your job something you generally enjoy, even if you don't like to do all of it? Does it reward you in a meaningful way? Do you gain some sense of satisfaction from doing it--even if some of it isn't fun or easy? I think those are the questions you have to ask yourself before you judge what line of work would be best for you. For me, the periodic frustrations I experienced from writing plans that were never implemented, working in an office on a computer most of the time, dealing with divisive or unethical politics that I couldn't control or fix and struggling to support increasingly misunderstood and politically marginalized rural communities was far more unsatisfying or frustrating than the physical struggles and challenges I faced creating our farm and building our retirement house. Throughout my career, I would say that the farm work I did as child was hard, challenging and exhausting, but you slept well when you went to bed. By comparison, the work I did in my professional career was much less physically demanding, but it was mentally and emotionally stressful and challenged my core values, which kept me awake many nights. Many of the communities I served treated my work as though it was something they *had* to do--not necessarily that they *wanted* to do. As a result, my efforts did not always feel useful or beneficial. All work has its benefits and costs. What you decide to do—if you must work—should give you the lifestyle you desire to make the effort to earn it worthwhile.

    I'm sure it's very difficult for people who have never lived a farm lifestyle to understand why farmers prefer it. Sure, it's hard, demanding physical labor. Most small-scale farmers struggle to make ends meet and do not make a lot of money. Nevertheless, I have met many people who don't farm and never lived on a farm (some of whom work multiple part-time jobs), but also live paycheck to paycheck and struggle to make ends meet. Even my son is realizing how difficult it is to afford his basic cost of living by working a minimum wage job. However, there are a number of intangible benefits to farming--beyond the obvious health benefits I have mentioned--that most people today may not realize.

Perhaps the most gratifying and satisfying benefit from farming is the sense of independence you can gain from farming. While many small, family farmers may not earn a lot of money from their work, their work reduces their cost of living and gives them a greater sense of freedom than any low wage job in the outside world. Farmers don't have to take orders from or please superiors, who may not always have their best interests at heart. They rarely (depending on the farm work they do) have to deal with rude or angry customers. They don't have to deal with office politics. They do work that can have its own frustrations, but by and large, farmers are free to decide what they want to do, how to do it and when to do it. I know of no work that pays so little but offers such freedom of choice, especially when you can own your own land free and clear. Those who farm enjoy a sense of self-reliance and independence that they could not obtain from any alternative line of work that may be open to them.

Add to that the small, periodic joys that come from working with animals (farmers do find "comfort" from the animals they work with), the pleasure of working outdoors during nice weather, the more immediate satisfaction a farmer receives from a job well done, living and working close to the land and nature and the contentment obtained from living in a peaceful, scenic rural setting, and it becomes easier to understand why farmers enjoy the farming lifestyle. To them, the struggles of hard work are a small price to pay for such freedom and abundant serenity. These are the reasons why I chose to pursue this lifestyle in my retirement. After working a 30+ year professional career, I can appreciate those lifestyle benefits far more than I did during my childhood. I consider this farming lifestyle to be part of my reward for the stressful and unfulfilling work I did over my professional career.

Those of you, like my inquisitive colleague, who prefer living in cities, can be very grateful and appreciative that farmers desire to live that lifestyle. Without them, you might not be able to choose the lifestyle you wish to live because you'd have to do it all for yourself--assuming you have the land and time you'd need to do it all successfully. Remember, too, if farmers were paid as fairly as *you'd* want to be paid to do their work, many of you might find it a lot harder to make ends meet or live as well from paycheck to paycheck as you currently do. So, instead of questioning a farmer's choice of lifestyle, I would like to suggest that you just politely thank him for the work he does and alleviates you from doing for yourself. Also, please be mindful--as I was taught during my childhood--it's not polite to criticize or disparage farmers or farming while you are enjoying a plate full of fresh food.

Post 4: Final Arrangements

November 5, 2016

    This fall has become a battle between late summer and early winter. After our first frost of the season on October 11, the following week brought us five days of pleasant Indian summer weather, with high temperatures ranging from 77 to 85 degrees. Two days after our Indian summer extravaganza ended, I saw our first winter snow flakes mixed in with some light rain in the early morning hours of October 22. Then, on October 26, we got our first hard freeze (31 degrees). After that, we have received a few days of intermittent late summer warmth. Throughout this period, we received a lot of strong and gusty winds as alternating warm and cold fronts swept through the area. The raging clash between summer and winter temperatures and the rapidly declining daylight hours serve as sharp reminders that winter is on the way, and the opportunities we need to finish the final outdoor projects for our farm operation are slipping away. The long-range forecast for our area forebodes a potentially hard winter with frequent snow storms.

    With all this encouragement, Barb and I have been preparing for winter and working aggressively on the final construction projects for our farm. We still need to install permanent fencing for our orchard, garden and goat pen, so we have been buying our materials and working on the fencing plans. We are also installing a back-up LP gas generator and I am actively trying to find a good wood stove for our garage. With a neighbor's help, we added antifreeze to our tractor tires to keep the water in them (used as a counterbalance for the front loader) from freezing. All the while, I hear the steady ticking of the clock in my mind. Less than four months remain until our official retirement.

    The spirit of our final farming preparations also helped focus our attention on our final end-of-life arrangements. I have always said since we purchased our retirement property in 2006 that the gravestones will go up with the house. Now we have taken steps to make that happen. We began discussing those arrangements on October 27 with David Basagic, owner of Basagic Funeral Home in Franklin.

    I must admit that making final arrangements for my eventual demise was not a high priority through most of my early life. I actually faced death late in my childhood on the farm and came to terms with my mortality through it. It has been so long since I harbored any fear of death that I never felt compelled to plan for it. I just figured I would die, be cremated and have my ashes scattered somewhere. I couldn't see much reason to fuss about it.

That thinking began to change for me when I began researching my biological father's family genealogy in 1999. I learned that my great-grandfather died a pauper in New Castle, PA, half a world away from his entire family and was buried in an unmarked grave. No one knows for sure where it is, and there are no records to use in finding it. To me, this was a shameful legacy for a man who risked his life to seek work in America so that he could earn the money he needed to rebuild his family's vineyard in eastern Hungary. You see, my father and his family are Transylvanian Saxons, who emigrated from what was Hungarian land, but was later ceded to Romania as a spoil of war at the end of World War I.

After gaining control of Transylvania, the Romanian government initiated an agricultural reform program, during which many of the region's Hungarian and Saxon ancestral lands were systematically transferred to Romanians and official records of their lives and property ownership were destroyed. Over time and regime changes, the program evolved into an ethnic cleansing campaign, where many ethnic minorities were murdered or relocated. So, when my genealogical research took me back to Transylvania, there were no records to aid me in my search. I found references in Hungarian history to some Umlings from the 1700's who were well known artists, but I could not find any genealogical records to determine how we were related to them. I eventually learned that the only surviving records I could search are the cemetery gravestones that may remain in my ancestral homeland. So far, I haven't had the opportunity to go there, but the realization that gravestones are the only possible ancestral records left to understand my heritage—and even that isn't enough to find my great-grandfather's grave—helped persuade me to think more carefully about what I leave behind for my future descendants.

Now that we have decided that West Virginia is where we will complete our lives, we determined it was time to make our final arrangements and choose our burial site. My first thought was to start a family plot on a portion of our farm. Eventually, I learned that would not be a permanent solution, since any future property owner could have our remains removed. My second choice was to be buried in the cemetery adjacent to Wilson Chapel, which we can see from our house whenever the leaves are not on the trees. However, that cemetery is filled. Consequently, we chose to be buried in Cherry Hill Cemetery in the village of Upper Tract, five miles from our home. We drove through the cemetery after our meeting with David Basagic and were impressed with the majestic view of Cave Mountain to the north. Our farm is located almost directly below the summit of Cave Mountain, and the knowledge that you could almost see where we live was very reaffirming.

I guess I really don't know who will remember us or how we will be remembered after we have passed away. All I can say is that it is one thing for our descendants to forget us on through their own neglect, but it is quite a different thing for us to care so little about them that we casually deny them any knowledge of us. I guess I've learned why it is important to leave something lasting and more permanent behind after we are gone, when nothing remains but a few fleeting memories. Perhaps it will be reassuring to my descendants to discover that we lived in a beautiful place and left a small token behind to give them an attachment to it—something to make them feel that it is a part of them, too. Isn't that what makes the "sense of community" so meaningful? Now that we have attended to our final arrangements, I hope we can focus on the challenge of making our life at Peeper Pond Farm worth remembering. The only remaining question I can leave for you is what will you leave behind for future generations to remember you?

Post 5: The Fine Art of Fencing

November 9, 2016

Barb and I are on vacation this week. The weather forecast called for beautiful conditions for outdoor work (for the Appalachian Mountains)—a mix of sun and clouds with crisp, cool mornings and afternoon highs around 60 degrees each day. You can't order better weather for farm fencing work from a catalog. So, while Barb traveled to visit her mother, I made arrangements to install the fencing we need for our orchard, vegetable garden and goats.

I stopped at Tri-County tool rental to discuss heavy equipment needs for the job. I said that, as a child, I had watched and helped my father install electric and barbed wire fencing, but having studied woven wire fences in our area at a distance, I knew this work would be different. The owner removed a business card and hastily scribbled a name and telephone number on the back before handing it firmly to me. All he said was, "He's the best." This is the kind of simple and direct recommendation I have come to expect from native West Virginians. Now that I have spent a couple of days working with Richard B and, I understand why he is worthy of such high praise.

Richard is a soft-spoken, but imposing and muscular man. An Army veteran and a multi-generational West Virginia native from a family whose name is engraved on all Pendleton County maps, his determination to work hard and do the job to the best of his ability is ever apparent. No matter how simple the immediate task may seem with respect to the overall job, his attention to detail is thorough and unwavering. No task is meaningless to the successful outcome of the work. As he explained each step in the process, I could sense the pride and satisfaction he gains from his handiwork. He smiles frequently as he discusses it. This is not the attitude of a laborer who does a job to earn a living. This is the demeanor of a true craftsman who treats his job as a fine art and finds great personal joy and pleasure in it. Some may see the work as installing a fence. However, Richard approaches his work as crafting the most attractive and functional fence possible into the farm landscape.

Throughout our work together, Richard talked about all the finish work (such as trimming the installed fenceposts so that they are all a similar height). That is the dedication to detail that characterizes a man who truly appreciates his work. I have felt that way about many jobs I have done in the past—most recently when I built our retirement house—even as I am not the craftsman that Richard is. This is a man with a work ethic I can truly admire, so I have thoroughly enjoyed the experience of working with him.

Michelangelo, who was likewise dedicated to his craft, left us with many famous quotes regarding his sculpting talent. When asked about his work, he would humbly explain, *"Every block of stone has a statue inside it and it is the task of the sculptor to discover it,"* and *"I saw the angel in the marble and carved until I set him free."* Such words make sculpting sound simple—perhaps divinely inspired. However, I think we can all be honest enough about our own artistic limitations to admit that our hands lack the talent of such a master. When it comes to his fencing work, Richard is a truly gifted master craftsman. He made his own specialized tools and devised his own strategy to strengthen the bracing that supports each gate and corner post. He carefully positioned each post so that any slight warp in the wood would run with the fence line instead of against it. Rather than telling me to spend a little extra money to buy pre-sharpened fenceposts (which might save some labor), he invested the time to carve a point at the end each fencepost with his chainsaw, so we could use the residual pointed slivers of wood as wedges to straighten every post that was shifted from plumb by a boulder deep in the ground. He is as resourceful as he is talented.

Yesterday, we rented a track loader with a post driver to pile-drive the fenceposts in the boulder-laden ground on our hardscrabble farm. Richard brought his son, Brock, with him to drive the machine. Brock has driven the machine for him many times over the past, and they have honed their communication and working skills to great efficiency. Again, Richard demonstrated his skill as both a craftsman and a teacher. I watched as he placed his large artist's hand against each post as it was driven into the ground. It was obvious he wasn't simply holding it in place for the post driver. He was feeling every movement of the fenceposts—how fast and true they were being driven into the ground. When a post struck a buried rock or boulder, he would feel it shift and call a simple direction to his son, "forward," "back," "to your left," "towards me," and his son would shift the lumbering machine as deftly and delicately as the situation required to straighten the post and keep it plumb. Brock exhibited the driving skill of an expert more than twice his age— even though he is only sixteen and a sophomore in high school. Together, they drove 59 fenceposts into the stony West Virginia soil across our farm in about six-and-a-half hours—an average of slightly less than one post every six minutes! Brock aspires to become a large crane operator, and his father is trying to help him land a longshoreman job at the Port of Baltimore. There should be plenty of opportunities for his skill with all the additional shipping traffic that will use the port now that the Panama Canal widening is complete.

We are getting some much-needed showers this morning (although it's not enough), so we will resume working a little late today. Nevertheless, I am eager to work with Richard again today—the hard work of fencing made a pleasant and rewarding experience by the skill and talent of a master craftsmen. We will probably spend the rest of the week carving our Peeper Pond fences out of and into the rural West Virginia landscape. Some people earn praise and fame from the things they build. I now have the honor to know an artist whose skill and craftsmanship is proclaimed not just by the work he does, but how he does it. Think of how much better our world would be if we could all enjoy and take pride in our work as much as Richard Bland does.

Post 6: A Three Season Weekend

November 20, 2016

When I was growing up in the Appalachian Mountains we always said, "if you don't like the weather, just wait five minutes." It still holds true today. This past weekend (November 18-20), we experienced three different seasons in three days. Friday afternoon I was enjoying a beautiful early or late summer day with clear skies, a light, lazy breeze and temperatures that topped out around 73 degrees. It was one of those days that made the drive through the mountains to Peeper Pond Farm a really pleasurable ride. The most difficult part of the drive was the last leg of the trip south of Petersburg when I struggled to see around the setting sun. However, as darkness settled over our farm and the embracing warmth of the day began to fade, I was treated to a spectacular view of the starry sky backlit by the ethereal, silky glow of the Milky Way galaxy.

Saturday morning, I awoke before sunrise. The weather forecast warned of a strong cold front that would sweep through our area around mid-day, heralded by strong, gusty winds and showers. The daytime temperatures were predicted to drop by 25-30 degrees in a matter of a few hours. Anticipating the drastic change, I scrambled to complete the tasks I had set forth for the day in the early morning hours, while the air was calm and the conditions were conducive to outdoor work. Even so, I crunched across the frosty ground on a fine fall morning as I headed for the orchard. It was about an hour before the sun would rise over the mountains, but close enough to sunrise that I could see what I was doing in the early morning twilight. It was time to remove the fence cages that we had placed around each fruit tree to protect them from the deer and rabbits when we planted them five-seven years ago. Now that we had completed our fencing around the orchard, the cages were no longer necessary and I was concerned that the coming winds would further bruise the branches as they rubbed against the wires. It took me two hours to remove all the cages, flatten the wire and store them in the garage for recycling.

Then I fired up the tractor and drove it into the garden to finish my morning chores. We had ordered and received four dump truck loads of mushroom soil from Grant County Mulch, which sat in piles in the garden. We needed the soft, rich soil to amend the clay loam in our garden. I decided it would be wise to spread it around the garden with the bucket loader to reduce the chance that it would blow away in the gusty winds. After another two hours of dragging and pushing the soil around with the tractor, I had spread the piles over three-quarters of the garden plot. We will need another two loads to cover the rest of the garden. As I parked the tractor and climbed off, I felt the first drops of rain and the winds began to build. It was just after 11:00 AM and dark, foreboding gray clouds were racing across the sky. Within an hour, the temperature had dropped from the mid-50s (about average for this time of the year) into the mid-40s. Strong winds and rainy squalls governed the afternoon weather. As we went to bed, we could hear the wind gusts roaring over Cave Mountain just before they slammed into the house.

We awoke in the morning to an early winter scene. The ground was covered with a dusting of snow and frequent flurries and squalls refreshed the dusting as fast as the warm ground struggled to melt it. Frequent wind gusts swirled the snowfall into brief white-outs. Our night-time low tonight is forecast to be in the low-to-mid 20s, with wind chills in the low teens. Maybe we had to wait a little longer that five minutes for the weather to change, but change it did. Three distinct seasons in the span of three days. It reminds me of another weather saying we used to tell people when I was growing up on the farm in rural New Hampshire. Our summers there were really short; last year it fell on a Wednesday.

Post 7: A New Day Dawns

February 4, 2017

    It's hard for me to believe it has been two months since my last post. Barb and I have been so busy shopping for farm supplies and outfitting our goat barn and garage to support our homestead dairy operation that I haven't had adequate time to just sit down and update our website. Barb even discovered that she has two customers for quilting projects and is spending much of her spare time filling those orders. However, our retirement date will arrive at the end of this month and we still have much to do.

    I know that this farming lifestyle will be very different for Barb, since she has no experience living on a farm. Back when we started planning for our retirement, she wasn't even sure we could build our own home, much less afford to establish a farm operation in addition to that. Now that our planned retirement date is only weeks away and we're putting the final touches on our operation, the end is in sight and reality is gradually taking root.

    I haven't been very outspoken about it, but I truly appreciate her dedicated support and help in achieving this major lifestyle change. She certainly had plenty to fear—the hard work involved, the cost and the transition to a very different way of life—but she never questioned my confidence that we could eventually do it. We both can look back on our professional careers and see the good and bad influences they have had on our life together. Sometimes, you need to look back to find the determination and confidence you need to make major changes to your life. Fortunately, she can sense and appreciate the benefits we are seeking from a simpler, more self-reliant lifestyle enough to subdue the fears that this change incites. Her unwavering faith in our ability to make it all work has been an inspiration to me, and I have come to appreciate it more than mere words can explain.

    Like all marriages I have known, we have had our disagreements and arguments. It is hard for me to believe that you can live with someone for 25 years without discovering some things you can't agree on. We have certainly struggled through our share of them and continue to do so today. Yet, through it all, we have never lost sight of how much we love and depend upon each other. Those are the ties that inevitably bind us together and make it more likely that we will eventually succeed. They are also the resources we have to draw upon as we face the inevitable challenges of our new lifestyle.

    Some people fear the idea of retirement because it implies that life is coming to an end. For us, it represents just another transition to a different lifestyle that has its own challenges, adventures and rewards. It is Barb's ability to see that and face the unknown with confidence that I find to be her greatest strength and most admirable virtue. Thank you, Barb, for that inner strength and support. It has been the wellspring of my determination to build this new life for us as well as the foundation of my lasting love for you. As we stand together admiring the sunrise of our retirement, I just wanted to make sure I gave you credit for your courage and devotion as best I can when words just can't say enough.

Post 8: Early Signs of Spring

February 18, 2017

We heard them for the first time this season on Sunday afternoon, February 12, a few hours after the sun emerged from the early morning clouds. It started with just one, but we eventually heard three or so. It was the first spring peepers in our little peeper pond. Apparently, the weekend sun had warmed the water just enough to begin rousing them from their winter slumber in the submerged silt at the bottom of the pond. It was the first audible sign that spring might be coming early to Peeper Pond Farm this year. However, one "sign" does not, in and of itself, herald an early spring. Since then, we have seen a number of other clear signs that spring weather is beginning to take hold.

When I returned to our farm on Friday afternoon, February 17—following my last day of work at my career job before retirement—I saw and heard the second sign. I walked out on the front porch in anticipation of Barb's arrival and I saw a flock of black birds circling over our peeper pond. They were about 350 feet from me, so I couldn't see the signature reddish/orange blaze on the front of their wings. At first, I thought they were crows, but they soon settled down into the cat o' nine tails and red cedar trees that frame the pond. Then, all at once, they began to sing. At that moment, I realized I was seeing and hearing the first flock of red-wing blackbirds to return to our peeper pond for the coming summer season! Oh, how we enjoy their distinctive and playful songs every summer.

Today, we discovered several other clear signs of the changing season. We were watching the goldfinches feeding at our sock feeder just outside the dining room window. They have begun shedding their heavy gray winter plumage, exposing the bright golden feathers beneath. Then we noticed that the crocuses at the end of our driveway were emerging from the ground and the buds on our lilac and forsythia bushes were swelling to burst. When we visited our next-door neighbor for lunch today, she drew our attention to the hellebores that were beginning to bloom beside her garage. Most everyone knows that blooming crocuses are an early sign of spring, but hellebores, which are deer resistant and popular in our area for that quality, will also poke through the late winter snow to bloom. When you consider all of these "signs" occurring within the span of a week—along with the forecasted 60-degree highs over the next six days—they provide sound and unmistakable evidence that the season is changing.

Although, coincidentally, I am celebrating the first full day of my retirement, I have more farming supplies to purchase before we receive our dairy goats.

That's what I'll be working to do in the coming week, along with organizing our garage, moving our belongings from the Keyser apartment that has been our workweek home for the past ten months, preparing our garden soil for spring planting and whatever else I may later realize I need to do. So much for retirement. At least, I can look forward to the first true rite of spring—our annual mid-March pilgrimage to Eagle's sugar camp in Highland County, VA to experience the sight, smell, taste and embracing warmth of the year's maple syrup harvest! The season is changing along with the daily patterns of our life as we begin to chart the course of our retirement. Nothing could feel or be more reassuring or affirming than that. Now the real adventure that we have been working to realize over the past eleven years begins! We hope you'll continue to follow us as we carry you along for the ride.

Post 9: Angel's Breath

February 21, 2017

    Yesterday, February 20, was the third day of my retirement. Warm, sunny weather was predicted. I first decided to harrow the garden to loosen and mix the soil in preparation for spring planting. It's a little early, but the weather and soil conditions were right so I decided to get a jump-start on the season. With Barb's help, I attached the harrow to the tractor and "Zambonied" the garden plot—driving down one edge, turning sharply, driving down the center, then shifting the next loop into the garden gradually working my way to the opposite side. It is an efficient way to work the soil when your turn-around mobility with the tractor is constrained on the sides by the garden fence.

    As the temperature warmed to a high of 67 degrees, I decided to supplement the dirt floor of my goat barn by adding several wheel-barrow loads of sandy loam. The sandy dirt floor makes a perfect bedding base for the goat barn, allowing urine to drain down to a thick gravel bed deep beneath the soil, minimizing the acidic ammonia odor that can cause lung problems in goats. I will add a bedding layer of hay before the goats arrive, and I will need to add lime periodically to minimize fly larvae.

    I finished the day by mixing and setting out some sugar syrup (50% sugar and 50% water by content) in buckets to feed our honey bees. Extended warm periods during the winter will stimulate the bees to leave the hives and begin searching for pollen, which is not yet available. The extra energy the bees expend during the futile searches will cause them to drain their winter stores of honey at a faster rate, exposing them to the threat of starvation if the cold weather returns and traps them in the hive with diminished food supplies. The sugar syrup will give them a source of food that they can use during the warm spell. I guess you could say it was my first full day of retirement farming, and it felt so good to work outside on such a lovely and pleasant day.

    After supper, I decided to relax on the front porch for a while and enjoy the view as the sun was setting. The fading light from the sun (which had already descended behind Cave Mountain) cast an azure glow along the horizon against which a brush-stroke of orange-red cirrus clouds blazed. The spring peepers were chirping cheerfully in celebration of the scene, and I was drawn off the porch to soak in the subtle beauty of the nightfall that was settling in around me. My eyes were drawn up into the sky by the bright, lonely white shimmer of Venus hanging over Cave Mountain. As I glanced even higher into the evening sky to study the streaking contrail of a passing jet, I felt the chilly brush of a gentle breeze against my cheeks. If the trees were in leaf, I would have seen the delicate branches bobbing up and down instead of swaying side to side, as would happen if a breeze were blowing along the land.

That gentle kiss of cool air settling into our valley revived childhood memories of warm, starry summer nights on our Connecticut River Valley dairy farm in New Hampshire, when our family would collect on the back lawn and relish the descending chill from the heavens. My adoptive grandmother always called this condition an *"Angel's Breath."* As she would explain to us, it was on nights like that when the angels above would draw down so close to the earth that you could feel their gentle breath brushing against your face. Many times, the descending air would stir the hair on the top of my arms and send a chill up my spine at the thought that the spirits of our ancestors were closing in on us from heaven above.

As I grew older, I read many books on meteorology. Those books taught me that the atmospheric condition I just described is caused by a temperature inversion when cool, heavy, dense, evening air settles into the valleys, leaving the mountaintops warmer during the night than the valley floor. The science behind that explanation makes sense, but it lacks the colorful and haunting suspense of her explanation. Although she lived to be 100 years old, she passed away about fifteen years ago and is now only a memory, like her Angel's Breath story. Still, the memory of those pleasant evening outings from my childhood brought a wistful smile to my face. Even though I understand the science behind it, I entertained the thought that perhaps it was her breath that I felt brushing against my face.

Post 10: Our First Goat Kids Are Born!

March 7, 2017

Spring continues to unfold here at Peeper Pond Farm. Our daffodils are in full bloom, Bradford Pear trees are blooming in Petersburg, large flocks of geese are flying north, and the ducks have returned to our peeper pond. The spring peepers are chirping gleefully on warm days and nights. We are also receiving two new neighboring families to homes that have sold in our small community. Both houses, which have stood vacant for several months, sold within the past week. Everything, including two empty houses in our neighborhood, is coming back to life.

I am also pleased to announce that we will soon receive our first Oberhasli doe kids! Esmeralda (who we will nickname "Essie") was born on February 28, 2017. Our second doe kid, which Barb wants to name Gertie, was born on March 5, 2017. They will be coming to our farm courtesy of Steve and Linda Anders at Blue Ridge Dairy Goats. Unfortunately, we don't have pictures of our new kids yet.

Steve and Linda have been raising American Dairy Goat Association (ADGA) registered Oberhasli goats for more than 30 years, many of which have received awards at regional goat shows. They have graciously offered to sell us some of their adult milking goats, which would allow us to build a pure Oberhasli herd from the start. We anticipate making our first trip to pick up our new goat kids in the next 2-3 weeks. Of course, we are very excited about the prospect of getting our milking adults on that trip as well.

Our preparations to receive our goats are just about complete. I finished ordering the last of our initial goat supplies on March 5 and I will be working this week and next to acquire the hay, grain and minerals we will need to feed our goats. I have waited to purchase the feed last because I want it to be as fresh as possible when the stars of our farm operation arrive. Finally, our homestead farming operation, which we have been planning and building for the past eleven years, will be in full operation by the beginning of April. That knowledge alone is the most rewarding sign of renewed life here at peeper pond farm this spring. Please stay tuned for more news and pictures!

Post 11: Sugarin' Time

March 12, 2017

    When I was growing up on our North Charlestown, NH dairy farm, the winters were long and harsh. The first snowfall would typically occur sometime in October and by the end of the first week of December, a thick blanket of snow would accumulate and linger uninterrupted across the frozen landscape into the month of April. Our family spent a lot of time during those cold, dark, snowy winter months in our large eat-in kitchen, which was heated by an old-fashioned Home Comfort wood stove. The long winter confinement would inevitably result in a severe case of cabin fever that gradually intensified our thirst for spring.

    Perhaps the best cure for cabin fever that I can recall was a trip to our local sugar house in March for a taste of the season's maple syrup crop. It was a treat for the senses. The steam rising from a wood-fired evaporator would fill the sugar camp with a soft haze thick with the sugary-sweet aroma of boiling sap and the smoky scent of burning wood. The embracing warmth generated by the evaporator would thaw the deepest winter chill. Then, the ultimate anticipation—the taste of a free sample of maple syrup, a maple sugar candy, or a cup of sugar on snow. After months of winter interment, a visit to the sugar camp was a welcome and reassuring awakening of the senses.

    The winters here at Peeper Pond Farm pale in comparison with those I experienced growing up in New Hampshire. Maple sap, once collected in buckets using a horse-drawn sled, is now fed directly to the sugar camp through a network of vacuum hoses. Yet, despite changes in time, location and technology, we have been making our annual March pilgrimage to Eagle's Sugar Camp in Doe Hill, VA for the Highland County Maple Sugar Festival every year since 2006. This year (today), we were joined by our friends, Jim and Donna Boyd for their very first trip. We shared stories and laughed as we ate our maple donuts and toured the craft fair. While the local sugar camps no longer offer free samples and I'm not sure any of them have ever heard of sugar on snow, we still enjoy buying our half-gallon of real maple syrup, a box of maple donuts and a package of maple sugar candy. Sugarin' time remains an important rite of spring, as the maple trees awaken from their winter slumber and sap begins to run through their veins. Hopefully, we have passed along the tradition to our friends.

Post 12: Winter's Snowy Reprieve

March 14, 2017

I must admit, it was difficult to believe the weather forecast for today. We have experienced a snow drought throughout the winter—having received only 6.5 inches of total snowfall from the first snowfall in late October until one week before the first day of spring. Our biggest snowfall this season was a mere two inches and we have had no need to plow our driveway this year. Consequently, when the weather forecast called for five-eight inches last night into this morning, we received it with a grain of salt. However, as the picture that accompanies this post clearly shows, we awoke to a six-inch blanket of white. Even with that amount, we were lucky. The coastal cities to our east were expected to receive a foot or more of snow and even higher totals were forecasted for New England. We still may not be finished with snow for the season. The forecast is calling for an additional lighter spring snowfall a week from this Thursday.

This storm raises our seasonal snowfall total to 12.5 inches making it a tie (with the 2011-2012 winter season) for the least winter snowfall in the ten years I have tracked since we moved to the Potomac Highlands. The 30-year average snowfall for our area is about 25 inches. Just ten miles (as the crow flies) west of us on the Allegheny Front, the 30-year average winter snowfall is over 100 inches and can exceed 200 inches in heavy snow seasons. Last season, we received 28 inches here at Peeper Pond Farm during a two-day storm in January, 2016. In case you're wondering, the highest seasonal snowfall total I recorded over the past decade was in 2009-2010 when we received just over 100 inches, including three storms that dumped more than a foot of snow each.

It was a pleasure to step out on our front porch this morning to take pictures of the ethereal snowy scene. With a morning low of 27 degrees and light, intermittent winds, it was fairly comfortable to admire the beauty. It was a wet, heavy snow that clung to the tree branches like a fresh coat of white paint. The boughs of the cedar and pine trees drooped reverently under the weight of their silky burden. The more distant mountains that frame our landscape were gently shrouded by a snowy haze that would make you wonder if they were really there or not. It was easy to see the bright red plumage of one of our male cardinals sitting on our fence, waiting patiently for his turn at our bird feeders. The thick blanket of snow on the ground forces the ground feeders to vie for a spot on the bird feeder for their morning sunflower seed feast. The dark blue water in our peeper pond was easy to spot against the snow blanketing our field. It was a picture of winter beauty at its best and a delight for the senses. I just wish it had been here for Christmas, rather than Saint Patrick's Day. I'm sure the weather will be better and more predictable when I'm elected President of the climate.

My primary job for the day will be to plow out our driveway with the tractor. We will spend most of the day indoors rearranging and reorganizing the house to make way for the rest of our belongings from our transitional Keyser apartment. We are also making final arrangements to receive our first doe kids, Esmeralda and Gertie. We are scheduled to pick them up at Blue Ridge Dairy Goats on Saturday, March 18. Finally, (weather permitting) we will be receiving the first of our dairy goat herd that will make our homestead farm operation complete. Hopefully, when we bring our doe kids to their new home at Peeper Pond Farm, we will bring a return to spring with us.

You can find additional photos of the snowfall on the "Dave's Pictures" page of our website.

Post 13: Essie & Gertie Come Home

March 19, 2017

    It was a foggy, dreary Saturday morning yesterday, as we headed out to Blue Ridge Dairy Goat farm to pick up our first two Oberhasli goat kids and bring them to their new home here at Peeper Pond Farm. The skies remained dull and gloomy until we crested Shenandoah Mountain on Corridor H (U.S. Route 48), just past Moorefield. Then, the skies cleared and the sun emerged from the haze, guiding us along for the rest of our journey. We arrived at Blue Ridge Dairy Goats around 1:15 PM and met Steve Anders as he was parking his Kubota tractor to disconnect his snow plow blade. We compared snowfall totals (we both received six inches from the storm despite being about 110 miles apart), as Steve led us to his garage to meet our goats for the first time. There in the garage holding pen we saw four exuberant Oberhasli goat kids, each about the size of an average hound dog. As we approached the pen, all four kids stood up on their hind legs and enthusiastically pawed at the top rail of the pen begging for their share of Steve's attention. Finally, after years of preparation and anticipation, we met our two-plus-week-old Esmeralda and Gertie for the first time.

    We picked them up and cradled them in our arms briefly as they squirmed and sniffed our faces, then carried them to the large dog cage in the back of our truck and loaded them in for their 2.5-hour ride through the mountains. After they were safely loaded, I took my first picture of them, which appears in this post. Steve then showed us some of his adult Oberhasli does that he was willing to sell us after they give birth. We selected two friendly does, five-year old Cara and four-year old Emerald as our first milking does, both of which are due to give birth around mid-April. We will return to Blue Ridge Dairy Goats soon thereafter to bring them home to share our barn with Essie and Gertie. We wish to express our great appreciation to Steve and Linda Anders for helping us build our initial dairy goat herd.

    Essie and Gertie appeared to enjoy their first riding adventure as they watched the cars and mountains drift by the rear window of our capped truck bed. Their tranquility was disturbed periodically by the sudden change in the sound of the tires on the pavement as we crossed over some concrete bridges. Each time the tires whined on the concrete pavement, I could see their heads and ears perk up in the rear-view mirror to make sure all was okay.

    We arrived home shortly after 4:30 PM and carried the now excited goats into their new goat barn. Since we have no adults yet, I was able to give them free run of the barn. Once turned loose on the bed of coarse hay, they began to bounce and dart nervously around the barn, expending their stores of energy to explore their new surroundings. They began to settle down as we fed them their first bottles of pasteurized goat milk from Steve's farm. He provided us with two gallons of fresh milk, which we will use as we transition them gradually over the coming weeks onto goat milk replacer and dry feed (hay and grain). After a reassuring bottle of warm milk, we gave them as much attention as we could as they pranced jubilantly around the barn tasting hay and nibbling gently at our clothes and fingers. People think that goats will eat anything, but they are really quite finicky eaters. However, they will nibble at most anything as they use their lips and sense of taste to augment their sense of smell even though they will only eat food that will pass their considered inspection. This nibbling behavior leads casual observers to believe that goats will eat anything, even though it is just one of many goat myths.

Now we face the challenge of raising our goat kids and building our homestead dairy herd. So far, Essie and Gertie appear to have adjusted well to their new setting and when I entered the barn before sunrise this morning for their morning feeding, they greeted me eagerly. We look forward to sharing the story of their growth and antics in future posts. We also hope to add Cara and Emerald in late April or early May. In addition to the picture that appears with this post, I took several more which you will find posted on the "Dave's Pictures" page of our website. I will also post Essie and Gertie's information on the "Our Livestock" pages. We hope you'll continue following our progress as we embark on our homestead farming adventure.

Post 14: Introducing Essie & Gertie To the Great Outdoors

March 20, 2017

Esmeralda and Gertie's second full day at Peeper Pond Farm was heralded by a bright red and orange sunrise and a return to spring-like warmth after more than a week of winter cold and snow. March came in like the proverbial lion, but the first day of spring arrived like a lamb. With the irresistible sunny skies and 58-degree afternoon warmth, we decided it was time for Essie and Gertie to get their first experience in the great outdoors at Peeper Pond Farm.

When I first opened the eight-foot sliding door leading to the main goat pen, Essie and Gertie stood at the entrance in awe. For the first time, there was no barrier between them and the open pen. I had to coax them outdoors before they would believe they were free to go. Once their feet hit the grassy ground, there was no turning back. They raced down the hill, leaping, romping and braying enthusiastically along the way. After several minutes of energetic darting about and chasing each other, they reached the rockpile I had built for them near the center of the pen. They stared at the jumbled rocks in eager anticipation, as they tried to decide the best way to conquer it. After approaching it from several angles, Esmeralda carefully and deftly climbed her way to the top. Not to be outdone, Gertie followed after several shaky attempts to climb the rocks. The rockpile was the highlight of their first afternoon in the sun.

Our girls got their first taste of the green weeds and plants that will eventually become an important part of their summer diet. Our goat pens abound in plants that goats love to eat, including red clover, daisies, multi-flora rose, thistle, chicory, dandelion and nettles. We even plan to plant some tasty sunflower plants along the north fence line (so the fencing will help support the plant stems against the south winds). Our goats will find a veritable smorgasbord of tasty vegetation to browse in our adult and kid pens throughout the summer.

Essie and Gertie spent between two and three hours outdoors today before we returned them to the safety of their warm, dry goat barn. We hope they'll have happy dreams of their first outdoors adventure and will be ready to hit the ground running tomorrow. For us, watching them frolic and play in the open air was one of the memorable side benefits of our new farming lifestyle. Please visit our "Dave's Pictures" page for additional photos of their antics.

Post 15: Preparing the Garden for Spring Planting

March 25, 2017

    Spring weather appears to be settling in for the long haul at Peeper Pond Farm. Our high temperatures topped out in the '70s for two straight days, and they are forecasted to stay in the '60s and '70s for the next ten days. Even the spring peepers are now in full symphony celebrating the arrival of spring. We have enjoyed a dry spell since the snow storm last week and, with the forecast for rain next week, the time was ripe to prepare our 4,500-square foot vegetable garden for spring planting.

    Last spring, we hired one of our neighbors to plow (using a two-blade bottom plow) and harrow our garden plot. He plowed the garden twice (once lengthwise and again widthwise) to turn the soil and allow us to remove the largest boulders and rocks. If you do not know West Virginia well, I will tell you that rocks grow well in our soil. In fact, I have told many people that when you buy land in West Virginia you pay for the rocks—the soil is free.

    You should also know that West Virginia rocks can be classified by size. The boulders are very large rocks that challenge the ability of one person to move. We pulled several of them from our garden plot, one of which required some help from the tractor. The next general size category is plain rocks, which still require two hands to move, but can be lifted and hauled. They generally range in weight from ten to fifty pounds. The next category is stones, which weigh less than ten pounds, but are no smaller than a clenched fist. After that, come the pebbles, which are smaller than your fist. After nearly a dozen rock-picking efforts, we believe we have removed all of the boulders, rocks and stones. They (along with a number of palm-sized pebbles) have been placed in a line of rock rubble stretching the length of our garden between the garden fence and the driveway. Since the garden is located on a slope below the driveway, the line of loose rocks helps slow and minimize the washing effect of storm water runoff from the driveway.

    After plowing the soil and picking out the large rocks, we used a disk harrow to break up the clay soil chunks and furrows left by the plow. We harrowed it four times (again in both directions)—twice in the late spring and again in the fall, just before we installed the fencing. Then we brought in six dump truck loads of mushroom soil to improve fertility by enriching the clay and reducing the soil density. I spread the piles of mushroom soil over the garden plot and allowed it to lay fallow throughout the winter, so that the winter rains and snow melt would allow the fertile top layer to slowly filter into the broken clay base. I did decide to harrow the garden for a fifth time in late February to loosen the compacted soil for the final step. The last task before planting was to roto-till the garden, thereby further refining and mixing the soil layers into a deep, soft composite layer that will support plant growth. I did that work today, tilling it once widthwise and a second time lengthwise. Our soil is now so soft and loose that my feet sunk at least three inches as I walked the width and length of the garden behind the tiller. Any experience gardener would be eager to work with it. The rain we expect to receive next week will further promote consolidation and settling of the rich planting soil.

If we had lived 100 years ago, the garden preparation work would have been done using one or two draft horses, pulling a single blade bottom plow, followed by a disk or spike harrow. The final mixing of the soil would be done either by the farmer using a hoe or a horse drawn cultivator, which would have two wheels, a seat for the driver and a set of curved jagged metal tines in the back that would dig into and mix the soil. My roto-tiller does a better job of mixing the soil as the rotating tines efficiently mix the soil in the same way that a mixer blends eggs. The mixing effect allows us to blend the fertile compost with the clay base that will help hold beneficial rainwater in the soil. In addition, I can use the roto-tiller during the growing season to periodically cultivate out the weeds in the walking paths between the vegetable rows.

Barb is putting the final touches on her garden plan and buying our seeds. The size of our garden (4,500 square feet) may seem large for two people, but we plan to grow enough excess vegetables to can and preserve so that they will support us throughout the winter. We would rather sell any excess vegetables we don't need than to grow only enough to eat during the growing season and have to buy canned vegetables from the store through the long winter months (which in our part of West Virginia can last five-six months). When I was growing up on our New Hampshire dairy farm, we planted an 11,250-square foot garden each year to support a family of seven, plus a little extra for our grandparents. Based on our smaller household size, our garden should be just about the right size. Now we'll see how well we can grow our vegetable bounty.

Post 16: Peeper Pond Farm Comes to Life

March 30, 2017

It's been a very busy week here on the farm. As spring weather firmly takes control, everything is coming to life—including our farm. The blossoms on one of the red haven peach trees in our fruit tree grove are bursting with delicate color. That was my signal to spray the fruit trees for the first time this year. I would prefer not to treat them, but we have many red cedar trees on our property and on neighboring properties that are a winter host to red cedar rust spores, which causes orange-red spots on our apple tree leaves, impeding their growth and ability to support a healthy apple crop. This blight has become prevalent throughout the traditional apple growing areas in the northern South Branch (of the Potomac River) and Shenandoah valleys. During our drive to pick up our goat kids on March 18, we passed through the northern Shenandoah valley around the Winchester Area where apple groves are common. This year, all of the mature trees on two large orchards we passed had been bulldozed down—perhaps a reflection of the struggles that apple growers face with all the pests and blights they must battle and the escalating cost of treatment they must absorb to protect their trees.

I must admit, we have struggled to maintain our own small orchard (thirteen apple trees and four peach trees). Although the orchard was the first element of our farm operation that we established back in 2007, we have replaced more than eight trees (some of them twice). Our apple trees have yet to produce more than a dozen apples in any year and our peach trees first began producing fruit last season. This year, we have to replace two more peach trees and at least two apple trees. We are pinning our hopes to salvage our fruit grove on two changes that will occur this year. We have retired, so we can work on the trees full-time rather than just on the weekends and we now have our honey bees to help pollinate the trees. Nevertheless, I will still have to aggressively treat our apple and peach trees to help them survive the red cedar rust. If the situation does not improve over the next two growing seasons, we may have to replace our own apple trees with grapes, blueberries, raspberries, or other fruits to augment our diet. It would be a shame to lose all of the family and commercial orchards that have been such a major component of our region's agricultural heritage.

With respect to our bee hives, we spent portions of two days this week getting them ready for spring. Our friend, Jim Boyd warned us that the winter has been hard on his hives and that we need to begin spring maintenance early so that they can survive until the flowering trees and plants begin producing the pollen they need. Supported by the warm, sunny weather we had yesterday, Barb and I opened both hives to check on their honey levels and to restack the hives so that the bees can begin rebuilding their stores of honey. During the winter months, the honey bees gradually migrate from the bottom box in the hive to the top box as they consume their summer honey supplies. By the beginning of the spring season, the bees are concentrated in the top box, so beekeepers need to take the top box off and place it at the bottom of the hive— so that the bees can begin building both their brood to gather pollen and their stores of honey. I also went back to the hives this morning to rotate the entrance guard to the hive so that the wider opening is available to them.

I am concerned about our Carniolan hive, which has only a small number of surviving bees. While I cannot count them, it was apparent that their colony is precariously small and their honey supply has been exhausted. I am supplying them with sugar water and pollen patties to give them a source of food to help them survive into the pollen season. They didn't exhaust their food supply because the winter was too cold; it was quite the opposite. The extended warm spells we experienced sporadically throughout the winter caused the bees to be more active searching for pollen when it wasn't available, thereby causing them to consume their precious supply of honey faster. This impacted our smaller Carniolan colony worse than it did our larger Italian bee colony.

Because our Italian colony was larger, more active during the summer and produced more honey, their hive is much healthier, and they have significant honey stores left in the outer frames. I am more optimistic they will survive until the pollen season is in full swing. However, I am feeding them sugar water and pollen patties as well. Hopefully, with our fruit trees beginning to bloom early, the bees will be able to begin collecting pollen again and, in doing so, ensure that our apple and peach trees will produce more fruit. I can only wait and see if we'll get lucky.

We also spent time staking out and beginning to plant our garden. On Sunday (four days ago) we planted two rows of potatoes (Yukon Golds and Kennebecs), one row of peas and a row of lettuce. We planted those seeds one day before we received a beneficial one-half inch of soaking rain on Monday, which will give them a good start. While we were working around the garden fence earlier today, Barb noticed that some of the peas are beginning to sprout. Barb is hoping to begin planting carrots and spinach sometime next week after we get through the next round of rain.

Our two goat kids (Essie and Gertie) are growing fast and gaining weight. I am shifting them out of the adult goat pen and into their kid pen, where (two days ago) I built a tree platform for them in a forked trunk red cedar tree located just beyond the barn. I built another rock pile (smaller than the one I constructed in the adult goat pen) to give them a raised access point from which to jump up onto the tree platform. They love to leap onto the platform and chew bark off the trunks of the cedar tree. I am keeping them in the kid pen for several days, so I can sow some red clover seeds in the adult pen for the adults to eat when they arrive in late April or early May. I wanted to give the clover seeds a chance to sprout before I let the kids romp around in that pen again.

All this spring work and activity is bringing our farm operation to life. It is an exciting start to the new season for us, as well as for our retirement life. Within the next few months, we will be producing fresh goat milk as well as some cheese, yogurt, soap, butter and other sundries. By the middle of June, we should be harvesting our early vegetables. With a little luck, we may be bottling our first jars of honey by mid-summer and harvesting some fruit from our orchard in the early fall so we can preserve some applesauce, apple jelly and apple pie filling for the winter. This is the life we are working to build here at Peeper Pond Farm. I hope to have many stories of our successes and mistakes to share with you along the way. Such is life on a farm. Now, if we can only find the time to finish moving our belongings out of the apartment we rented in Keyser to finish out our professional careers.

Post 17: Dignity

April 12, 2017

We've been busy lately finishing our move out of our temporary Keyser apartment (which we completed last week), organizing our house, shed and garage, planting our garden, mowing yards for the first time this season and preparing to receive our adult goats. It has been a lot of work, but the weather has been very pleasant (fair skies with highs mostly in the low-to-mid 70s). Still, we have a lot to do before our adult goats arrive. So, we decided to take the better part of a day off yesterday (Tuesday) for a trip to the Grafton, WV area. Barb wanted to chat with her former co-workers at the Grafton office of her credit union (whom she had not seen since her retirement), and I decided it would be a good opportunity for us to visit my biological father's grave at the West Virginia National Cemetery in the adjoining community of Pruntytown. We paid our respects and left some red roses before his gravestone.

The visit gave me cause to think about dignity. When my former coworkers would ask me why I was pursuing early retirement when I was young enough to work longer at my professional career, I would tell them that I was aware of the gradual decline in my mental capacity to do my work competently. I was forgetting legal deadlines and procedures, struggling with simple math and misspelling words that others used to ask me how to spell. I have always been very conscientious about my work, so I explained that I wanted to retire with dignity, rather than lingering on at the job until I was forced to retire because I was no longer able to do the work competently. Dignity has always been a difficult thing for me to achieve (by my own standards) because I struggled so long with my own self-esteem. I simply didn't want to become someone who had to depend on my *past* work achievements to salvage my professional reputation because I stayed in the job longer than the quality of my current work could justify. Simply put, I wanted to retire with my own dignity intact.

Dignity is an important virtue to people like me who strive to live as self-reliantly as possible. It can be a double-edged sword, as I know a lot of people whose dignity is based more on vanity than on their competence or abilities. Such people feel that money, their appearance and the brand names on their possessions make them dignified in the minds of others. I am speaking of the dignity that derives from the personal integrity that you demonstrate to others by the way you conduct yourself and the way you live according to your core values. To me, this is the dignity that you *earn*, not demand from others. I guess I view dignity that you demand from others, rather than earn from them, as another aspect of excessive personal vanity.

I did not have the opportunity to grow up with my biological father. I was raised by an adoptive family on a small dairy farm on the opposite side of state from where my biological family lived. I found my birth family when I was 36 years old and was only able to know my biological father for six years before he died in 2004. According to what my mother, brothers and sisters told me about him, he may not have been the best father to them or even the best father he could have been. In some respects, I guess I have not done much better. However, I developed a good measure of respect for the father I was able to know during the final six years of his life.

He served in the Air Force for 23 years and saw active combat in World War II and the Korean War, eventually retiring in the earliest years of the Vietnam War. He told me that he survived the Bataan Death March (which he escaped with the help of some native Filipinos - aboriginals), fought during the battle of Okinawa and was trapped behind enemy lines for more than seven months during the Korean War. His struggle to survive his entrapment during the Korean War left him with a scar on his face from an enemy rifle butt during hand-to-hand combat for his life, the loss of three quarters of his stomach after living on grubs during the ordeal and a steel plate in his head to repair skull fractures. He placed his life on the line numerous times during his military service, and I would not have been born if he hadn't served bravely and with distinction. By the time he died of cancer in 2004, he had suffered a number of heart attacks and strokes. In fact, I was with him when he suffered the last of his strokes and managed to get him to the hospital in time to save him. He spoke six languages (most of them fluently), although he dropped out of high school. As the cancer began to affect his mind, he would suddenly start speaking Japanese.

I learned from my discussions with him over his final years that he had indeed earned a good measure of dignity. After he died, his body was cremated (in accordance with his request) and my mother kept his remains in an urn that sat on a pedestal in her home. Occasionally, she would argue with his remains (a rather one-sided fight) over a number of alleged transgressions she felt he committed over the 41 years of their marriage—some of which I learned were not fully justified. When Barb and I visited her in late 2012, she slipped into one of her arguments with my father's remains and threatened to dump them in a ravine behind her apartment building. It was then that I offered to take his remains with us so that they could be laid to rest with some measure of dignity. I had hoped that removing his remains would help end her arguments with him, but I guess it wasn't enough. When I returned home to WV, I had his remains interred at the WV National Cemetery with full military honors. I felt it was the least I could do to show respect for the father who gave me life and served his country va iantly. As far as I know, my wife and I and one of my biological brothers (who now lives in our area of WV) are the only family members who have visited his grave. Perhaps now he can rest in peace.

Now I am working to establish a small, homestead dairy farm at Peeper Pond Farm. I hope I can do it all successfully and with dignity. That is one characteristic I have never been able to give myself, but that I hope I can earn. I see it as the least I can do for the two fathers I have had—the one who gave me life and the one who raised me. It is also something I must do to bring integrity to the value of self-reliance that has guided my life and brought me to this beautiful and bountiful place that we all know as West Virginia. May we all live our lives with dignity and earn that assessment from our friends. Then we can all rest assured that we have lived a good and meaningful life.

Post 18: Welcoming Cara

April 22, 2017

    We are working with Steve Anders at Blue Ridge Dairy Goats on arrangements to pick up the first of our milking adult goats sometime around the first week of May. Cara has given birth and is ready to be transferred to us. She is a five-year-old Oberhasli doe with a very gentle disposition, and we are very eager to receive her. We will also be purchasing Emerald, a four-year-old adult, but she is nursing her newborn buck, and Steve needs to keep her to take care of him until he can find a home for him. He offered the buck to us, but we are not equipped to raise bucks at this time as we are concentrating on building our small milking herd. We will have more to say about Cara once she has settled in here at Peeper Pond Farm.

    In the meantime, we have been spending a lot of time raising our first two goat kids, Essie and Gertie. They are doing very well and are enjoying free run of the entire goat barn and both outdoor pens. They actually choose to spend most of their time in the kid pen that we built for them, even though the adult pen is much larger and has a plentiful supply of tasty grass and weeds. Essie and Gertie love to eat the multi-flora rose bushes that grow freely in our open field. They also love to climb onto the tree platform I built for them in the kid pen and chew bark off the red cedar trees that support it.

    For the past six weeks that we have raised them, we have been feeding them Sav-A-Kid milk replacer, which they really enjoy. We have been offering them hay, alfalfa pellets and sweet goat meal to encourage development of their rumens, which is the chamber of their stomach that will help them digest the majority of the food they will eat as adults. Within the next couple of weeks, we will be weaning them from the milk replacer and they will depend on adult foods (wild browse, hay, alfalfa pellets and sweet goat meal) until they are ready to be bred for the first time at about twenty months of age. Unfortunately, Essie and Gertie seem to like the milk replacer so much that I think they are trying to fool us into thinking we shouldn't wean them from it. Although we offer them free choice water and the adult feeds I mentioned, they try to drink water and eat the food only when we are not watching them. They like to spill their alfalfa pellet and sweet goat feed bowls occasionally during the night so we can't tell how much they have eaten. They also like to poop in the barn immediately after we have cleaned up all the poop piles they left for us overnight. Indeed, they seem to behave very much like human infants.

    In our spare time, we are planting our garden and working with our bees. We finished setting up our hives for the spring/summer pollen season yesterday and we have seen our bees visiting our fruit trees and flowering plants. We have already planted peas, lettuce, spinach, carrots, potatoes, onions, red cabbage, strawberries and peppers in our garden and are looking forward to adding some squash, cucumbers, tomatoes and corn. We will be waiting until early May to plant the tomatoes and corn, since they are most vulnerable to late frosts. All the while, we continue to enjoy daily evening serenades from the spring peepers in our pond. Life here at Peeper Pond Farm just couldn't be better.

Post 19: Forty Shades of Green

April 27, 2017

When Johnny Cash wrote the lyrics to the song named in the title of this post, he was writing about Donaghadee in Northern Ireland. However, when I look out our windows at the fields, flowers, trees and mountains of West Virginia, I see the same pastoral scene. The generous spring rains we received this past Saturday, Monday and Tuesday brought the leaves out on all the remaining trees and turned our view into a pastoral palate of countless shades of green—from the brilliant yellow greens of the sprouting lettuce in our garden, to the bright spring greens of the various deciduous trees, to the deep blue-greens of the cedars and pines. Each species of tree seems to announce its arrival on the scene with its own shade of green.

It always seems to me it is the yellows that first bring spring color to our landscape. The daffodils and dandelions are the first to appear, followed by the wild mustard in the meadows and along the creeks and the forsythia bushes in front yards around our area. Then, the grass begins to revive and the trees begin to leaf out returning green to the landscape. Now we have a complete celebration of greens, dappled with the lavender of the lilac bushes, the reddish purple of the red bud trees, the whites and pinks of the flowering dogwoods and the blues, whites and purples of the wild phlox. Springtime in West Virginia is a celebration of color, but it is the forty shades of green that proudly stands front and center before us now. Soon, the deciduous tree leaves will darken with age and assume a more similar shade, perhaps to give the wildflowers a chance to command our attention. To everything there is a season.

We celebrate not only the return of color to our landscape, but also the sounds of spring. The summer birds have returned and the chorus of their songs fills the early morning and evening air. While our spring peepers continue their courting songs, other species of frogs are joining the concert. To accompany their choir, we can hear the occasional cow lowing, rooster crowing, horse neighing, and of course, our goats bleating. Visitors often remark about how quiet and peaceful it seems at our farm, but in reality, the rural silence is filled with sounds—the sounds of silence. You just have to listen closely. That's why I often tell visitors to our front porch to close their eyes and *hear* the view. The majestic beauty of the mountains often steals your attention, and you forget to hear the sounds that waft across the landscape. It is during spring that we most appreciate the full beauty of our rural landscape. We look forward to sharing this stunning visual and auditory experience with you when you come to visit us here at Peeper Pond Farm.

Post 20: Blackwater

April 30, 2017

No, I'm not writing about a federal government subcontractor, I'm writing about Blackwater Falls State Park—one of the finest in the state of West Virginia. With the hot weather forecasted for today, Barb and I decided to cool off by taking a trip to our favorite state park near Davis, WV. With elevations ranging from 2,500 to 3,000 feet above sea level, temperatures in the park remained in the low-to-mid 70s during our visit, as opposed to the 85-degree high we experienced today at Peeper Pond Farm. It was also a good way to celebrate the anticipated arrival of our adult milking goats sometime in the coming week. The Blackwater River and its associated waterfalls and 1,000-foot-deep canyon provide some of the most dramatic, spectacular and majestic mountain scenery in West Virginia. Even though I did my best to take pictures of the falls and the canyon, I'm afraid they can't do justice to the experience you get from a visit to the park.

I took two pictures of the main falls of the Blackwater River, one of which appears in this post. The characteristic tawny color of the water is the reason why the river was named Blackwater. The tea coloring of the water is not caused by upstream contamination or soil erosion. Rather, the color is caused by the gradual decomposition of hemlock and spruce needles from Canaan Valley, through which the river's headwaters flow. Canaan Valley (pronounced differently in WV than its biblical namesake) is the highest mountain valley east of the Mississippi River and is forested with many hemlock and red spruce trees found only at the highest altitudes in WV. Each year, needles from these trees are dropped in the valley swamp through which the river passes, and their seasonal decomposition gives the water its dark coloring. As it leaves the valley, the water plummets 62 feet over the falls and descends into the canyon the river has carved over the millennia. At its greatest depths, the eight-mile-long canyon is at least 1,000 feet deep.

Another minor tributary stream creates Elakala Falls along the deep canyon walls. Elakala Falls is marked by several boulder-strewn cascades as it spills into the canyon to join the Blackwater River. Because trees crowd the steep canyon walls, Elakala Falls can be hard to see during low flow periods, but the rains we received over the past week swelled the creek and made the falls easy to both see and hear. In fact, Blackwater River was so swollen by storm water runoff that the two separate curtains of water that we typically see were joined into one single waterfall that thundered into the canyon.

We spent more than three hours in the park touring the various waterfall and canyon vantage points and enjoying the picnic lunch we packed for the trip. Over the past decade that we have lived in West Virginia, we have camped at and visited the park many times. During one of our camping trips, we were informed that two black bears had walked past our tent while we were sleeping! Fortunately, we were not interesting enough to draw their interest. Blackwater Falls State Park is one of the most scenic gems in our region that we hope you will take the time to visit for yourself—perhaps as part of a future trip to Peeper Pond Farm. You will not regret the experience. You can access more detailed information on the park on the Attractions/Events page of website under the "Our Community" header.

Post 21: A Year of Goat Experience in One Day

May 7, 2017

We have had a very busy week to say the least. It all started off innocently and pleasantly enough, but before it ended, I was left scratching my head asking, "What was that?" After thinking about it all for a while and laughing about it with our goat colleagues, I have come to the conclusion that we got a year's worth of goat-keeping experience in one 24-hour period. Let me explain.

Tuesday, May 2 started off with bright sunshine and a lot of anticipation. After twelve years of planning, sacrifice and hard work, we were heading off to Blue Ridge Dairy Goats to pick up our first milking goats. Finally, Peeper Pond Farm would be in full operation. At least four of the fruit trees in our orchard are producing abundantly (which seems like a miracle), all of the herbs in Barb's herb garden are growing well, our vegetable garden is nearly planted and we have already harvested some spring lettuce, we have installed a honey super on one of our bee hives, and I would begin milking my dairy goats. This would finally be our reward for all the work we've done to build and equip our fledgling homestead farm operation. What could possibly go wrong at this point? I shouldn't have asked myself that question. I guess I was tempting fate.

The 2.5-hour drive to Blue Ridge Dairy Goat Farm was very pleasant and went without a hitch. We loaded three goats, Cara, Emerald and her three-week- old buck (who we have named Billy The Kid) into our vintage Chevy truck and returned home by about 5:00 PM. Since Emerald has been feeding her newborn buck, she would not need to be milked again until the next morning. Her buck consumes most of the milk she is now producing, but not all of it, and it is a good idea to milk her once per day to make sure that she is being milked evenly. However, Cara is not nursing a kid, so she needed to be milked as soon as we got her home. We fed both of our new adults some sweet feed (high in protein) and gave them about 45 minutes to investigate the new barn and outdoor pen that would become their home. I realize that's not enough time to fully adjust, but I needed to make sure Cara was milked before too much time had passed from her traditional evening milking time at her prior home.

I brought Cara to the milking stand in our garage and fed her some sweet feed while I cleaned her udder and prepared to milk her. Cara was not expected to produce a lot of milk because the kid she birthed a couple of weeks earlier had been taken from her too late and she was still experiencing anxiety from the separation. When I first began to milk her, I could tell that her udder was full, but I struggled to get her to let her milk down. I talked calmly to her, caressed her neck and did everything I could to calm her, but I was only able to get about one and one-third cup of milk from her after more than twenty minutes of effort. At that point, she began to fidget and tried to kick at the milk pail, indicating that she was not willing to be milked any more. I was disappointed and concerned, as I knew she still had milk to give, but I took her back to the barn under the assumption that she might calm down by the next morning. My childhood experience with milking cows taught me not to push an animal to milk when it is unwilling because it may eventually learn to resent you and will resist your future milking efforts. After all, she was experiencing a lot of stress from the recent loss of her kid, the long ride to our farm, adjustment to a new and unfamiliar living environment and the transition from machine milking at her former home to hand milking here at Peeper Pond Farm. To compound this situation, this was my first hand-milking experience in nearly 40 years and Cara has rather small teats, which are more difficult to milk by hand.

    I started off eagerly at dawn on Wednesday morning to milk both Cara and Emerald. I started with Emerald, and despite the fact that her udder felt full, I could not get her to release any milk. I decided to put her back with her buck kid for a while thinking that her kid would be very hungry (since her full udder was a clear sign she had not fed him at all overnight) and he would get her to release her milk better than I could. So, I brought Cara in to milk her for the second time. However, she resisted my milking efforts and I could only get a few squirts of milk from both teats. Now I was genuinely concerned. Was I doing something wrong, or was the stress of the move and new surroundings too much for my goats? I knew it was critical to get them milked soon or the growing pressure of milk production would cause them to begin the process of drying off or might cause mastitis, a malady that causes clotting of the milk and makes it undrinkable. I returned Cara to the barn and called Steve Anders and our friend, Shelley Hutcheson, for some much-needed goat advice.

    As I was standing on our front porch talking with Shelley, I glanced back towards the goat barn and I noticed that Cara, Emerald and her buck were walking in circles in the barnyard. They had managed to get loose from the barn! Had I not closed the barn door securely? They didn't answer—they just stood there staring at me as if to ask innocently, "Where are we supposed to go now?" Shelley laughed as I tried to explain what was happening, and she concluded our brief conversation by saying, "Welcome to the goat world!" Barb and I dropped what we were doing and managed to corral them and get them back in the barn. The only remaining question was, how did they get out? The barn door was closed. All three outdoor fence gates were latched securely. While it was possible that the buck could have leapt over the fence, the adults were far too heavy to clear the four-foot-high fence without injuring themselves. Perhaps I failed to close the barn door securely, but how did they manage to close it after they got out? All we or our goat colleagues could do was laugh at the situation. We were learning just how clever and sneaky goats can be.

After taking with Steve Anders later that day, we learned that some of his goats know how to open a door with a round nob. He has several such doors at his farm and the door we use to go in and out of the goat barn also has a round knob. Apparently, goats can learn how to put their mouths around a door knob and twist it just enough to open it. I also recalled that after I put the goats in the barn and returned to the house to call Steve and Shelley for guidance, a sudden, strong gust of wind blew down off the mountain. If that gust of wind blew after the goats got out of the barn, it might have blown the door shut. To the best of our sleuthing abilities, we determined that is how the goats got out of the barn. Hopefully, we have remedied this situation by installing a child-proof plastic guard over the door knob that has only two small finger holes in opposing sides that we can use to pinch the door knob to turn it. Our goats should not be able to twist the knob with their mouths.

After talking over my milking problems with Steve Anders, we decided it would be best for me to purchase a hand-milking device that would make it easier for me to milk Cara and make it feel more like the machine milking that the goats are used to. In the meantime, I would bring the goats back to Steve's farm so they could be machine-milked in a familiar environment until I could get the hand-milking device. Since their udders were very tight, they needed to be successfully milked as soon as possible, and only Steve could do that. So, I loaded the goats back into my truck and drove them all the way back to Blue Ridge Dairy Goat farm, eventually arriving there around 1:30 PM that afternoon.

Steve and Linda brought Cara and Emerald into their milk room and successfully managed to get them to produce about half a gallon of milk combined. In fact, Emerald had begun letting her milk down during the trip and was leaking milk when I arrived. They also gave me some good advice regarding hand-milking goats. I was beginning to feel that we had the problem under control until I could take a different approach. I would have to make another trip to Blue Ridge Dairy Goats to pick them up again, but that was better than keeping them and creating a problem that would deprive us of any milk. I was determined to do whatever would be best for our goats. When I spoke to Steve again at the end of the week, he indicated that the goats were having problems readjusting to his farm again. Clearly, stress was one of the causes, but we decided that I was having problems milking Cara because of her small teats.

As I returned home from the unexpected trip to Blue Ridge Dairy Goats, I felt better about the situation because I knew that Steve would give them the care that they needed, and I could try it all again when I had the new equipment I needed. Although I wanted to avoid purchasing a milking machine, I knew all along that the arthritis I have been struggling with over the past decade would eventually make it increasingly difficult to hand milk my goats even if I gained enough experience to do it correctly.

However, I no sooner arrived home from the trip when I found Barb on the telephone talking to our vet. Apparently, sometime around 5:30 PM that day Barb discovered that one of our goat kids, Gertie, was down and not willing to drink her evening bottle of milk. When I went into the goat barn, Gertie was lying on the floor, moaning as she breathed and foaming slightly at the mouth. She was listless and could not stand up for more than 30 seconds at a time without lying down again. Although she was not producing diarrhea, her stools were very soft. I got my stethoscope and listened to her stomach. I could hear a gurgling sound on her left side, where her rumen is located. Gertie was clearly experiencing a case of bloat, which can be fatal for a young kid.

Once again, I was calling Steve and Shelley for advice on how to handle our new problem. We were told to get her to take some baking soda. We tried offering it to her by hand, but she wasn't interested in eating anything. I tried mixing the baking soda with some warm water and giving it to her using an oral drench syringe, but we weren't sure we were getting enough into her or even getting it in the right stomach chamber. Our vet advised us not to try again because, without proper experience, we might accidentally get it in her lungs, which would make matters worse. I eventually poured a couple of tablespoons of baking soda into the palm of my hand, forced her mouth open and fed it into her. I did it a second time, then stayed with her for another 45 minutes.

Suddenly, shortly after 7:00 PM, I noticed that she was perking up a bit and was able to stand again. I fed her some loose hay, which she ate eagerly and normally. By 7:30 PM, she drank her bottle of milk and was acting as though nothing had happened. Fortunately, it was a mild case of bloat, perhaps caused by eating too much green feed earlier in the day. We are working to wean Essie and Gertie from the milk replacer we have been feeding them over the past two months, and we decided to adjust their feedings as we cut the volume back to help them wean more gradually. Hopefully, that will solve that problem.

Although we had been raising Essie and Gertie successfully and without any problems for nearly two months, we experienced several complex and scary goat problems in one 24-hour span of time. You just never know when a cloudburst is going to rain on your parade. Consequently, we learned more about goat-keeping in one day that we had over the two previous months. Hopefully, the experience, while both frightening and funny, will make us better and more successful goat owners in the future. Perhaps I can take some solace in that thought—at least until our next disaster day occurs. We are looking forward to our next trip to Blue Ridge Dairy Goats (sometime in the coming week) when we can bring our goats back to their new home at Peeper Pond Farm for the final time. Wish us luck. Clearly, we need it!

Post 22: Presenting Our Dancing Lady

May 11, 2017

Armed with our new hand-operated milking device, Barb and I ventured off to Blue Ridge Dairy Goat Farm in Keedysville, MD on a sunny Wednesday morning (May 10) to bring our milking does (Cara and Emerald) and another dry adult doe (Dancing Lady) home to Peeper Pond Farm. The Henry Milker we purchased operates on the same basic principle as an electric vacuum pump milking machine, except that the pump is hand-operated. We tested it when it arrived on May 9 and it operated simply and efficiently. I needed this device to milk Cara successfully because she has small teats, which can be difficult to milk by hand. We have already modified the device, and it works perfectly. I also have arthritis in my hands and fingers that bothers me under certain weather conditions, so the new milking device will allow me to hand-milk my goats far longer than I might be able to without it.

Steve and Linda were able to get Cara and Emerald settled after their stressful trip to and from our farm on May 2 and 3. The adjustment to a new farm environment and owners is stressful for any dairy animal, but our goats also had to adjust to hand milking as well. Steve even had some problems getting Cara to settle down after her return, but he felt confident that she and Emerald were better prepared for the transition. We also arrived earlier in the day yesterday so we could get them home a few hours before their scheduled afternoon milking time. This gave them some additional time to relax and explore their new surroundings before having to be milked in the evening. The hand-operated milking device would also feel more like the machine milking they were accustomed to. All in all, the transition worked this time and Cara and Emerald produced nearly half a gallon of milk (combined) on their first evening milking and a full half-gallon the next morning. We are now producing fresh goat milk and preparing to experiment with various ways to utilize the excess volume of milk they will be producing. Barb is planning to make her first batch of hand lotion and some fresh cream and butter today.

Also, during our trip, we purchased another adult doe--four-year old Dancing Lady (who we call Lady for short). Her picture accompanies this post. She is one of Steve's show goats and has won a number of awards. She is currently dry, which means that she is not producing milk at this time. We will breed her in the late summer/early fall so that she can give birth this coming winter and begin producing milk for us next year. In the meantime, she seems quite content to enjoy her work vacation and stroll through our goat yard eating succulent grass and weeds.

After all the difficulties we faced last week during our initial attempt to bring our adults home, as documented in my previous post, we are enjoying the success we are having this time around. It is a great feeling to have our farm in full operation and to finally enjoy the peace and serenity of our retirement farming lifestyle. It is raining today, so we are taking a break from our outdoor work. However, once this rainy spell ends, we will be back in the garden to finish our soring planting and working with our bee hives. Our life is once again in harmony with the ebb and flow of our rural environment. As spring matures and our peeper frogs end their daily serenades, we can enjoy the beauty of the wild phlox and the locust tree blossoms as they dot the landscape with color. We hope you can find your own relief from the stress and madness of modern life in the beauty of the surrounding natural environment that embraces and nurtures us all.

Post 23: Goats & Tractors Are People Too

May 22, 2017

If you don't believe me, just own some for a while and they will teach you who's really the boss. Now that we have been milking our new adult goats for nearly two weeks, we are getting to know them better. Cara, the elder goat, is the queen of the herd. She exerts her influence over the other goats by pushing them around and charging them. She has terrorized Dancing Lady (our dry adult) to the point that she often spends a lot of her time standing alone in the pen outside our goat barn. I plan to install a fence divider in the designated sleeping area to create two open stalls that I hope will provide some separation within the barn between Cara and Lady. Only time will tell if it will work, but I can't get started on the improvement right away. Before I set the post for the divider, I need to clean out the bedding from the barn. For that project, I need some help from our 2004 33-HP Massey Ferguson tractor, which I have affectionately named "Ferguson." Unfortunately, Ferguson won't be much help until I can replace his hydraulic oil filter and give him a refill. I am waiting for the unexpectedly rare filter to be shipped to us. Maybe it seems like I am working for myself, but I'm still at the mercy of the weather, availability of essential supplies and cooperation from my livestock to get the work done.

It also occurs to me that our livestock and equipment have their own characters and idiosyncrasies—or "idiotsyncrasies" as they often appear to be. For example, soon after our adults returned, I noticed some shallow pits in the sandy-loam flooring in our goat barn. Within a few more days, I was standing on the front porch of our house looking at the goat barn, when I saw puffs of sand flying out the open door. It was then that I realized Cara was digging holes in the sand. I asked her former owner, Steve Anders, about this behavior and he said, "Oh yeah, Cara likes to dig in the barn bedding so she can sleep on the dirt. It's just her way." She's the only goat who does this. However, she digs so hard with her rear hooves that she digs craters up to a foot deep in the sandy dirt floor. You can imagine how it feels to enter the barn carrying a five-gallon bucket of water only to find the level of the floor has been lowered by an additional six to twelve inches. Fortunately, Emerald's buck kid (Billy The Kid) tries to help me control the problem. Barb has seen him digging in the dirt to fill in the golf course that Cara is working to build. The result is a dirt floor that shifts as frequently as the landscape of a wind-swept desert. I believe Cara was also the goat who managed to open the door I use to go in and out of the barn by turning the doorknob with her mouth. The plastic child protector I installed over the doorknob seems to have frustrated her at the expense of making it harder for me to open the door.

Each of our goats have their own unique character and behavior patterns, just as people do. Lady actually managed to remove her collar and tags. We discovered them missing when we entered the barn for the daily morning feeding. We don't know how she did it, but we searched the barn and pen and couldn't find them. Several days later, Barb was raking over the bedding and discovered one of her two tags, but no evidence of the other tag or the chain she was wearing. How did she managed to separate them? Barb was jokingly afraid she had eaten them, but I highly doubt that. Eventually, I just gave up looking and gave her a new collar. I thought if I replaced it, the original would suddenly appear, but that hasn't happened yet. Goats manage to do the strangest things.

As for Ferguson, he is resting peacefully in the driveway at our Peeper Pond Farm Tractor Spa. Ever since we bought him last July, he has been our faithful beast of burden. Oh, he would protest from time-to-time by refusing to start or reluctantly belching puffs of grey smoke when being urged to work, but he would always manage to get the job done. Given his choice, though, I think Ferguson would rather sleep than do a job for me that I am unable or unwilling to do for myself. I started to give him an overhaul in mid-March, when I lubed all of his grease fittings—at least those fittings that weren't broken off in some past job. I had to replace one of the fittings on his bucket loader. Then, I discovered that he had not been fully maintained by his prior owner. So, I began to give him a complete workover. I supplemented his coolant level, changed the antifreeze in his rear tires, cleaned his air filter (a new one is hard to find and very expensive), replaced his diesel fuel filter, replaced the engine oil and filter, replaced his front wheel drive gear oil and replaced a front tire that went flat. My final overhaul task was to replace his hydraulic oil and filter. After I had drained out all of the old oil, I discovered that I had been sold the wrong hydraulic oil filter. I spent a good part of the day this past Sunday calling auto part stores in search of the correct filter only to discover that it, like the air filter, is hard to find. Fortunately, I managed to find an affordable source on the Internet and ordered two so I would have the next replacement on hand when I should need it. When you live in a very rural area like we do, you need to be prepared for emergency situations.

Consequently, Ferguson is getting the extended vacation from work that I'm sure he was secretly plotting. I even think I could hear him snickering at me out of the corner of his grill. Either that, or farm work is gradually making me paranoid. I sincerely hope I can successfully finish Ferguson's overhaul so I can earn the cherished grease monkey degree from my correspondence course in tractor maintenance.

All I can say from all my recent experiences with goats and tractors is that they can act a lot like people. They can be strange, unpredictable, finicky, uncooperative and tricky—sometimes all at once. I think they know who's really in control and manage to find ways to throw you a curve when you least expect it. Consider this realization a lesson in the true nature of farm work. The State of West Virginia may call me the proprietor of Peeper Pond Farm, but the real bosses are the livestock and equipment. Just try to succeed at farming without their cooperation!

Post 24: Memories

May 24, 2017

Today is one of those cool, sullen, dreary days where the landscape is shrouded in fog. It rained most of the night, and the forecast is for more rain late this afternoon and through the day tomorrow. Whenever these periods occur, life and outdoor work at Peeper Pond Farm slow to a crawl in the muck-- the clay topsoil that fills the gaps between the rocks in our hardscrabble soil. Even the goats spend most of their time loafing in the barn to avoid venturing into the rain and muddy soil. Goats don't like to get wet. However, they do poop prolifically, and the visible traces of their presence in the barn gives new meaning to the term, "party poopers."

During these rainy days, we focus on indoor activities, such as house, garage, or barn maintenance (as needs may dictate). Barb has been hard at work in our kitchen (also known as the Peeper Pond Farm Laboratory) working on various different recipes to make creative use of our excess goat milk. Over the past few weeks, she has successfully made soap, cream, butter and a couple of cheeses from the milk our goats produce. We still need to work on the yogurt and hand lotion, both of which were too runny, but we will keep trying and will eventually f gure out how to get them right. We even had some delicious buttermilk pancakes made from the residual milk produced from the butter we churned.

We also do a lot of reading. Barb has been reading a book that she bought at the library book sale during the Pendleton County Spring Fest a couple of weeks ago. The book is, <u>Wasn't the Grass Greener?</u> by Barbara Holland. In it, Ms. Holland shares her laments about the gradual loss or disappearance of cherished features and activities from the past as the 20th century drew to a close, such as pianos (and piano playing), picnicking, clotheslines, desks and other things that have either been replaced or forgotten with the passage of time. I realize that, during my lifespan, transistor radios, eight-track tapes, floppy disks and video rental stores were invented and faded away into history. As Barb read passages from the book to me, I was inspired to think of all the changes I have seen since my childhood.

For instance, we used to take recreational rides through the countryside and perhaps stop for a casual picnic lunch at a "roadside stand," which Ms. Holland also discussed in her book. Some of these highway pullouts and their picnic tables remain in the New Hampshire, Vermont and West Virginia countryside, however they are seldom used and, more often than not, the picnic tables are severely worn out or chained to the ground to prevent theft. I can even remember playing car games on these trips, such as I Spy, car Bingo with cards filled randomly with features you could find along the road, or highway alphabet, where we would scan signs along the road to be the first to find (in order) all the letters of the alphabet. We would even compete to see how many different license plates we could see as we traveled along. Many of you who are my age or older would certainly remember these family activities. Maybe they sound quaint today, but they were fun activities at the time and helped make the drive feel like an adventure.

Today, people rarely go on a recreational drive. There is either too much traffic on the highways or people live so confined to their urban settings that they don't even think of taking trips into the countryside. Even if they did go for a drive, the kids would be too busy watching a DVD or playing with their cell phones to engage in such simple social activities. We seem to have little idle time that is not governed or absorbed by technological toys like computers, video games and cell phones. Social media has become the focus of most of our "social interaction," and our declining social skills appear to reflect it. It's very easy to be insensitive to someone when you communicate remotely and anonymously with people and can't see the hurt in their faces. Yes, modern technology can be empowering, but it can also be alienating, with consequences that are apparent in the daily headlines.

When I think back to the different ways we played as children, I am reminded that there is value to the simpler lifestyle we have chosen in retirement. Perhaps my family didn't always get along well and wasn't the model of rural living represented by <u>The Waltons</u>, but we did find great pleasure in outdoor activities and games. When we couldn't afford expensive toys, we used our imaginations to turn a fallen tree into a great tall sailing ship, or a roadside snow bank into a fort, or an abandoned well house into a wilderness cabin. We chased each other around the yard playing tag, hide and seek, fox and geese, and cowboys and Indians (which might be considered sacrilegious to play in today's politically censored world). We caught fireflies in the summer, jumped in piles of raked leaves in the fall and had snowball fights in the winter. We even climbed the stacks of hay in our hayloft and pretended we were scaling mountain cliffs. When there was nothing better to do, we would sit and talk on the porch while we watched the sunset, the clouds, or the traffic go by. How often do you see children interacting in any of these ways today?

Some of you may feel that my sentiments are misplaced and that I am just "wallowing in the past." That's certainly your prerogative to think that way. Although my memory for names and numbers doesn't last more than a few fleeting minutes, these memories from the distant past remain fresh in my mind. It's hard not to think about them fondly and regret their gradual loss over time. It's frustrating to consider the social consequences of those changes and know that most young people won't even make the effort to try to understand. I just ask you to remember one important point. At some point in the now distant future (perhaps long after I am gone), *you* will be the person who notices how the cherished lifestyles and activities of the past have vanished into the fog that now shrouds our mountain view. When you reflect upon them, you also may wonder why it was necessary for them to disappear when they could still have value. You may also realize that society has experienced some unintended and regrettable consequences from their losses that were ignored in the lust for change.

If you can think today about how that experience will affect you in the future, then perhaps you can have some understanding for how I and others like me feel—and the tiresome laments of those who have passed before you may not seem so irrational and unreasonable after all. We *all* want what's best for the future and future generations, even if our experiences teach us that they are tied to the past. Whether we really understand what it is or not, time is simply the greatest equalizer in the universe, and if you're thoughtful and lucky, you may come to understand that.

Post 25: Thank You PPF Website Patrons

May 29, 2017

Hello everyone. I'm sorry that I don't have any pictures to accompany this post, but I wanted to express our appreciation to the people who have been reading and commenting on our journal posts. Some of you have wondered if I am checking our site regularly, probably because I have not responded to any comments before today (I just replied to one for the first time). Please let me say that I have not ignored your thoughts and comments. I simply am not computer or Internet savvy, so I didn't know what I was supposed to do with the comments I was receiving.

The first few comments I received to our earliest posts appeared to be spam solicitations bearing requests for me to access their accounts with no specific comments on my post. Since I didn't know what threats "approving" or responding to these initial comments would expose me to, I simply trashed them. I didn't want to naively encourage a hacker or virus to damage the website I worked so hard to construct. I built the Peeper Pond Farm website on my own with no previous experience (just as I built our retirement home at Peeper Pond Farm), so I am very careful not to do anything that might jeopardize my work. I'm sorry if that fear led me to ignore some early genuine comments, and I am trying to figure out how to rectify that. To those of you who may have felt ignored, please accept my sincere apologies. You should also know that I have some technological limitations. We live in a very rural area (about ten people per square mile county-wide) and I only have access to satellite Internet, which is not a very fast or reliable platform. Our home computer is also a laptop, which has significant storage and processing constraints that only complicates matters and requires more of my time to access and communicate through the Internet.

As for my attention to our website, I don't make it a point to check the website daily, but there are many days where I access it more than once. As a farmer in retirement, I have many work responsibilities--milking and tending to our goats, managing our bee hives, and maintaining our garden and orchard, to name a few. Some days, I don't have enough time to check it or my e-mail, but I work hard to make sure I don't neglect it more than two days in a row. Some of you have commented with surprise on the size and scope of our website. To tell you the truth, I made it as large as I did as much for myself as for the viewing public. You see, my memory is progressively failing as I age, which was an important factor in my decision to retire. I posted information on my website that I could use to quickly find a business telephone number I might need (as you will find on my links page), to remind myself when important seasonal tasks need to be done (my calendar) and to review the local weather forecast when I need it (my almanac listings). I actually use my website as my "computer memory," which also gives me an incentive to keep it up-to-date. Since I am not very knowledgeable about our computer or how it all works, I don't always know how to improve or enhance it beyond what I've already learned to do. I just try to keep it up-to-date. That is my personal shortcoming, and with the limited time I have to experiment, I don't go out of my way to do some of the things you folks have suggested. I am getting too old and technically challenged to do much more. I'm sorry for that limitation, but I hope you will understand. As I've said in a past post, I'm someone who probably should have gotten off the train before it passed into the 21st century; I just didn't realize that before I arrived here.

One commenter asked if I have any concerns about plagiarism of my work. Not really, primarily because it's not something I can control. If someone decides to plagiarize something I have written, I won't even find out about it until after it has occurred. I am more diligent about making sure I don't knowingly plagiarize anyone else by always citing original sources. If someone uses my original work without my consent, they would be vulnerable to a civil suit because all original work that is published is automatically copyrighted (and thus protected) by that publication--as I understand it. Therefore, I don't concern myself with it, nor am I bothered if someone likes what I say and uses it, as long as it they are not doing it to profit from me. There are a lot of people in this world and even more who have lived before us, and it is actually hard for me to believe there are many truly original thoughts. We may just think of it or say it in different ways.

Another commenter suggested I include more pictures in my posts. I do try to do so from time to time, but I again have limitations on time and access to my camera. In doing farming work, it can be dangerous to have a camera around my neck and carrying one with me may expose it to damage. Therefore, my camera is not always handy when the opportunity to take additional pictures may occur. I do like to take pictures, especially of scenery, sunrises and other natural phenomena that occur here on a daily basis. I did take some pictures of the most scenic amenities in Pendleton County today, which I will include in the next post I write. Please watch for it, as it will appear on our website tomorrow or in a couple of days--depending on my workload.

I was quite surprised to learn how many people we have never met are accessing our website. I'm even more encouraged to see that you are enjoying our posts. I expected to write these journals primarily for the benefit of our family, friends and former professional colleagues, who expressed an interest in knowing what we are doing and following our progress. I know they have been accessing our site. I was truly surprised to learn that others who knew nothing of us before we retired three months ago have managed to find our rather obscure website. This is a very rewarding realization to us, regardless of how you managed to find us, because our primary business objective in operating this farm is to encourage and teach others about our traditional way of living. I truly believe that our simple, traditional lifestyle is a healthier, less stressful and more environmentally sound way to live. It fosters a closer and more intimate relationship with nature and the environment while teaching us how to live more self-reliantly. I was never very comfortable with all the conveniences of modern society that deprive us of a better understanding of how things really work. I hope that our message resonates with some of you and my writings encourage you to think more creatively about our true purpose in life.

Again, please accept my sincere apologies for not being more responsive to you. I will try to do better, but I wanted you to know why I may not be able to respond personally to all of you. Now that our farming operation is fully active, we anticipate opening our home to visitors who are interested in learning more about what we do. I am an "autodidact" by nature, so I like to learn and teach by doing. I'm sorry to use such an outdated word, and I realize some of you may have to look it up in the dictionary. I believe there are very few people who learn that way today, but I would be happy to teach you. Thank you again for your interest in Peeper Pond Farm, and I will do my best to entertain you with my future posts. I also hope you will invest the time to explore Pendleton County and the Potomac Highlands region of West Virginia. I promise you will not be disappointed. I will try to prove that to you with my next post. Please stay tuned!

Post 26: Legendary Pendleton County

May 31, 2017

When I was growing up on our family dairy farm in North Charlestown, New Hampshire, I attended a small two-room stone schoolhouse for first, second and third grades. Only two years before I began school there, it housed a total of six grades. This school had been built in the late 1800's and I believe that the two teachers who taught there during my tenure were born in the closing years of that century. It was a different time, and they were considered old-fashioned teachers even for my era. However, I do remember that, in addition to the required curriculum, they took the time to teach us about the legends of New Hampshire and our local area. We were treated to occasional impromptu stories of Indian raids and kidnappings, German spies using the summit of Mount Monadnock during World War II to signal their subs lurking just outside Boston Harbor, and the haunting story of a young pioneer lady who died in a frightful winter storm while desperately searching for her lover. Even our small school had its own legend. One of the rocks in the south wall of the school was said to have been a meteorite. As far as we were concerned, it certainly looked like one.

While these stories were not considered an important part of the basic curriculum that would help us succeed as adults, and I can't even tell you now which (if any of them) were true, I do recall that they were spellbinding and important in their own right. They taught us that we were part of a special, distinct place that had a treasured heritage. They made us feel that we had a birthright to our community and state as part of its cherished history. We didn't just live there for the moment. We were part of a long and storied history that instilled in us a pride of place. I remember those stories and the impact they had on my imagination all those years ago. Even today, they make me feel like I belonged there because I understood our state's unique heritage more intimately than any outsider who moved there. In sharing those stories amongst ourselves as children, they made us feel closer to each other as well as to our forebears and in some cases, ancestors. What I'm trying to say is that, regardless of how true they were, those legends became an important part of our understanding and sense of place, even if they taught us no useful skills. They taught us what it meant to be a New Hampshirite. I'm sorry to say that much of that sense of place has been lost now that so many suburbanites from Boston have moved in and disrupted the continuity of the State's history and heritage. Many if not most of those newcomers have no knowledge of (and perhaps no interest in or concern about) those cherished legends. People seem more concerned about what's new than what happened in the past.

One of the things I appreciate most about our adopted home of Pendleton County, West Virginia (and the State itself) is that it has so many colorful legends that are still vital and cherished parts of the public conscience. People still repeat the old stories about their community and identify with them as a meaningful part of their shared community heritage. Even the county's biggest annual festival, Treasure Mountain Festival (conducted each September) is based on the story of a French and Indian War raid and the legendary buried treasure that the Indians confiscated from the first European settlers.

Old-time story telling is also a central activity at the festival. Pendleton County's legends are tied to prominent natural features of the county, which rank among the most iconic in the State of West Virginia, including Smoke Hole and Seneca Rocks. One cannot understand the depth to which these features are tied to the generations of families who have lived in this county until these legends are known and understood. Many of these prominent natural features bear the names of multigenerational families. Therefore, when Barb wanted to go on a trip for her birthday this past week, I took the opportunity to photograph a number of the most iconic scenes in Pendleton County to share them with you in my post, along with a brief recounting of their legends. In sharing all of this with you, I am inviting you to understand what Pendleton County means to its native citizens and what defines it as a unique and distinctive community. The legends embrace not only their shared history but their shared values as well. That is how you learn what it means to be from Pendleton County. Please bear with me as this will not be a brief post.

The first stop on our journey around Pendleton County was the 1,000-foot deep Smoke Hole Canyon. It is located between North Fork and Cave Mountains along the South Branch of the Potomac River and extends for 25 miles across north-central Pendleton County and into neighboring Grant County. The main canyon entrance is about three miles south of Peeper Pond Farm, but it is only a mile away as the crow flies west over Cave Mountain, the summit of which looms above our farm. There are so many fascinating and thrilling stories and legends about Smoke Hole Canyon that it is impossible to even list them all in this post. Dona Bardon Shreve, a multi-generational native of Smoke Hole, recounted many of them in his Smoke Hole book trilogy (1997-2005).

For instance, the imposing cliff of Eagle Rock is named for one of the canyon's earliest pioneer settlers, Revolutionary War veteran William Eagle, whose grave is located in the shadow of the cliff. As the William Eagle legend is recounted by Dona Shreve, William's chickens were being killed by an eagle that had nested high on the cliff wall. In order to protect his livestock, Mr. Eagle climbed to the top of the cliff and attached a long rope to a tree, in order to scale down the cliff and destroy the nest with a long knife. As he scaled the cliff face, the mother eagle attacked him fiercely, causing him to thrash his knife at the great bird in self-defense. However, in doing so, he accidentally started slashing his own hemp rope, cutting through it strand by strand until he dangled from only one remaining strand. Fortunately, his companions managed to pull him up to safety before the rope gave out, saving his life. Although the final outcome of the battle was never documented, all we can say is that when Eagle fought eagle, only one eagle won.

Our next stop was a highway overlook on U.S. Route 33 near the summit of North Fork Mountain to enjoy an iconic view of Germany Valley, which was one of the earliest settled valleys in Pendleton County. The view is framed by Spruce Mountain, the summit of which is the highest point in West Virginia, the Alleghany Mountains and the Potomac River Watershed at 4,863 feet above mean sea level. Germany Valley includes Seneca Caverns and the Stratosphere, two commercial caves that are among the most visited attractions in the county. The caverns may be part of a complex of caves in the valley, the full extent and inter-connectivity of which has not been completely charted. This complex may include the alleged home of Batboy, Pendleton County's two-foot-tall boy with a face and ears resembling a bat. According to the West Virginia Encyclopedia, a publication of the West Virginia Humanities Council, Batboy was first reported in 1992, and his story was actually made into an off-Broadway musical that completed its New York run in 2001.

Our final stop was at Seneca Rocks, a 900-foot rock fin of Tuscarora Sandstone that towers above the small community that now bears its name. The face of the imposing cliff is a favorite rock-climbing attraction and was used as a military training location during World War II. According to legend, the cliff was chosen by a Seneca Indian princess, Snowbird, as a test for the many warrior suiters who wished to marry her. She challenged them to follow her as she scaled the cliff with the sole winner being awarded her hand in marriage.

These legends and many, many more, illustrate the depth and breadth of Pendleton County's history and heritage. They add color and intrigue to our history as they help define the community's special character. I hope these brief accounts, along with my pictures of the places from which they emerge, will instill in you an interest in exploring our area further. Perhaps you will eventually discover what I have said in another part of our website—that the *real* reason West Virginia is called "Almost Heaven" is because it can't *all* be Pendleton County. Nevertheless, you may inevitably learn what I did more than a decade ago, that West Virginia has a sense of community and continuity of heritage that is rapidly becoming unique in our increasingly faceless, modern, urban society. It is something to be discovered, understood and cherished. I also hope it will stimulate your interest in visiting us at Peeper Pond Farm. I have a library with shelves of books about the Potomac Highlands region and its history. I'd love to discuss our heritage with you in greater detail and, perhaps, learn something of your own.

Post 27: Goat Milking Basics

June 3, 2017

One of the most important aspects of our mission at Peeper Pond Farm is to help encourage and teach our followers to live more simply and self-reliantly. Now that I've been milking our goats successfully for more than three weeks (twice daily), I think it's about time that I passed along some of the lessons I've learned about it. Hopefully, this information will help you avoid some of the mistakes and misconceptions I made so that those of you interested in acquiring your own dairy goats will be better prepared for the task.

When I finally decided to pursue a dairy goat operation, I mistakenly assumed that my childhood experiences milking cows would transfer easily to goats. That is not entirely correct. While both cows and goats are ruminants (meaning they have multi-chambered digestive systems and rechew their food [cud] before fully digesting it), cows and goats have different feeding patterns and have different mammary characteristics that can affect how you milk them. Cows are grazers, which mean they feed primarily from ground level grasses. Goats are browsers, which mean they feed primarily from taller weeds and plants and will actually rise up on their hind legs to feed from low branches. They can also climb or scramble up onto low lying tree limbs and ground structures that cows are not designed to negotiate and would avoid. The primary reason for this difference in feeding preferences is because the parasites that can harm a goat's digestive system live within the first four inches from the ground, so goats seek food that is taller or higher to minimize their exposure. The most important ramification of this fundamental difference is that it affects how you feed goats to keep them healthy and producing good milk.

I certainly can't claim to have a thorough knowledge base on proper feeding practices yet, and we've had our share of initial problems. Our young kids have experienced some mild cases of bloat because we may have given them access to fresh green feed (in our outdoor pens) before their rumens had properly developed. We also have had problems finding a reliable source of good quality (leafy legume) hay, so we have been supplementing their feed with alfalfa pellets. So far, the milk volume and quality from our adults has been good, so we are hopeful that we are doing fine given our food limitations. However, our goats do occasionally have soft stools indicative of our dependency on green feed.

I learned another important difference between goats and cows by milking them. Although we used milking machines to milk our cows (primarily because we had at least 30 cows to milk twice daily), I did gain experience hand-milking them during power or equipment failures. It doesn't take long to learn how to hand-milk cows when you have to milk 30 cows with four teats each. However, cow teats are much more uniform in shape and size. They tend to be long and narrow, making it easy to get your fingers around the teats the same way each time. One of our milking goats, Cara, has relatively narrow and short teats when compared to Emerald's stout and large teats. When you hand milk a goat (or a cow for that matter), you must squeeze tightly first at the base of the udder to close off the milk artery that conducts milk from the udder to the tip of the teat. Doing so traps milk in the teat so that you can gradually squeeze your other fingers down the teat (one at a time) to force the milk out.

I had problems milking Cara initially, because I couldn't hold her small teats properly and, consequently, was inadvertently tugging down on her teats when I attempted to milk her. Her teats are so short, that I can only get two or three fingers around them. I had to learn to hold her teats differently in order to milk her. Emerald's teats are easier to handle, but they are so wide at the base of the udder that it can be difficult to constrict her milk artery tightly enough so that you can squeeze the milk down from her teat. I quickly learned that I needed a new hand-milking technique for each goat in order to milk them successfully. I have now leaned how to do that through trial and error, but I decided to use a hand-milking device (a Henry Milker) because my hands are becoming arthritic, and it would only be a matter of time before it would be quite painful to milk my goats using only my fingers. The new device is driven by a hand-operated pump that I must squeeze periodically, but it is much less stressful on my fingers to operate.

As for the actual milking process I follow, it all begins when I bring each goat to the milking stand, which can be seen in the picture accompanying this post. The stand includes a feed bowl in front of the stanchion, which I fill with sweet goat feed (high in protein to support milk production) before securing them on the stand. The rich food entices them to get onto the milking stand and put their heads into the stanchion. After the goat is locked into the stanchion, I brush her to remove chaff and debris that could fall off her during milking and contaminate the milk. It also helps calm her, which aids in the release of her milk. I then wash her teats and udder to remove any manure, dirt or debris that she may have collected between milkings. I am using a rag and warm iodine wash (sanitary iodine and water) rather than teat wipes to sanitize the teats, because I find that the wipes dry out too fast and don't stay moist in the packaging long enough when I am milking so few goats. The wipes are also too small to effectively clean debris that clings to the udder, and I want my goats to be thoroughly washed before milking. I also believe, from my prior experience milking cows, that the warm udder wash helps them release their milk more fully.

The next step is to use a "strip cup" to test and inspect the quality of their milk. A strip cup is a stainless-steel cup with a fine, removable screen on top. I hand-milk a couple of squirts from each teat onto the screen and inspect it. If the milk leaves clots or blood on the strip cup screen, I would check to determine if she has mastitis (an infection of the udder caused by unsanitary conditions), and I would not be able to keep or use her milk. She would then have to be isolated from the rest of the milking herd and treated. If the strip test indicates that the milk is clean (doesn't stand on the screen), then I can proceed to milk her, one teat at a time. As I milk her, I stroke her neck and belly to further calm her. A calm goat is a productive goat. Once she has fully released the milk from her udder, both her teat and udder become soft and limp. The final task is to apply a sanitizing teat dip to each teat after milking to guard against infection of the milk artery until the orifice of the teat has had sufficient time to constrict and close it off.

The first 30 minutes after milking is the most sensitive time for handling fresh, whole goat milk. The temperature of milk fresh from the goat is about 110 degrees Fahrenheit. In order to minimize contamination from the bacteria (both good and bad) that are inherent in the milk, the temperature of the milk must be reduced from 110 to about 38-40 degrees within 30 minutes from milking. I have already experimented with several ways to do this and have settled on using a large ice chest filled with water, ice and ice blocks. I place my jars of milk in the cooler and keep them there for at least 30-40 minutes before straining the milk (using a small strainer containing a fine mesh straining pad) into final storage jars to store in the refrigerator. If we are going to process the milk into cream, yogurt, or other products that require heating, I don't bother cooling the milk in the ice chest. We just get it into the house and begin pasteurization or processing right away to minimize the amount of cooling and reheating energy that is required. It is important to understand that unpasteurized milk must be stored continuously at 38-40 degrees Fahrenheit (to minimize bacterial growth) and, even if that temperature can be properly maintained, the total shelf life is about ten or so days, not the two weeks or longer that you may have come to expect from store-bought milk (which has been pasteurized). That's why we process so much of our milk into other products. Fortunately, we can also pasteurize the milk ourselves, if necessary, by placing it in a double boiler and heating it to 165 degrees for fifteen seconds. To date, we have done this successfully several times.

This process works well for us and allows us to enjoy fresh whole goat milk for consumption, cooking, and processing into cheese, soap, yogurt, hand lotion, ice cream and other dairy-based products. To date, Barb has been successful making everything but hand lotion, which has been a little too runny to satisfy her. However, we have no doubt that, with additional practice, we will find a solution to the problem. Our two milking adults, Cara and Emerald, are producing a little over a gallon of milk daily, so we have plenty to drink and use for processing. The only remaining question I have is whether or not we can manage the ongoing cost of our operation so that the savings we can achieve from our milk and dairy products will be affordable over the long run (given our limited retirement income). We won't be able to answer that question for some time to come, but we are working hard to determine the most affordable ways to manage our operation so that we minimize our costs without compromising the quality of our milk products.

If you would be interested in understanding the milking process better or gaining some first-hand experience of your own, please feel free to contact us and arrange a visit or an extended stay. We are eager to help anyone interested in home milk production learn how to do this time-honored, traditional practice. We hope you'll continue to follow our homesteading adventures at Peeper Pond Farm.

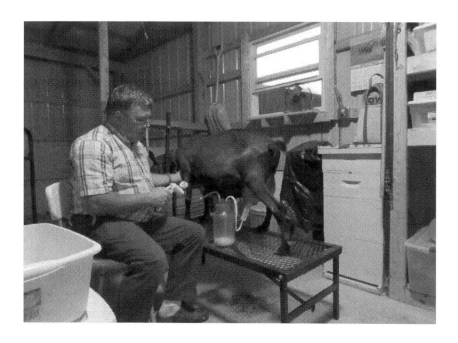

Post 28: Trout Fishing in Smoke Hole Canyon

June 4, 2017

    Just over Cave Mountain from our farm lies a mystical canyon. The local natives say it was named Smoke Hole (actually, they usually refer to it as "Smoke Ho es") because of the caves in the canyon that the Native Americans used to smoke or cure their meat. The storied history of the canyon's evolution over time is the subject of many colorful legends lovingly recounted by multi-generational native Dona Bardon Shreve in his Smoke Hole book trilogy. The narrow canyon is 1,000 feet deep and is being slowly carved deeper by the South Branch of the Potomac River which thunders through it as it descends more than 400 feet in elevation over its 25-mile course through the canyon. At one point (Big Bend) the river doubles back on itself, appearing on one side of the road flowing east and, after passing over a narrow crest in the road, suddenly reappearing on the opposite side flowing west. Although the river's flow through the rugged, precipitous canyon is twisted, tortured and littered with cataracts, it is widely recognized as one of the best trout rivers in the Eastern United States.

    Consequently, when we asked Barb's former co-workers, Garett and Stacey Roderick, to teach us what they know about trout fishing, Smoke Hole Canyon was the best site. As Barb says, Garett loves to hunt or fish anything that West Virginia issues a license for, so their shared experiences provided us with a wealth of knowledge about trout fishing. This was something we wanted to learn to supplement our basic self-reliant living skills and, therefore, is something we are eager to share with you. After all, we all know the oft-quoted biblical proverb, "Give a man a fish and you will feed him for a day; teach a man to fish and you will feed him for a lifetime."

    While I did gain some fishing experience during my childhood, I hadn't been fishing in over 45 years. Our farm included over 3,000 linear feet of Connecticut River frontage, so we would fish for bass and perch in the river to stock our two swimming ponds. They, in turn, helped control the various bugs that lived in and around our ponds. We never cleaned and ate our fish because the river was considered to be too contaminated. As a result, I had a lot to learn and relearn about fishing.

    Garett and Stacey led us to all their favorite fishing spots through the spectacular canyon and generously shared the wealth of their knowledge about trout fishing. Trout, unlike the bass and perch I fished as a child, are cold water fish and like to feed in swift flowing waters with abundant shade and rocky hiding shelters. The South Branch River possesses all these qualities in abundance throughout its course in the canyon. They taught us to use small (size twelve or fourteen) treble hooks, colorful bait that will float in the current, and to weight our line with sinkers, so that it will rest on the bottom with the bait floating about four-to-six inches above—where trout prefer to live and search for food. They also taught us to let the bait sit near the river bottom for 30 or so seconds at a time, as trout can be especially cautious feeders. My past fishing experience taught me to snap the line as soon as I felt a solid bite, but that approach does not work for trout. You have to be more patient with trout and let them nibble at the bait for a while to lure them to take it. This guidance was quite different from the approach I learned as a child. While Garett and Stacey were quite successful catching brown, golden and rainbow trout, Barb and I struggled. I managed to get a few good bites, but my timing wasn't polished enough to land any fish. All I did was feed them my bait. Clearly, we will need a lot more practice. Fortunately, the experience of fishing in the dramatic and serene landscape of Smoke Hole Canyon is well worth it—even if you don't catch a mess of fish.

Towards the end of our trout fishing expedition, Garett decided to demonstrate his fly-fishing prowess for us. While his casting skills are fascinating to watch, I think I'll concentrate more on my basic casting skills. After all, I guess I prefer to kill flies with a fly swatter, rather than fish for them. Our thanks to Garett and Stacey for a very pleasant and enjoyable day in Smoke Hole Canyon. We look forward to our next fishing adventure.

Post 29: Swarm!

June 5, 2017

    I asked Jim Boyd, our friend and owner of Middle Mountain Apiary in Petersburg, to stop by our farm in late May to inspect our Italian bee hive with me. During the course of routine hive inspections, I had noticed that our Italian bees were not working to build comb and store honey in our honey super (the top box on the hive which would contain the honey we could eventually harvest for ourselves later in the season). That, in and of itself, was unusual during the peak blooming time of the season when the pollen they collect to make honey is abundant. However, I had also noticed some irregular brood cell patterns in the hive and a lot of drone cells. Since we are still bee-keeping novices, I wanted to get Jim's experienced advice to understand if what I was seeing in the hive was normal or peculiar behavior.

    Upon inspecting the hive together, Jim quickly determined that the hive was preparing to swarm sometime within the next 2-3 weeks. We found evidence of new queen cells on several frames, an indication that the hive was preparing to replace the existing queen in the hive. When the bees in a hive feel too confined because they don't have room to expand or the queen is not producing enough larvae or pheromones to prevent the workers from feeding and raising one or more replacement queens, the hive will eventually swarm. Swarming occurs after a new queen hatches and challenges the former queen (who laid her egg) for supremacy. Eventually, the older queen will be killed or forced out. If the former queen leaves the hive, a swarm can occur. The queen, who can't travel far from the original hive, will settle in on a nearby tree branch or other secure structure along with roughly half the worker bees in the hive. Our swarm settled on a nearby peach tree branch in our small fruit orchard, where our hives are stationed. We didn't notice the swarm until after we returned from our Smoke Hole fishing trip yesterday afternoon (June 4), roughly three weeks after Jim predicted that it would occur.

    A swarm is a problem for beekeepers who depend on honey production for their livelihood. Since a swarm can reduce the population of a beehive by roughly half, it can have a significant impact on honey production from the affected hive. Our hives are clearly visible from our house, so we were able to discover it soon after it occurred. Within another 24 hours, the swarm would have sought out a new permanent location and would have disappeared. We called Jim as soon as we saw the swarm, and he came by to collect the bees. He can use them to start a new hive, although it will take a while (perhaps another season) for the new colony to become established and large enough to produce excess honey for him to harvest.

The swarm caused me to think carefully about our bee management strategy. As I noted in an earlier post, I have been having difficulties locating the queens in our hives because I can't focus on individual bees easily when so many of them are moving around on each frame. Being able to monitor the queen and her activities within a hive is an important part of bee management, if you want to be successful in producing excess honey to harvest. In my case, my first interest in establishing a couple of beehives was to provide a home for bees on our property to help pollinate our fruit trees and garden plants. Harvesting honey was an additional interest, but not our primary motivation. Bees can be a challenge to raise, especially with all the threats and pests they face today, so we could not be guaranteed a stable source of honey from just one or two hives. The only reason I wanted two hives was to have a backup if one of them were to fail or swarm, as occurred yesterday.

Given the competing demands on our time and the physical demand of all our farm work, I decided to reduce our honey production expectations and make them secondary to the primary management objective of pollinating our trees and plants. Since it is difficult to prevent a swarm from occurring, I simply can't afford the time to manage the expanding number of bee colonies that swarms can produce. It was better for us to let Jim capture the swarm and to manage our remaining hive to keep the bees for pollination. Our Carniolan hive seems fine, but they may not be able to produce honey for us this season. They did not winter over well and will need to rebuild their worker population to produce enough honey for their own survival needs this winter.

I will keep monitoring our hives through the year, and if I feel the Carniolans are producing enough honey stores for their needs, I may add a honey super to their hive. Otherwise, we'll probably have to see if we can produce some extra honey for our own use next year. I'm just not going to worry about producing enough honey for us to sell. We have enough work to do now just trying to make use of all the milk our goats are producing each day. If you have an interest in starting some beehives, you should think carefully about your hive management priorities and objectives, because they will have a direct impact on the cost of your operation and the amount of time you will need to commit to your bees.

Post 30: Bear Rocks

June 7, 2017

The Allegheny Front, a 200-mile-long mountain escarpment extending northeast to southwest from central Pennsylvania to its elevational climax of 4,770 feet above sea level at Mount Porte Crayon in the Potomac Highlands of West Virginia, is one of the geological marvels of the Eastern United States. In Western Grant County, the Front first reaches 4,000 feet at Bear Rocks, which is owned and managed by the Nature Conservancy. It is a landscape of broken sandstone and quartz rock boulders and outcrops shattered by repeated frost and freeze cycles over thousands of years. Immediately west of Bear Rocks is a ten-mile-wide plateau known as Dolly Sods. The sods were first farmed by a German family named Dahle (later anglicized to "Dolly") that settled in the area shortly after the Revolutionary War. The land was later cleared by timber barons in the late 1800's, which removed the virgin red spruce, hemlock and black cherry forest. This exposed the underlying humus soil to drying and repeated fires from sparks and cinders ejected by the steam engines that transported away the timber. After the top soil burned away, the underlying rocks were exposed, resulting in the boulder-strewn landscape of Bear Rocks today. All that remains at Bear Rocks today is a dense growth of wild cranberry plants punctuated by scattered second growth red spruce trees that are "flagged" by the persistent west-northwest winds that sweep across the plateau stunting the growth of limbs on the west side of each tree and leaving branches only on the downwind side pointing to the east.

I have stood at Bear Rocks on days when the landscape was shrouded in a misty fog, swept into columns of clouds by gusty west winds that last touched the surface of the earth in the western Great Plains, somewhere east of the Rocky Mountains. I've felt the mist wash across my face as it condenses on my flesh and shivered in the chilly temperatures, even though the weather was hot and humid some 2,000 or more feet below in the valley at the base of the Front. When the clouds clear and the sun emerges, an other-worldly landscape of boulders and flagged spruce trees is revealed, and you can stand on the cliff at what seems like the edge of the earth and overlook waves of mountains rippling east as far away as the highest peaks of Shenandoah National Park. It is a stunning view that inspires solemn contemplation and awe. Children scamper and clamber over the rocks, thrilled by the adventure. It is a place for all ages to enjoy and appreciate the wonders of nature.

So, it was when our son, Michael, asked us to show him how to get there last week, so he and his girlfriend, Isabella (or Bella as she prefers to be called) could visit there together. Although Bella was born and raised in West Virginia, she has never seen Bear Rocks and Michael wanted some nearby places to take her where they could share their affection for the great outdoors. Barb and I packed a picnic lunch and met him in Maysville, where we picked him up and drove him to Bear Rocks. As he leapt from boulder to boulder admiring each vantage point, we saw the child in him emerge again, inspired by the enticing, playful landscape. It is one of those places and images that you will never forget. If you wish to visit, take care not to plan a winter trip. The gravel access roads are not maintained during the winter because the average annual winter snowfall at Dolly Sods is about 160 inches (13+ feet), but can total well over 200 inches, and wind chills can easily dip to thirty or forty degrees below zero Fahrenheit. Nevertheless, the thrill is well worth the effort to get there. It will take your breath away and make you feel young again, no matter how old you may be. Bear Rocks is one of the many natural wonders that we enjoy by living here in the Potomac Highlands of West Virginia.

Post 31: Ferguson Is Back on the Job

June 10, 2017

I guess it's high time for a Peeper Pond Farm news update. After a three-week vacation, our trusty tractor, Ferguson, is back at work. It took me a long time to track down and buy the correct hydraulic fuel filter that I needed to replace. I talked to at least ten different engine part suppliers all around our region and purchased two filters that were not correct before I finally found the right one at a Massey Ferguson dealer in Harrisonburg, VA. Apparently, it is a difficult part to locate and the one I found cost me $72.00, which was more than twice the cost of the oil and fuel filters I bought.

After I finally replaced the filter last Friday and fed him with eight gallons of fresh hydraulic fluid, I started him up and his hydraulic system wouldn't work. After further consultations with our Harrisonburg supplier this past Tuesday (June 6), I learned that I needed to bleed air out of the hydraulic system before the pump would work. Of course, this step and how to do it were not mentioned in my owner's manual. I think I heard Ferguson chuckling to himself over the issue. However, his vacation and his luck ran out on Tuesday morning, when he reluctantly admitted I had successfully completed his spring overhaul. We used him to clean out and replace the bedding in our goat barn (a chore that must be done periodically to remove manure and urine-laden bedding) on Wednesday and to carry bucketloads of topsoil to our orchard on Thursday so we would fill some holes we made by removing dead trees and rocks that were an impediment to mowing the grass. It is clear that our apple trees are losing the battle against the persistent red cedar rust, and we are considering giving up on apples and replanting with cherry trees. Our Red Haven peach trees are hanging in because they appear to be less susceptible to the leaf rust. One of our three peach trees is producing a healthy number of peaches for its age.

Our vegetable and herb gardens are doing very well and are producing a lot of healthy plants. We have already harvested some lettuce and peas from the garden, and we have eight nearly complete rows of corn growing well. We had some spotty losses of corn plants in some of the rows due to rainfall runoff erosion from the heavy storms we had in May. Fortunately, the losses were inconsequential. Now we are facing our first hot and humid heat wave next week, so we are setting up a couple of tower sprinklers (elevated on tripod legs) to water the garden. All of our other vegetables are doing well, however the rabbits have been feasting on our broccoli. Barb tried using some rabbit and deer repellent to discourage them, but they ignored it. Our next line of defense was to buy some one-half inch Pex tubing that we can cut into six-foot lengths and install along the row as hoops over which we can stretch some fine mesh netting that we hope will protect the broccoli plants. Surprisingly, the rabbits bypassed our lettuce, which we expected them to enjoy most of all—especially considering that it is all mature now. The broccoli hasn't headed out yet.

As I noted in our June 5 post, our Italian bee hive swarmed this past Sunday, and we lost about half the colony of bees. This reduces our chance of obtaining honey from the Italian hive. I opened both hives on Tuesday, June 6 and discovered that our Carniolan hive is doing very well and the bees have filled all but one frame in all three supers (boxes) that that are available to them. I placed an excluder screen on top of the third box to keep the queen from laying brood above that level and installed a fourth box on the hive. This new top box will be a honey super that we may be able to remove in mid-summer to harvest some fresh honey. We are hoping that the wildflower season will continue to provide abundant pollen so our Carniolan bees can fill the honey super before the early wildflowers die back in the second half of the summer.

We also took some time this past week to pressure-wash the house and shed and then re-stain the three porch decks on our house and a ramp on our shed. That was a big job, as the front porch on our house has a deck that is ten feet deep and 64 feet long, running the full length of our house. I also mowed over an acre of yards around our farm, including the orchard. Our mower is supposed to be self-propelled, but after nine years of service, its get up and go has long since got up and went. It's more of a push mower now, and the slopes of our lawn areas and orchard make it a challenging exercise for an aging retiree.

Our goats continue to produce a good supply of milk for us, with Cara and Emerald teaming up to provide an average of a gallon of milk per day. Barb used some of our excess milk this week to make a gallon of rich vanilla ice cream, which I will use to make some sweet chocolate frappes during the heat wave. Barb plans to begin making some farmhouse cheddar cheese tomorrow. It will be a good two months for that to age before we can enjoy it.

Our infant buck, Billy The Kid, is growing rapidly and weighed 47 pounds just five days before he turns two months old. We anticipate selling him sometime before the end of June. Since he has been feeding on milk from both Cara and his mother, Emerald, we expect that we will gain a brief increase in milk production after he is sold.

Of course, our spring peepers have ceased their nightly serenades, but we are seeing our first fireflies of the season on the warmer nights, and we are being entertained by crickets and tree frogs throughout the days and nights. As you can see, we've had a very busy week here at Peeper Pond Farm. Hopefully, we have caught up with the most labor-intensive tasks so we can take life a little easier during the coming heat wave. We wish all of you a happy and healthy summer as the season unfolds.

Post 32: Spruce Knob

June 13, 2017

It's no wonder to me why so many of our states establish great parks at their highest summits to celebrate the grand views that unfold from them. Nowhere else is the sense of standing at the top of the world more palpable. Many of the Native American legends regarding those lofty heights regard them as sacred places that were to be cherished and protected from desecration. I have visited many of them in the places where I have lived along the great, twisted spine of the Appalachian Mountain chain—Mount Washington in New Hampshire, Mount Mansfield in Vermont, Brasstown Bald in Georgia, Mount Mitchell in North Carolina, Clingman's Dome in Tennessee, Cheaha Mountain in Alabama, Backbone Mountain in Maryland and now Spruce Knob in West Virginia. At each of those places, the Appalachian Mountain panorama is breathtaking, revealing a seemingly boundless forest that rises and falls over the mountains and hills like storm-churned waves on a great ocean of land. Even the earliest European pioneers and settlers were struck with awe and fear of the mountain landscapes they discovered as they pushed west. In recording the Batts and Fallam expedition through the mountains of western Virginia in the fall of 1671, Robert Fallam wrote...

"When we were got up to the top of the mountain and setdown very weary we saw very high mountains lying to the north and south as far as we could discern...It was a pleasing tho' dreadful sight to see the mountains and hills as if piled one upon another."

These words still accurately describe the view from Spruce Knob, the loftiest point in West Virginia, the Allegheny Mountains and Pendleton County nearly 250 years later. I thought about them yesterday (June 12), as Barb and I stood at the summit of Spruce Knob to escape the building heat in the valleys below. Living in a society that has conquered and transformed much of the American wilderness that marveled Robert Fallam, it is reassuring to find a few remaining sacred places that evoke the sense of awe and fear that the earliest pioneers first felt when they contemplated their desperate westward treks across the Appalachian Mountains. Even the dark night skies above the mountain provide glorious views of the heavens. It feels like you could just pluck the stars from the sky.

Spruce Knob's comparatively modest summit height (4,863 feet above mean sea level) does not garner as much public attention as the highest peaks of the Blue Ridge and White Mountain ranges of the Appalachians. Mount Washington (6,288 feet above sea level) in my native New Hampshire is notorious for the ferocity of its foul weather and has recorded sustained wind speeds up to 231 miles per hour. While the winds on Spruce Knob are not as vigorous, they are strong and persistent enough to stunt the growth of the summit Red Spruce trees so that their limbs grow only on the downwind (east) side of the trees creating what are known as flagged spruces.

The summit temperatures during our June 12 visit peaked at about 70 degrees, while our high temperature for the day at Peeper Pond Farm (at 1,375 feet above sea level) was 90 degrees. Spruce Knob has an alpine feel about it, not just in terms of the relatively cool temperatures and persistent winds, but also in terms of the vegetation it supports. The summit is dominated by a dense spruce forest with undergrowth vegetation and wildlife more characteristic of northern New England and southern Canada than the Southern Appalachians which the mountain graces. Many of the northern species that inhabit Spruce Knob became established there during the last major glaciation. During that epoch, the climate of Spruce Knob and most of West Virginia more closely resembled New England today. As the climate rapidly transformed during the climactic maximum that followed, the boreal habitats became gradually confined to the highest elevations, where the cooler temperatures prevailed, including Spruce Knob. Many of the species that now inhabit the summit are living at the southernmost fringe of their natural ranges. The summit is home to a number of endangered species, some of which live only on the summit and other peaks of similar height (over 4,500 feet in elevation) in Pocahontas, Randolph and Tucker Counties in West Virginia.

Spruce Knob is yet another of the natural wonders that abound in Pendleton County and the larger Potomac Highlands. We hope you will choose to visit and cherish them as we do—perhaps as part of your next visit to Peeper Pond Farm.

Post 33: Our Canaan Valley Escape

June 30, 2017

June was a very busy month for us at Peeper Pond Farm. We worked all or most of eleven days over the past twelve. During that span, we mowed our acre-plus of yards and orchard, inspected and tended the bee hives, weeded the garden, sprayed all the fruit trees, mucked out the entrance to the goat barn, repainted all the trim around the shed, two porches and the crawlspace bulkhead doors. We also started repainting all the trim on our large front porch, rebuilt and replaced one of the doors on our shed, cleaned the house and finished a score of lesser work projects. We also have been dealing with Nin's declining health, but I will discuss that later when we can determine the cause. All of this work was in addition to our daily chores of tending and milking our goats.

Fortunately, we had six straight days of dry and cool weather to make it comfortable for all the outdoor work. Our Wednesday (June 28) morning low temperature was 44 degrees—only three degrees above the record low for the date! We had five straight days with morning lows below 60 degrees and seven straight days with high temperatures below 85 degrees. That all ended abruptly today, when the typical summer humidity returned and the high temperature topped out at 88 degrees. That was more than we could bear, and we needed a break from our determined work routine, so we decided to find a cooler escape from the farm and the heat.

Our local get-away of choice for today was Canaan Valley. In West Virginia, the name 'Canaan' is spelled like the Biblical land, but pronounced differently. We pronounce it 'kuh-NANE,' with the stress on the second syllable. With a base elevation of 3,200 feet above mean sea level, Canaan Valley has the highest elevation of any major valley east of the Mississippi River, and it is framed by two mountains (Canaan Mountain on the west and Cabin Mountain on the east) each of which has a summit in excess of 4,000 feet. Weiss Knob, the highest point on Cabin Mountain, has an elevation of 4,470 feet—almost 1,300 feet above the valley floor. The high, remote location of the valley made it one of the last wilderness areas of West Virginia to be explored, settled and developed. One of the earliest explorations of the valley occurred in 1851, as documented in Phillip Pendleton Kennedy's humorous account, <u>The Blackwater Chronicle</u>.

The valley is the headwaters of Blackwater River and is home to plants and animals that are more common to southern Canada than West Virginia today, just like Dolly Sods, which is located on the east side of Cabin Mountain (see my

June 7, 2017 post entitled, "Bear Rocks)." Portions of the valley (especially the most sensitive wetland areas adjoining the Blackwater River) are protected and managed today by Canaan Valley State Park, the Canaan Valley National Wildlife Refuge and the Nature Conservancy. While we experienced a high temperature of 88 degrees at Peeper Pond Farm, the temperature in Canaan Valley never exceeded 75, making it a wonderfully pleasant escape from the intense summer heat of the lower valleys.

Two relatively large ski areas grace the slopes of Cabin Mountain above the valley—Caraan Valley and Timberline, with the former being owned and operated by the State of West Virginia. During the summer months, the state operates one of the chair lifts to the summit of Bald Knob (with an elevation of 4,370 feet above sea level). The expansive view of the valley from the top of the mountain is truly breathtaking. Having been there many times before, we packed a picnic lunch and dined at a lonely picnic table at the top of the highest ski slope. As we were eating our lunch, a whitetail buck strolled past us, taking us by surprise. We didn't even have enough advance warning of its presence to take a picture before it disappeared into the woods.

After eating, we walked around the summit of the knob and discovered that, last fall, the state created a new hang gliding and parasailing launch on the southern edge of the Knob, opposite from the ski area. As we stood at the top of the launching site, we enjoyed a dramatic, sweeping view of the rugged valleys below Canaan. The third highest mountain in our state, Mount Porte Crayon (named for WV's famous native artist, David Hunter Strother), with a peak elevation of 4,770 feet, frames the view to the left, with Rich Mountain in the near background and Cheat Mountain stretching out in the distance behind it. Because the summit was always densely shrouded in trees, we never realized that view existed in our previous visits.

The Canaan Valley State Park and resort supports a wide range of winter and summer outdoor activities, including downhill skiing, snowboarding, tubing and cross-country skiing during the winter months, and horse-back riding, hiking, wildlife tours (at the Canaan Valley Wildlife Management Area), hang-gliding, parasailing and scenic chairlift rides to the summit during the warmer months. Special seasonal events are scheduled throughout the year at the park lodge. With everything it has to offer, Canaan Valley is yet another major outdoor recreational attraction that we enjoy in our larger Potomac Highlands Region. We hope you will enjoy exploring it for yourself.

Post 34: Our Garden of Plenty

July 14, 2017

Perhaps our best farming success story has been our vegetable garden. Our corn crop is maturing, and the garden is full of fresh vegetables. Most of everything we planted has grown well this season, even though it has been quite dry. The corn rows we planted early this season have tasseled and are producing abundant ears. We have already harvested lettuce, peas, peppers, broccoli, red cabbage, spinach, wax beans, onions, and Barb picked the first cucumber off the vine earlier this morning. We anticipate harvesting tomatoes, potatoes, carrots, green beans and corn by the end of July. Earlier this month, Barb canned five pints of red cabbage, and our freezer now contains several servings of frozen peas and wax beans. Our pumpkin and butternut squash patches are taking over a large section of the garden, and we have found many pumpkins and squashes ripening in the tangle of leaves and vines. We certainly expect to have pumpkins and squash to sell this year. All the work we did last fall to amend and prepare our soil appears to be paying off.

Our goats are still producing more than a gallon of fresh milk daily and Barb has succeeded in producing soap, yogurt, several varieties of cheese, ice cream and butter from the excess milk we can't drink or use for cooking. All who have asked to taste our goat milk have said it is every bit as fresh and delicious as store-bought milk. Now that we have more than two full months of milking experience under our belts, we have settled into a system that works very well for us and our goats.

While we can do the all the farming work and produce our milk and milk products successfully, we are struggling to manage the cost of our operation. We are still working with the Health Department to determine if our proposed lodging and dairy operation can be permitted so that we can house visitors for extensive lifestyle skills training and sell products made from our goat milk. The permitting costs, liability insurance cost and increased property taxes that we will incur are significantly higher than we anticipated, which reduces the annual farm income we can raise to subsidize and offset our operating costs. Our feed and supply costs for the milking operation are a significant drain on our retirement income, and we still can't be sure that we could maintain such a small operating scale without the training business operation. This issue remains our greatest concern for the future viability of our farm, even though we have enjoyed a great deal of success with it.

I inspected our bee hives yesterday, and although our bees now appear to be doing well and are storing sufficient honey reserves for the winter, they are not producing enough honey to fill the honey supers we had hoped to harvest for our own use. Three weeks ago, I decided to take a frame of honey from our Carniolan hive and place it in the honey super to encourage them to build and fill up that box. However, when I checked the hive yesterday, I discovered that the bees have removed all the honey from the frame I relocated and moved it down into the hive. It now appears that we won't be harvesting any honey this year. However, that should not be viewed as a failure, because the bees have helped us pollinate the fruit trees in our orchard, the herbs in our small herb garden and our flowering vegetables.

Our orchard remains our biggest disappointment, largely because of the tenacity of red cedar rust. The blight has stunted our trees over the years by attacking the leaves with a reddish-orange rust that renders them unproductive. Our apple trees produced very little fruit, and all of it is either damaged or immature. One of our peach trees managed to produce a few mature peaches, which Barb harvested yesterday evening. Although many of them are blemished or cracked, the fruit is generally edible. Barb used them to make some delicious peach cobbler. We had planted some grapes and blueberries in our orchard this year to begin a transition away from apples, but the deer managed to leap over our fence and eat them. We built some cages around the blueberry plants to save them, but the all of the grapes are lost. Overall, our small orchard has been our biggest disappointment, but at least we managed to produce some peaches. As I've said in earlier posts, farming can be a lot of work with no guarantee of success.

We are continuing our efforts to bring our cat, Ninny, back to health. The fungus that has infected her lungs appears to be in remission, but we still need to have x-rays taken to be sure. By all appearances, she is breathing easier now and her appetite is improving, although she still has a lengthy recovery ahead.

It now appears that we have mastered the skills we need to make our farm successful, but our finances remain uncertain. That situation should not seem unfamiliar or unusual to those who have farmed or have farm experience. As many of our local farm friends have reminded us, farming is the best way to take two million dollars and turn it into one million. Barb and I have determined that we will not allow our farming venture to compromise our retirement finances, so we will have to monitor our costs carefully as we proceed. We have made arrangements for a meeting with Health Department officials to evaluate our milking operation on July 25, and the results from that visit will have a significant impact on our ability to package and sell goat cheese. We are trying to remain hopeful that all will work out for the best, but we must admit that our future financial success remains uncertain at this time. I'm sure many farmers will understand and sympathize with our struggle.

Post 35: Livestock Fugitives

July 18, 2017

    Lady did it to me again during the morning milking earlier today. I had just brought Cara back to the goat barn after she had finished milking and was trying to switch the leash over to Emerald when Lady squeezed past her and scampered out the barn door. It's the second time she has escaped when I was trying to bring one or the other adult in to be milked. Fortunately, I knew where she was going. As before, she made a quick dash across the barnyard to the garage, where she knew that the high protein sweet grain that I feed our milking goats would be waiting in the milking stand for the next goat. Although Lady is dry (not producing milk this season), she knew there would be grain in the milking stand feed bowl because she had been in the stand twice previously to have her hooves trimmed. When I followed her into the milking area, she greeted me with a momentary "Who, me?" innocent look, before she drove her face into the feed bowl to devour the evidence. All I could do was laugh as I grabbed her chain and led her back to the goat barn where she belonged.

    Lady's quick escape maneuver reminded me of my first morning with the milking adults, when Cara, Emerald and her buck, Billy The Kid, escaped from the goat barn and wandered around the yard as stunned by their new surroundings as I was to see them loose. It took some time to figure out how they managed to get out when all the fence gates and the barn door were closed tight. As it turned out, Cara had learned at her previous home how to clamp her mouth around a round doorknob and twist her head to open the door. I had to install a plastic child-proof doorknob protector to keep the goats from repeating that escape act. One thing I learned about goats from both the books I read and the other goat owners I met is that goats are clever and persistent in their efforts to escape any enclosure you may place them in. While I don't have an electric fence, I have been told that goats will actually encourage their kids to test the electric fence for weaknesses. I guess they don't mind seeing their kids get shocked, as long as they don't feel it.

    I guess cows can be just about as creative in their efforts to escape their enclosures as are my goats. I recall many times during my childhood when we had to get up late at night and chase our cows back into their fenced paddocks because they had found some weakness in the fencing. The most unpleasant retrieval experience I recall was when our cows escaped from a pasture seven miles from our home during the wee hours of the morning. The call came in sometime between midnight and 1:00 AM from the Richardsons—the people who owned the land we rented for several summers to pasture our dry cows and first-year heifers. The pasture was actually a series of seven adjoining open meadows separated by dense hedgerows and stone walls that was enclosed along the entire perimeter by fencing that consisted of three rows of barbed wire topped by an electric fence wire. This fencing was considered to be escape proof and had served adequately for at least three prior summers. However, they finally managed to figure out how to escape and had disappeared into the woods. We searched for hours that morning responding to scattered random sightings by neighbors and travelers along the well-worn Unity Stage Road that only led us to believe they could be anywhere.

After four or more hours of searching, we finally determined that they had split into two groups, each apparently led by one of the two dry adult cows. We broke up into two search teams of two each and, using walkie-talkies for communication, tried to flank them on both sides of the pasture perimeter fence working our way into the woods from the road. After another hour or two of searching, we finally met on the back side of the pasture having found nothing more than scattered cow chips they had left behind during their aimless wanderings. Eventually, my father glanced into one of the pasture meadows and there they were standing innocently in the field staring back at us like we were the poor lost souls. Actually, I think they had been laughing at us for hours, as they must have heard us calling from the woods and shaking pails of grain. Somehow, they had managed get out and back into the pasture without leaving any evidence as to where or how they managed to escape. We had spent roughly five-to-six hours traipsing through the woods and puckerbrush with flashlights and walkie-talkies searching frantically for two groups of escaped cows that had mysteriously let themselves back in. We never did learn how they escaped, and they never repeated the trick. The electric fence was active the entire time we were searching, and we could find no loose wires. All I recall getting for my trouble was a bad case of poison ivy from wandering around in the dark woods.

We had many more livestock chasing adventures during my years growing up on a dairy farm. Fortunately, our goats have been satisfied to stay on our farm when they escape and have not become night-time fugitives. I guess I should knock on wood when I say that. I certainly don't mean to challenge them by that admission. After all, I have learned well enough just how clever and creative cows and goats can be.

Post 36: Bye, Bye Billie

July 19, 2017

When Emerald's buck, who we affectionately named Billy The Kid, first arrived at Peeper Pond Farm, he was barely three weeks old. At the time, he was afraid of people and his new surroundings. We kept and raised him for nearly two-and-a-half months. Over that time, he gained over 40 pounds and grew three times as big as he was when he arrived. We also earned his trust and affection. However, we have no separate facilities to raise a buck, and the time had come to give him a new home. He was entering his "adolescent" stage and was trying to ride our does.

We advertised him for sale and eventually connected with a new goat farm in the Uniontown, PA area who saw his picture and wanted to buy him. When we originally purchased him along with his mother, Emerald, he was destined for the livestock market. However, we managed to find a farm where he would have a meaningful life of his own, so we decided to let him go there rather than sell him for meat. As soon as we finished the morning milking today, we collected Billy, loaded him into the back of our truck and delivered him to a rendezvous with his new owner near Cumberland, MD.

When we returned home this afternoon, we received a message from Lynda, the lady who bought him. Billy had arrived safely at his new farm and was being introduced to the other animals that he will be living with. When he lived with us, he only met the other goats in our herd and the wild deer that frequent our farm in the evenings and mornings. He had come to be curious of the deer, but Lynda discovered that he was afraid of her cat and didn't know what to make of her chickens. He will have a good life at his new home with plenty of browse to feed upon.

Although we will miss him and his antics, we can already appreciate the fact that we won't be sharing our goat milk with him. He had been feeding on his mother's milk since he was born. Today, with Billy not sharing the pen with his mother, Emerald produced 11.5 cups of milk—a new one-day production record for her. Now we can see that she has the potential to be a very productive doe. Thanks Billy, for being a memorable part of Peeper Pond Farm. We wish you the best in your new life.

Post 37: Remembering Ninny

July 20, 2017

When you live on a farm, you can experience all aspects of life from birth to death on any given day. That doesn't mean that death isn't a sad and mournful event. However, after experiencing death many times, you begin to accept it as an essential and necessary part of the life cycle, rather than just a loss. We must remember that virtually all life forms we have discovered, studied and understand, with the exception of some of the simplest and earliest forms of life, gain their life-sustaining nourishment from the death of other living things. The rich soil that sustains our farm and crops is, basically, an accumulation of formerly living plants and animals mixed with dirt and sand. The goats we raise gain their nourishment by killing and eating the plants that grow in the soil. Our goats, in turn, feed us life-sustaining milk and provide a source of meat, rich in the protein and essential nutrients humans need to thrive. All of those living things eventually die to nourish the soil and begin the cycle anew. Ashes to ashes, dust to dust. Consequently, even when death occurs, the energy that gave us life survives and nourishes the life of surviving and future plants and animals. It is one of the fundamental principles of our universe that energy can be converted to or from matter, but it cannot be destroyed.

Such is the nature and inherent beauty of the life cycle that we all must remember when we mourn the loss of those we love. Our lives were nourished by the passing of previous living beings, and our deaths will return that life-sustaining favor to those that survive us. If it didn't work that way, then the cycle that gave us life would expire with us. In essence, I am trying to explain why I feel that death is not the end of life, but just a transition from one form of life to another. We are just passing the baton on to the next living thing. There really isn't an end to life, just to the life we once knew.

I find this way of thinking reassuring as I work to accept the loss of our beloved cat, Ninny. She had been ill for the past two months and was gradually losing her appetite and her energy. On occasion, she would show signs of recovering, only to decline again after a few days. The past six days were one of those brief recovery periods when she would eat her meals and seek attention from us. However, unbeknownst to us, she took a tragic turn last night, and we found her this morning under our bed largely unresponsive and barely alive. Her breathing was labored—short and rapid—and it was very apparent that she was dying. The dazed and tired look we could see in her eyes made it obvious to me that she was suffering. So, we carefully laid her on a towel and carried her back to the vet's office. Ultimately, her vet had worked hard to treat her infection.

I see and hear of many people today who struggle desperately to preserve the life of one they love at all or any cost—as though it would be compassionless to allow death to occur if there was *any* hope of survival, irrespective of how desperately futile it may be. I couldn't feel right doing that. I guess I feel that such people are showing more compassion for their own feelings and fear of death than for the well-being of the one who is suffering and will eventually die anyway. As I told our Veterinarian, I don't think Ninny needs us to hold out more hope at her expense, she needs to be getting better at our expense. My core value of self-reliance allows me to understand that death can be a relief for one that has exhausted his or her useful lifespan.

Ninny was nearly fourteen years and nine months old when we had to put her to sleep. That is a long life for a cat. Out of compassion for her suffering and the fullness and richness of her life (which we knew she could never recover), we chose to put her to sleep. Having enjoyed her company for so many years, it was not easy to make that decision; in fact, it was very painful. What made it easier for me to accept was to think about what we would put her through simply to extend our own emotional attachment to her. Ultimately, her life belongs to her, not to us. I was just fortunate to have been there to share in it. We decided it would be cruel and heartless—not a measure of devotion—for us to prolong her suffering just to relieve my own. We had to let her go because we cherished her, not because we could not find the compassion to extend her life beyond its natural course. Now I am reminding myself that her passing will preserve life for countless future generations, as I have explained above.

Life can be as tough as it is real. At some point, it will inevitably toss adversity in our paths. We all have to make very difficult decisions when that occurs. We just can't allow our emotional weaknesses to make the tough decisions for us. We simply don't make our best decisions when that happens, and that only leaves the opportunity to feel later regret. These are some of the important and reassuring lessons that I feel we can all learn from farming.

Over time, I will fondly remember all the funny and entertaining things that Ninny did during the time our lives intersected. I will never forget her first hunting attempt. We were living in Oxford, AL at the time and she couldn't have been much more than a year old. She was stalking a squirrel that was feeding on spilled bird seed that had collected at the base of our feeder. The squirrel's back was turned to Ninny when she first saw it, so it didn't know she was stalking it. She managed to creep up unseen beneath the squirrel, which was sitting near the edge of a raised landscape bed (built from old railroad ties) as it sorted through the deposit of spilled sunflower seeds. All the while, Nin carefully tracked the movement of the squirrel's tail, which she could see over the top of the railroad tie without being seen by the squirrel. What she failed to realize is that, as she was creeping up on the squirrel, it was gradually turning around so that it was facing her as she prepared to pounce. Consequently, she misjudged her leap and when she pounced, her paws landed on both sides of the squirrel and they bumped heads, catching both of them by surprise. Both Ninny and the squirrel leapt straight into the air and turned and raced away from each other in opposing directions. She had "kissed" it instead of catching it.

For many years after that incident, Ninny was a frustrated hunter. In her fourteen years of life, she never caught a bird, mouse, or squirrel, despite all the hunting successes of our other housecats. That's why it seems so ironic that, in her final two months of life, Nin actually caught a wild bunny that was feeding on the plants in our garden. It wasn't very big, but it was her very first kill. We discovered her trophy when we found it laying at the door to our front porch, where she had left it as if to say, "There, I finally did it! Aren't you proud of me now?" It took most of her life, but she finally managed to prove she was the hunter she had always strived to be. I guess I can consider that one success to be the satisfaction she needed to make her own life complete.

We still have the fuzzy heart toy that Ninny would carry around the house in her mouth, as she meowed plaintively for attention. We would return home from some trip knowing that she missed us because the fuzzy heart toy would be in some new location around the house (usually on our bed). I don't know what we'll do with it now. Perhaps one of our future cats will appreciate it as she did. It was actually a cat toy that Ninny inherited from her predecessor, Isis, who lived to be sixteen-and-a-half years old before she, too, passed away. I guess we will keep it because it is a reminder that the life cycle continues. That toy has already passed from one cherished cat to another. Who are we to disrupt the life cycle that sustains and preserves us all? It's just another reminder of how I will cherish the memory of our long-time companion, Nin. I hope you will take the time to read Nin's page under our website's "Our Livestock" header, which I will leave active as her memorial. I also hope you will understand how we feel and remember to find solace in the fact that life goes on here at Peeper Pond Farm, just as it does everywhere else.

Post 38: The Great Pumpkins Are Coming!

July 28, 2017

As I mentioned in a recent journal post, our garden is one of our best success stories at Peeper Pond Farm. We are now harvesting some delicious sweet corn from our garden, along with cucumbers and tomatoes. Today is a rainy day, so Barb is planning to can some more red cabbage that she harvested yesterday. However, we also have some large pumpkins growing in our pumpkin patch as well. We measured two of the largest pumpkins in our garden, and they already measure about eleven inches in diameter. With all the rain forecasted over the next few days, they will be putting on weight fast. Even our honey bees are enjoying a pumpkin feast, as we could hear and see them buzzing about the golden pumpkin blossoms while I was taking pictures. Many more new pumpkins will be starting soon. If all goes well with them, we will have beautiful great pumpkins to sell at our local farmer's market in September.

Everything we planted in our garden is producing crops, although the rabbits and deer have taken their share of our bounty. We only managed to get a few carrots, but our potatoes and tomatoes are doing very well. We had a few early potatoes from our garden for supper two days ago, and they were superb. Barb will be making pickles from our cucumbers, soon, once she has harvested enough for a batch. The broccoli is going by, but we have enjoyed what we harvested. We are eating fresh corn on the cob most evenings for supper, but we are hoping to dry or freeze some for corn meal (to use in making honey cornbread) and for winter vegetables. It has been a challenge for us to keep up with the weeds, given all the hot and humid weather we have had this summer, but we are managing. We always plan to do most our heavy outdoor work early in the day after the morning milking. I have been calling it "wet t-shirt work," because I like to wear a water-soaked t-shirt when doing active outdoor work on warm days to keep my body cool and reduce sweating. If you haven't done this before, it works well. After I'm done working, I can just take it off and hang it on our clothesline to dry out.

Now that we have sold Billy The Kid, his mother's milk production has increased dramatically. Yesterday, Emerald produced 14.5 cups of milk in two milkings—seven-and-a-half cups in the morning and seven cups in the evening. It was a one-day record for her and our farm. Our other producing goat, Cara, has produced seven cups once in a day, but not twice. Emerald's milk production was consistently lower than Cara's while she was feeding her buck kid, even though he would occasionally feed from Cara as well. Now that Emerald has given us more than a full week of production since Billy was sold, I can see she has the potential to be a great milker. She is only two years old and has not reached her peak production potential yet.

Despite the successes we have had producing good, fresh milk, we are still struggling to manage the feed and supply costs for our goat operation. Our meeting yesterday with the Milk Sanitation Program Manager from the Department of Health in Charleston did not leave us with any hope that we can satisfy their requirements so that we could sell any aged cheese we can produce. We produce so little milk (and even less cheese) that we could never recoup the costs we would have to incur to upgrade our operation to satisfy their standards. Our state, unlike most others, still treats unpasteurized milk as an "elixir of death," which results in very strict restrictions on sales of fresh milk and milk products. This prevailing attitude greatly restricts our business opportunities and jeopardizes our ability to afford the ongoing operating costs of our milking operation. It should come as no surprise to anyone that, as these milk standards and regulations have evolved and strengthened over the decades, small, family-operated dairy farms (like the one on which I was raised) have declined and large, industrial-scale dairy operations (whether owned by a single family or a larger corporation) have taken their place. The market price a farmer receives for fresh milk, now controlled by dairy processing companies, is insufficient to support the smallest dairy farming operations like our, and it is becoming very clear that we cannot afford to maintain it over the long run. Our modern money- and technology-driven society, along the rules and standards that govern it, continue to strangle small family farms and ultimately, our most basic rural lifestyle choices.

Post 39: Deluge

July 29, 2017

    Over the past three months, I've had to muddle through rainfalls during at least four milkings, but none like the last two. Our rain gauge recorded the full four inches of rain that fell between 5:00 PM yesterday (July 28) and noon today (July 29). However, that figure doesn't include the 0.68 inches of rain that had fallen in the hour prior to 5:00 PM on July 28. We experienced two gully-washers during those milkings that dropped roughly one inch of rain each in spans of 30-45 minutes. I didn't just get wet during those downpours, I was drenched as I filled and lugged water buckets and feed to the goat barn, prepared and staged all the milking equipment, and led the goats to and from our milking parlor. Our goats, who don't like to get wet, didn't enjoy the bath they received walking between the goat barn and the milking parlor, even though they may have needed it. Overall, we received 4.68 inches of rain from the storm in a twenty-hour period!

    The 24-hour deluge that we received impacted all aspects of life here at Peeper Pond Farm. Although we experienced no flooding (due to our elevation), the runoff from the storm carved a drainage ditch through our garden, and a flock of hungry hummingbirds declared a truce so that they could all drink briefly from our nectar feeder during a brief lull in the storm. When I went to the goat barn to check on our goats (who were loafing the day away), I was startled by a rain-soaked, mud-caked skunk that was desperately searching for refuge in the goat barn. It didn't appreciate the thought of sharing the barn with our goats, but fortunately, it chose not to spray them. My approach to the open entrance apparently was the last straw for the skunk, so it turned away from the barn and crawled under our 350-gallon LP gas tank. After another brief period of indecision about what to do next, it scampered away into the woods beyond our garage to seek its refuge elsewhere. I tried to get a picture of it as it fled, but my camera couldn't focus clearly enough on it before it disappeared into the puckerbrush at the edge of our ravine.

    We have heard radio reports of severe flooding in six West Virginia counties, but not ours. Some areas of our state received over five inches of rain in a much shorter span of time. Rainfalls of that magnitude cause the mountain rivers to swell into the valley floodplains where many homes hug the narrow roads that wind through the mountain hollows. Our house is elevated over 130 feet above Brushy Run, Stony Creek and North Mill Creek—the principal streams that combine to drain our relatively narrow valley. That means we are very safe from any major floods. Although this storm is not the worst our county has seen (that occurred during November of 1985 and is known throughout our area as the Election Day Flood), it was the heaviest rainfall we have experienced since the remnants of Hurricane Sandy struck our former home in New Creek, WV in late October of 2012. That was the last time I measured four inches or more of rain from one storm, but it fell over a four-day period. Although this wasn't a record storm in our area, I'm sure it will be remembered for a long time to come.

Post 40: And Then There Were Four

August 1, 2017

It is another sad day here at Peeper Pond Farm. One of our two initial kid goats, Gertie, had to be put to sleep this morning. About two weeks ago, we noticed that she was looking a little thin and lethargic. At first, we thought that her problems were caused by competition for food with our other kid goat, Essie. Beginning soon after they arrived at our farm this past March, Essie established herself as the dominant doe. She was born six days before Gertie, and she was very aggressive in establishing her dominance by challenging Gertie as they played and romped around the barn and outdoor pen. More recently, we had noticed that Essie would push Gertie's face out of the feed bowls, even though we had installed a second bowl so they would each have one of their own. No matter which feed bowl Gertie selected, Essie would crowd her out of it. If Gertie moved to the other bowl, Essie would decide she wanted that one, too. This is not uncommon behavior for goats. We have seen many instances when a goat that was offered something to eat would turn away or ignore it until a different goat showed interest in it. Then she'd decide she wanted it, too.

We felt that Essie had been making it difficult to compete for the food she needed. Consequently, we decided to feed Gertie separately with a bucket of grain all her own. However, after a few more days passed, we noticed that Gertie was becoming weak and wobbly in her hind legs, and she would periodically stumble or struggle to stand up on her hind legs to reach into the cedar trees for browse. At that point, we decided to take her to our vet in Petersburg. The vet took a sample of her stools for a fecal test and determined that she had Coccidiosis, a parasite that attacks the intestinal lining causing weakness and lethargy. Young kids are more susceptible to the parasite than adults, which develop a resistance with age. We treated both her and Essie for it, even though Essie showed no symptoms, because they were housed together. The vet also tested for Caprine Arthritis Encephalitis (CAE), a debilitating and deadly disease in goats, and for deficiencies in selenium and thiamine to see if they might be contributing causes of her overall weakness.

We waited a week for the test results. All of them were negative (which was a relief). Gertie's overall energy levels rebounded after the Coccidiosis treatment was administered, but the weakness in her hind legs persisted. Some of our goat colleagues suggested that the weakness might be a sign of Meningeal Worm, another parasite transmitted from deer to goats through contact with deer feces. The parasite initially attacks the intestines, but migrates into the spine as it develops. Once in the spine it attacks the nervous system, gradually weakening and paralyzing the goat. Since there is no reliable test to determine if a goat is infected or not, many goat owners treat their herd for intestinal parasites (including Meningeal Worm) during the late summer and early fall months as a precautionary method. However, this pretreatment is not without controversy. Many goat owners fear that the parasites will develop an immunity to the deworming agents, just as the overuse of antibiotics in humans have resulted in the evolution of drug-resistant super-bugs. There is no clear right or wrong way to approach this potential health problem.

Since Gertie had initially tested positive for Coccidiosis, her treatment was focused on that. Unfortunately, it is likely that she had also contracted Meningeal Worm, the symptoms for which were not clear due to the complications from Coccidiosis. By the time we had narrowed her health problems down to Meningeal Worm, the parasite had migrated to her spine and she quickly lost the ability to walk or stand up. Once the parasite has attacked the nervous system, there is no guarantee that the treatment will be effective, and the goat is unlikely to ever regain full health. Due to her rapidly declining health and the risk of further contamination, we decided it was best to put her to sleep and administer deworming treatment to our other goats. Our vet will be arriving tomorrow to treat our remaining goats. It was another painful choice for us to face after losing our cat, Ninny, less than two weeks earlier. However, Gertie would have suffered greatly as the parasite advanced, and there was little hope of recovery.

Now our goat herd has been reduced to four—our three adults and Essie. As if that wasn't heartbreaking enough, we had decided only days earlier that we needed to sell our dairy goat herd to reduce the cost burden on our retirement finances. Our inability to establish a meaningful business operation to offset our operating cost has been straining our monthly finances to the point that we would not be able to afford the long-term operating and supply costs of our milking operation. We simply don't produce enough milk to generate the income we need through milk or milk product sales, and the permitting and liability insurance costs, increased property tax burden and regulatory restrictions on milk and milk product sales effectively destroy any hope of establishing a supporting business operation. We have identified a buyer for our adults and will be selling them within the week. That day will be a sad end to our hopes and plans to operate a manageable homestead dairy farm operation here at Peeper Pond Farm.

Unfortunately, as farm life teaches, life can be a harsh and unsympathetic teacher, and hard work is no guarantee of success. We are further disheartened by the fact that we were very successful in producing good quality milk and milk products, such as soap, cheese, yogurt, ice cream and butter. Barb is hopeful that we can continue to make many of these products after our goats are sold because we can still use store-bought milk to make them and some of the products, such as soap, do not always require milk. Nevertheless, we are greatly disappointed with this unavoidable outcome, and we will miss all of our goats dearly—especially our Gertie, whose life was cut painfully short by a tragic disease. We will always remember you, Gertie.

Post 41: Tri-County Fair

August 2, 2017

Having persevered the tragedies of the past couple of weeks (the untimely deaths of our cat, Ninny and one of our doe kids, Gertie), Barb and I decided we needed a diversion. So, we decided to attend the 97th annual Tri-County Fair in Petersburg yesterday evening. The fair serves Grant, Hardy and Pendleton Counties, although Pendleton County still conducts its own much smaller county fair.

County fair week is one of the major traditional events each year for the local agricultural community, as it gives everyone an opportunity to show their work and equipment, relax in a festive event, and catch up with their friends and colleagues. While at the fair, we met our friend, Jim Boyd, who was teaching people about his bee business (Middle Mountain Apiary) and selling his products. The highlighted evening event of the day was the Lumberjack Competition, which we wanted to see. The timbering and wood products industry has been and remains one of the principle economic engines of the local economy. One wood processing plant (Allegheny Wood Products) is a large employer in Petersburg. Ironically, the timber harvesting and processing industry was also one of the major industries in my hometown community in New Hampshire.

The Lumberjack competition featured crosscutting, wood chopping, and ax throwing competitions, and drew a large crowd. One of the wood chopping competitors was 84 years old and, even though he finished last in his heat, he accomplished his work and received a huge applause from the audience. The physical strength and hard work required to be a lumberjack are embodied deeply in the values of our local culture.

We also took time to view the home and garden displays in the Exhibition Hall. The display featured hand-made quilts, canning, baking, flower arrangements, photography and painting, and garden produce, all of which was judged. We had considered submitting some of our own garden produce, but we were too busy to meet the deadline.

When I was a child growing up on our dairy farm, all of us children would submit crafts and farm products we had made or grown at the Cornish Fair—our annual county fair. It was always exciting to go through the exhibits and see if we won a ribbon for our work. Back then, ribbons (blue for first prize, red for second and yellow for third) were given out far more sparingly than they are today. That was also an era when losing a competition gracefully was a sign of personal integrity, respect and dignity.

Finally, we toured the livestock barns and viewed the cows, sheep and goats, which comprise the largest share of the Potomac Highland region's livestock market. Although we decided to raise milk goats, most of the goats and cows raised in our region are market stock sold for meat. In the distant past (more than fifty years ago) the Moorefield and Petersburg area featured a number of dairy farms and a couple of milk processing plants. Those operations gradually ended over time, as in my childhood hometown, and are disappearing from the landscape—just as our own fledgling operation will soon join them. Consequently, the goats that are now raised here in the Potomac Highlands are primarily Boers and Kikos, which are breeds well suited for meat production.

We always enjoy our annual pilgrimage to the fair, and we intend to visit the State Fair of West Virginia in a couple of weeks. We have attended it for more than five years and find it to be the best State Fair we have ever known. We at Peeper Pond Farm encourage you to attend the annual agricultural fairs in your area to show continued support for your local agricultural community and, especially, small, family owned and operated farms.

Post 42: The Old Ways

August 3, 2017

    I must first apologize for the length of this post, but I have been waiting to write it for a long time. Now that we are approaching the end of our dairy operation, I wanted to comment on our historic agricultural folkways, or as they may be more commonly known, "the old ways." When we began planning for our farm, I wanted to practice and teach, to the extent possible and practical, our time-honored, traditional farm practices, which I consider to be fading into a forgotten and largely devalued history. Perhaps the most important aspect of our Peeper Pond Farm mission is to train future farmers to respect and honor our traditional folkways and practices.

    There was a time, not too many generations ago, when farm work was done primarily by hand, horse, or ox—not by tractor, computers and other farm technology. While the manual labor was great and time-consuming, the work was more rewarding and healthier, building the strong men and women who founded our society with little more than an ax. Today, we have created modern machines and other labor-saving technologies that have changed the face of agriculture, with some good and some bad consequences. Our new computers and heavy equipment can increase and maximize agricultural productivity greatly, while decreasing the amount of manual labor required to farm. We have also learned how to genetically engineer crops to increase yields and the quality of production.

    However, we must remember that these advances also result in unintended, and perhaps poorly considered, consequences that may offset many of those benefits. Consider the ongoing controversy and debate over genetically engineered farm products. There remains considerable debate in the agricultural community over the long-term health ramifications of these food to both humans and livestock. I would also note that the high cost of these new technologies has raised the overhead and operating costs of farming to such a high level that small, family owned and operated farms have been driven out of the market. In making this assertion, I refer to small, diverse homestead farms where the work was done almost exclusively by the family members who lived there and who obtained most of their food and sustenance from it. Such farms may specialize in one aspect of production that provides an outside income for the family (such as meat, dairy, or cash crops), but they also produce additional products to support their own living needs. Our small scale of operation and limited production capability made my childhood homestead farm one of those victims.

Farms that have invested heavily in new advanced technologies require significant capital and have greatly intensified and expanded their farming operations to produce the product sales they need to generate a positive return on investment. Many of them may have expanded from the small family farms I once knew. They may still be owned by a single family, but they have become "industrial farms" in scale and require outside and migrant labor to operate successfully. They also consume huge volumes of power and fuel to operate, which creates new and greater farming impacts on the environment. Many of them have become so large in scale and intensity that they are known as Concentrated Animal Feeding Operations (CAFOs), which have come under increasing regulatory scrutiny because of their environmental impacts. Additionally, there is a health impact to many farmers and farm operators from the labor-saving conveniences that these new technologies afford. Workers on an industrial farm can do more of their work from a chair or an air-conditioned tractor cab that earlier generations did by hand or on their feet. While these new technologies may make the work safer, they also make it so much easier that farm workers gain less exercise and muscle tone from it.

I could cite many more negative consequences from our prideful admiration of modern technology and the alleged conveniences it bestows, but I trust I have made my point. In a time when technology advances by great leaps and bounds over shorter and shorter periods of time, we would be wise to devote more consideration and critical thinking to the potential negative consequences they may cause, or we may suffer from them later—perhaps when it is too late to avoid or correct them.

Just because something is old or has been outdated by new technology does *not* mean it has no inherent value. In making this statement, I echo one of my literary idols, Eric Sloane, who recognized and repeatedly documented this point in his extensive research and writing about traditional early American lifestyles, customs, values, tools and folkways. In his book, *Eric Sloane's Do: A Little Book of Early American Know-How*, he wrote:

"One of the first delights of life was when the child learned to button up his own pants, but the zipper eliminated that satisfying exercise of dexterity. Grinding coffee, making ice cream, shining shoes, and nearly all the small movements that made up the continuous ballet of daily life a few years back are now being done by plugging into a socket or flipping a switch. Even the satisfaction of knowing where that electric power comes from is kept from us and sometimes the power company doesn't know either. I still recall the extraordinary pleasure of pumping spring water and carrying it for the household; now I turn on a faucet and I am too lazy to wonder where the stuff is coming from. Perhaps if I really knew, I wouldn't drink it. We used to pray to God for our needs to be fulfilled; now we depend upon the establishment.

"Years ago, when I contemplated the difference between the early American and his modern counterpart, I made some interesting finds. The old-timer was smaller, about twenty to fifty pounds lighter than the average man of today, but he was wiry and very much stronger. Bread was as solid and hard as the people who ate it, but now the 'staff of life' is so fat and spongy and full of air as we have become. The 'sports fan' of today seldom does his own thing; instead, he watches others do their things, eating and drinking at the TV while sitting on a behind that would have shamed great-grandfather.

"There is no doubt about it, doing things by and for ourselves has become a lost art, and the joy of doing things not just 'the old-fashioned way' but plainly the right way is a nearly vanished satisfaction. Living in the country where you have to chop your own firewood, pump your own water, and do a lot of your own repairing is worth the trouble; the psychiatrists make less profit but life is seldom a bore."

I would note that Eric Sloane made this assessment prior to 1972, when his book was first published. I find great irony in the realization that his appraisal remains fully as relevant in 2017—45 years later—as it was when he first wrote it. After a 30-year professional career where I spent the majority of my time sitting on my butt in front of a computer, I must admit that my physical condition has deteriorated greatly, and I have struggled over the past decade to build our home and do the manual farm work that many lifelong farmers my age can do without thinking. Nevertheless, we hand-milk our goats, lug five-gallon water buckets to and from the goat barn, clean out the barn with pitch forks, successfully make our own cheese, soap, yogurt, ice cream and butter from the fresh, unprocessed goat milk we produce, and we grow vegetables and herbs in our garden—all by hand. We live in a house without air conditioning or central heat; our house is heated by a pellet stove and a wood cookstove supplemented by an LP gas heater. Our water comes from a drilled well and our wastewater is treated by a septic system. I have been mowing our yards with a push mower, and when we first began to build our house and establish our orchard, I used a scythe to mow the tall grass and weeds. We don't live our lives as simply as is possible, only as simply as we can, based on our advancing age and declining physical capabilities—much of which has been accelerated by the modern conveniences and reduced exercise afforded by our professional careers and life in the modern society. Yet, even though we burn wood for heat, I would contend and argue that our overall 'carbon footprint' and our overall environmental impact is far less than it is for the average urban-dweller who lives in constant fear of such things—all the while living in a home that consumes rapidly increasing volumes of energy with poor air circulation and virtually no windows that open and spending most of his spare time sitting in front of a home theater, playing on a computer, or communicating with faceless friends on his mobile device. The very lifestyle that our modern society values most tends to emphasize the lack of integrity in the basic values of physical health and environmental quality that it espouses. It is from an understanding of those lifestyle idiosyncrasies (or as I like to refer to them— 'idiotsyncrasies') that I espouse and value our traditional lifestyles and folkways.

    I only hope that, as you travel around our remaining rural areas and see the aging barns, overgrown farm fields, abandoned mills and dilapidated farmhouses, you will think carefully about the 'old ways' that gave these relics their former vitality and relevance. Perhaps in doing so, you will also gain greater respect for the way people used to live and will work to make sure that those old ways—our traditional folkways and cultural heritage—do not become a lifestyle lost to a forgotten and unappreciated history. That is one of the principal values we desperately tried to convey through our determined efforts here at Peeper Pond Farm. Please don't let it all die simply because we couldn't succeed. Our heritage deserves far greater respect than that.

Post 43: Fox Hunt

August 4, 2017

Our son, Michael, just got a new kitten to replace his long-time cat, Toni, who had to be put to sleep in early March. Since our cat, Ninny passed away a couple of weeks ago, we decided to make a trip to visit him in Keyser and give him our remaining unused cat food, treats, cat litter and deodorizer. We don't intend to seek another house cat for a while, so we thought it would be wise to let him make good use of them. We also delivered to him a half gallon of fresh vanilla ice cream that we made from goat milk obtained during one of our final milkings. We hadn't seen him in over two weeks, so we decided to put together a picnic lunch and share it at the beach on nearby Jennings Randolph Lake in Mineral County.

After we returned home to Peeper Pond Farm, we began preparing for the evening milking. As I was mixing some warm iodine udder wash at the kitchen sink, I glanced out the window and saw a small brown fox in our hayfield. The tall grass had been mowed by Scott Kimble's hired hand earlier this week and the fox was hunting in the dried hay for field mice and/or small rabbits. This was the first fox we had seen on our farm property. Barb and I watched with interest (along with some of our neighbors) as the fox pounced at prey that it had found scurrying under the hay. It appeared to us and our neighbor that the fox was suffering from mange that had left its tail almost hairless except for the white spot at the tip. However, the long, pointed ears were unmistakable as those of a fox.

The hungry fox relentlessly pursued its small prey throughout our small field for more than an hour, unfazed by our periodic presence on the porch. I got my camera and managed to capture a few pictures of it, one of which I have included in this post. Unfortunately, the fox was more than 300 feet out into the field, which required the use of my telephoto lens, resulting in pictures that are somewhat less than perfectly sharp and clear. However, it is not too difficult to see that it was a fox.

It eventually retreated into the wooded ravine on the east side of our field, as if sensing the approach of a severe thunderstorm that struck with strong winds. The storm dumped half an inch of rain in twenty minutes, urging the now drenched fox to trot back towards our house in the hope of seeking shelter under our front porch. When it came within about twenty feet of the house, I scared it back to the woods. Knowing that it was suffering from a bad case of mange, I was concerned that the animal could be afflicted with other diseases—perhaps even rabies. In all reality, we have no way to know that the fox has not been sleeping under our porch on other recent occasions, as we did not attach any skirting to restrict access below the porch.

We have seen many wild animals at our farm over the past decade, including deer, skunks, raccoons, groundhogs, opossums, ducks, bald eagles, and now a brown fox. Although we have never seen a black bear, we know that they have visited our farm during the night because we found their unmistakable scat in our driveway the next morning. One of the most rewarding aspects of farming in such a rich and bountiful rural area is the opportunity to see and study all manner of wildlife. Now we are waiting for a chance to see an elk, which, beginning last year, have been reintroduced into West Virginia for the first time since they were wiped out in the 1860s. Despite popular stereotypes about our state, based largely on its coal production, most of the West Virginia we have come to know is truly wild and wonderful.

Post 44: Kaput

August 5, 2017

    I knew this day would arrive someday, I just never expected it would happen this soon. It swept in ushered by a dry, cool, almost fall-like breeze capped by puffy, broken clouds with slate gray bases. With all the summer humidity gone, the morning air felt refreshing as we trudged out to the goat barn to prepare for our final milking. Today is the day that our remaining adult goats would be sold to the Stover Homestead Farm in Slippery Rock, PA. Our retirement dream of operating a homestead dairy farm on our property in Pendleton County was finally broken by our inability to establish a business operation that would effectively subsidize our operating costs and keep us financially solvent. State health regulations and standards, designed to govern large farm operations, proved to be too inflexible and expensive for us to satisfy. We were ultimately unable to sell our fresh milk or any products made from our milk for human consumption. Along with it, our plans to house and train people seeking to learn how to live more self-reliantly were frustrated by the permitting costs and potential impact on our property taxes, which would increase because our house would be reclassified as a bed and breakfast use. With the added cost of liability insurance to protect our business operation, we simply couldn't afford it all. Therefore, we made the inevitable, heart-wrenching decision to abandon our dairy operation and sell our goats before our retirement income and savings were exhausted. It was the only decision we could make, as the dairy operation was the most expensive element of our overall farm operating costs.

    We will continue to keep our bees, vegetable and herb gardens, and our struggling fruit orchard, but Peeper Pond Farm won't be the same anymore without our goats. By abandoning our goat operation, we will also lose the future income potential from sales of goat kids, but the cost of feeding and breeding our goats until that point in the spring would be more than we could afford on our retirement income. Our garden may produce some vegetables that we could sell at the local farmer's markets, but that potential income isn't enough to offset the extra monthly expenses we have been incurring for feed, supplies, medications, and electricity to power the barn fans on hot days and to pump and treat the thirty-plus gallons of water we have been using daily to provide drinking water for the goats, wash and sanitize the milking equipment, and clean the goats' udders prior to each milking. We worked to the best of our abilities and found as many ways to minimize our operating costs as we could, but it wasn't enough to keep us solvent without a meaningful subsidy from our planned business operation.

In the final analysis, our overall goat operation lasted nearly five months, from March until early August. During that time, we gained experience raising three goat kids, hand-milking goats twice daily over three months, trimming hooves, trimming teat and udder hair on our milking adults, treating several simple goat maladies, mucking out the barn, vaccinating our goats, and successfully processing our milk into useful household products, including soap, cheese, butter, yogurt and ice cream. We are somewhat consoled by the fact that we can continue making soap, cheese and ice cream even after we cease our milking operation. Barb was able to freeze enough five-ounce packages of goat milk to use in making future batches of soap for more than a year. We can also use store-bought whole milk which we haven't purchased for more than three months, to continue making as much cheese and ice cream as we desire. While the loss of our goats does not bring an abrupt end to our overall homestead farm operation, it diminishes it significantly.

I will also miss working with our goats. We had developed a good working rapport with them over the past three months. Where they were nervous and afraid of us at first, they now trust us implicitly and seek attention from us whenever we are in the barn or pens. Some of our friends who operate market livestock farms in our area felt that we were treating them more like pets than livestock, but when you milk goats for a living, you work more closely with them and need to make them feel at ease with you or they won't produce the milk you need. Dairy farming is very different from raising goats or cows for meat. We are proud to have been successful in producing a steady flow of high-quality milk that all who tasted agreed was as good to drink as store-bought milk. Neither of us became ill from drinking our own milk. I can say the same of my childhood on our dairy farm in New Hampshire, as all of us kids had better attendance records at school than most other students. To my knowledge, none of us ever became sick from a milk-induced illness throughout my eighteen-year childhood on the farm. Obviously, none of us died from it.

I am also pleased with our efforts to teach our followers about farm life and our beloved Pendleton County through our website posts. I was surprised to discover how many people from around the globe have been reading and enjoying our periodic posts. I really don't know how many of you found us, but we really appreciate your dedicated interest and support. We have worked hard to convey the values and benefits of rural, self-reliant living, and we have used our five-month dairy goat operation as a tool to do that.

As for my future after milking, I will be dedicating my efforts to build support for the future adoption in West Virginia of a Farm Freedom Act, similar to the one first adopted by Wyoming in 2015. I do not object to basic regulations in principle, but I can't support agricultural regulations that destroy or frustrate one scale of farming (small, family owned and operated homestead farms) in favor of the modern, industrial farming of today. We need a better way to establish basic standards without discriminating against the smallest farm operations. I plan to use my professional research skills to evaluate this issue further so that future homestead and small farmers will have a better chance to succeed than we did. At this point in my life, I cannot afford to rebuild our dairy goat operation, but I can work to make it easier for the next person. That will become my next mission in life.

Post 45: As the Seasons Turn

August 13, 2017

The march of the seasons is like a slow-motion ballet. There is a subtle beauty to the changing sounds of the days and nights as the seasons transition from one to another. If you listen carefully to the cicadas during the day and the katydids in the evening, you will be convinced that the dog days of summer still hold sway. However, I have noticed that the nights are becoming perceptibly longer, cooler and dryer as the summer humidity begins to melt away. We refer to the hottest days of midsummer as the "dog days," but few of us have any way to know exactly when they begin and end. The generally accepted timeframe is between early July (about three weeks prior to the average hottest day of the year) and mid-August (about three weeks after the average hottest day of the year).

The term dates back to ancient Egypt and Greece, where sky observers noted that the warmest part of summer coincided with the dominance of the brightest star, Sirius, in the night sky. Sirius is known as the "dog star" because it is located in the constellation Canis Major—the dog constellation. This constellation is high in the night sky during the months of July and August, which is the climactic peak of summer. Although Sirius is relatively large and close to us, as neighboring stars go, it is too far away to have any direct impact on our planet's temperature. However, its consistent appearance during the peak of summer heat forever engrained it in the human consciousness as the primary cause as well as the reason why this time of the year is known as the "dog days of summer."

If the most common six-week timeframe is accepted to define the dog days of summer, then they are now ending (sometime around the 11th of August). That may explain why we have seen so many deer in our field during the early evening hours lately. Our visiting Peeper Pond Farm deer herd has gradually grown to more than ten deer and now includes two bucks. Barb actually watched them engaged in combat for a few minutes, signaling the start of rutting season, when the bucks fight to win the hearts of the accompanying does. The start of rutting season is a clear sign that the days are getting shorter, the summer heat is waning, and the fall mating season is just around the corner. Of course, come November, the hunters will follow. Even our goat does, which we sold one week ago, had shown signs of their early heat cycle weeks earlier.

Having recently sold our goat herd, I have felt lonely in the overwhelming stillness of our empty goat barn. Where once our goats would call to us when they heard us approaching the barn door, I now only hear a few lingering crickets chirping away at the deafening silence. Within the walls of our barn, fall--the dying season--has already settled in. Fortunately, I sold our remaining doe kid, Essie, to a small goat farm located only three miles above our farm at the entrance to Smoke Hole Canyon. We decided to visit her at her new home yesterday and deliver to her new owners some of the remaining feed that we had in our milking parlor cabinet. When we arrived, she recognized my call to her immediately and replied by braying back to me from inside her new barn. It was wonderfully reassuring to see that she was healthy and content in her new home as she affectionately pressed her head and shoulders against us to beg for attention. Essie displays a beautiful form for a dairy goat, and I remain firm in my conviction that she will become a champion show goat someday. When I look into her eyes, I can still see the glimmer of loving recognition that she held for us during the nearly six months that we raised her. Although I truly regret losing her, I try to find solace in the knowledge that she will be well appreciated and cared for by her new owners. May the changing seasons and future years be kind to you, Essie. You will always be remembered fondly by us as the queen of Peeper Pond Farm.

Post 46: The State Fair of West Virginia

August 17, 2017

    We attended the State Fair of West Virginia yesterday (August 16). We have attended State Fairs in New Hampshire, Georgia, Alabama and Maryland, but we find the West Virginia State Fair to be the best. The weather was perfect for the long drive through the mountains to the Lewisburg area. We took a rural route through Highland County, VA and Pocahontas and Greenbrier Counties in WV that inevitably led us to Anthony Road. Anthony Road is a very rural stretch of road that connects WV Route 92 in Neola to U.S. Route 219 in Frankford across Round Mountain and the Greenbrier River. Although it is used as a mountain gap cutoff route between two valleys frequented by locals, it is a type of narrow rural road known in West Virginia as a "Layover Road." It consists of a two-lane wide gravel base overlaid down the center with a one-lane wide asphalt surface. Since the traffic volume using the road is typically low, drivers can drive slowly along the single lane of black top until they encounter an oncoming vehicle—which explains why you have to drive along it slowly. In order to avoid a collision, both vehicles must then "lay over" their right tires onto the gravel shoulders so they can safely pass each other—hence the name. It is a traditional and affordable way to maintain a partially paved roadway along a very rural stretch of highway. When I was growing up in New Hampshire, we had a number of roads like this, but many have since been widened and expanded into full two-lane paved highways.

    After arriving at the State Fair, we attended the Dairy Goat show. Judging from the contestants, French Alpine goats are far more popular than other breeds. We found only one Oberhasli goat entry in the show, which was disappointing to us. Our Oberhasli goats proved to be very productive milkers and gave us quality milk with high butterfat levels. We couldn't stay to watch the entire show, as it was running late, and there is a lot to more see at our State Fair.

    We toured several of the livestock barns to see the dairy cows, horses and sheep. Holsteins and Jerseys were the predominant breeds of dairy cows exhibited at the fair, both of which we raised on my childhood dairy farm. Most of our average herd of 30 cows were Holsteins, although we also kept one or two Jerseys to raise the butterfat levels in our milk. Although Jerseys produce relatively high butterfat levels in their milk, our Oberhasli goats can produce even higher levels of butterfat than a typical Jersey cow. Butterfat helps make the milk creamier and richer, allowing us to produce very rich ice cream.

We also toured the horse barns, where we watched two horses being bathed. They appeared to enjoy the attention and the cooling rinse water during the heat of the afternoon. We also watched a Bengal Tiger demonstration show at the fair, and our son, Michael, fed some raw meat to one of the tigers. Of course, we made sure we attended the home and garden exhibits, as Barb loves to view all the quilts. We decided that we need to enroll some of our garden vegetables and canned goods in next year's Tri-County fair, as the vegetables we have grown in our Peeper Pond Farm garden would be very competitive with those we have seen displayed at the fairs we attended this season.

After a long day of walking around the fairgrounds in the blazing sun, we returned home. Today, Barb is planning to prepare some dill and sweet pickles from the cucumbers we recently harvested from our garden. We have grown some fine cucumbers. Perhaps they will win some ribbons during the fair season next year. We look forward to the competition. Now if we can only make use of all the cucumbers yet to be harvested from our garden.

Post 47: The Total Solar Eclipse of 2017

August 22, 2017

When we were milking our dairy goats, we couldn't travel more than a three-hour drive from our farm without interfering with our established morning and evening milking times. I have always been an early riser and a morning worker. I enjoy working outdoors in the early morning hours, when I am most refreshed and have the energy and cool air to make the work comfortable. I derive more satisfaction and can relax more peacefully when the hard work is behind me than I can when I have procrastinated and left the hard work for late in the day. That Is a true farmer's attitude and behavior. Although I now have far more free time during the day than I did during the first six months of my retirement, I find that time less rewarding or relaxing than when we were raising our goats.

We had known that a total solar eclipse would occur in 2017 for some time, but we would have never planned to watch it from within the path of totality while we were milking goats because it was too far away to be within our reach. Here at Peeper Pond Farm, the moon's shadow would have covered only about 80-90 percent of the sun's disk. While that would be more impressive than any other solar eclipse I have known in my life, it wouldn't have afforded us the experience of a true total eclipse. However, after we sold all our dairy goats on August 5, I found myself thinking more carefully about the eclipse and checking the date, time and location of the path of totality. As far as I knew with all our focused farm work, it might have already occurred and we missed it completely.

Fortunately, it had not (perhaps one of the few fortunes we had during our final few weeks of goat farming), and I was able to determine that, if the weather conditions were good, we could travel to the path of totality in Tennessee from our farm and return home in a single day. That was enough to convince me that it would be worth the effort for a "once-in-a-lifetime experience." True, I had seen pictures and television videos of many past solar eclipses, but they only served to whet my appetite to understand the whole experience—the sights and sounds of the entire event. My curiosity and inherent interest in celestial events made the driving sacrifice a minimal concern, as long as we could pack our own lunch and pay for little more than the gas needed for the journey. So, off we went on at 5:42 AM on our drive to Loudon, Tennessee (Exit 72 on Interstate 75) for our great adventure.

The traffic along Interstates 81, 40, and 75 (our most expedient driving route) worked to our advantage. The only slowdowns we experienced along the route (both going and returning) were in the immediate Knoxville area. I had planned an extra hour for our journey because we had passed through Knoxville so many times when we were living in Georgia and Alabama (13 years) that I was very familiar with the frequent traffic jams along the stretch of Interstate highway shared by both I-40 and I-75. In the twenty or more times I have driven through Knoxville on my way north or south, I believe I have passed through without a slowdown or traffic jam only once—regardless of the day of the week or time of day. I won't tell you this, but I have often sarcastically referred to the city as "Knoxiousville" because of the distaste I have for those predictable and annoying traffic jams. I fully expected that I would need to allow extra time to suffer that fate on our way to the see the eclipse. We were pleasantly relieved to find that I had allowed more than enough time, and we arrived at our planned exit just as the moon's shadow was taking its first tempting bites out of the sun.

We were armed with everything we needed—several cell phone cameras, our 35 mm Canon Powershot camera and a solar eclipse projector that I handcrafted using a Cheerios cereal box, some aluminum foil and some duct tape (the handyman's secret weapon, as the Canadian television character Red Green always proclaimed). While I was refueling our car at a gas station on the northbound side of the exit, two gentlemen in a bright red pick-up truck drove by us in the parking lot and graciously offered my son (who accompanied us on our trip) two solar eclipse glasses that they didn't want. We drove our son's 2008 Hyundai Sonata because it had cruise control (to make the long Interstate drive a little easier) and a tinted sun roof through which I could comfortably shoot stable pictures of the total eclipse. Regardless of the ad nauseum radio and television warnings we heard not to look directly at the eclipse, I knew that viewing the eclipse during the time that the sun's disk was completely obscured by the moon's shadow would not cause damage to my eyes or my camera. The damage to which they were referring, with an overabundance of caution, is caused by prolonged direct exposure to high intensity ultraviolet light rays, which would be completely obscured by the moon's disc at the peak of the eclipse. My basic knowledge of astronomy and my common sense understanding of the geometry involved in an eclipse allowed me to read safely between the lines of their warnings. If we want to have a truly informed understanding of the strategically qualified information and statistics we are typically force-fed, we need to apply substantially more critical thinking and personal research to the issues than the average person appears to do. As for the car sunroof, I wanted to use it to reduce the impact of atmospheric glare on my view of the sun's corona, or the sun's plasma-charged atmosphere. That is the essential beauty of the total eclipse, which I clearly captured in the picture accompanying this post—one of several I took during the two or more minutes of totality. I am pleased to announce that my eyes and camera still function as well the day after the eclipse as they did before.

However, we did not make the trip solely to view the interaction between the sun and moon. An eclipse event embodies much more than that, if you choose to experience it all. All during the eclipse (including the time before and after the peak of totality), I kept drawing attention to the sights and sounds all around us that accompanied it. I noted how short the peak of totality was when compared to the time it took for the moon to creep completely across the sun's disk (roughly 90 minutes, by our estimate). I drew attention to the very gradual decline in light levels, as though someone had gently turned down the brightness with a dimmer switch. That experience is different from the approach of a large cloud shadow, which creates a more sudden and more immediately conspicuous change in light levels. As the sunlight subtly faded, I observed how the colors on the landscape (from the shade of the grass to the colors of the buildings) intensified, the solar-activated signs and streetlights lit up, and wispy, ethereal cirrus clouds began to appear in the sky, which although present all along, were previously obscured by scattered glare that resulted from atmospheric haze.

I also noted the gentle drop in air temperature. The air in Loudon, Tennessee was essentially too humid for an extreme overall temperature change to occur. I'm sure that observers at the higher elevations (thinner and dryer air) of the path of totality in the western states experienced a more dramatic temperature change than we did (roughly five or six degrees). Barb noted how we could feel the relative humidity increase, as the temperature fell relative to the more stable dew point of the air. I also pointed out the increased noise from birds and crickets, that were fooled into thinking that night was approaching. These were all observations that even a blind person could experience and appreciate.

However, the atmospheric haze (combined with local particulate levels in the air), created another interesting sight to behold. The atmospheric glow along the horizon surrounding the shadow of totality changed slowly from a typically haze-induced milky azure color to a subtle orange-red color that provided a striking backdrop to the overhead darkness of the eclipse itself—like a ring of sunset around the horizon. We observed only two intensely bright celestial points of light around the eclipse, the glow of Venus to the right (the morning star I could see through my garage window during my final weeks of milking our goats) and another that I wasn't able to immediately identify to the left (which I would assume to have been Jupiter). Finally, I noticed that the tops of the small, billowing cumulus clouds dotting the sky in the distance remained fully illuminated by the sun, adding to the glow of the atmosphere along the horizon.

These observations were the real material benefit we sought and obtained by making the long trip to observe the eclipse for ourselves. During past eclipses of which I have heard or read accounts, I never learned nor could I have seen and experienced all of these subtle environmental effects to the depth and comprehensive detail that I have taken in this post to explain so carefully to you. From my observations of all the other people around us, everyone was too focused on watching the actual eclipse through their protective glasses have to noticed everything we observed. I also had the privileged opportunity to share them with my wife and son—my family—who accompanied me on the journey. For those two or so minutes, we experienced the most conscious period of our day in a special time and place. Every element of the natural world around us— all the way into the limitless depths of the heavens—was ours for the taking. Those observations are the sum total of our experience from the 2017 solar eclipse that I will carry in my memory and share with others for the rest of my life. That's what the day-long adventure was truly all about.

Human life may seem long while it is lived, but it is painfully short by cosmic standards. I have no way to assure you or to be certain that I will survive to attend the next 2024 total solar eclipse in the eastern U.S., or even that the observing conditions where I could reach it would be as ideal as they were yesterday. We weren't fortunate in that our goat farming experience at Peeper Pond Farm was so painfully brief. However, I greatly appreciate and dearly miss the opportunity I had to enjoy it. It is often the briefest experiences in our lives that we cherish and remember the most. At least I can say that the loss of our dairy goats gave us the opportunity as a family to share another great, but brief once-in-a-lifetime event—the full sensual experience of a total solar eclipse. May each of you enjoy every subtle aspect of the brief, but grand, farming and celestial events in your life. Only in them will you be truly aware of the full richness of life that you will experience. Only then will you understand and appreciate the remarkable beauty that surrounds us and makes our lives worth living fully.

Post 48: Brandywine Lake

August 23, 2017

Using our periodic website posts, I have introduced you to many of the special natural and scenic landmarks in Pendleton County. Yesterday, Barb and I visited another to escape the 92-degree heat of the day on our farm, the warmest temperature we have seen in more than a month. Fortunately, the humidity levels were relatively low, thereby preventing the hazy skies so common on the hottest days of the year and allowing clear views of the surrounding mountains. This time, we decided to go swimming at a small, peaceful public beach on the nine-acre Brandywine Lake, the namesake centerpiece of a day use area and campground in the George Washington National Forest, about three miles up U.S. Route 33 from the village of Brandywine, WV at the foot of Shenandoah Mountain. We were lacking sleep from our hectic dash to see the solar eclipse on Monday (August 21), and we decided that a peaceful afternoon rest at the lake would be the perfect recuperative medicine.

The lake and day use area are located in a heavily wooded section of forest. The lake's placid waters had warmed to a comfortable swimming temperature (around 70 degrees) and the delicate late summer wildflowers were blooming in abundance, including golden yellow wingstem and soft lavender Joe Pye Weed. All of the wildflowers we saw at the lake can also be found here on Peeper Pond Farm.

I waded casually into the fresh, creek-fed waters of the lake until I was neck-deep (nearly five feet) in the water. The lake was so clear and calm, I could still see my toes at that depth. As I stood there, I watched tiny water bugs as they darted and skimmed along the shimmering surface of the water as gracefully as figure skaters on ice. All around me dragonflies and their larger cousins, which we used to call "darning needles" when we were young, buzzed about busily in search of prey, while just below the surface hungry fish were lurking lazily in the water and leaping above the surface for a quick meal. The scene and water were so enticing that Barb actually waded chest-deep into the lake, something she rarely does unless the water is bathtub warm.

After a brief swim, we walked around the park, enjoying the gentle afternoon breeze that made the shady areas very pleasant to enjoy. We even watched a couple of kayakers casually paddle along the shore. No one was in a rush at Brandywine Lake. I wished we could have spent more time enjoying the lake to fish, picnic and walk more of the forest trails, but Barb has been busy lately canning and freezing the rest of the green beans harvested from our garden. Reluctantly, we packed up our belongings and returned to our home at Peeper Pond Farm. Reality sets in hard and fast when you live on a farm.

Now that we have introduced you to many of the local and nearby special places and natural wonders we frequent in our area to escape the summer heat—Blackwater Falls State Park, Bear Rocks, Spruce Knob, Seneca Rocks, Smoke Hole Canyon and Brandywine Lake—perhaps you can appreciate why I assert that the *real* reason why West Virginia is called "Almost Heaven" is because it can't *all* be Pendleton County. If so, then you can truly understand why we love our home at Peeper Pond Farm.

Post 49: Harvesting the Bounty of the Land

August 28, 2017

Some may call us nuts, but we like to harvest the natural bounty of our land here at Peeper Pond Farm. We are fortunate to have a small Shagbark Hickory grove along the ravine that divides our two adjoining properties. Not only do hickory trees produce dense hardwood timber for boards and firewood, but the nuts are good to eat. This year, the trees produced a lot of nuts, many of which had been eaten by the squirrels and deer that also love them. With all the wildlife surrounding our farm, the competition to collect the nuts can be rather fierce. Still, we managed to collect a good number of edible nuts along the bank of our ravine.

Hickory nuts are hard to crack open. We use a hand-held nutcracker, but you have to apply a lot of strength to split the outer hulls. We have used these outer hulls in a charcoal grill to add a rich, smoky taste to our barbecued meat. I have also thrown them in the firebox of our wood cookstove to enhance the smell of the firewood we burn during the winter.

The inner shell is equally tough to break open, but the meat that hides inside is worth the effort. The inner shell is divided into several twisted chambers from which you must dig out the meat with a nut picker. Two years ago, we harvested enough nuts to provide us with a full cup of nut meat. Judging from the number of nuts we harvested earlier today, I'd say we'll fall a little short of that amount this year—perhaps three-quarters of a cup. We have used the hickory nut meat to enhance the flavor of our banana bread, which is prepared from an age-old scratch recipe that pre-dated ingredient measurements and baking temperatures.

In past years, we have also harvested some walnuts from our neighbor's property and, of course, Barb has occasionally harvested the wildflowers that grow abundantly around our farm. We especially love the wild phlox that grows in our ravine. Many of these flowers have medicinal properties, if you know how to prepare them. We have books on the subject, but we haven't experimented with that yet.

One of the most wonderful aspects of life on our farm and in our Appalachian Mountains is the incredible variety of plants and animals that have supported generations of homesteaders in our area. We cherish the fact that one can still wander through the woods and find an abundance of edible mushrooms, nuts and plants to support your diet and your health. It is one of the many benefits we obtain from a simple lifestyle. We hope you can take the time to appreciate the environment around you and discover how our ancestors carved a satisfying life out of the wilderness.

Post 50: Treasure Mountain Festival

September 16, 2017

We attended our 11th Treasure Mountain Festival today (September 16, 2017). Treasure Mountain Festival is Pendleton County's biggest annual heritage event attracting tens of thousands to Franklin and surrounding communities over four days during the third weekend of September.

The festival is based on an old Indian legend from the 1758 attack and burning of Fort Seybert, the construction of which was commissioned by General George Washington in the early years of the French and Indian War. According to the legend, the raiding Indians plundered the fort before burning it to the ground. They executed half of the settlers they captured at the fort and decided to march the rest of them back to their home territory in Ohio. They placed the valuables they collected from the fort in a large iron kettle to carry back with them on their journey. However, as they began their march back to their Ohio home, the two warriors carrying the laden kettle began to fall behind under the weight of their burden. Fearing the pursuit of Colonial forces, they decided to bury the pot along the trail that they were following to quicken their pace. Since no Indians ever returned to Pendleton County after the raid to collect their treasure, it has remained buried somewhere in the county. Although many have searched for the lost treasure over the centuries that have passed, it has never been recovered. The culmination of the annual festival includes a ceremonial reenactment of the burning of Fort Seybert.

This year, we decided to attend the walking tour of historic buildings in downtown Franklin. We were fortunate to view restoration work on the General Boggs House (built in 1820), which may be the oldest standing house in the Town of Franklin. The house was purchased during the past few months, and the new owner has been carefully peeling back layers of wallpaper and plaster that had been added over the years to reveal the original plaster walls and ceiling in the house. The original plaster walls and ceilings were decorated by colorfully hand-painted designs. We also saw the elegant Queen Anne design of the Anderson House, built in 1900, which overlooks the village of Franklin from a steep hill. The view of the town from the front porch was stunning.

Barb enjoyed the quilt show, which is hosted by the local quilting guild, Sew and Sew quilters. The display included fine quilting projects from across the region. We also toured the flea market and artisan displays at the festival's Country Store just below the village as well as the book sale at the Pendleton County Library. We were pleased to meet several of our friends and neighbors from the region. While we couldn't attend all the scheduled events, we try to experience something new each year. Maybe next year we will attend the fort burning, the parade, the Country Store Opry, the beard and mustache contest, or the horseshoe pitch. Whatever your interests may be, Pendleton County's annual Treasure Mountain Festival offers something fun and entertaining to do.

Post 51: The Peeper Pond Farm Story

September 21, 2017

When we sold our dairy goats in early August, I said that I would be turning my attention to documenting our problems and working to change the regulations that frustrated our dairy business plans. Since then, I have been working on my third book, <u>The Peeper Pond Farm Story: Where Did All the Family Dairy Farms Go?</u> I finished writing and editing the first draft last week. The book picks up where my first book, <u>Lifestyle Lost</u> (2012), left off by explaining how our farm operation plans evolved as we were building our retirement home. By incorporating the website posts from our first year of operation (September 2016 – August 2017), it explains what we planned to do, how we got it all started, what worked well and what didn't, our traditional farming practices, and why we were ultimately unable to make our lifestyle skills training program work which inevitably led to the demise of our dairy operation. The book also provides an historical context for the plight we share with so many other small family dairy farms and explains how we feel the regulations that govern dairy farm operations should be changed to help small homestead farms survive. I will now begin working on getting it published to help bring public attention to the gradual decline of small family farms.

As a first step in my efforts to obtain regulatory relief, Barb and I traveled to Charleston, WV to meet with WV Department of Agriculture Commissioner Kent Leonhardt in his State Capitol office on Monday, September 18. It was a lovely four-hour ride through the mountains of our state. The cool and dry weather we have experienced over the past three or more weeks has brought out the fall foliage colors in the higher elevations that we traversed along the way, making the long journey a truly pleasant and scenic ride. We spent roughly 45 minutes talking to Commissioner Leonhardt about the difficulties we experienced and the strict regulations that govern dairy milk sales and pasteurization procedures. Although I can't say for certain how strongly he supports our cause, he assured us that our interests align well with his legislative agenda. This was an important first step in determining that our concerns will not be opposed by the WV Department of Agriculture. My next step is to begin networking with our local legislative delegation in both the State Senate and House of Delegates. I will need to discuss with them the legislative changes I am seeking to determine if a bill can be introduced. At the same time, I will be sharing draft copies of my book with them and seeking support for publication by a WV publishing house. After writing two other books, I have learned that, as competitive as the publishing industry has become, it is almost impossible to get the attention of a publishing house without some demonstrated support from distinguished citizens that will command their attention.

Despite all my work on the book, our farming work continues. We are working hard to finish harvesting the bounty from our garden and getting it preserved for the coming winter. Most of the vegetables we planted have died back already, but we have been harvesting a great crop of butternut squash (we have filled two carts with them already and still have a few more to pick) and some rather large pumpkins. Barb also has some herbs (thyme and sage) ready for sale and some goat milk soap that she made from the goat milk we preserved before selling our goats. We plan to sell as many of these products as we can at the Petersburg and Keyser Farmer's Markets during the coming week. We will be at the Petersburg Farmer's Market on Saturday morning, September 23 and, if our inventory holds out, the Keyser Farmer's Market on Tuesday afternoon, September 26. If you can stop by, we'd be eager to meet you. I will post more pictures from our first farmer's market sale before the end of the month.

Post 52: Peeper Pond Farm Goes Leaf Peeping

September 24, 2017

The cool mornings we received in the first two weeks of September (AM lows around 40 degrees) appear to have convinced the higher elevation trees in our area to shed their summer green for some early autumn colors. Unfortunately, the three weeks of dry weather that accompanied it has shortened the brilliant color display and is causing the trees to drop their leaves after an all-too-brief display. The result is some early color at the higher elevations that lasts but a few days. Barb and I decided to do our best to take advantage of the finicky early fall display by visiting our favored high elevation viewing areas—Blackwater Falls in Tucker County, Highland Scenic Byway in Pocahontas County, and the North Fork Valley in Pendleton County—to seek out the best colors we could find. Although our results were less than spectacular, we did manage to capture some respectable color in each of those areas.

We visited Blackwater Falls State Park first this past Thursday (September 21). Although the color was spotty, we managed to find some pretty trees along the canyon at the Pendleton overlook and along the falls themselves. The dry weather had reduced the water flow at the falls significantly since our last visit in late April (see our April 30 Blackwater post), but you could still hear the river thundering through the canyon.

We took a second longer trip today (September 24) through Highland County, VA and Pocahontas County, WV to scout out the high elevation colors in those counties. Unfortunately, we found very little color in Highland County, VA, even though we passed through the highest elevation valley in the county. It appeared that many of the trees that changed early had dropped their leaves, and the later bearing trees were just beginning to change. The color wasn't much better in Pocahontas County, although the slopes of the Yew Mountains as viewed from the Highland Scenic Byway (Route 150) displayed some decent colors.

We returned home through the North Fork Valley of Pendleton County. Although we found little color along Spruce Knob, as viewed from the valley floor, North Fork Mountain displayed some of the most brilliant colors we found along our entire journey. Even though the display was very spotty for the mileage we drove, the mountain scenery was a delight in its own right.

We also had a decent volume of sales during our first appearance at the Petersburg Farmer's Market on Saturday morning (September 23), but we still have a lot of products to sell. We will be appearing at the Keyser Farmer's

Market in the Keyser Assembly of God parking lot Tuesday afternoon (September 26). If we still have enough left over from that sale, we will try to appear again at the Petersburg Farmer's Market on Wednesday morning (September 27). I will update you on our success with some pictures in a later post. Please plan to visit us if you will be in the area. We'd love to see you.

Post 53: To Market, To Market

September 27, 2017

    Our vegetable and herb gardens have been very productive this year, but they are nearly exhausted. The warm, dry weather we have had over the past three weeks has stressed the remaining plants. We are still waiting for our tomatoes to mature and our peppers are still productive, but the rest of our vegetables have dried out or died back. What corn we did not eat during the summer has dried on the stalks and we are harvesting some of the remaining ears to harvest corn kernels that we can grind into corn meal. Barb has been finding some remaining potatoes in the soil, but other than that, we are about finished for the season.

    Now that we know what excess vegetables we have to sell, we have been attending the farmer's markets in Petersburg and Keyser to earn a little extra cash from the bounty. We have been selling a bumper crop of butternut squash, some large pumpkins, tomatoes, peppers, onions and some herbs (sage, basil and thyme). Barb has supplemented our produce with goat milk soap she produced (both bar and liquid), small loaves of banana bread, and some hot pads that she sewed from her quilting material. I am also offering PDF file copies of my recent book, <u>The Peeper Pond Farm Story</u>, which documents our first year of farming and the ultimate loss of our dairy goat operation.

    We packed up all of our sale items in the back of our 1987 Chevy S10 and traveled around to the local farmer's markets. Our first sale was at the Grant County Farmer's Market in the Petersburg City Park parking lot on Saturday morning, September 23. We returned there again earlier this morning (September 27). We also plan to return for the final time on Saturday morning, September 30. We also attended the Mineral County Farmer's Market at the Keyser Assembly of God parking lot on Tuesday afternoon, September 26. Our sales have not been very impressive, but we are doing as well as can be expected for this late in the season. We have yet to share the market with more than two other vendors, and we were the sole vendor at the Keyser Farmer's Market yesterday afternoon. Most of the other vendors have sold their produce, so participation is waning and, apparently, the customers know it. Unfortunately, we weren't able to participate earlier in the season because we were either consuming or canning the produce we need for the year. Only at the end of the season did we know for certain what we could afford to sell. I guess we'll have to plan to attend earlier in the season next year, perhaps before the end of August when the customer traffic is a little more favorable.

We did get to meet some nice customers, and we also got to chat with some of the regular vendors in Petersburg. Many of them have interesting stories to tell. Although the weather has been quite warm, the humidity has been very low making it quite comfortable to sit under our portable canopy. Our experience has taught us that the most popular items are tomatoes and peppers. Some customers have been asking about cucumbers, but they expired much earlier in the season and none of us have any to sell. Another popular item are green beans, but we didn't have enough to sell. Some producers are planting multiple crops of certain popular vegetables, so they can have some to sell after most gardens have been exhausted. We may try to use that planting strategy next year.

We will test our luck one more time this season at the Petersburg Farmer's Market on Saturday morning, September 30. If you're going to be in the area, please stop by and visit for a while. We always appreciate the company.

Post 54: Putting the Garden to Bed

October 4, 2017

Now that we've had our first two hard frosts (October 1 and 2, 2017), the growing season has ended here at Peeper Pond Farm. Although we heard no frost warnings, we covered all of our remaining tomato plants in preparation for the freezing temperatures and managed to save them. Our pepper plants withstood the frosts and remain productive. However, all of our other vegetables have expired, and we are now making preparations to put the garden to bed for the season.

Over the past three mornings, Barb and I have removed the remains of many vegetables and weeds in the garden. I pulled our eight 50-foot rows of dried cornstalks, and Barb pulled the pumpkin and squash vines. The only remaining plants are the tomatoes and a short row of peppers. I harvested some of the dried corn ears from the stalks I pulled so that we can grind the kernels into corn meal that we can use to make honey cornbread over the winter months. Barb managed to harvest fifteen pounds of Roma tomatoes that she will use to make and can tomato sauce. When those tasks are completed, we will have harvested all we can from our productive garden.

Once we have cleaned up the rest of the weeds and debris, it will be time to use Ferguson (our tractor) to disc harrow the garden. I brought him out of the goat barn yesterday (where he has been resting lately) to get him ready for the job. Afterward, Barb and I dressed him up with his backhoe, as we have a buyer for it and I need to demonstrate to him that it functions properly—which we proved to be the case yesterday afternoon. Once our buyer arrives to pick up the backhoe (sometime before the end of the week), Ferguson will be free to harrow the garden.

After the soil has been loosened by the harrow, we are planning to plant a crop of winter rye. The rye will help hold the soil in the garden during the winter snows and rains, and when the rye begins to grow early in the spring, it will help restore nitrogen levels for the spring replanting. Sometime in late March or early April, we will plow the garden to turn and mix the soil, harrow it to break up the clods, apply some lime, then rototill the soil to mix and loosen it up for the spring planting. Then the cycle will begin anew.

As I've noted before, our garden was the most successful aspect of our farm operation this year. We are working hard now to ensure that it will serve us well again next year. With any luck, we'll see you at the farmer's market sometime during the summer. We wish everyone a pleasant fall and a joyous holiday season. Now I have to end this post so I can tend to the hot water tank. I am draining it today to remove calcium build-up on the heating coils. This is another traditional fall and spring maintenance ritual we perform here at Peeper Pond Farm.

Post 55: Making Cider – A Pressing Issue

October 8, 2017

Yesterday (October 7, 2017), on our way to the Dayton, VA autumn festival, we stopped at a nearby fruit farm on Onyx Hill Road in Rockingham County. We were looking for freshly harvested apples to put our fruit press to work making fresh apple cider. As I've said in past posts, our apple trees failed to produce any mature apples again this year, so we needed to buy some from a commercial grower. The farmer sold us some bargain culls—apples that were picked from the trees but had various blemishes or were malformed making them undesirable for eating. We bought two bushels of apples—a mix of Staymen, Rome and Red Delicious for a good mix of sweet and tart apples. Tree-picked culls are preferable to use over drops (apples that were collected off the ground), because apples that fall on the ground may become contaminated from animal feces left by the deer and squirrels that scrounge around for them after dark. Since today was forecasted to be a rainy day, we decided to crush and press our apples into fresh cider.

Although we never made cider during my childhood on our New Hampshire dairy farm, I recall several fall trips we made to a nearby water-powered cider mill that we visited to learn how cider was made and to buy fresh cider. I recall how impressive the giant water-powered wooden cogs and mechanisms within the mill were to watch as they clicked and clacked in tempo to the water splashing over the outside waterwheel. It was an awe-inspiring sight to watch the large crusher process the apples and deposit the pomace into the giant wooden press. Although the mill could make more gallons of cider in an average day than I could count, my father informed me that cider sales was not what kept the mill in operation. Apparently, the owner used some of the cider to make what we called "Applejack"—a form of apple brandy that was much more lucrative. Now, I don't wish to speculate on whether or not the owner paid the required liquor taxes on the brandy he may have sold, so I will just assume he did. However, he did make very good apple cider and apple juice, and my father always left satisfied with his purchases.

Fortunately, apple cider is very easy to make, even without a water or electric powered cider mill. The first step is to carefully wash the apples and cut them into halves and quarters to make them easier for the apple crusher on our fruit press to crush them. We don't have to peel the apples or remove the cores, but we do remove the stems and we cut out any portions of the apples that were damaged by insects, bruises, or scars.

The next step was to take the sliced apples out to our garage and to feed them into the crusher, which ground the slices into pomace and deposited it into a pressing bag suspended in a porous metal basket through which the cider will be squeezed out by the press. Our fruit press contains both a crusher and a press to make the processing easy.

After the pressing bag was filled with pomace, I swung the hand-operated crusher out of the way, twisted the top of the pressing bag closed, and tipped the press up onto the top of the bag. Once it was clamped into place, I turned the auger to drive the metal press onto the bag and force the cider juice out of the basket, where it drained into a bucket at the base of the press. No other additives are required. By the time we had crushed and pressed the apples we purchased, we had collected four-and-a-half gallons of fresh, sweet cider from two bushels of apples.

We discussed fermenting some of our cider into apple cider vinegar, but that would require a lengthy, multi-step fermenting process. I'm afraid the cider we made tastes too good to wait that long. Maybe we'll think about doing that next year. For now, we placed two-and-a-half gallons of the cider in our chest freezer for safe keeping. There it will keep for Thanksgiving and Christmas dinners.

Post 56: Anyone Want Some Fresh Honey Cornbread?

October 9, 2017

Whenever we have soup for supper, Barb likes to make some honey cornbread. Nothing goes better with soup than her cornbread. With all the excess corn we grew in our garden this year, we decided it would be wise to grind some corn meal for use in making cornbread over the cold winter months. About two weeks ago now, we harvested some of the remaining ears of corn that we left to dry on the stalk. I removed the husks and placed the ears in a brown paper bag to dry for the intervening two weeks. This morning, I took the now thoroughly dry ears and carefully removed the healthy kernels of corn and filled a colander. We then rinsed off all the corn and set it out to dry in the sun on cookie sheets.

After the corn was dry, I ground it using our hand-operated corn mill—turning it into a granular powder, which is corn meal. Our corn mill is much smaller than the water-powered grain mills that used to dot the West Virginia landscape in the late 1800's, but for the amount of corn we had to process, it did the trick just fine. The State of West Virginia actually operates a water-powered grain mill (the Glade Creek Mill) at Babcock State Park near Fayetteville, where you can see it operate and actually purchase small bags of corn meal that have been ground by the mill. You may have seen pictures of it without realizing it, as the mill is one of the state's iconic landmarks.

By the time I had finished grinding our corn, I had converted what was a half a brown paper grocery bag of dried corn ears into roughly four pounds of corn meal, ready for use in making our next batch of honey cornbread. I can't wait to taste the results. This is just another simple way we can make practical use of the excess production from our garden. It's amazing to realize how easy it can be to get more food value from your own vegetable garden. We hope that by telling you how we did it, you'll be encouraged to make use of the traditional homesteading skills that we continue to practice here at Peeper Pond Farm.

Post 57: A Peeper Pond Farm Ghost Story?

October 16, 2017

 Our farm has existed now for only two years on land that was subdivided in 2000. It doesn't seem possible that our farm could be associated with a ghost story, but, in the spirit of Halloween, anything that the mind can imagine can be possible. West Virginia and especially our long-settled Potomac Highlands Region, harbor many ghost stories and legends that stretch throughout recorded history. Perhaps our property is connected to one, even if the key events did not occur here. I'll just ask you to pull up a chair, tell you the story, and let you decide. After all, what I have to tell you is all hearsay, and I have no way to validate it or refute it. To protect the identities of those who entrusted me with the story, I will not reveal any of the real names of the persons involved.

 Although I wasn't born here, I have come to know a number of old-timers from families that have lived in our area for generations. I love to listen to the stories they have to tell, even though it can be difficult at times to make them comfortable about sharing them. Many of them don't like to discuss deeply held community secrets with outsiders who may only make fun of them or use them to perpetuate long-held derogatory stereotypes about the locals. Fortunately, the impetus for the telling of this tale emerged from my own curiosity about a somewhat mysterious discovery we made on our property soon after we had purchased it in 2006.

 The very first element of our future farm operation that we began to establish in early 2007 was our fruit orchard. Barb, Michael and I spent our 2007 Memorial Day weekend in Petersburg to plant our first apple trees on the north side of our open field. I dug the holes and removed a seemingly countless number of large rocks so that Barb could plant the five-foot tall saplings. Since I didn't want to deposit the rocks anywhere in the field, where they might get in the way of future work, I carried as many as I could over to the ravine and let them roll down the bank until they found a stable resting place along the run. It was then that I first discovered what appeared to be the front driver's side corner of an old car protruding from the bank. So little of the car was exposed that it was very hard to know what it might have been (and I don't claim to be a car expert by any stretch of the imagination). However, my initial impression of it reminded me very much of the first car I could remember from my childhood—an Oldsmobile Delta 88. The car was buried in our ravine many years ago and covered over with heavy clay soil, brush and even small trees.

How long it had been there and why it was abandoned there and covered up were mysteries to us.

About a year later, one of my neighbors invited us to one of her church's social functions, where I met a few of the older families in our community. While I was talking with a man who was roughly 70 years old, I happened to mention our discovery of the car we found buried in the bank of our ravine. He asked what kind of car it was, and I told him I honestly didn't know for sure because so little of it was exposed, but it reminded me of the Olds Delta 88 my family owned when I was a child. His eyes suddenly lit up, and he became more intensely engaged in our casual conversation. He asked if I could tell him what color it was or how old it might be. I told him that the exposed corner of the car had a lot of rust and mud caked on it, but I thought it might have originally been a white or cream color. I wasn't at all sure of how old it was, but if it reminded me so much of my childhood car, it must have been a 1960s era model or older.

I watched him rub his chin as he considered the information I gave him, and I noticed that he began to look at me more critically and the wrinkles on his forehead became more pronounced, as if he were deciding the wisdom of discussing the matter with me further. After a few moments of careful thought, he relaxed, leaned back in his chair, and said, "Son, I'll tell you a little story if you promise not to tell anyone where you heard it." Puzzled but intrigued, I looked him squarely in the eye and assured him I would not reveal his identity. What he didn't know at the time was that I have a terrible time remembering the names of people I have not met many times, so his identity was never in danger with me. Thus reassured, he began his tale (which I will attempt to recount to you as accurately as my aging memory will allow).

"Although I've lived all of my life in Upper Tract, my mother and father were raised in Smoke Holes and moved to Upper Tract when they got married. I'm sure you've heard many tales of the moonshiners who operated there. Some of them are true, but many are exaggerated. My Pa told some of those stories, including one that occurred when I was just a kid. You see, there was one particularly reclusive old shiner who lived in an old homesteader's cabin down along the South Branch River. Although he kept to himself as much as he could, he was known to have a fiery temper. He and his wife ran a still way up on the slopes of Cave Mountain well into the 1950s. He inherited a love of fast cars from his Pa, who taught him how to modify the engines so that he could always outrun the local law when he had to make a delivery. Well, towards the end of his career, he bought and modified a white 1950 Oldsmobile Rocket 88 that he used for many years."

At this point in the story, he leaned towards me, as the tone of his voice became more serious, and he spoke more covertly. "My Pa told me that sometime around 1960, this shiner's wife suddenly disappeared. She was a good friend of my Ma's and had confided in her about the fights they would have and how she wanted to leave him, but she was afraid he'd never let her go and feared that he would kill her to keep his shining operation secret. When his wife suddenly stopped appearing at church, members of the congregation, including my Ma and Pa, started asking him questions. Pa always said that he'd just wave his hand and say she was off in Tennessee visiting her sister who had been feeling poorly for a long time. However, Ma never believed him and said she knew in her heart that mean-hearted old man had murdered her and probably stuffed her body in the trunk of that car so he could bury her somewhere deep in the forest. After a few more days, the Sheriff's office took an interest in all the scuttlebutt and went looking for him to make him answer some questions. But, by the time they got to his cabin, they found it empty and the car was gone. Everyone kept an eye out for that white Rocket 88, but as far as I know, it was never seen again. Most folks figured he was on the run and would eventually be caught, but if he was, no one ever heard about it.

"Now some people in the community said that the real reason they were fighting in the first place was because that old moonshiner was having a fling with the wife of another man who lived in Smoke Holes. Once his wife learned of the affair, she finally threatened to leave him, and in a wild fit of anger and fear, he killed her. When the rumor about the affair circulated around the community in the days following her disappearance, the unfaithful woman's husband went to the moonshiner's cabin, killed him, stuffed his body in the trunk of the car, and got rid of it somewhere. Whatever really happened, everyone figured the truth would only be known when that missing car was found."

That story lived in the dark recesses of my mind and made me very uncomfortable about the abandoned car buried on our land. What if it was linked to one or two murders? Now that I had told someone in the community about our discovery, I knew it could spread like wildfire. As I've said many times, the only mills still operating in these mountains are the rumor mills. I just needed to resolve the mystery for myself, rather than wait until the Sheriff knocked on my door with a search warrant.

In 2016, we were preparing to build our garage and goat barn, the placement of which would make it very difficult (if not technically impossible) to remove the car. Over the years, continued erosion of the bank had exposed more of the car, so I decided it was time to have it winched out of the ravine so we could know for certain what it was. I hired a local tow truck driver to see if he could pull it out of the ravine, but I was very careful not to discuss the story I'd heard. After all, I couldn't be sure if any of it was true, but the thought of it had haunted me for years. He wasn't sure if he could pull it out of the ravine, but he said he'd try. On April 28, 2016, he and his son managed to retrieve the crushed and rusty remains of the car. As soon as he had pulled it up the bank, we confirmed from the identification plate on the dashboard that the car was indeed a 1950 Oldsmobile Rocket 88, and it indeed appeared to have been white. I studied the interior of the car and trunk (or what was left of them), but most of it had either rotted away or broke off deep in the mud and clay that had buried it for decades. I satisfied myself that there was no evidence of any bodies in the car, so I had the tow truck driver take it away. I never asked where he would be taking it.

    I guess I can't say for certain if the abandoned car buried on our farm was part of that double murder story I was told, but I'm sure relieved to know it's gone. However, once in a while, on dark and gloomy nights when the moon is the only source of light to illuminate the fog that rises from our ravine, we could swear that we can see a shadowy figure walking along the edge of the bank. Maybe it's only one of the deer that feast on the grass and clover in our field. Then again, maybe it's the ghost of one of those tortured souls searching for the lost car that served as the only marker for its grave. With any luck, I'll never know for sure. Happy Halloween and pleasant dreams to everyone from Peeper Pond Farm.

Post 58: As Fall Fades Away

November 9, 2017

November has always been my least favorite month. Throughout my childhood on our dairy farm in New Hampshire, November was the cloudiest and gloomiest month of the year. It was the month that marked the final transition from fall to winter, as the air gradually turned cold and dank. The cold, raw air that accompanied November rain and snow storms always seemed to drill all the way to my bones—quite often feeling far colder than calm and sunny days in the depth of winter. Such has been the pattern we are experiencing this November, which has brought the season's first sullen, dank weather to Peeper Pond Farm, with frosty nights and a persistent drizzle that hangs in the air with the fog that drapes across our mountains. We still have some brilliant fall foliage that clings to the most stubborn trees, but the fierce northerly winds that push each progressively colder storm front through our region have stripped most of the fading color from the ridgeline trees at the highest elevations. Winter is knocking on our door, as we have already seen our first heavy snowfall along the 3,124-foot summit of Spring Mountain. Now that we are burning our pellet stove, the satisfying warmth of our house is a welcome retreat against the winter storms that are sure to come. I remember that we received eleven inches of snow on the day before our first Thanksgiving we celebrated at Peeper Pond Farm in 2014. It's only a matter of time.

Fortunately, time has become a more abundant resource now that we have completed all our winter farm preparations. Our vegetable garden, which provided a bounty of abundant crops during the summer, now lays fallow for the winter. Ferguson (our tractor) has found a secure winter home in our lonely goat barn, now that we have sold our dairy goats. I have installed the wind screens in front of our bee hives and replaced the fall sugar water feeders with winter patties to provide a supplemental winter food supply for our bees. I will now inspect them only on the warmest days in each month to ensure that they are wintering over well.

Barb is busying herself with indoor projects, baking bread and sticky buns, quilting, and making soap from the goat milk reserves we froze before selling our goats. I have finished all of the outdoor improvement projects I had planned for the fall, and I am now concentrating on my efforts to encourage changes to West Virginia's dairy farming standards and regulations, which I feel to be unfairly and unnecessarily restrictive on family homestead farm operations, thereby expediting their extinction and constraining our traditional lifestyle choices. My first meeting with State officials and our local Delegate to discuss these issues has been scheduled for November 15. All of this work is merely a prelude to Thanksgiving, which may be the last we can celebrate as a family. Our son is contemplating a move to Arkansas in 2018, and we don't know if that Thanksgiving will be his first away from home. That thought is a reminder that more changes will come with the new year. Clearly, the sun is setting on 2017. As we await the arrival of winter, our hopes for a better year in 2018 are pinned to the return of spring. That is when life and activity will return to Peeper Pond Farm. We wish all of you many reasons to be thankful this Thanksgiving.

Post 59: Reunions

November 17, 2017

    This has been an exciting and difficult year for us. Our long-anticipated retirement came to fruition at the end of February, and we bought our first dairy goats in March. It seemed as though our retirement dreams were just being realized, when we were struck by a number of tragedies. First, our loyal housecat of nearly fifteen years (Nin) became ill in late May and passed away at on July 20. Less than two weeks later, on August 1, we had to put down one of our two initial doe kids (Gertie), who had fallen victim to Meningeal Worm, an insidious parasite that attacked her nervous system and left her paralyzed in the hind legs. Only four days later, on August 5, I milked our adult goats for the final time. We were compelled to sell them because we could not afford to sustain our dairy operation without any reasonable way to derive a supporting income. Our retirement income simply wasn't enough to cover the operating costs from our dairy goat operation. In less than three weeks, we lost our faithful companion and six dairy goats. Now our house and barn are quiet in a way they haven't been before.

    The losses were a severe shock to us. It seemed that everything we had worked so hard to realize was suddenly slipping through our grasp. It has been difficult at times to know what we can hold onto. We are still working to bring our retirement finances under control, but at least it appears that we are winning the battle. What we can plan to do in 2018 is still uncertain. Fortunately, I had what I believe to be a very promising initial meeting this past Wednesday with our State Delegate (Allen V. Evans) and two State officials, where I explained my concerns about the future of homestead dairy farming in West Virginia. It appears that there was agreement that the issues I raised deserve further consideration. Where that will lead remains uncertain, but I am cautiously optimistic that progress can be made over time.

    Yesterday, Barb and I traveled to Spencer, WV to visit two of my dairy goat colleagues, Don and Shelley Hutcheson, who were very supportive and helpful in the planning and operation of our short-lived dairy goat operation. As a token of appreciation, we delivered a box of butternut squash from our garden. Goats love to eat butternut squash. Shelley has owned and milked goats for nine years now and has been my most trusted adviser. We first met them on March 19, 2016 for a tour of her operation and a long discussion of goat rearing and milking tips. Shelley and Don later visited us on July 21, 2017, the day after we lost Nin, to see our farm, meet our goats and console us as we struggled to decide the ultimate fate of our dairy goat operation. In addition to these visits, we talked many times over the phone and shared e-mail messages to give us guidance on various aspects of our dairy operation.

    We spent part of these last two days with the Hutchesons at their new Spencer home engaged in lively conversation regarding all aspects of our growing friendship and learning how much we share in common despite the very different lives we have lived. Barb and Shelley commandeered the kitchen until late in the evening making a large block of Chihuahua Cheddar cheese from Shelley's goat milk stores. The reunion visit affirmed our friendship and left us with pleasant memories to be thankful for this Thanksgiving—a time when I have struggled to decide what we have achieved.

    At one point during our conversation, Don talked to me about his love for his alma mater, Berea College in Kentucky. I mentioned that I had heard similar comments from another friend and associate of mine, Wayne Spiggle, who lives in Mineral County and also attended Berea College. As it turns out, Don remembered a Wayne Spiggle who had been a classmate of his during his years there. We quickly determined that we were talking about the same person, more than 60 years after they had attended the school. Ironically, I had last talked with Wayne less than 24 hours before leaving to visit Don and Shelley. After we all arose this morning, I placed another telephone call to Wayne, and the two college friends were reunited for the first time since their college days. They laughed and shared memories as they relived that special time in their early lives. I felt honored to bring them together for the first time in over six decades.

    Now that we are only days from the Thanksgiving holiday, I find myself reminded that we all have things to be thankful for this year. Although our farm operation took some serious hits, significant portions of it will continue into 2018. I am hopeful that the loss of our cherished dairy operation will result in positive changes to the state laws and standards that frustrated it. We have renewed and deepened our relationship with our good friends and helped reunite two of them after years of separation. Everything that happened this week has restored my faith in new opportunities for the coming year. Perhaps, at some time in the near future, we will be able to test our luck with dairy goats again with greater wisdom and a more manageable plan based on the lessons we learned this year. Rather than an end, our experiences in 2017 may eventually serve as the foundation for another attempt—hopefully within the context of a more supportive regulatory environment. Only time, enduring faith and dedicated, determined work can make that happen. Such is the essential nature of farming. It never happens by itself. I guess we may have a lot more to discuss and share with our good friends, Don, Shelley and Wayne.

We here at Peeper Pond Farm wish all of you a happy Thanksgiving shared with family and dear friends. Remember that, no matter what happens to us, we all have things to be thankful for this and every year—even if you do have to dig a little deeper to find them.

Post 60: Christmas Spirit

December 2, 2017

    No place that we have ever lived before has captured and extolled the traditional Christmas Spirit as fervently as our Potomac Highlands region of West Virginia. From Christmas parades to brilliant lighting displays to festive events, our rural region embraces the holiday fully and warmly. For the past ten weeks, Barb has volunteered her time to sing on the newly reconstituted Petersburg Community Chorus, which performed a free 1.5-hour Christmas music program last night to an audience of hundreds at the Landes Art Center. It was an inspiring performance that enticed many in the audience to sing quietly with them as the chorus sang its rendition of traditional carols and hymns to the sole accompaniment of a piano. During the chorus' musical performance of "'Twas The Night Before Christmas," the children of the audience were invited to approach the stage to enjoy the story before Santa Claus. The performance was a reaffirming testament to the talent and spirit of a small city of 2,500 people to have successfully organized a group of dedicated volunteers to conduct a free public concert.

    This was merely one element of a broader celebration of Christmas throughout our region. Each Monday evening between Thanksgiving and Christmas, Santa Claus appears on our local radio station, WELD, to read children's letters and speak to those who call in. Both Petersburg City Park and Welton Park in Petersburg Gap are decked out with colorful lighting displays that will run throughout the holiday season. On December 7, area residents are invited to bring decorations to hang on the city Christmas tree at Petersburg square and tour the display of illuminated snowmen at City Park provided by local sponsors, which will be auctioned off the following weekend as a fundraising event.

    Later this evening, the annual Keyser Christmas parade will be conducted, and Moorefield has scheduled its annual tree lighting ceremony and Christmas parade on the first Sunday of the month. A local benefactor, Denver The Elf, climbs to the roof of a sponsoring business on the hill in Petersburg and refuses to come down until a specified number of toys have been donated to "Toys for Happiness." Annual Christmas bazaars abound in churches and community centers throughout the region. All of these festivities and more are celebrated throughout a rural, five-county region with a combined population of 85,000.

    We treasure the inspiring natural beauty and community spirit of our special region. Regardless of the fickle whims of our winter weather, the warmth and engaging spirit of our area residents provide sound confirmation that the

Christmas season has arrived. We at Peeper Pond Farm wish all of our dedicated readers a truly Merry Christmas and a Happy New Year in 2018.

Post 61: Meet Our New Kitten, Calli

December 11, 2017

    It's been nearly five months since our beloved cat, Ninny, died and we lost all of our dairy goats. Earlier last week, I also discovered that our two bee colonies will not survive the winter. The Carniolans died out sometime in mid-November and our Italian hive is barely alive. We are not alone in losing hives this winter. Our friends Jim and Donna Boyd have lost a number of their own bee colonies, and they told us that a many of their local colleagues have lost bee hives. The most likely cause appears to be Varroa mites. I would guess that the mild winter last year allowed mite populations to explode. This is a very difficult infestation to treat because the standard treatments cause a lot of stress on the bee colony. We managed to maintain our hives for just over 1.5 years, but now we seem to be losing that battle as well.

    With all of the losses we experienced this year, we decided it was time to bring some life back to our home and farm. We need to do so carefully so that we can manage our retirement expenses properly. On Wednesday, December 6, we decided to take our first step by adopting a new kitten. We heard an ad on WELD-FM's Pet Corner program for kittens to adopt, one of which was a black calico female. Our last two cats have been calicos, so we decided to continue the line with our newest kitten. We decided to name her Calli and she has been a welcome addition. She is full of vigor and vim and enjoys playing with all the cat toys that have been handed down to her from our previous cats. She especially loves to play with a mouse toy that squeaks and any plastic shopping bag that might fall on the floor.

    It was especially interesting to discover that she is not afraid of plastic shopping bags, as Ninny would always run and hide at the first rustling sound of any plastic bag. Ninny had been a stray cat that we adopted from the humane shelter and we always felt that she was probably placed in a plastic bag by her original owner and dumped out on the streets of Anniston, Alabama (where we lived when we adopted her). It's hard to be sure of that, since Ninny was always afraid of any sudden noise, but she had a very pronounced fear of plastic bags. Fortunately, Calli loves to pounce on them when she sees them fall and push herself around the floor on them with her hind legs.

    Calli eats very well and appears to appreciate her new home very much, as she is always affectionate and likes to be held when she wears out from all her playing. If our prior two housecats, Ninny and Isis, are any indication, we hope to have her for a long time. I adopted Isis when she was one year old in 1988 and kept her until she died in 2003 – a 16.5-year lifespan! We adopted Ninny in late 2003 and kept her for nearly fifteen years, until she had to be put to sleep on July 20, 2017. Now that we have made Calli our new queen of Peeper Pond Farm, we hope she will keep us company for another fifteen or so years. We also hope she will be but the first new life we bring back to our farm. We hope you enjoy the first picture of her that I have included in this post. Best wishes and Merry Christmas to all from all of us at Peeper Pond Farm.

Post 62: Caring for the Carroll Farm

December 26, 2017

We hope everyone had a Merry Christmas yesterday! Our son, Michael, spent the day and Christmas Eve with us, and we all had a good time. We were very surprised and fortunate to enjoy our first white Christmas since 2012! We received a surprise 0.5-1.0 inch of snow during the night on Christmas Eve and the sky spit snow flurries and squalls well into the afternoon on Christmas. A fierce wind blew gusts of twenty-forty MPH intermittently throughout the night and day making it virtually impossible to get an accurate snowfall measurement. The wind left over an inch of snow in sheltered locations and a dusting in the more exposed areas, but the ground was completely covered and the snowfall was persistent enough for me to call it an inch overall.

Over the past three mornings (Christmas Eve, Christmas Day and today), we have been feeding and watering the livestock at Dale and Merrily Carroll's homestead farm about three miles from our house at the entrance to Smoke Hole Canyon. They travelled to Georgia to visit Merrily's mother for the holiday and asked us to take care of the livestock for them. It also gave me a chance to spend some quality time with our former goat kid, Essie, who greeted me eagerly and boisterously each and every morning. Essie is looking great with her thick winter coat. We brushed her on Christmas morning, and her coat was as soft and silky as it was when she was born. She is a beautiful goat, and I anticipate that she will be a show champion someday.

The Carrolls are raising a number of cows (mostly Angus steer), goats, bees and chickens of various breeds. With the visible exception of Essie (who is an Oberhasli), all of the Carroll's goats are Dwarf Nigerians about half of Essie's size. Four of the goats are bucks and the rest are does. I found it nearly impossible to get an accurate count of their Dwarf Nigerians because they never stood still long enough for me to avoid double counting, but the entire herd totals at least 25, not including Essie. Five of the Dwarf Nigerians are yearlings, born earlier this year. The same is true for all the chickens, which include several species from Icelandic to Rhode Island Reds.

They also have fifteen Angus cows (most of which are market steer) and two Jersey cows, which they milk from time to time. They are both dry now. Feeding all of this livestock was not difficult, but furnishing them with sufficient water was a real challenge. The cold wave that is settling in over our area has frozen the ground and all of the various waterlines we needed to use to replenish the water supplies. Even one or two of the heated watering troughs had frozen solid this morning. Fortunately, the Carrolls are returning home today, and I have advised Dale of the issue so he can make that his first priority to address this afternoon.

I wish to thank Dale and Merrily for the privilege of caring for their farm. It was a great Christmas gift for me to tend their livestock and spend some time with Essie. As she did when we raised her, she clung to my side everywhere I went in the goat pen and lovingly rubbed against me to beg for attention. She clearly remembers me even 4.5 months after she left our farm. I will continue to visit her routinely as I hope, someday, I can repurchase her and/or one or two of her future kids so we can enjoy the fresh goat milk we produced while we milked our goats. Having discovered last week that our Italian bee colony had died out, we look forward eagerly to a better year in 2018. We wish everyone a Happy New Year from Peeper Pond Farm.

Post 63: The Pit of Winter

January 26, 2018

Happy New Year, everyone. I'm sorry to be so lax in my website journal postings lately, but we sent our computer in for some much-needed upgrades and file management. I am not very computer savvy, so I asked my friend in Mount Savage, Maryland, Chase Green, to do the work. He doubled our RAM and cleaned up all the apps that were of no use to us but were chewing up our active memory and slowing down our computer's operating speed. Chase is a computer expert, and we appreciate all of his trustworthy assistance.

I guess there's little to write about at this time of the year as it is a significant down-time for us. We have decided to begin attending local craft shows this year to display and sell some of Barb's talented work. She has been making quilted hot pads, pot holders, coffee coasters, table runners and lap quilts that she can sell. I have been taking over our goat soap-making operations to free her from that responsibility. Soon, we will have an inventory of soap and quilt products to sell when the outdoor craft fair season kicks into gear. We anticipate that our first appearance will be at the Spring Mountain Festival in Petersburg during the last weekend in April. We will hope to see some of you there.

The biggest news this January has been the brutally cold weather and ferocious winds. It all began with our first white Christmas since 2012. We only received an inch of snow (our largest snowfall accumulation so far this season), but it turned so cold that a good portion of it lasted through January 8 more than two weeks later. In fact, we have had two extended periods in January where the temperatures never rose above 32 degrees. The first one began on December 24, 2017 and lasted into January 8, 2018—a total of fifteen consecutive days! During that span of time, we set four record low temperatures (including our coldest reading in the last three winter seasons of five degrees below zero on January 5). We also set a few record cool high temperatures. The worst aspect of it has been the wind chill factors, which fell below zero on six of the first seven days of January. This is not the New Year's weather resolution we were hoping for.

After a brief five-day respite from the cold, the thermometer dove below freezing again in the early morning hours of January 13 and remained there for another 5.5 days until if finally struggled above the freezing mark late in the afternoon on January 18. During the second cold snap, we experienced a few more days of single digit wind chills. Our ten-day forecast is now calling for some measurable snowfalls in the first few days of February, which is the one aspect of winter from which we have been spared this season. I was wondering when the snow would catch up with us, as we have only recorded 2.5 total inches of snow this season at Peeper Pond Farm.

My father always referred to this period as the pit of winter. As he would always remind us, "when the days begin to lengthen (after the winter solstice), the cold begins to strengthen". It certainly did so this season, hitting us hard and early on December 24 only three days after the winter solstice. What my father termed as the pit of winter was the four coldest weeks of the year centered around the date in January that falls one month after the winter solstice (which falls on January 21 this year). It is during this four-week period (January 7 through February 11) that we should expect to see the coldest temperature readings of the year. You can think of it as winter's counterpart to the dog days of summer. Well, in 2018, I believe we hit that mark two days early on January 5. Still, I am looking forward to February 11 when the pit of winter should end and we can begin looking forward to the gradual return of spring. I'm sure many of our neighbors and friends will agree. Until then, we hope you can remain warm and cozy. Best wishes to you in 2018 from all of us here at Peeper Pond farm.

Post 64: What the Reaper Sowed
February 17, 2018

 With the arrival of the first 70-plus degree day since November 6, 2017, Barb and I decided to take a trip to Steeles Tavern, Virginia to visit the famed McCormick Farm Museum. This is the farm where, in 1831, Cyrus McCormick built and demonstrated the first practical mechanical wheat reaper. McCormick's device, along with several other early labor-saving agricultural equipment, including Eli Whitney's Cotton Gin (1793) and John Deere's self-scouring steel plow (1837), revolutionized farming and made it more productive and efficient. The device evolved over the years as McCormick made improvements so that the harvester could also bind the wheat into sheaves. Eventually, the horse-drawn mechanical reaper reduced the number of workers needed to harvest a crop of wheat from five to two.

 We don't often regard the importance of farm innovations with the same awe and significance as the invention of the light bulb, automobile, or the airplane, but they truly were as transformative to our society and modern lifestyles as any of those more modern devices. In fact, I would argue (as I did in my 2017 book, The Peeper Pond Farm Story), that society's ability to make the advanced technological strides born of the Industrial Revolution was fundamentally dependent on the labor-saving agricultural innovations that preceded them. Agriculture made it possible for people to produce the food they needed where they lived, which in turn, allowed the first permanent towns and cities to form. The invention of labor-saving mechanical farm implements, such as the cotton gin, plow and reaper, made it further possible for professional farmers to produce more food with fewer workers. Those people who no longer had to produce food for themselves were free to devote their time and energy to other non-farming pursuits, such as inventing light bulbs, automobiles and airplanes.

 Most people have simply become so many generations removed from life on a farm that they have no clue about how their food is produced or where it comes from. Consequently, they don't place as much importance on ground-breaking (pun intended) agricultural innovations as they do the release of a new major film or a new pair of athlete-endorsed sneakers. If only people today could realize how impossible it would be for them to live their technologically-driven lifestyle of convenience without the invention of Cyrus McCormick's wheat reaper, then perhaps farmers and the rural communities they live in would not be as politically and socially marginalized as they are today. However, should the economy that supports our modern lifestyle suddenly collapse, I firmly believe that those living that comfortable urban lifestyle would form longer lines to be fed than to see a new movie or buy a new pair of overpriced sneakers. Do you remember the Great Depression of the 1930s? Our perspective on the important issues in life seems to be influenced more by our personal vanities than any understanding of our most basic needs and the people who toil in relative obscurity to satisfy them.

The museum includes the restored original gristmill and farm workshop within which McCormick built his reapers until 1847, when he moved his operation to Chicago following the opening of the Great Plains for wheat production. The original farmhouse remains on the farm, but has been converted into a local office for the Virginia Cooperative Education System. The grist mill, which was operated by an overshot waterwheel, is still capable of grinding wheat. A visit to the farm is free of charge, so there is no reason not to broaden your understanding of farming and its importance to your life and lifestyle. I would suggest you owe it to the farmers who support you and who we so casually take for granted. I urge you to understand your local farmers and their concerns while they can still support you.

Post 65: Spring Returns to Peeper Pond Farm

February 22, 2018

The record cold of December and January has finally yielded to some record warmth at Peeper Pond Farm. Over the past two days, our high temperatures have topped 70 degrees and signs of Spring have emerged this week. It all began with a huge flock of robins that descended on our field to search for worms. One or two days later, we saw our first redwing blackbirds and turkey buzzards return to the skies. Barb noticed that her crocuses are emerging from the ground and, perhaps most reassuringly of all, our signature spring peepers began singing their mating calls from our pond on Monday. The convergence of all these signs in the span of one week is welcome confirmation of the initial arrival of spring. It all makes me eager for my annual pilgrimage to the maple sugarhouse in the coming weeks. Now, if only the pleasant weather will hold for us.

With the temperature rising to 80 degrees yesterday, Barb and I got the urge to visit Blackwater Falls State Park for the day. We packed a picnic lunch and toddled off through the high Alleghenies to our lofty destination on the canyon rim to enjoy the view. The transition from winter to spring was evident in the remaining ice flows we found along the canyon walls and the raging torrents of spring runoff that washed down the river. It was a joy to see a rainbow form in the mist at the base of Blackwater Falls.

Even Elakala Falls, downstream from Blackwater Falls, was easily visible across the canyon. The volume of water in this stream varies greatly throughout the year. On this day, it was running full, painting a foamy white path down the canyon's rocky walls. The lack of tree foliage helped make the falls easier to see. The thundering flow of water down the canyon added a pleasant white noise to the peaceful scene. There is truly no place in West Virginia like Blackwater Falls.

After returning home, we spent a few hours on our front porch enjoying our peeper pond serenade. We even introduced our new kitten, Calli, to the great outdoors, and I led her on a walk across our small field. She followed me obediently and played among the bushes and broom sedge that bordered the ravine, chasing every insect that dared move in her field of vision. After her romp, she collapsed on the porch and enjoyed some peaceful sleep, satisfied by her wild kitty exploits. Spring truly does renew the spirit as much as it renews all the flowering plants and trees. Life at Peeper Pond Farm is never more satisfying than it is throughout this season.

Post 66: Essie's First Doe Kid

February 27, 2018

    We are proud to announce that the first doe kid born to our farm has given birth to her first doe kid. She will celebrate her first birthday tomorrow, February 28, so we guess that she decided to give herself an early birthday present. Her doe is half Nigerian Dwarf and half Oberhasli, and has very pretty blue eyes. The Carrolls, to whom we sold her last August, bred her to one of their Dwarf Nigerian bucks last fall. Since she was in her first year of life, breeding her to a smaller goat breed made the pregnancy and birth easier on her. She required no assistance with the birth.

    Essie was my favorite prized goat, and I looked forward to raising her as my own. She still recognizes me even more than six months after I sold her. She has a wonderful, affectionate disposition, a beautiful silky coat and fine body composition. Her udder has developed a good shape, although she appears to have relatively small teats. So far, she appears to have good motherly instincts and is very attentive to her offspring. Her kid appears to be very healthy and enthusiastic.

    We still regret having to sell our goats late last summer, but we remain hopeful that, if we can find a more effective way to manage our costs and the State of West Virginia will take a more progressive stance on unprocessed milk sales for small dairies, that we can eventually restart our dairy goat operation. I will say that I remain hopeful for that, but I won't hold my breath for it. We face a very difficult obstacle with the State of West Virginia, which views fresh unprocessed farm milk as an elixir of death, even though 31 other states (including California, New York and Massachusetts) allow it to be sold. Unfortunately, there are no legal restrictions on ignorance and intolerance.

Post 67: The Lion Roars

March 2, 2018

It is said that the month of March comes in like a lion and leaves like a lamb. Despite the fact that this winter season has given us an average of more than one day of strong winds each week, the ferocious storm we received last night and today outdid them all. The first day of March began calmly with low, grey clouds, per odic showers and sporadic gentle breezes. However, behind that gentle overture, a deep low-pressure system was taking shape over northern Ohio that wound itself into an intense storm as the sun began to set. By 9:00 PM, a stiff breeze began to blow at us from the SSE that rapidly built to steady winds of 25-35 MPH with gusts of 45-60 MPH that slammed into our house with the frequency of ocean waves against a breakwater. I was awakened at 11:30 PM by a monster gust of 59 MPH that roared down our valley like an approaching freight train, rattled the walls that resisted its force, and whistled like a teapot, as it squeezed through the narrowest air gaps around our exterior doors.

The pun shing winds howled continuously at us for the next four hours as each new gust tested the integrity of our house for the slightest weakness. At 12:00 AM, the power suddenly failed and our back-up generator snapped to life. It shut down only briefly around 1:15 AM when a sudden surge of electricity in the grid tricked the generator into its shut-down mode, but it restarted immediately after completing that cycle and has operated continuously for twelve hours. This is now the longest continuous period of time that our neighborhood has lost electrical service since the June 29, 2012 derecho storm, and we don't yet know how long it will ultimately be before power is restored.

Around 2:00 AM, we were roused again by loud scraping and banging noises that sounded as though the house was being ripped apart. I jumped out of bed and surveyed the house for damage. When I turned on the front porch lights, I discovered that the winds had pushed our barbecue grill 40 feet along the porch into the picnic table at the other end. In the process it had collided with a chaise lounge and shoved it into one of the picnic table benches that was now pinned against the north railing. I fought against the stiffening gale in my bathrobe and jacket to move the grill and chaise tight against the house where they would be better shielded from the winds. As I looked out from the porch, the only reassuring sound I could hear in the wind was the steady chorus of the spring peepers rising out of our small frog pond. Although it was very dark, I could see the even darker masses of red cedar trees snapping to and fro as they were battered by the punishing winds.

The winds only began to subside slightly around 3:30 AM as they shifted around to the west where the mass of Cave Mountain could shield our house from the strongest gusts. However, they are expected to strengthen again this afternoon as the main low-pressure system merges with another coastal low, forming a massive nor'easter that will gradually slide away from us along the eastern seaboard. The winds are not expected to die down completely until Saturday night.

I didn't awaken again until after 6:00 AM, when the sky began to brighten from the approaching sunrise. I could still hear the winds howling over the summit of Cave Mountain, but they only slammed into our house periodically now. The back-up generator was still running, and I discovered that it was snowing outside with a wind-blown dusting on the ground. I also saw that the storm had blown many limbs out of our dying American Elm Tree in front of our porch. If the winds had blown out of the east, all of those heavy limbs would have landed on our house. Regrettably, it appears that we will have to remove the tree this year.

At 8:30 AM, we drove to the Mill Creek Veterinary Clinic to pick up our cat, Calli, who was spayed yesterday. She is resting peacefully in the security of our house as she recovers from her surgery. Along the way, we saw a number of fallen limbs, but there was no evidence of significant building damage. We have been very lucky thus far, but we still have a lot of blustery weather to persevere. It is now approaching noon-time and it has not stopped snowing yet. We would have received a measurable amount of snowfall, but the ground is too warm to support it. The sun is now struggling to shine through the clouds.

We are now entering the time of the year where our weather is no longer dominated by winter, but it is still influenced periodically by winter's revenge. March has blown in on the back of a prolonged, ferocious gale, and we are eager to meet the lamb waiting for us at its conclusion. Now if we can only survive tax season.

Post 68: A Lackluster Snowfall Season

March 13, 2018

    We are being grazed by another Nor'easter storm today. It left us with a total of about 1.5 inches of snowfall, most of it accumulating during the early morning hours today, even though the snow started falling yesterday. This is typical of the lackluster snowfalls we have received so far this winter, with the biggest snowfall occurring earlier this month when we received a total of two inches. The vast majority of these storms dropped snow when the ground and air temperatures were both above 32 degrees, so our accumulation totals have been less than the amount of snow that actually fell. Consequently, my snowfall totals for each storm and the season as a whole are very conservative relative to the amount of snow that actually fell, but I am only able to measure the actual accumulated totals with any accuracy. As of today, my running accumulated snowfall total is 7.5 inches—the least I have tracked in a single season since I began keeping records in the winter of 2008-09.

    Some people may be quick to call this a confirmation of global warming. That's not an issue I wish to debate. After all, over the Earth's long history, the climate has changed from a period when the entire planet's surface was completely covered with glaciers (the so-called "Snowball Earth" period) to periods when there was almost no surface ice anywhere on the planet (during the reign of the dinosaurs). I expect it will continue to change in the future as the Earth's climate seems to be influenced by a wide range of independent variables, from solar luminosity, variable sunspot cycles, and volcanic eruptions to precession in the Earth's axial tilt, atmospheric composition changes caused by life (as with the eras dominated by humans and the dinosaurs), and cataclysmic cosmic and planetary-scale events (like asteroid impacts).

    I can't say for certain how accurately and reliably our current climate models reflect all of these possible influences (and many others I haven't specifically listed) or what critical assumptions have been made about them because I've never heard any of those factors publicly discussed or debated—just the model predictions and the resulting public policy debate surrounding them. We seem to have lost our ability to apply critical thinking to the models themselves. Many assert that because they were compiled by scientists and loaded into a computer, they are considered infallible and irrefutable. I, however, remain interested in and willing to evaluate the real operative factors—the assumptions made to simplify complex environmental factors that drive each model's predictions. Perhaps, if I were able to evaluate those assumptions, I could understand and determine more precisely why our sophisticated meteorological models don't agree with each other and why they had such a difficult time predicting the storms we received this winter—even within 24 hours of each event. If we want to know (with any firm accuracy and reliability) what is going to happen to the climate in the next 50 years, I think we'd better do a much better job of predicting what's going to happen in the next three days. Remember, any prediction of future events based exclusively on what happened in the past should always be subject to some healthy measure of skepticism. There is an important technical difference between a projection (a mathematical extrapolation of future trends based on historic data) and a forecast (an interpolated projection of future events, some of which may not be accurately represented in mathematical terms). This distinction may help explain why computer models are not always able to make accurate weather forecasts.

As for the snowfalls we've had this season, I can say with a great deal of accuracy (and without the use of any computer model) that our total seasonal snowfall is less than I have measured over the past ten seasons. However, does that statistic alone make me confident that it's been a mild winter? Admittedly, we set two record high temperatures so far this season, but we also set four record lows and we had many more record cool daily high temperature readings than record warm low temperature readings. We also experienced far more days of high winds this winter than in any other season I have experienced over the past decade with a highest measured wind gust of 65 MPH in Upper Tract on March 3. These winds have produced very cold wind chill temperatures on many days. I have also noticed a number of morning frosts that is well above average for the other winter seasons I have experienced, even despite the large number of windy days that make it difficult for frost to form. The total number of days on which snow has fallen is tracking consistently with the average over the past ten years. Although we have received no days where I have measured more than two inches of fallen snow, I have witnessed a well above average number of days when the ground has been dusted with an amount of snow too small for me to accurately measure. In many ways, this winter has been above average in severity, even though it ranks below average in others. What data you choose to discuss will have a significant impact on your overall appraisal of it—which is a situation that I find governs most political debates on our changing climate.

All I know for certain is that I can't intelligently debate the *predictions* of any computer model until I know the universe of *assumptions* as well as the *precision* (margin of error over time) and *historic consistency* (reliability) of the data that went into its construction. All I can tell you is that each assumption we make begins with an "ass," and that any *truly objective* science regarding complex systems is never as simple as it seems and should *always* be subjected to critical thought and debate. In fact, the fundamental resiliency of our science depends upon rigorous and unfettered theoretical debate and challenge. That is because *all* assumptions are made to simplify variables that are too complex to lock down or that our understanding of them is too limited to know for certain. If that wasn't true, then I would expect to receive far more perfect short-term weather forecasts than I receive. I believe that any scientist who refuses reasoned challenges to his or her theories should be considered to be excessively egotistical or politically motivated.

Perhaps I shouldn't expect too much from meteorologists who don't seem to understand the technical difference between "average" temperatures and "normal" temperatures. Please correct me if I'm wrong, but there are no such things as normal temperatures. The term "normal" refers to what a temperature *should be* on any given day. However, the figures frequently touted as normal are really calculated as an "average" of all daily temperatures that were recorded over a 30-year period. Who decided that any given 30-year historic average should actually dictate the temperatures we should consider "normal" and expect to attain on any future day? Which 30-year historic period should we use to decide what the normal temperature on any given day should be—the one that concluded most recently, the one before it, or the one to come? Can the weather that we accept as "normal" be predicted with any accuracy over just one 30-year period? The term "normal" is *not* an appropriate synonym to use in place of "average," as far as daily temperatures are concerned, and its casual misuse by meteorologists today says far less about their scientific integrity than it does about their political ideologies. Regardless of what you may think I believe, that fact should be a cause for concern and a good reason to apply more critical thinking to your own beliefs.

Beliefs are a funny thing. No matter whether you believe in God or you are an atheist, your position is fundamentally based on a belief that is founded more in faith than in fact. To my knowledge, no one has been able to empirically prove that God does or does not exist, despite the fact that this issue has been debated philosophically for centuries. If so, the matter would not be debated further today. Even our best empirical scientific thinking regarding complex systems governed by many independent variables is founded on a set of assumptions that, because of the inherently complex nature that governs them, resemble beliefs more than they do fact and require a greater measure of faith than understanding to model. Until that is no longer the case, then all science should be subject to reasoned skepticism, critical thinking and debate. Knowledge cannot lead to reasoned understanding until it has been subjected to thorough and objective (unbiased) testing and critique. That is my personal position and I will stand by it. Because of what I have said, I have no interest in, nor do I see, any conclusive value in debating the politics on global climate.

You may choose to believe whatever your faith dictates as long as you understand that no one knows precisely or reliably what the weather will be one month from today, regardless of what you feel the weather should be. That is what I believe. I don't know if I have explained my thinking clearly, but I hope that the points I am trying to make will be understood and given fair consideration.

Post 69: "Udder" Disappointment

March 23, 2018

    Since my first journal posting on this website in September 2016, I have addressed many subjects. I have done instructional postings on farming, exposés on the stunning natural amenities that abound in our area, somewhat whimsical and/or philosophical discussions of traditional values, updates on our farming activities, humorous accounts of farm life and even a ghost story. Throughout it all, I have tried to keep my posts entertaining, educational and thoughtful. Farming and traditional rural living framed my childhood upbringing and became my chosen retirement lifestyle. I feel it is important to convey why I cherish it so and why it represents an important pursuit and lifestyle choice that should endure. In order to maintain that focus, I have tried to minimize political commentary. Today, however, I have decided that I can't achieve my primary farming objectives without making a political statement on our state government's abject lack of focus on the survival and ultimate success of small, family owned and operated dairy farms.

    In early August 2017, I was forced to sell our dairy goats and end our milking operation because the laws and regulations in West Virginia made it cost prohibitive for us to sell our farm fresh, unprocessed milk and dairy products, and we couldn't afford to finance the cost of our operation solely on our retirement income. I then dedicated my energy to work for positive, progressive changes to those laws in an effort to salvage what was left of small family dairy farming as well as to promote agricultural diversification and profitability in West Virginia. I even wrote a book about those issues, <u>The Peeper Pond Farm Story: Where Have All the Small Family Dairy Farms Gone</u>, last August and September. In it, I explained the critical issues as they affected our farm and dairy farming throughout the Potomac Highlands region. I further discussed what positive changes we needed to make to improve the situation and make small-scale dairy farming a more viable lifestyle choice. I even made multiple trips to Charleston (our state capital) to discuss with Department of Agriculture officials and my legislators why these issues were important and needed to be addressed. During those efforts, I encountered a state government with an institutionalized regulatory culture so dismissively entrenched in its own lack of concern for the continuing demise of small family dairy farms that they could hardly show any interest in, much less be bothered to listen to my concerns.

    I can understand that my legislators have to address a wide range of important issues to govern our state, and that the concerns I raised may not be something that they could prioritize at this moment in time. However, I cannot excuse the West Virginia Department of Agriculture for not recognizing the importance and critical nature of my concerns. Critical nature, you may ask? Yes, because in my August 2017 book, I noted quite factually that only two-family dairy farms remained in our tri-county region of Grant, Hardy and Pendleton Counties. As I write this post today, neither of them remains. The last multi-generational family dairy farm in the region, owned and operated by Chris Keller, ceased operation in December 2017. The Maryland company that collected and transported his milk daily, decided that it was no longer profitable to collect it and severed his contract with them. Yet, according to the Hardy County Cooperative Extension Agent, there were a total of 28 commercial dairy farms operating in Hardy County alone when the 1985 Whole Herd Buyout program was introduced. Since the State of West Virginia remains one of only nineteen states that prohibit direct customer sales of unprocessed milk directly to a growing number of consumers eager to purchase such milk, Chris was forced to sell all but eight of his 35-cow milking herd to avoid impending bankruptcy. He was left with eight cows because the buyer wouldn't accept them. Chris now milks his remaining milk cows, at his own expense, twice daily and dumps whatever milk he can't consume or use in his home. I have referred to dairy farming as a lifestyle, rather than just a business pursuit because of its time and work demands. In Chris' case, the farm was his family's heritage as well.

The news of this tragic and unanticipated loss made front page news in the February 6, 2018 edition of the Grant County Press, even though Chris' farm is actually located in neighboring Hardy County. Steve Davis, a radio personality for our local radio station, WELD, invited Chris and I to participate in a series of interviews regarding the ongoing demise of family dairy farms and the changes we feel need to be made to salvage what may be left of it. However, the Department of Agriculture's own state-wide farming newsletter, the Market Bulletin, has yet to even acknowledge it occurred, much less devote any attention to what, if anything, should be done about it.

To place this abject neglect in perspective, you should know that when I met with Department of Agriculture Commissioner, Kent Leonhardt, on September 18, 2017, he was very concerned about the Health Department staff's lack of responsiveness in giving Chris the most recent sanitary milk quality test results on his herd's production. Chris told me he had been waiting on those results for several months. Commissioner Leonhardt asked me to tell Chris that he was working on this issue and that he hoped to get those results to him as soon as possible. It was only two months later that his dairy farm was put out of business by the dairy processing industry without so much as an official expression of sorrow regarding the loss from anyone at the Department of Agriculture. No one from the State of West Virginia has approached Chris to offer any financial help or technical assistance in deciding what, if anything, can be done to salvage his family farm. The ultimate *magnitude* of this loss—the last dairy farm in the Tri-County region—has not even been acknowledged by the state. In fact, a deafening silence was the response from the one state department that is focused *exclusively* on agricultural issues and needs. The Health Department's untimely response in issuing required sanitary milk quality test results was the only concern ever expressed by the Department of Agriculture. By the way, Commissioner, Chris still hasn't received those long overdue test results. Perhaps, at this point, it just doesn't really matter anymore, does it?

Yet, it is the state's onerous sanitary milk regulations that prohibit Chris from selling any of his fresh, natural milk to a willing customer base without first sending it to a dairy processing plant. This is why I argue that those regulatory prohibitions leave small dairy farmers subject to the financial whims of a dairy processing monopoly. A regulatory monopoly that allows dairy processors to control the wholesale prices they pay for the farmer's milk and leaves the farmer with no dairy sale options if the milk processor decides they no longer want the farmer's milk. Even the states of California, New York and Massachusetts—highly urbanized states known to impose more restrictive regulations than those of West Virginia—have amended their laws to allow direct farm-to-consumer sales of unprocessed milk. It appears that our state has no concern about this situation, which would be untenable to any other line of business, much less a business that immediately impacts a family's life and livelihood. Not to mention the fact that dairy farming was an important element of the state's agribusiness industry only forty years ago. I recognize the fact that it was when I drive around the South Branch Valley and see the deteriorating remains of long-abandoned dairy barns across the landscape. What value do regulations serve, if they have the ultimate consequence of destroying the activity they seek to govern? Perhaps the state's remaining embarrassment will fade when the last of them collapses and disappears into some distant landfill. What then, I ask, will be left of our traditional farming and rural landscape?

Once again, I apologize to my readers for this lapse into the disgraceful state of our political system. However, I hope that by explaining my concerns, you will understand my reasons and need for doing so. How much does the survival and/or potential rebirth of this cherished, traditional lifestyle choice mean to you? I wish to enlist your help in educating the State of West Virginia to the fact that fresh, unprocessed milk is NOT an elixir of death. At least it never made me or Chris Keller sick, even after consuming it for years. If it was truly the dangerous, potential killer our state regulators fear it to be, neither of us would be here to tell you about it today.

Post 70: Spring Fever

April 15, 2018

    Well, what initially appeared to be a lackluster snowfall season when I wrote my March 13, 2018 website post redeemed itself later in the month. We received our biggest snowstorm on March 20-21 when 7.5 additional inches fell. Overall, our March snowfall total was at least 12.5 inches, raising our seasonal total to 17.5 inches. Because all of the March snow fell when ground and air temperatures were above freezing, my figures are likely to be very conservative. Nevertheless, what was shaping up to be, as of March 13, our least snowy winter in the prior ten years now ranks fourth over that decade. What a difference the second half of March can make!

    The bitter cold and fierce winds of March ultimately forced us to postpone our usual spring preparation activities until April 10, when the temperatures began to stabilize and better reflect the 30-year average. We responded by rushing to prepare our vegetable garden for spring planting. I serviced our tractor, Ferguson, on April 10, which included replacing motor oil, the oil filter and the fuel filter, adding some hydraulic fluid, cleaning the air filter, lubing all fittings and checking coolant levels. I then put Ferguson to work harrowing the garden to loosen the soil and spread some pellet and wood stove ashes in the areas that required low-acid soil to grow our vegetables. On April 11, I mowed the grass at either end of the garden and rototilled the garden soil twice—once widthwise and once lengthwise—to make sure it was broken up and well mixed. Then we staked out all of the planting areas. By April 13, we were planting our first early vegetables—cabbage and onions. Rain is moving in today to further delay our spring planting, so we will have to wait until it can dry out sometime next week.

    We managed to enjoy some early summer weather in the latter half of the week by making our first excursion to find Douglas Falls near Thomas, which I have been told is West Virginia's second highest waterfall (after nearby Blackwater Falls). With all the runoff from the recent March snowfalls, the waterfall was roaring at deafening levels. We had to carefully scale down the steep walls of the North Branch of Blackwater River bank to view it. Luckily, our efforts were aided by a heavy knotted rope to keep us from losing our footing on the steepest grade of our descent into the rocky gorge. The refreshing trip was well worth it. Now it will be back to work for us.

    We hope you have a good and productive spring.

Post 71: The Demise of a Legacy

April 25, 2018

During the past year, we suffered a number of losses—the passing of our fifteen-year-old housecat, the loss of our dairy goat operation, and the collapse of our two beehives. However, we also realized that our magnificent American Elm tree, which provided shade for the northern end of our front porch, began to die last year and was not producing any buds this spring. I don't yet know how old this tree was, but the best estimates that we have been given range from 100-125 years. Therefore, it may date back to the closing years of the nineteenth century. It clearly survived when most of the largest and most elegant American Elm trees were being destroyed by Dutch Elm Disease. If you look back at postcards from that era, you will find images of city streets lined with stately elm trees, which explains why so many cities have Elm Streets named for them.

The large American Elm tree that graced our front yard was one of three such trees that exist on our Peeper Pond Farm property. I believe that all three of them were offspring from an even bigger American Elm tree on our upslope neighbor's property. We struggled hard to help our front yard tree survive the ravages of American Elm disease and bug infestations by treating it each year, but the bugs finally defeated us. The fierce winter and early spring winds that we faced this year stripped away loose bark and snapped off many branches making its rapid decline immediately apparent. It was with great regret that we have finally decided to have it removed.

We haven't decided how we will replace it or what type of tree we want to plant. It would be nice to have a colorful maple tree, if the deer that visit our farm most nights will let it grow. For now, we're just disappointed to watch it come down, marking the end of a natural legacy here at Peeper Pond Farm. Instead, we are turning our immediate attention to the planting of our vegetable garden, which we hope will fulfill the promise of life renewed at our farm.

Post 72: Sacred Places

May 4, 2018

Now that warm spring weather has firmly taken control, Barb and I have taken some time to enjoy the special outdoor places we like to patronize in Pendleton County. Today, we took another trip deep into Smoke Hole Canyon, the entrance to which is a three-mile drive from our house but is less than half that distance if you go out our main door and proceed due west over the 2,801-foot summit of Cave Mountain. Just a drive through the canyon is an ideal sensory toric to cure the most tenacious cabin fever bug. We drove past the iconic Eagle Rocks to Big Bend campground and visited a small sandy beach along the South Branch of the Potomac River where we like to picnic and swim on hot summer days. The sense of scale that strikes you as your eyes wander up the precipitous, rocky canyon walls to the top of Cave Mountain, some 1,200 feet above the river, reassures me that this is a truly sacred place; a place that humbles you by making you feel small and insignificant amidst the natural grandeur of the world that closes in about you. It reminds me of an old German saying I learned when I researched my biological family's heritage two decades ago, "People think a hunter is a sinner because he seldom goes to church, but in the forest, a glance up to the heavens is better than a false prayer." I may not be a hunter, but I certainly understand and appreciate its meaning.

We have found numerous places in Pendleton County that make you feel that way, such as Seneca Rocks, Germany Valley, Spruce Knob and Greenwalt Gap. Many of these places are legendary elements of Pendleton County's history and cultural heritage, as I explained last year in my May 31, 2017 post on our Peeper Pond Farm website. I appreciate them all, as they define what makes Pendleton County so distinct from other places we have lived in throughout our lives. These sacred places remind me of the real reason why West Virginia is called 'Almost Heaven.' It's because it can't *all* be Pendleton County.

One of our recent acquaintances in Pendleton County was reading my website musings regarding the scenic natural places in our region and said he felt I was a true Naturalist. I admit, people have told me that I am many things in my life, but that was the first time I was classified as a Naturalist. It felt strange and somewhat uncomfortable to me because my vision of a Naturalist was Euell Gibbons, and I couldn't embrace that image. After all, I have never eaten Grape Nuts for breakfast. I do have a deep and profound respect for our natural environment, but I can't fully accept the perspective I hear from many so-called or self-professed "environmentalists" that we must avoid any impacts on the natural environment—as though we are not entitled to have any impact on it.

My own environmental thinking was influenced significantly (but not dictated) by a little known (and long challenged) free thinker by the name of James Lovelock and his Gaia theory. He acknowledged that the environment on our planet has profound and subtle influences on the evolution of the life it supports, but he also theorizes that life, in turn, has subtle influences that can shape the environment that supports it. I still carry with me copies of a 1989 article describing his theory that I have shared with my friends and colleagues throughout my professional career. His views, which are far too complex for me to explain in this post, recognize that life can, as it proliferates, influence the environmental and climactic conditions that support it and can, in subtle ways, help regulate environmental conditions. If you accept this theory, you can understand the essential influence living organisms have had in making our planet suitable for it to proliferate and evolve. While that view doesn't excuse humans from being negligent and casually disrespectful of the natural environment and our resources, it does provide a reason to accept the fact that we don't have to live like we are not entitled to have *some* impact on the environment by virtue of living in it.

As I have always said, "it is not a question of whether or not we will (by virtue of our existence) have an impact on the environment but of what impact we can or should have. Even the staunchest environmentalist owns and uses a wastebasket and eats other life forms to survive." We want to believe that our sentience and our technological abilities makes us superior to other life forms that share the planet with us. That ego-driven superiority complex enables us to believe that we can ultimately live as though we are separate from the environment in ways that can give us complete dominion over it to either exploit it as we wish to serve our desires (opportunists) or to preserve it as it is and fully mitigate our impacts on it (preservationists). I tend to feel that both of these extreme views on how we relate to our environment are, in many ways, contrary to the true nature of it.

While many environmentalists I hear today espouse a preservationist perspective, I feel that we have no more right to decide how the world should look or what species should survive than we do to casually exploit its resources without any concern for the impacts that may have on the other life forms that share the planet with us. I freely admit that our lives will impact the natural world and perhaps cause the incidental extinction of other life forms. I believe that other 'higher order' life forms, such as the dinosaurs, altered the world and in doing so caused the extinction of other life forms, even though they too eventually became extinct.

    I believe that our environment and its physical limitations, can and will eventually decide our own fate because it is beautifully and powerfully designed to balance the basic needs of the life forms it nourishes. To preserve it as it is today or as we feel it should be may deny the opportunity for the next higher order life form to emerge and take its place after we are gone. I simply don't believe we have that right any more than I believe we have the right to exploit it all as we may wish. Both of these perspectives are extreme opposites as I see them. I prefer to believe we should live responsibly and let the awesome power of the natural world decide our fate for us—thumbs up or thumbs down. I think we tend to delude ourselves with a false sense of power or righteousness simply because we happen to be the highest order of life on the planet today. In doing so, we may forget that we are much less smart and powerful than we think we are, even as we learn again and again that we don't really understand it all or its humbling complexity. I am confident that, in due time, nature will set us straight. What right do we have to think otherwise?

    I have heard it said that at least 99 percent of all life forms that have ever lived on this planet are now extinct. At some point in time, humans, like many other species, will likely face an environmental tipping point that will end our own existence. It may be caused by natural forces/constraints or we could become the cause of our own extinction. How soon that may occur will depend on how responsibly we conduct our lives and satisfy our basic needs. One way or another, the history of life on our planet suggests that we, too, will become extinct and we will leave a niche for some other life form to fill—perhaps one that does not even exist today. I only hope we will have the wisdom to respect and appreciate our most sacred places. That's why I prefer to call myself a Conservationist—not to be confused with many Environmentalists today who I prefer to classify as Preservationists. I feel that the growing preservationist perspective is what makes modern environmentalism too extreme for me. However, if you can accept my way of thinking about our environment and the natural world, then perhaps I can also accept being called a Naturalist. After all, it is the indomitable power of the natural world that will ultimately teach us how we should live within it.

Post 73: How's the garden doing, Mary?

May 16, 2018

Do you remember the old English rhyme? ...
   Mistress Mary, quite contrary
   How does your garden grow?
   With silver bells and cockle shells,
   And so, my garden grows.

This old rhyme came to mind as we contemplated the rapid growth of our freshly planted garden. Spring weather came so late this season that it seems all the trees, plants and flowers finally decided they weren't going to wait any longer. All of the buds just burst into life this year in firm defiance of the intemperate weather. Now we're experiencing some hot and wet weather, as though the climate has conceded in defeat. Our planting rows can be seen against the rich, dark soil in our garden as they celebrate spring's victory over winter. We still have to plant a few more tomato plants and two rows of late corn, but other than that, our Peeper Pond Farm garden has been planted for the season. The plants currently sprouting in our garden include pumpkins, squash, cucumbers, peppers, broccoli, cabbage, onions, corn, peas, beans, carrots, peppers, potatoes and tomatoes. We actually have multiple varieties of cucumbers, cabbage, potatoes, beans and tomatoes, including nine West Virginia (heirloom) tomato plants. We found that particular variety of tomato to be very popular at the Grant County Farmer's Market last year. We hope to have some sale vegetables ready for the big grand opening of the Farmer's Market in Petersburg this June (date unknown due to the late growing season this year). We hope we'll see you there and throughout the summer.

As I think back on the old English rhyme I quoted at the start of this post, I am reminded how often we used to recite many of them during my childhood on our dairy farm, and yet how forgotten they are today. We had old sayings that we used to guide our weather observations and just humorous poems that we would recite just for pleasure. All of them seem to be forgotten today. I still use the old weather sayings to judge weather conditions because they were rooted in fact, such as...

"Red sky at night, sailor's delight; red sky at morn, sailors be warned."

"Fog on the hills brings water to the mills."

"As the days begin to lengthen (in late December), the cold begins to strengthen."

"A heavy dew at night foretells a clear morrow; a dry night lawn predicts rain on the morrow."

"When smoke rises quickly, good weather prevails, but when smoke curls downward and lingers near the ground, a storm awaits."

...and many more. Eric Sloane, who I have quoted from time to time on my website, documents many of them. They actually work because they were based on observations of actual weather phenomena. Old-time farmers knew them and used them because they had no access to weather forecasts, and the success of a farm depends on good knowledge of the fickle and often adverse whims of the local climate.

However, I also remember many old stories, poems and parables our family recited on long, stormy, winter days when we huddled around the kitchen table in front of our Home Comfort wood cookstove because the rest of our house would be so cold. If a winter storm caused our power to fail after dark, we might also spend some time learning how to make shadow figures on the wall in the soft, flickering glow of lamplight. Other times, we would take turns recounting embarrassing memories of our lives on the farm or reciting humorous or clever anecdotes to relieve our sheltered boredom. Although I knew most of the old rhymes and tales by heart as a child, I had to look them up some 45 years later because my memory is failing, and I haven't heard them recounted since then. Reciting them during my childhood gave us something to laugh about in the face of dreary and dreadful weather, although some of them might strain the increasingly fragile sensitivities of people today who are easily offended.

I can easily recall one old riddle we used to tell. Let's see if you can guess the correct answer. It will challenge your math skills.

"As I was going to St. Ives,
I met a man with seven wives.
Each wife had seven sacks.
Each sack had seven cats.
Each cat had seven kits.
Kits, cats, sacks and wives,
How many were going to St. Ives?"

If you read or listened carefully, you would know the correct answer is one—the person who was telling the story. If he was 'going to St. Ives' and met the others, they were either traveling in the opposite direction or simply staying put. Consequently, he was the only one who was 'going to St. Ives.'

Here's an old parable that I remember hearing as a child that I believe may have been one of Aesop's original fables, although I don't know for certain. I always like this one and recounted it many times to my coworkers who were often puzzled by the unpredictable and often hypocritical attitudes of elected officials we served. Only one person of the many I have told it to (including young and old) actually remembered hearing it once many years before.

"A fox and scorpion met each other at a wide and deep river. Both wished to get to the other side. Being small and unable to swim, the scorpion asked the fox to carry him across the river on his back. The sly fox said it would be stupid for him to do so because the scorpion could sting him and he'd drown. The scorpion noted it would be foolish for him to do so because they'd both drown. The fox thought about it further and decided there was no reason to fear. He allowed the scorpion to climb up his tail onto his back and then proceeded to swim across the river. When the fox was half way across the river, the scorpion suddenly stung him. 'Why did you do that you fool, now we'll both drown!' the fox cried. As the fox gasped for air, the scorpion casually replied, 'Because it's my nature.'"

I heard these little traditional ditties and many others like them when I was a child. Most of them, including the traditional child nursery rhymes, were English in origin, although I've forgotten or never knew who first recorded them. People today seem so casually disinterested in their heritage and the old and traditional ways of doing things that they have little interest in remembering and preserving them. To me, this is a tragic waste. I have always said that the specific bits of knowledge and education you learn do not become wisdom until they can be fully understood and applied in some meaningful way to real life experiences. I have known too many educated people in my life who sound smart because of their advanced knowledge of some specialized trade or profession but were unable to balance a checkbook or find their way out of the woods. Going to college to get an education means nothing if you don't know how to apply the knowledge you learned. That is the essence of what I refer to as 'common sense.' In the past, it was called, 'horse sense.' That is also the skill that I believe the people who did write all these little ditties had and that has become a lost art in our modern, ego- and convenience-driven society. It is also why I try so hard to discuss it in my website posts. Perhaps, someday, that loss will become our Achille's heal. Do you know that old story?

Post 74: Waterworld

May 19, 2018

What a wild week of rain and storms we've had! It all started on Monday afternoon. Barb and I were in the Grafton area visiting one of her former Chessie Federal Credit Union co-workers who she hired to use her long-arm sewing machine to stitch a flame pattern into the Harley Davidson lap quilt Barb was making. The stitching took a little longer than expected, so we didn't leave her friend's house until about 3:00 PM. As we were driving east of Grafton towards Laurel Mountain on U.S. Route 50, we encountered the brunt of a severe afternoon thunderstorm that was passing through the area. Our car was lashed with heavy, driving rain, strong wind gusts and pea-sized hail that greatly reduced visibility and caused us to turn on our flashers. The storm subsided as we climbed Laurel Mountain, but we knew from the weather forecast and radar image that we would be following it all the way home to Pendleton County.

As we descended the east face of the Allegheny Front, Barb had to swerve to avoid a tree that had fallen onto the highway. The rest of the way home, we saw multiple trees blown down by the storm as well as limb and leaf debris stripped from the trees. We arrived home just after 6:00 PM to find our whole-house LP gas generator running. Our electric power service had been out since 5:00 PM. We did not realize at that time that we would be without electric service until 5:30 AM on Wednesday morning—a 35.5-hour outage! Fortunately, our trusty generator kept our home powered during the entire outage.

That storm was only the leading edge of a weather front that stalled over our immediate area for the rest of the week. Although it wavered slightly north and south during its unwelcome visit, waves of rain and thunderstorms trained along it giving us daily rains that totaled 4.86 inches of rainfall before the front was swept away on Saturday morning! The worst single day was Thursday, when 2.9 inches fell in 24 hours. Our total rainfall for the month stands at 7.11 inches as of the writing of this post on Saturday morning (May 19) and more rain is in the forecast, even though that forecast doesn't extend to the end of the month. The 30-year average monthly rainfall for May in Upper Tract, WV (our nearest village and the driest community in all of West Virginia) is 3.78 inches. Although we still have nearly half of the month left, we have already received nearly twice the average rainfall for the full month. When considering the magnitude of that, you should realize that our April rainfall total was 4.64 inches (which included a 2.82-inch rainfall event on April 16), even though the 30-year average for that month is 2.66 inches. The upshot of all this is that we are living in a virtual waterworld here in eastern West Virginia.

The past week of storms turned the intermittent stream that traverses our farm into a fervent, babbling run. Although the stream is never closer to our house than 200 feet (and sets in a deep ravine), we can hear it gushing down from Cave Mountain from our front porch. All the creeks and rivers in our area are full to overflowing, and periodic road flooding has been a problem. Our local schools closed early on Thursday afternoon out of fear that highway flooding would make it impossible for the buses to safely deliver school children home. Our cat Calli still managed to enjoy her daily periodic outdoor hunting excursions, even though she would return each time to the house soaking wet from the tips of her ears to the tip of her tail. She certainly appears to have no fear of water. At least our tree frogs thoroughly enjoyed the weather. We've heard them celebrating loudly day and night throughout the storm siege. While the rain has helped our garden vegetables grow, it has also helped our lawn and field grass grow, two factors which inconveniently offset each other in terms of their impacts on my overall workload.

Fortunately, we experienced no damage at our farm from the wind and rain. The trenching work I did earlier this month around our garden effectively prevented any runoff damage to our infant vegetable plants. Everything in the garden looks fine, even though we noticed water ponding in a few locations. We lost no more trees to the storms, probably because the fierce winds during the winter and earlier this spring had already taken down four or five of the most vulnerable trees. I don't know how much rainfall we will eventually accumulate this May, but I'll bet we won't see another month with as much excess rainfall during this year. I hope that doesn't mean we'll end up with a dry, hot summer. I guess only time will tell.

Post 75: Man, I Lived It, Too

May 22, 2018

 The persistent rain we've experienced this May has made the ground too soggy for outdoor work and driven us indoors. When I last reported our total rainfall for the month in my last (May 19) website post, we had received 7.11 inches. Our 30-year average for the entire month is about 3.78 inches. Well, it's been three days since I gave you that report and our current total rainfall amount has increased to 8.74 inches with more rain in the forecast for today and the rest of the month. At our current pace, we could easily top ten inches of rainfall by the end of the month. If the actual amount of rain we've received hasn't made life dreary enough, the lack of remaining indoor work to do has made it downright boring.

 Despite the rain and fog, I have been spending more time on our front porch enjoying the beauty of our mountain view in quiet contemplation. Yesterday afternoon, had the pleasure of watching a distant thunderstorm develop and drift towards us. I could clearly see the sweeping path of the heavy downpour as it crept north along our valley and obscured my view of the mountains and hills in its path. Knowing how far away and high those peaks are made it possible for me to know how fast it was approaching and how high the cloud deck was. This is one of the old observational skills I learned growing up on our family dairy farm that still gives me pleasure today.

 That scene brought my wandering thoughts back to a new song by Blake Shelton that is rising up the Country music charts and that I really appreciate, *I Lived It*. In the song, Blake recounts a number of traditional living experiences that he allegedly experienced growing up, such as riding in the back of his grandfather's truck, having his uncle put tobacco on yellow jacket stings, and his mother putting 100,000 miles on a Sears box fan to cool the house. These images are so forgotten today that, as he sings...

> "Oh, you think I'm talking crazy
> In a different language you might not understand.
> Oh, that's alright
> That's just the kind of life that made me what I am.
> Just takin' my mind on a visit
> Back in time 'cause I miss it.
> You wouldn't know how to love it like I love it
> Unless you lived it."

I like to sing that chorus with him when I hear the song, because that sentiment means a great deal to me. The only unfortunate aspect of the song is that I sincerely doubt that Blake Shelton is old enough to have actually lived it. The song's lyrics were not written by him, and I bet that the actual authors are considerably older. I often tell Barb that, although I can really appreciate the sentiments of many of today's popular Country hits (especially *Dirt, Back at Momma's, In Color, I Hold On, You Should Be Here, Automatic* and *How I'll Always Be*), I realize that they may represent more image than substance to the artists that sing them. Most of the artists that sing the songs I just listed, with the notable exception of Tim McGraw, are too young and too many generations removed from that lifestyle to have actually lived the experiences they extoll in their songs. In fact, I have noted many "inconsistencies" in them.

For example, in the song, *Heartbeat*, Carrie Underwood sings about a quiet dance with her lover deep in the wilderness. In describing the setting, she sings, "…I love the way you look in a firefly glow," and "…a cricket choir in the background, underneath a harvest moon." If you've truly spent time in a rural environment, you would know that the fireflies "glow" in the early summer months (June, in our area), but the "harvest moon" typically occurs in mid-to-late September, and sometimes in early October. The lyrics evoke a warm, romantic 'country' image that works for the spirit of the song (and the artist's pocketbook), but lacks substance in reality. It may sound nitpicky of me to point that out, but anyone who truly lived in and understood that environment, as I did, would cringe at that, just as a skilled singer would cringe at a missed note. When I see the lavish and ostentatious lifestyle that today's young Country artists live, it doesn't make it easy for me to imagine them growing up the way I did.

When I think back more than forty years ago to my childhood on our family owned and operated dairy farm, I can recall many traditional lifestyle experiences, most of which were long outdated to many of my own peers. I can also recall riding around in the back of our flatbed pickup truck holding onto nothing but a headboard, but I also remember…

- hanging laundry on our clothesline to dry,
- 'rolling' glazing putty for my grandfather to use in replacing a window pane,
- heating soap stone blocks in our wood cookstove to wrap in towels and place under the covers of a bed in an upstairs, unheated bedroom to warm it up before going to sleep,

- using an outhouse at my grandparent's camp and when staying with a babysitter who lived in a house without running water or electricity,
- milking cows by hand for days when the electricity was out,
- mowing a three-acre hayfield by hand using a scythe (I still use one today),
- picking rocks out of a freshly plowed field on a raw, dank spring day,
- being told by my first grade teach not to use my left hand to write because it was "the devil's work,"
- raking fall leaves into black plastic bags and placing them around the foundation of our house as insulation against the winter (trust me, it never worked as well as we hoped it would),
- swimming in a natural pond to cool off in the summer,
- riding in a horse-drawn sleigh before Christmas to sing carols to the shut-ins in our village,
- listening to wilderness hunting stories told by a great-uncle who was born just after the end of the Civil War,
- watching a great-aunt demonstrate how a spinning wheel and hand-operated wooden loom were used,
- helping shear a neighbor's sheep and cut the horns off our own heifers,
- earning $2.50 per seven-day week of work for doing my farm chores,
- having only one station to watch on a black and white TV (at least it was a solid-state TV in my later childhood—if you know what that means),
- collecting maple sap in galvanized buckets in an attempt to boil our own syrup (which we failed to perfect),
- being given the town cemetery keys to open and lock the entrance gate each day during the snow-free months,
- trying (often unsuccessfully) to ride our cows,
- laying on warm, dry hay in the hayloft of our barn on rainy days,
- fishing in the Connecticut River to stock our swimming pond (to keep the mosquitoes down),
- driving a circa 1955 John Deere B tractor with a flywheel on the side (I'll bet you have no idea what that is or what it was used for),
- attending school in a classroom that housed two grades at the same time,

- going to visit a neighboring farm so my father could "see a man about a horse," even though we always ended up acquiring something else in trade,
- going to the town (open burning) dump less than once per month and often returning with something someone else had thrown away, but would be useful to us,
- drinking our own unprocessed cow milk dipped daily out of the bulk tank,
- splitting wood on a sunny, below-zero winter day because the wood was easier to split when the moisture in it was frozen,
- and hand-churning milk into butter.

Although I have a list of traditional life experiences that could turn Blake Shelton's song into a novel, I could tell you many more. What I remember most about these experiences was how the people I would meet during my college and later professional working years would find it hard to believe that I actually lived them. Our parents had told us we were not to aspire to live as we did and that I would have to go to college, get an education and make a living in the outside world like everyone else. They told us there was no future in farming, so we could not expect to inherit the farm. That farm is now lost to time, and like so many other farm children during my era, we moved on to find our way in the modern society. What I did not realize when making that transition was how the stories and memories of my childhood upbringing would be treated by my peers, most of whom were generations removed from any farm experiences.

I attended a college in Hartford, Connecticut (a big city to me) with students who were the children of professional families that were well "above my station," as we used to say. One of my freshman classmates was Jack Klugman's daughter, who was driven to and from campus weekly in her father's limousine. Although I never met her and she transferred out later in our freshman year, I and a couple of my friends, would run out and sit on the hood of the limousine while the driver went in the dorm to collect her luggage, until he returned to chase us off.

Most of my college friends found my experiences funny or "quaint" in a pitiful sense. I had never used an escalator in my life, and my first awkward attempt at a shopping mall was a source of great amusement to my new college friends. I used many rural mountain terms that my classmates did not understand but were just second nature to me. I also learned quite early on that my baseball cap was not proper attire for a college student. For all appearances, I felt as though I was fresh off the cast of Green Acres. I remember one particularly aloof student asking me if I needed a visa to attend school in Connecticut. I quickly became very conscious of my manner of speaking and the memories I discussed. I became ashamed of my rural upbringing and sought to distance myself from it any way that I could. I knew that those experiences and mannerisms would not help me connect with my peers, and I had no choice but to change if I was going to find any acceptance or success in the outside world. Even though I was from rural New Hampshire, my experiences transitioning to the outside world make it easy for me to understand how native West Virginians feel about the perceptions that outsiders have of them. You see, I lived that, too.

When I discovered West Virginia in 2006, I felt a sense of great relief. I always felt out of place living in modern society during my professional career. I always told Barb (my wife) that the way we lived didn't seem real to me, and that the suit I wore to work felt like a costume I had to wear to play a part in the professional world. My exposure to other professionals I met and worked with in the course of doing my job taught me that they lived by very different values than I internalized from my childhood upbringing. Although we moved many times during my career, I never found a place that felt like a home to me—that is, until I discovered West Virginia. That's why we chose to retire here. In West Virginia, my childhood experiences are typical, the way I used to talk is understood, and I can dress as I did growing up on the farm and not feel conscientious about my appearance. For once in my long, lost life, I can feel like I belong, even if I'm still a "come-here" to many of the natives.

Actually, I find that some natives I've come to know actually have a hard time believing I once had a professional career and lived in or near cities. I remember meeting one elderly man from Hampshire County, WV when I was living in our home in New Creek, WV. He was a former farmer, and I was sharing with him some of my long-hidden childhood farm experiences. He asked me where I was from, so I told him I was from New Hampshire--although, as a native New Hampshirite, I tend to say the name so casually that it sounds like I'm really saying Ne' Hampshire. At any rate, he misheard what I said and, based on his first impression that I was a native West Virginian, he asked me if I grew up somewhere near Romney, which is the seat of Hampshire County, WV. I snickered with appreciation at his question, and I told him, "No, I grew up in Charlestown, New Hampshire." My clarification only appeared to confuse him further. After taking a second to figure out how to politely respond, he leaned closer to me and said in a soft, fatherly tone, "Son, you really need to get your story straight. Everyone here knows that Charles Town (WV) is in Jefferson County, not Hampshire County." I was overjoyed that he could be so convinced I was a native West Virginian that he completely misunderstood my attempts to explain that I was actually from the State of New Hampshire. I've felt truly at home here in my adoptive state ever since. It is, to me, a home where the lifestyle I lived during my childhood can be a source of honor, rather than shame. That's also why I proudly sing the chorus to "*I Lived It*" whenever I hear it play on the radio, even if I think that Blake Shelton probably didn't. It is also why I strive, to the best of my ability, to relive it today at Peeper Pond Farm.

Post 76: Calli's Catch

May 30, 2018

    It's so easy to marvel at the profound beauty of nature. I find it to be impressive in its grandeur, breadth and complexity. I often let my mind wander in the sweeping majesty of the rolling, mountain landscape from our front porch. It always amazes me how far and wide it carries my thoughts and helps me place them into perspective. However, nature is much more than a pretty view. It also embraces the symphony of life and death and the balanced complexity of the wildlife and plants that live within it. The natural world is a fascinating learning environment in its own right that inspires wonder and awe as we contemplate how it all works. It often refreshes and nourishes the soul to think about it and appreciate it for what it is.

    As spring ushers in the annual renewal of life at our farm, we have enjoyed the transition. It began with raucous mating calls from the spring peepers that live in our pond and the morning chorus of summer birds returning to the trees. As the leaves and flowers burst, a palette of colors returned to our landscape. Then, we noticed the playful celebration of the various wild animals as they emerged from their winter retreats. The deer, rabbits, butterflies, and now the fireflies have each appeared in our field like actors gradually emerging from the wings to take center stage.

    Perhaps the most entertaining element of the choreography of life has been the growth and maturity of our new housecat, Calli. We took her in at the beginning of winter, when she was only a three-month-old kitten, full of energy and eager to play with any toy she could find. As she matured with the reluctant approach of spring, the focus of her play evolved. Her attention shifted from her cat toys to the houseflies that buzzed in the windows. It was funny to watch her leap up the window casing or creep up behind them to catch them. From time to time, she would be successful and enjoy a tiny morsel of protein. All the while, she was honing her hunting skills for the bigger game that would eventually emerge in our yard.

    By the time the weather made it possible for Calli to explore our farm, she was mature enough to apply her hunting skills. Her first prize was a field mouse that she caught in our front yard. Our former housecat, Ninny was more than fourteen years old and two months shy of death before she caught her first wild animal. Calli had mastered the skill when she was only seven months old. From that simple beginning, she moved on to birds and bunnies. She wasn't very successful with the birds, but she did eventually catch some baby bunnies. She learned that they would sneak into our freshly planted gardens to nibble on the vegetables that were emerging from the ground. She would sit on the porch overlooking the garden until she spotted just the right movement in the grass. Then, in a flash, she would leap from her perch on the railing and race toward her prey like an arrow shot from a bow. She returned from such a mission yesterday afternoon with her second bunny catch. I knew what she had caught from the desperate squeaks it made as it tried to evade her. The grass was too tall in the field to see the entire pursuit, but I could periodically see Calli leap above the grass as she repeatedly pounced on the bunny. After a brief chase, she carried her trophy triumphantly back to the freshly mowed yard and presented it to me for inspection and affirmation.

I guess many people today would think it cruel to watch our cat relentlessly pursue, catch and kill an innocent baby bunny. Even our own son felt sympathy for the bunny when we shared a picture of Calli and her catch with him. As I noted in an earlier post this month, I have known many environmentalists who feel that we should preserve nature as it is today and save every living thing from peril at the hands of evil, unnatural humans. I guess I just view Calli's success as a fulfillment of the natural order of predator and prey. Calli was only responding to her true nature as a hunter. Actually, the bunny would not have been caught had it not been responding to its nature by attempting to rob our vegetable garden of its delectable bounty. In that respect, the bunny was the predator seeking to kill an innocent vegetable that we had planted in our garden to feed ourselves. If we did not let Calli pursue her natural hunting talent, our field would be quickly overrun with bunnies (which breed like rabbits) and all our gardening efforts would only result in feeding an unsustainable bunny overpopulation on our farm.

Yes, nature can be cruel at times, but it's all part of the natural order of the cycle of life and death. All of the players in this incident—we who planted the garden, the bunny who tried to invade it, and Calli who intervened—were doing what we must do to survive. It is not a variable-sum game, where all the players can win something without having to take away from the other players. It is a zero-sum game where some win at the expense of others, but life inevitably goes on. To intervene and try to save the bunny may sound virtuous in one respect, but it may ultimately be cruel when it results in the survival of more bunnies than the natural environment can ultimately support. Nature has its own built-in check and balance system that works better on its own than any control I could exert over it, regardless of my intentions. I guess I just find solace in that natural simplicity and appreciate it for what it is. That's just the way it works, naturally.

The only problem I see is that Calli is now emboldened by her recent hunting success. Twice now, she has been fascinated with the deer that she sees from our porch in the early morning hours just before sunrise. I have watched her steely gaze lock onto them and, moments later, she tears off the porch in hot pursuit. Once, she managed to chase two bucks across our driveway and up the road from our farm. Perhaps she may be responding to her predatorial nature or she was just protecting her territory from competition by invaders, but I think, at some point, she will have to face the reality of scale—before she makes the unfortunate mistake of pursuing a buck during rutting season. As I said, nature is fascinating and powerful enough to teach us all important lessons. That is, if we're willing to understand and learn from it—and accept it for what it is.

Post 77: All Washed Up

June 3, 2018

In case you were wondering, we ended the month of May 2018 with 11.42 inches of rainfall here at Peeper Pond Farm. That's a little more than three times the 30-year average total rainfall for the month of 3.78 inches. We ended up receiving an inch or more of rain on four days, one of which dumped a total of 2.90 inches! As you might expect, we are hoping for some relief now that the month has officially ended. I know, good luck with that!

Thus far, after the first three days of June, we have received an additional 4.70 inches, 4.65 inches of which fell over the past 36 hours. The 30-year average rainfall for June in our area is 3.13 inches, so we received 1.5 inches more than the entire monthly average in the first three days of the month. After the soaking we received in May, the ground was too saturated to absorb the deluge. Although we sustained no significant damage here at Peeper Pond Farm, the river and stream flooding that resulted washed out roads throughout our area. Numerous mudslides also occurred, including one that closed a section of U.S. Route 220 south of Moorefield. Barb and I toured our immediate area and discovered that portions of four important roads in our area were closed due to high water or washouts—U.S. Route 220, Greenwalt Gap Road, Mozer Road (formerly Brushy Run Road) and North Mill Creek Road. Every road we travelled had some areas where runoff from individual properties and driveways actively flowed across our path.

Many young people will be quick to call this storm event a "500-year flood." However, our old-timers will remember that the 1985 Election Day flood was far worse. That epic flood was spawned by the remnants of Tropical Storm Juan and left record-high watermarks when the South Branch of the Potomac River spilled over its banks and wiped-out sections of Franklin, Petersburg and Moorefield. Pictures and stories of the devastation would simply take your breath away.

I wasn't living in West Virginia during the 1985 flood, but I do recall the most devastating flood that occurred in any place I have ever lived—the 1994 flood in west and central Georgia. At that time, I was the Planning Director for the Middle Georgia Regional Development Center in Macon. The storm, which was caused by Tropical Storm Beryl, washed out the Lake Wildwood dam and flooded the city's water plant. Everyone in the immediate Macon area lost public water service for 23 consecutive days while the mud and debris that buried the water treatment system was removed and the water lines were flushed. National Guard stations were set up across the city to distribute bottled water to affected residents. Just driving around the city made one feel as though it had fallen under marshall law.

I clearly remember how frequently and casually the term, "500-year flood", was used to characterize that flood. At the peak of the flooding, Emergency Management Agency and Army Corps of Engineers officials descended on our office to evaluate the extent of the flooding. They had taken helicopter aerial photos of the floodwaters and wanted to compare them directly to digital Flood Insurance Rate Maps using our new computer-based Geographic Information System. They scanned and digitized their aerial photos and overlaid them on the digital flood maps to see how they compared to the official floodplain boundaries. The results of that comparison were amazing. As the officials compared the data, they noted how far the floodwaters extended beyond the 100-year floodplain lines in many areas. However, I found other areas where the alleged 500-year floodwaters didn't even reach the 100-year floodplain lines (perhaps suggesting that the engineered flood boundaries were based on some errant assumptions). When I pointed that out, the officials agreed it was interesting, but they offered no explanation for it. They simply said, "Well, we have to call it something." As a former farmer, I had a thought to offer.

In the years that have passed since that historic Macon flood, I have had many opportunities to think about that assessment. If you think carefully and critically about it (a truly lost art these days), you will realize that we don't have enough accurate historic weather records to know what a 500-year storm or flood could be. The Commonwealth of Virginia (from which West Virginia was carved in 1863) was first settled permanently at Jamestown in 1607. That was 411 years ago now, and our area (Pendleton County) was not first settled until 1737 (130 years later). This means that historic weather data in our country has yet to span the first 500 years of our settlement, assuming accurate, comprehensive weather data began at first settlement, which is a very shaky (perhaps patently absurd) assumption at best. They didn't even have fully accurate maps of the colony at that time.

You must also consider the fact that any biggest flooding events in the first 500 years may or may not be representative of 500-year floods in prior 500-year periods. The word "average" means the average of all floods over a statistically reliable number of 500-year historic periods (whatever that may be). Even if you have reliably accurate data and maps for one 500-year period, how can you even argue it is representative of the floods that may have occurred in prior 500-year periods—much less those that will occur in future 500-year periods? The fact of the matter is that, even after we have kept 500-years' worth of flooding records, we have no basis to say that the biggest flood that occurred during that period is representative of any other "average 500-year flood."

That obvious point I'm making is one of the important baseline theoretical quandaries that we face when we discuss all climactic data. It also explains quite clearly why I would question the assumptions made for our climate models—not for political reasons, but in the name of proper scientific quality control assurance. What truly, unbiased, professional scientist would claim that such basic, rational reasoning does not entitle me to objective critical inquiry? Besides, if the science is truly justifiable, there should be no threat of consenting to it. After all, such critical analysis would only serve to further validate the model's (as well as the scientist's) scientific integrity, wouldn't it? I find it ironic that we understand the concept of "Garbage In, Garbage Out (GIGO)" when it applies to computers that impose no operative bias of their own, but we are told to implicitly trust the objectivity of the people who program them. Alas, there is no law that prohibits any scientist from being intentionally or unintentionally influenced by his or her own personal political beliefs or biases.

There's no doubt that the flooding we experienced in Pendleton County over the past month will be remembered for decades to come. It will become one of the stories that define what it means to be a grandparent. However, it also should remind us of the indominable power and elegant complexity of nature. Hopefully, we don't need too many more experiences like this to learn that.

Post 78: Practicing Hydroponics

June 13, 2018

...And the rain continues. As I write this post, we have received 5.93 inches of rain this month, with more expected early this afternoon. According to the 30-year average for nearby Upper Tract, we would expect 3.21 inches of rain for the entire month. We are not yet half way through June. Since the beginning of April, we have received 21.99 inches of rainfall here at Peeper Pond Farm. At this rate, we could go without rain for about three months and still achieve our yearly average rainfall.

We decided to make use of a cool and cloudy morning before the next storm to weed our garden. I used the rototiller to dig up the grass and weeds sprouting in our garden paths, while Barb (with some help from Calli and her bathroom impulses) dug out the weeds growing in our planting rows. The soil in the garden is so saturated that you can literally pull the weeds out of the ground with little effort and without breaking off the roots. It seems as though we are practicing hydroponics this year instead of traditional gardening. Fortunately, the drainage ditches I dug around three sides of our garden have been successful in reducing the amount of erosion and ponding that occurs in our planting area. Consequently, our garden looks to be very robust for the weather conditions it has persevered.

Our early corn should be knee high by the fourth of July. Our broccoli is mature, and we have been harvesting large heads from the plants. Some of our tomatoes and peepers have flowered and should begin producing soon. We are somewhat concerned about our peas. The remnants of Tropical Storm Alberto dragged some tropical weather with it, and the peas appear to be suffering from too much early heat, even though they were planted a little late.

Despite the excessive rain, we have kept busy. On Friday, June 1, a reporter, Marina Barnett, from WHSV-TV in Harrisonburg visited our farm to film a news segment on our attempted dairy goat operation and my ongoing efforts to change the law in West Virginia to permit unprocessed milk sales from farms. A portion of the segment was filmed on Dale and Merrily Carroll's farm about three miles south of us. In total, they shot about one and a half hours of footage, which are being edited down for the final broadcast. The final segment is scheduled to be broadcast as part of the 10:00 and 11:00 PM news on Tuesday, June 19. You can watch it live (as it airs) on the station's website (www.whsv.com), or you can view it in the following days as a news clip posted on the home page. I hope you get a chance to see it. You will see clips of our farm and our former doe, Essie, who now lives at the Carroll's farm. If you can't watch it, then please come and visit us at the Petersburg Farmer's Market during the anticipated grand opening sometime later in this month.

Post 79: Sinks of Gandy

June 20, 2018

First of all, I want to wish West Virginia a happy 155th birthday. Today is West Virginia Day in our state; a holiday we celebrate to commemorate the founding of West Virginia as the 35th state on June 20, 1863. You will hear it said that, when our state was born, it became the first state to be created from the boundaries of another, but that is an over-generalization—one of many I have tried to correct or clarify through my website posts. Actually, the states of Kentucky and Maine became the first and second states carved from the boundaries of another in 1792 and 1820, respectively. West Virginia simply became the first state carved out of another as a consequence of war (the Civil War, specifically). You see, Virginia had already seceded from the Union when West Virginia was formed, so technically speaking, we became a U.S. State carved from the bowels of a rebelling Confederate State.

Second, I have to correct an announcement I made in my previous post regarding the official broadcast date for the dairy farming news segment filmed at our farm on June 1 by WHSV-TV in Harrisonburg, VA. In my last post I said it would air on Tuesday, June 19. At the time I said that, it was correct. However, I received an e-mail yesterday afternoon from Marina Barnett, the reporter who is producing the segment, informing me that the broadcast date had to be postponed until the 10:00 and 11:00 PM news broadcasts on Tuesday, June 26. If you tried to view it last night and was disappointed to miss it, I apologize. It appears the segment required more time to edit than they anticipated. I am not surprised, as they filmed more than an hour's worth of interviews, plus some additional footage, that must be edited down to a three or so minute story. I knew that would be a difficult task, as I once served as a producer (and Board member) for the community access cable television station in Middlebury, VT nearly 30 years ago and struggled with my own editing decisions. I am eager to see the final news segment, and I hope you will "tune in" to view it live on the station's website, www.whsv.com. It should contain video of our first doe kid, Esmeralda (our Essie), who now lives at the Carroll's Nigerian Dwarf goat farm at the entrance to Smoke Hole Canyon. Now that I have taken care of immediate business, I wish to tell you about another of our local natural wonders, the Sinks of Gandy.

Our son, Michael, recently expressed an interest in touring a noncommercial cave with a small group of his friends. There are many such caves in our area, but the most renowned of them all is the Sinks of Gandy located high in easternmost Randolph County, close to the Pendleton County line. Although the main cave passage is only about 3,000 feet long, it is very unique in that it was carved through the slopes of a mountain knob by Gandy Creek. Gandy Creek, which begins on nearby Cunningham Knob and flows west towards Yokum Knob, which has a slightly lower summit elevation. Instead of winding around the summit of Yokum Knob, it carved a passage through it and emerges on the other side before wending its way along the eastern boundary of Randolph County. Although the cave is located within the purchase boundary of the Monongahela National Forest, it is located entirely on privately-owned lands. The upstream entrance is located on land owned by the Teter family, in whose trust it has been held since the earliest days of European settlement in that area. Therefore, sensitive respect for the property owners must be observed when visiting the cave, but they have generously allowed access to the Sinks for more than 150 years. I had toured the cave some six or seven years ago with a local group of cavers I know, so I knew it was a relatively easy cave to negotiate for first-time cavers.

However, when I say that, I am *not* encouraging inexperienced cavers to try it recklessly. ANY cave, regardless of the apparent ease or simplicity of it, poses life-threatening hazards and dangers, and should not be attempted without an experienced guide or prior training from an experienced guide and appropriate equipment. In the case of the Sinks of Gandy, the passage is a creek channel, so water levels in the cave as well as the strength and temperature of the current are important factors to anticipate. As it turned out (and as I had forewarned), these factors were *not* in our favor when I took Michael and his friends to see it this past Friday (June 15).

The cave has large, open entrances that make it very impressive to approach from either direction. The upstream side of the cave has one single entrance that serves as the iconic image of the cave. The first published illustration of the Sinks by West Virginia native David Hunter Strother (Porte Crayon), which appeared in Harper's Magazine in the 1870s, depicted this entrance. Although the landscape surrounding the cavern has changed significantly over the years, the rock entranceway has not and remains immediately recognizable. The downstream exit of the cave consists of both a dry and wet exit (along the creek). Because the dry exit is located above and away from the wet creek exit, it can be difficult for inexperienced visitors to find. Having toured the cave before, I could remember where to find it. While the natural condition of the cave has been undoubtedly impacted over the years by the many people who have toured it, I know of no "improvements" that have been made inside it. This makes it a good natural environment for aspiring cavers to explore.

The passage is quite large, especially at the upstream entrance, so it is easy to follow. Cavers must negotiate the creek several times, regardless of the water level, to traverse it. On the day we visited it, the water levels in the creek were so high, there was no dry land at the entrance. The depth, cold temperature and strong current of the water quickly ended any innocent interest my son and his friends had in touring the full length of the cave. Instead, they spent an hour or more studying the cavernous entrance and the cave environment. We noticed that a number of swallows had built nests in the cave, and they soared defensively about the entrance as we approached. (We have had to defend the front porch of our house against nesting swallows by placing rubber snakes along the railing and trim. This trick has encouraged them to seek alternate nesting sites.)

The kids (kids to me, but "young adults" by their own definition) also noticed scores of spiders along the roof and walls of the entrance, as well as crayfish in the creek bed. Mineral deposits in the cavern roof shimmered in the light of their headlamps and salamanders scampered along the rocks at the base of the walls. Although the air temperature outside the entrance was in the 80s, every breath we expelled hung in the dank cave air before our eyes as a thick mist. The water temperature probably hovered somewhere between 55 and 60 degrees, cold enough at the depth that day to pose a significant risk of hypothermia. I knew from my past visit that the main passage narrows near the middle of the cave and that the water level at that point might be above my head. Although it was too dangerous to attempt a tour of the cavern, they found plenty of features in the entranceway to satisfy their interest in visiting the cave. No one was disappointed because we decided to abandon our tour.

The Sinks of Gandy is another iconic and wonderous natural treasure of our Potomac Highlands region of West Virginia. It is a fabled natural curiosity that is tied to local folklore by many tales and stories. History records that Union forces chased a Confederate troop into the cave during the Civil War. Other stories of intrigue and mystery, too numerous to give proper attention in this post, enrich its heritage. If you wish to truly understand West Virginia and her impressively distinctive and colorful heritage, a visit to the Sinks of Gandy must be part of your bucket list.

Post 80: WHSV Tells Our Story

June 28, 2018

To begin, I need to give you a brief update on our ongoing rainfall saga. According to the official weather forecast this morning, we are not expected to receive any additional rainfall for the month. Based on that assumption (which, with two more days to go, is shaky at best) I can give you our rainfall total for June. As of the writing of this post (AM, June 28), we have received 9.72 inches, which is a hair over three times the 30-year average at nearby Upper Tract of 3.21 inches. As you may recall from my recent posts, we received just over triple the average rainfall in May with a total of 11.42 inches and slightly under double the April average with a total of 4.61 inches. That gives us a cumulative three-month rainfall total of 25.75 inches. This figure represents 73 percent of the 30-year average *annual* rainfall total for Upper Tract of 35.33 inches (ignoring the other nine months of the year). At this point, I would hazard a guess that we won't end up with a dry year here at Peeper Pond Farm. I hope West Virginia's monsoon season will be ending soon.

I also mentioned in a previous post that WHSV-TV, Channel 3 in Harrisonburg, VA, visited our farm on June 1 to film a news segment on our efforts to reform West Virginia's remaining legal restrictions on unprocessed milk sales from the farm to informed consumers. I began my work on this effort in September 2017 after we had to sell our dairy goat herd in early August because the current law would not give us the authority we needed to sell the milk, cheese, butter and other consumable dairy products we were producing, and we couldn't afford the ongoing feed and operating costs of our operation on our retirement income. During their visit to our farm and the Carroll farm, where our first doe goat, Essie, now lives, they filmed at least 1.5 hours of footage that was eventually edited down to a three-plus minute news segment. The final version aired during the 10:00 and 11:00 PM newscasts on Tuesday, June 26.

The story has received positive reviews from all of our supporters who have seen it, but I'd like to explain some of the details of my position that could not be captured in the WHSV story. They have time and information constraints that my website postings do not. I hope you will take the time to read and think about what I have to say.

I was especially pleased to see the clips of our Essie, who we had hoped to make the foundation of our future dairy goat herd. While we hope that we may be able to bring her back to our farm, someday, I know I first need to change the current law restricting farm-fresh milk sales to herd share agreements. The herd shares bill, which was signed into law in 2016, allowed dairy farmers to sell a "share" of their animal herd to willing milk consumers so they could take a portion of the milk produced. We considered this option but decided that it wouldn't work for our very small operation for at least two important reasons. First of all, anyone paying a farmer to invest in a portion of the dairy herd would certainly desire a regular and reliable volume of milk. Why would someone pay to own a portion of a dairy animal if they still had to pay for milk at the store because it isn't enough to satisfy their needs? Our operation, as with most homestead dairy goat farms, produced too little milk to fully satisfy the needs of multiple families. We were milking only two of our six goats and produced only about 1.5 – 2 gallons of milk daily. I was drinking roughly half a gallon of milk daily and we were processing much of the remaining excess into cheese, butter, ice cream, yogurt and goat soap. While we would end up with an extra half gallon or gallon to sell periodically, the excess was not reliable enough to be marketable to other customers, and the law did not embrace direct sales of the unprocessed milk products we were producing.

Our second concern was the lack of clarity in the bill's language regarding what level of "ownership" was granted by a herd share. Although I recognize that a herd share agreement could spell that out, the more complex the agreement has to be to address those and other legal issues, the less attractive they may become to potential customers—especially for small volumes of milk. Many of the customers that would be interested in buying our milk come from nearby major cities and their suburbs, including Washington and Baltimore. These customers desire what they consider to be the most pure and organic natural foods, and I can envision many of them wanting to control what we feed our goats and what vaccinations and treatments we use to keep them healthy. We didn't want to give the implication that we could provide that level of "ownership" to our customers, and we didn't want any claims for "compensation" when we had to sell or put down one of our goats—as we had to do with Gertie because she had contracted a terminal case of meningeal worm. There are many legal issues to consider when contracting to share the ownership of a goat herd that we felt were too complex for a such a small operation and volume of salable milk.

Ironically, the group that promoted and gained passage of the herd shares bill had originally lobbied for direct farm-to-consumer sales of unprocessed milk, which is what I am now seeking to expand milk sale options for the smallest dairy operations. However, they faced a strong, entrenched political lobby that opposed open sales because of "health concerns" that unpasteurized milk represents a grave public health threat. The battle over the issue lasted seven years, and the group had to settle for passage of the current herd shares bill. Since that option doesn't work well for all dairy operations (especially the smallest) it doesn't make it as easy for small start-up operations (like ours) to step in and fill the void that has resulted from fifty or more years of small dairy farm failures throughout West Virginia.

As I documented in my March 23, 2018 website post entitled *Udder Disappointment*, the last commercial family dairy farm in the tri-county region of Grant, Hardy and Pendleton Counties was put out of business in December 2017 because the farm's milk hauler decided it was no longer economically beneficial to transport their milk for processing. Yet, I can still drive around the South Branch valley and see the deteriorating remains of more than fifty dairy barns that once housed small herds of milking cows. West Virginia's rugged, mountain topography does not provide the large tracts of level land needed to support the huge, mechanized and technologically advanced dairy operations that produce a growing share of our nation's milk production. According to a 2016 USDA Report, Changing Structure, Financial Risks and Government Policy for the U.S. Dairy Industry (Economic Research Report 205), which documents this dramatic trend, the median herd size of dairy farms nationally has increased from 80 cows in 1987 (two years after the whole herd buyout program was initiated) to 570 in 1997 and 900 in 2012. The largest single dairy farm documented in the report (located in Oregon) milks 32,000 cows on 39,000 acres. Clearly, the land in West Virginia is not capable of supporting such large operations, and virtually none of the small herd (50 or fewer cows) operations that once dotted our landscape could compete. Virtually all of them have since failed. All that remains are the remnant, dilapidated dairy barns that still stand.

Yet changing times and a growing trend of families seeking farm-fresh foods have created a new market that the small, family owned and operated farms that once proliferated in West Virginia could serve—if only they could sell their unprocessed milk and milk products directly to informed consumers, rather than being forced to sell their milk to a processing industry that is only interested in buying high volumes of less expensive, industrial-scale raw milk. Pennsylvania farmers are already taking advantage of this new sales opportunity. This is why I began working on legislation to open unprocessed (raw) milk sales from the farm. To promote opportunities for new small start-up dairy farms to exploit that emerging market in West Virginia.

Our opposition is an army of health officials, special interest groups and elected officials who fear that unprocessed milk sales will unleash a Pandora's box of pathogens and "superbugs" on an unsuspecting public. They regard farm-fresh milk to be an "elixir of death" that may represent the greatest health threat of the food industry, despite the fact that I and many other people who were raised exclusively on farm-fresh, unprocessed milk survive today to tell you that this potential threat is grossly over-exaggerated. Can I guarantee that unprocessed (raw) milk sales will not cause illnesses? No, I can't, and I never will. However, no public health official can ever guarantee you that there will be no pathogens or public health illnesses caused by the consumption of *any* food product, even if it has been certified or inspected by the USDA. The daily news routinely documents food recalls, illnesses and deaths from processed food products that consumers expect to be safe. You don't have to consume my unprocessed milk to become deathly ill. Simply go to your local hospital—considered by many to be the most sanitary environment that people regularly encounter—and you may become one of the growing number of patients who contract deadly super-staph infections or flesh-eating bacteria. These are deadly pathogens that the same people don't encounter in their own homes.

I argue that the fear of so-called "superbugs" and pathogens that these officials are spreading is grossly excessive to the actual threat. Although these deadly germs and bacteria do exist, they are not typically found in the milk of dairy animals. Sure, many of their less-deadly precursors, such as e-coli, listeria, salmonella and other potentially "bad" bacteria, can be found naturally in milk at low levels that are not immediately dangerous. Some of these and other bacteria that can cause illnesses already exist in our bodies. These bacteria occur naturally and, at the low levels that they occur in impurity-free fresh milk, help strengthen our natural immune systems at an early age.

All mammals have natural immunity systems that help protect us from the germs and bacteria we routinely encounter in the course of our daily lives. They produce the antibodies that help kill the invading germs, diseases and bacteria that cause illnesses and death. Those individuals with the strongest immune systems are among the healthiest people in society. If your immune system is underdeveloped or weakened by disease, your threat of illness is greatly enhanced. Most people understand this, as it is common knowledge. Health officials insist that milk be pasteurized (heated to a specific temperature over a specific length of time) prior to consumption to kill any bad pathogens that may be in the milk. I agree that it does make the milk safer to consume. However, in making their argument against the sale of unpasteurized milk, the same public officials conveniently fail to acknowledge a number of other facts.

First of all, pasteurization is an indiscriminate killer. It not only kills the potentially bad bacteria; it also kills the potentially good bacteria that exists naturally in milk that can help build stronger bodies. In fact, even the presence of bad bacteria in milk can help strengthen human immune systems to reduce the threat of future illnesses. By preventing gentle exposure of our immune systems to these bad pathogens, we are shielding them from the low-level exposure they need to build the antibodies that make us stronger. This is why milk is the first and most basic food consumed by all mammals, from the smallest shrew to the biggest elephant or whale. It contains all the essential nutrients, proteins, vitamins and other elements that our bodies need for healthy growth. Many of the diseases we face today from weakened immune systems could be caused by our efforts to avoid natural childhood exposure to common bad pathogens and bacteria. Our growing fear of exposure to bad germs and bacteria are causing people to over-use antibiotic and antiseptic treatments to the point that we damage our flesh (from over-use of hand sanitizers) and cause the pathogens to eventually become resistant to treatment.

As I said, the most dangerous superbugs that public officials fear most, do not occur naturally in dairy animals. They actually emerge from our efforts to kill their less deadly ancestors. The second fact public health officials do not freely acknowledge is that our efforts to create stronger and stronger antibiotics to kill the most basic and common germs and bacteria cause them to mutate quickly into stronger and more deadly germs and bacteria. These pathogens are very simple organisms that have no immune systems, as do more complex creatures like humans. Their defense mechanism to ensure their survival against the things that threaten them is their very short lifespans and rapid reproduction rates. Virtually all of them create multiple generations of themselves in a single day. With that rate of reproduction, they are capable of mutating into stronger (and inherently more deadly or immune to treatment) forms at a much faster rate than we can develop new and stronger antibiotics to kill them. Therefore, it is the overuse of antibiotic treatments and vaccinations, as well as excessive use of sanitizing agents to clean food processing equipment, that can cause superbugs to get into the foods we produce and eat—including milk. That's why public health officials are now warning people not to overuse antibiotics and sanitizers. Unfortunately, they don't reveal to the public why they now issue those warnings.

As I learned how these deadly superbugs have emerged, I decided to call the process, "inverse engineering." You won't find that term in the dictionary (I looked it up to make sure), because I made it up. What I mean by it is that all of our determined efforts to develop drugs to kill bacteria that could cause human illness only results in making the bacteria mutate into more drug resistant and deadlier forms. We are not intending to make them stronger, but we are getting the "inverse result" because of their fundamental nature. As a result, our efforts to impose increasingly stricter sanitization in milk production, handling and processing can have the potentially inverse effect of increasing the public health threat from the end product. The same can, under the right circumstances, be true of some preventative treatments and vaccinations given to dairy animals. This effect should be studied more carefully and specifically by health officials before they conclude that unprocessed milk represents an elixir of death, although I won't hold my breath in anticipation that they will.

As a society, we essentially have two choices. We can either continue to feed our current frenzied germophobic fears by desperately working to create stronger and stronger antibiotics and drugs to kill off deadly superbugs before they can kill us, or we can find ways to strengthen our immune systems to protect us from the less deadly pathogens recognizing that a small number of us could become ill or die, but that we may avoid a future superbug apocalypse. My opponents choose the former course. I endorse and try to practice the latter. If you wish to have a choice, I encourage you to think about it carefully and quickly, before the CDC, local health officials and the pharmaceutical companies make the choice for us.

The legislation I am working to write would require farmers to follow specific best milking and milk handling procedures designed to minimize airborne contamination of raw milk from the time it is taken from the dairy animal to the time it is sold to the consumer. Regardless of the specific threat posed by any potential contaminant or pathogen, the steps I am working to prescribe represent the most any dairy farmer can do to minimize contamination of the milk and preserve its natural state. I also hope to avoid requirements that would promote excessive use of antibiotics and antiseptic treatments that would escalate mutation of common pathogens into the superbugs that health officials fear. This is how I hope to ensure that unprocessed milk is as safe as it can be for me and my potential consumers to drink.

I recognize that milk can pose a threat of illness to consumers regardless of how sanitary the production process may be. Any consumer can cause milk to become contaminated by letting it sit unrefrigerated after purchase (thereby providing an environment for pathogens to grow) or through direct contamination resulting from careless use. These risks can be greater for unpasteurized milk, which is why it has a shorter shelf life and must be maintained in a storage environment that maintains a constant temperature range. That's why we need to inform consumers of how to keep and use unprocessed milk. My proposed legislation includes requirements for farmers to provide written consumer milk handling and use guidelines to ensure that the customer is informed when purchasing unprocessed milk and to offer tours of his/her dairy operation to all prospective customers, so they can learn how the farmer is complying with all required best milking and milk handling procedures.

If I am successful in writing rules that farmers can satisfy and that will address the most serious public health and contamination issues, I see no reason why unprocessed milk would not be safe and healthy to sell and consume. Unfortunately, I have no assurance that the health officials and their advocates will be reasonable in debating these issues. That is simply the nature and state of politics today. Once you join a political party, it seems that you must suspend your critical thinking skills and simply "believe" whatever the party platform says you should—regardless of whether or not is it inherently defensible or thoroughly tested and considered. I do not accept that way of thinking. I am comfortable remaining, perhaps, one of the last free thinkers. I hope that my explanation of the issues covered briefly in the WHSV news segment will cause you to think more critically about these issues, and that you will want to help me preserve and promote a cherished traditional lifestyle choice that is rapidly becoming extinct, but that is a part of everyone's shared heritage. The health and survival of your descendants may ultimately depend upon it. If you do decide that my position on these issues has merit, I hope you will support my ongoing efforts. As always and either way, I appreciate your thoughtful consideration.

Post 81: Reaping Wheat – A Shocking Experience

July 6, 2018

This post is the first in a series discussing our adventures helping Jeff & Amanda Barger harvest and process an experimental plot of wheat into flour the traditional way—using traditional hand tools and equipment. This process requires a number of separate steps completed over a long period of time. The next segment in the series is Post 84: Bringing in the Sheaves.

I well remember the first time I used a scythe. It was nearly 45 years ago when I was a young child growing up on our family dairy farm in North Charlestown, NH. I can't tell you the date, but it occurred during our summer school vacation, which was a misnomer to any kid raised on a farm. Back then, a vacation from school was just an excuse to do more farm work.

I came to the breakfast table that morning and found my father sitting there waiting for me. As I sat down, he simply said, "I need you to help me with the haying today." Apparently, that was all I needed to know. My father was a man of very few words. At first, I let my mind fill in the details of his request. I became excited because I thought he was finally going to let me drive the tractor to mow some hay. That was what he had been doing the previous day, but he had never trusted me to mow with our side bar mower, which was a rather persnickety mechanical device that was powered by its own wheels, rather than the tractor that pulled it, and it was so old that it broke down frequently. My father felt I wasn't skilled enough to operate it without accidentally damaging it. Perhaps he was now ready to trust me with it. However, as with most times when I tried to read the hidden meaning between his words, I was wrong.

After finishing my breakfast, I learned that our mower broke down more seriously than before, and he had to order a lot of cutting teeth to repair it. It would be out of service for weeks, and we had only a brief window of time to finish mowing, raking and baling the rest of our hay crop before the next big rain. Weather in our area, as it is throughout the eastern U.S., changes frequently and often challenges your ability to finish outdoor work when it needs to be done. My father was trying to finish mowing our first cutting that day, and we had only one small three-acre field left to mow before we had to begin raking the next day. As I quietly followed him out the door of the house, he led me to the corn shed, where he produced an antique scythe that my grandfather had given him within the past year. He handed it to me and instructed me to sharpen it because I was being sent to the lower meadow to mow the last hay field with it.

    Before passing it on to us, my grandfather had demonstrated how to sharpen the blade and use it properly. I remembered his instructions on how to use a whetstone bar to sharpen the cutting edge of the long, curved blade using my wrist to make short scraping strokes down the length of the blade along both sides. "Make sure you work the stone with your wrist, not your arm," he instructed, "it's all in the wrist." Once sharpened, he demonstrated the mowing technique, teaching us to hold it low and level to the ground with our arms and swing it with our shoulders. "Never swing it with your arms, twist it into the grass you're mowing with your upper body." I replayed those instructions in my mind as I prepared to mow the field, because my father was never one to explain how he wanted me to do my work. He would only tell me to do it over, if I had failed to do it to his liking.

    I spent that entire day mowing the small hayfield, breaking only for lunch or to resharpen the blade. Mowing with a scythe didn't appear very difficult when my grandfather first demonstrated how to do it, but I found it much more difficult than I thought. I spent most of my first hour struggling with my cutting stance and technique. I quickly learned I was trying to mow too much grass on each stroke, which made it much harder to swing the scythe and complete my cut. However, as I exercised my vocabulary and adjusted my technique, I managed to make some clean strokes that "felt right" and realized I needed to swing the blade so that it sliced the grass along the length of the blade, rather than trying to hack it down like you would with a machete. I understood why my grandfather told me to swing with your upper body, as it helped me keep the blade level with the ground throughout each stroke, resulting in a clean and level cut. It took time, but I eventually learned to step into each cutting stroke I made with it as though it were a dance partner.

    Although I was *instructed* how to use the scythe before I began mowing, I realized it was something you had to practice until you got the "feel" of it. Using the old antique hand tools to do heavy work is more of an art than a science. The tool becomes an extension of your body and the work you do with it is as much artwork as is a sculpture. It requires skill and experience as you apply your mind to the physical task. Perhaps that's one reason why old-time craftsmen treasured their hand tools and maintained them so carefully. They were as delicate and important as an artist's paintbrush, and the work he did with them said as much about the artist's skill as a fine painting. Working with hand tools in those times was a craft, not a job.

The lessons I learned using a scythe that day so many years ago flashed through my mind the day that Jeff Barger asked me if I would be interested in helping him and his wife, Amanda, harvest and process an experimental plot of wheat they had planted at the edge of one of their fields using nothing but traditional tools and methods. I had never worked with wheat before, because none of the farmers I knew during my childhood grew any grain crops, such as wheat, buckwheat, rye, or barley. Since I now owned my own scythe, which I used occasionally to mow the grass and weeds in the small orchard we had planted more than six years before we finally retired, I felt I was well prepared for the task. This job sounded to me like an exciting new experience and challenge in traditional farming, so I eagerly accepted.

Barb and I had first met Jeff during one of our many visits to Central Tie and Lumber in Petersburg (where he works part-time) to buy materials to build our Peeper Pond Farm retirement house. I have told many people we bought our house from Central Tie one stick at a time. Some assembly was required. Apparently, during our brief informal encounters at the store, Jeff learned something about us and our plans that captured his interest. We were making one such trip to the store in January 2017 when he suddenly invited us to attend an old-fashioned pot-luck supper and bluegrass sing-a-long at his home the following month. We accepted, and at the event, we met his wife, Amanda, her parents, Bonnie and Wayne Ours, and a number of their local friends. Our efforts to start a dairy goat operation at our retirement farm was of great interest to Bonnie, who also grew up on a dairy farm and had raised goats. Over time and many subsequent visits, a close friendship blossomed founded largely upon our shared interests in farming and traditional folkways. Their desire to undertake this experiment was another exciting extension of those shared interests.

We arrived at Jeff and Amanda's farm on North Mill Creek Road in Grant County early yesterday morning (July 5). The air was heavy with humidity, which would build into oppressive summer heat by the afternoon, so an early start was essential for the work we had to do. The heat was already becoming quite intense by the time the morning dew had evaporated, which had to occur before we began reaping (mowing) the mature wheat. Although I brought my scythe as a back-up tool, we began cutting the wheat with Jeff's antique four-fingered cradle, which is essentially a scythe equipped with four wooden prongs above the blade (one of which had previously broken) that gently catches the wheat stems as they are cut to minimize the loss of grain from the stems by the mowing process. We sharpened the cradle blade with my whetstone and went to work reaping the wheat. I found the cradle to be more challenging to use than my scythe because the handle was short and lacked the ergonomic curvature that later models had to allow the reaper to stand more erect while mowing. As I began using it, I had to bend over closer to the ground with each swing than I was accustomed to make level cuts. Even so, my cuts were not very consistent, but I did the best I could. Unfortunately, the cradle was so old that the stress of active use eventually made the fingers loosen and fall apart, so we had to abandon it and finish our work using my scythe. I could make better cuts with it, but it wasn't the best implement to use for reaping wheat. I could not cut the stalks so that the heads would fall on the ground in the same direction, which the cradle was specifically designed to do. This made it harder for the rest of the crew to collect the cut wheat and bind them into sheaves.

    We had a work crew that included Barb and me, Jeff and Amanda, Wayne and Bonnie, and two of their close friends, Amy and Doug. While I was cutting the wheat, Barb, Amanda, Bonnie and Amy worked to collect the cut shafts into fist-sized bundles called sheaves. Jeff, Wayne and Doug bound each sheaf together and staked them into shocks for further drying. To build each shock, a number of sheaves were stood upright (erect) on the ground in a circle with the heads bearing the wheat grains leaning against one another at the top. Once the standing base of each stack was formed, a final sheaf was fanned into a flat disk and pressed into place on the top as a cap. This structure keeps the grain husks above the ground so they can be further dried by the breeze. We only managed to cut half of the wheat crop before the heat became too intense to finish the job. Unfortunately, I no longer have the stamina I had when I first mowed with a scythe due to my advancing age and declining physical condition, which I attribute to the deleterious effects of modern living and conveniences I have suffered from a 30-year professional career of office work. I often refer to my former office job as "butt work," because it was those muscles that I exercised most when doing it.

    Although we did not complete the reaping process, it is only the first step in producing wheat. The next step is to "flail" the wheat to separate the hulls containing the wheat grain from the shafts. This involves placing the sheaves on a tarp or sheet and beating them with a flail, which is a device constructed of two short shafts connected by a cord that most closely resembles nunchucks. Some people just stomp the sheaths like grapes to loosen the grains from the stocks.

    The third step is to winnow the wheat, which may involve tossing the flailed wheat into the air so that the breeze blows the chaff (husks that surround the wheat grains) and residue away while the heavier grains fall onto the tarp or sheet. Jeff plans to winnow the wheat using an antique, hand-cranked winnowing device he has acquired.

The fourth and final step is to grind the wheat grains into flour. Jeff has acquired a small, antique grain mill for that purpose. With any luck, we can process the wheat we reaped and shocked yesterday into a fine flour that can be used to bake a loaf of homemade bread. This explains the process by which bread, a staple food that everyone consumes today, is made.

For those people who lived two to three generations ago, this process was common knowledge. However, few people who are becoming adults today have an understanding of where the most basic foods they consume really come from. It is that understanding and knowledge that forms the foundation of our traditional, self-reliant lifestyle that we at Peeper Pond Farm cherish and hope to preserve for future generations. Who can say if or when our modern society (and the wealth-driven monetary economy that fuels it) will collapse leaving behind a society of people dependent on modern conveniences and failed technologies to relearn these basic skills for their very survival? This is the inherent, intrinsic value of our traditional lifestyle skills that all too many people (including my own adoptive parents) casually reject as outdated or regressive. I only hope that you will not be one of the people who may someday learn what a colossal mistake that attitude may create. It is for that reason that I work so determinedly to preserve and teach those traditional lifestyle skills and folkways. I hope you'll follow my later posts in this series to see if we can succeed in our efforts to turn a plot of wheat into a loaf of homemade bread. Thanks for *your* continued interest in our ongoing adventure.

Post 82: Farmer's market 2018 & Our Trash Bandit

July 8, 2018

Our garden is starting to produce abundant vegetables. It all started a few weeks ago when we were able to harvest our first peas, red cabbage and broccoli. It was only able to produce enough peas for a few meals because the hot weather kicked in early and, combined with the excessive rainfall, was too much for the plants to endure. However, we did take some broccoli, cabbage, some early yellow onions, and a few green (early) tomatoes and peppers to our first sale at the Grant County Farmer's Market in the Petersburg City Park parking lot on Saturday, June 30. We set up along with several other early producers on another hot and steamy day. Despite the heat, our sales were much better than we expected, and we sold all our vegetables except for one red cabbage.

We complemented our produce with some of our homemade goat soap and Barb's quilting products (lap quilts, table runners, pot holders, hot pads and mug mats). These are items that set us apart from some of our colleagues at the market. We also set up at the farmer's market on Saturday, July 7 with an expanded produce selection, which now includes bags of green and wax beans, cucumbers and banana peppers. The weather on July 7 was perfect with abundant sunshine, temperatures in the low 70s, very low humidity and a gentle breeze. It felt like a glorious spring day in early summer, which was a greatly appreciated gift after days of hot and humid mid-summer weather. The number of producers at the market increased significantly, but our sales were not as good. That's how it goes at a farmer's market. You just can't predict what combination of weather and produce selection will generate descent sales. We just hope our loyal readers will come and visit us at the farmer's market. We will be selling our wares most Saturdays from 8 AM to noon at the parking lot adjacent to the Petersburg City Park on South Main Street, just before the South Branch River Bridge.

As a side note, an interesting incident occurred in our garage when I was loading our farmer's market equipment and produce into the pick-up truck—which I affectionately refer to as our "flivver." I noticed that one of the garbage bags we temporarily store our rubbish in until our next trip to the transfer station had been chewed by some animal searching for food scraps. I had found a groundhog in our garage last summer, but I didn't feel that a vegetarian would be trying to chew its way into a garbage bag. My first thought was that it might be a field mouse, which can get rather large and wouldn't hesitate to feed on any refuse it could scavenge. I decided I needed to keep a close watch on it to see what was after our rubbish.

A couple of days later, I discovered that the hole in the trash bag was larger and some rubbish had been pulled out. The mystery grew as it appeared that a trash bandit had taken up residence in our garage, because the doors had been shut tight for nearly 24 hours. Then I caught a glimpse of some movement along the front wall of the garage, and I called to Barb, who was also in the garage with me. She said she thought she saw a young opossum scamper behind the storage cabinet in the milking area. I peeked into the space between the wall and the cabinet and even tried to coax it out with a pry bar, but I didn't see, hear, or feel anything.

I remembered back to the time we were living in Oxford, AL (1996-2004). We had a partially enclosed (on three sides) carport in which we parked our vehicles and stored our yard maintenance equipment. We used to leave some dry cat food and water in that carport for our two housecats when we would take a day trip away from the house, so that the cats would have something to eat and drink while we were gone. However, we often discovered that the cats were eating far more dry cat food when we left it outdoors than they would when we fed them in the house. One day, we returned home just after dark and pulled into the garage. There, in the glow of the headlights, was an opossum that had been feeding on the dry cat food. We knew that opossums can be rather viscous and will hiss at you and bite to defend themselves. If you're not properly equipped to deal with them, it's best to scare them away rather than try to touch or capture them. So, we just left him alone until he left and then stopped filling the cat dish for a while.

After a few more daytime visits to check on the cat food supply in the carport bowl, the opossum became so accustomed to seeing us that it didn't run away or hiss at us when we were present. It just ignored us and went about its business searching our home and carport for any dry cat food or spilled sunflower seeds beneath our front yard bird feeder. We eventually named him "Bandit" for his/her frequent raids and the dark bands around his/her eyes, and he became just another outdoor wild pet that made our home part of its daily feeding range. I thought again of Bandit after Barb said she thought the scavenger that had taken up residence in our garage was another opossum.

When I opened the garage door this morning, before we left for church, I noticed even more trash had been removed from the bag. However, this time, I saw something moving in the bottom of the bag. I touched it with my hand, and it moved some more. I had caught our trash bandit in the act. I put on some heavy work gloves and called Barb to the garage, as I slowly opened the outer garbage back and removed the inner bag containing the trash. Sure enough, when I removed the inner bag, the opossum fought its way out of the outer bag and dashed out the garage door before I could capture it and hid under the wooden step adjacent to the barnyard porch.

We brought Calli outdoors to keep it occupied and trapped under the porch step. She made sure to keep her distance, but she managed to captivate its attention. After sealing off the porch to make sure it couldn't hide there, I took out our animal trap and set it up on one side of the step, while I coaxed it out with a pry bar from the opposite side of the step. Luckily the opossum dashed into the trap, while I triggered the back door of the cage to drop. We had safely trapped the rascal! I carried it to the far end of our meadow and released it along the run. The opossum raced along the bank and disappeared into the woods. Now that it is on the opposite side of the stream from our house, I hope it will find more a more convenient and less risky food source than the household rubbish stored in our garage.

This incident also helped explain two recent injuries Calli had received, both of which required a visit to the local vet. In early June, she had been bitten at the base of her tail, as though she had been in a struggle with some unknown animal. About three weeks later, we discovered she had a laceration on the pad of her left front paw, which suggested she had tried to swat something that ended up cutting her. After I relocated bandit and let Calli outdoors again, I noticed she went directly into the garage to look around. That caught my attention, because I knew she was looking for that opossum, but she didn't know we had chased it out of the garage. After a brief survey of the garage, she came out and continued her search around the back side of the building and on towards the ravine. She was obviously searching for the opossum and knew where it could be found. That was all the evidence I needed to conclude that she had been hunting for the opossum, which had bitten her twice previously.

Hopefully, this incident will be all the evidence you need to learn two important rural living lessons regarding wildlife. First, never leave household trash lying around where wildlife can get to it. If you have to store it as we do (because we have to make a special trip to deliver it to the transfer station), make sure that you rinse off any food containers and seal any food scraps in a zip-lock bag. We had not done that enough times. The second lesson is to take great care in dealing with wild animals, regardless of how innocent or cute they may appear. Even the cutest little animal knows how to defend itself and does not understand any words of endearment you may use to make it feel safe in your presence. To them, you are merely another predator that it must guard against—especially if it feels threatened by you or is protecting its young. Rabies is one of the most common rural killers, even if the threatened animal is not. Such are the hard lessons that the cold realities of rural life teach us, whether you choose to live in the country or not. Never make the mistake of thinking that we are so intellectually superior to the wildlife around us that we don't have to respect it. Sooner or later, you may end up paying for the cost of your own intellectual ignorance or arrogance. That's just another piece of advice we have learned and continue to learn from our life at Peeper Pond Farm.

Post 83: Coalwood

July 11, 2018

Barb and I took our first full day-trip of the summer on Monday, July 9 down to the Southern Coalfields on what was, for me, a pilgrimage to the mining town of Coalwood, WV. This former company town was the boyhood home of the native author and NASA employee, Homer Hickam, Jr., during the 1940s and 1950s. Homer wrote a trilogy of books about his former home that I have avidly read.

Although we had very different childhood upbringings—Homer was the son of a highly respected Olga Mine Superintendent, while I grew up on our family dairy farm in New Hampshire—I discovered in the pages of his books that we shared a lot in common. We both were raised in the mountains by fathers totally dedicated to their respective lines work. They were both philosophically conservative men of few words who rarely offered encouragement and displayed little respect for their children's different interests. Both of us were affected by the emerging space age advances of the mid-to-late 1900's. Homer became the founding father of Coalwood's "Rocket Boys," as documented in the 1999 movie, *October Sky*, and was inspired to build and test experimental rockets by the 1957 launch of the Soviet Sputnik satellite.

I, on the other hand, inspired with awe by the 1969 Apollo moon landings, spent many cool summer nights laying on a bank (after walking our cows up to their holding pen from the evening milking) watching streaking meteors, the stars, the moon, and occasionally, the subtle, wispy glow of the northern lights. My father taught me what caused the phases of the moon using a pair of burned-out barn light bulbs to represent the changing positions (and resulting shadow effects) of the earth and moon in the glow of a working light bulb representing the sun. A few years later I had a friend, Dubber Dobbs—a true science fiction fanatic—who built a "fort" with me in a portion of our abandoned chicken house and launched a model rocket he had made from our driveway. I certainly was more of a social outcast than Homer was during my later school years, due in large part to my awkwardness and fear of social situations from isolation on the farm. However, what really captured my fascination in his books was how Homer described his feelings about his strained relationship with his father and how he struggled to understand them. I went through the same curious soul-searching process during my own childhood, and I could immediately relate to his soul-searching questions and thoughts about it as described in his books. Upon reading his childhood accounts, I began to feel that we were almost twin sons from different backgrounds raised two full decades apart in different states. That, in addition to seeing firsthand the coalfields of southern West Virginia that form the core stereotypical impressions outsiders have of our state, is why I felt so compelled to visit his childhood home.

As we traveled into the southern coalfields south of the New River, I was very impressed by the changes in topography that unfolded. Both parts of the state, our Potomac Highlands and the southern coalfields region, are dominated by forested mountains. The mountains in Pendleton county are the highest in the state, reaching nearly 5,000 feet in elevation, separated by relatively narrow valleys. While the mountains of the southern coalfields are not as tall, ranging between 2,000 and 3,200 feet, they crowd in more tightly against the rivers, which makes them feel more confining, rugged and steep. The valleys in the southern region are far narrower than our valleys, leaving only enough room for a winding road, a railroad, and a few homes and businesses that cling to the base slopes of the hills and mountains. There are almost no farm fields to open the views and break up the dark forest expanse. Everywhere you travel, the viewscape is framed exclusively by the closest hills and mountains, and you are unable to see anything beyond them. In our area, the occasional valley farms, fields and meadows open the landscape and provide vistas up and down the length of the valleys and to the higher mountains beyond the immediate defining ridgelines.

We saw the scarred evidence of only one surface mine (in Wyoming County) over the 100 miles we traveled through the coalfields. It emerged gradually as we drove along the incomplete Southern Coalfields Expressway from Beckley. The steep, dull, terraced bedrock slopes littered with rubble stood out starkly against the green-carpeted mountains that framed it. Many of the towns and villages through which we passed seemed largely abandoned and worn with boarded-up businesses and storefronts. Clearly, our Potomac Highlands Region and its towns are far more economically stable and vibrant than the remnant communities of the southern coalfields. However, we discovered that more of the homes we passed were surprisingly better maintained and tidy than we were led to expect. Obviously, many of the people who linger behind care about the appearance of their homes and property.

After passing through Welch and over Welch Mountain we arrived in Coalwood and stopped at the country store directly across the street from Homer's boyhood home during the time of the Rocket Boys. His earliest childhood years were lived in a different house. An enclosed back porch had been recently added (within the past decade) to the house and the original fence (a portion of which he blew up with his first experimental rocket), had long been replaced. The mine tipple and superintendent's office where his father worked had been removed many years ago. We stopped at the store briefly, then turned northwest to Coalwood Main, the former town center of the mining community. There we parked on the former sites of the company Club House and Post Office and took pictures of the adjacent Community Church. Across the main street from our parking location were the deteriorating remains of the Olga Mine Office framed to the rear by the brick and glass machine shops (where many of Homer's rockets were manufactured) and to the right by the Tudor-style company apartments mentioned in his books. A park now marks the site where the Coalwood Big Store once stood. That park houses a model of a space shuttle, representing the program that later employed Homer to train the shuttle pilots that repaired the Hubble Space Telescope.

We drove on to find the Mudhole Church (with its distinctive round window and listing steeple) and Cape Coalwood, the slack dump that the Rocket Boys used to launch most of their rockets. The former launch site has been restored to a natural state, which made it impossible for us to find the precise location. We traveled as far up the barely passable gravel road as we could to locate it and felt lucky to find a wide enough spot to turn around. We continued on to the City of War in an attempt to find the site of the former Big Creek High School (which Homer attended) but were unable to find it before we had to begin the return trip home.

It was a very pleasant day and excursion. The weather was warm and dry with low humidity, which made it very comfortable for driving. Although we found many of the sites mentioned prominently in his books, much of the town has changed and deteriorated. In that particular respect, it is much like the small village of North Charlestown, NH where I was raised (by an unavoidable accident of birth). What we were able to see made it easier for me to visualize in my mind the descriptions Homer wrote in his books of the former Coalwood community. In my own writings about my farm upbringing (Lifestyle Lost), I tried to do the same for my old hometown. From that standpoint, I was satisfied with our brief one-to-two-hour visit. I now look forward to rereading his books with a much clearer vision and context of the sights and sounds he vividly described in the memoirs of his upbringing, which are now an important and cherished part of the true rural heritage of our adopted West Virginia home at Peeper Pond Farm. It was a trip that I will remember fondly for many years to come.

Post 84: Bringing in the Sheaves

July 20, 2018

This post is the second in a series discussing our adventures helping Jeff & Amanda Barger harvest and process an experimental plot of wheat into flour the traditional way—using traditional hand tools and equipment. This process requires a number of separate steps completed over a long period of time. The next segment in the series is Post 89: Winnowing It All Down.

<u>Previous posts in this series</u>:

Post 81: Reaping Wheat – A Shocking Experience (July 5, 2018)

Yesterday morning, July 19, 2018, Barb and I returned to Jeff and Amanda Barger's homestead farm on North Mill Creek Road to continue helping them process their small experimental wheat crop. It was a much finer day for outdoor work than when we first helped reap the wheat on July 5. The skies were clear and the air was crisp and dry, with temperatures in the mid-70s and a gentle, refreshing breeze. The next step in the harvesting process was to dismantle the wheat shocks we had built in the field and flail the wheat seeds and husks off the stems. We took each sheaf that was used to build the shocks and broke it apart on large tarps staged in the shade of some yard trees. We then used some antique flails and hay rakes to beat the piles of wheat, which dislodged the wheat seeds and the husks (chaff) that enshrouded them. A flail is a device consisting of two staffs of wood connected by a rope or cord. They resemble nunchucks. Grabbing the narrower handle, you swing the flail onto the pile of wheat, making sure that the beating staff is level to the ground when it strikes the wheat. As we beat repeatedly on the piles of loose wheat stems, the seeds and husks collected on the tarp. We only had two flails to use, so we also used some antique wooden rakes as flails. In the distant past, some farmers would stomp on the wheat to dislodge the seeds, in the same way that winemakers would stomp on grapes in a large vat to crush them.

With each flailing stroke, we could hear the seed husks falling onto the tarp. We continued flailing the wheat until the sounds of the wheat husks hitting the tarp diminished, like heating popcorn until it's finished popping. We then removed as much of the overlying stems as was possible by hand and sifted the seeds and husks through a square wooden frame with a base of chicken-wire mesh to separate more of the remaining stem fragments. Once we were satisfied that we had removed as much of the stems as possible, we lifted the tarp and dumped the wheat seeds and husks into a cloth sack. The sacks were then hung in a barn for further drying, which would allow the husks encasing the seeds to open so that the seeds will drop out freely. It is the seeds that we will eventually grind into flour, after we remove the chaff using a winnowing device—which is the next step in the process.

Flailing wheat the traditional way requires a lot of time and energy. To speed up the process a little, because the volunteer help had other time commitments, Amanda decided to demonstrate how her 21st century wheat flailing machine (an ATV) could speed up the process. She and a friend drove their ATVs repeatedly over the tarps, while the rest of us raked the stems back onto the tarp after each pass to make sure we weren't losing too many of the valuable wheat seeds. Admittedly, the sight was somewhat amusing to behold. After careful consideration and debate, we concluded that the ATVs were effectively producing what would eventually amount to about one quarter pound of flour per gallon of unleaded fuel. Ah, the labor-saving convenience of our consumptive modern technology. Just think of all the valuable time it frees for you to watch television or pay for a gym membership to reclaim all the free exercise you avoided.

We will leave the bags of wheat to air dry for an extended period of time. Some of the wheat was still damp from the morning dew when we flailed it, but the shocks had dried very effectively. The next stage of the process will be to run the bags of wheat seeds through an antique hand-cranked winnowing device to separate the wheat [seeds] from the chaff or husks, which is the root of that old saying. The winnow uses a series of wooden blades, operated by a hand-crank, to fan the husks from the wheat seeds as they pass through the device. I will explain its operation in greater detail in the next post of this series. The final step will be to grind the wheat seeds (grain) onto flour, which can be used for baking. That's the actual process by which all flour is made.

Although the traditional ways take time and energy, they make it easier for people to understand where our food comes from and to appreciate the amount of work it takes to make it. Nevertheless, we find it far less stressful than the work required today to earn the money necessary to buy the food we eat from the store. It also is an inherently healthier way to obtain food than driving to the store and buying it. When we consider how lazy and unhealthy our modern technological conveniences have made us, and the enormous health costs and reduced active and useful lifespans that imposes on our society, it makes it easier to appreciate the intrinsic value of our traditional, self-reliant lifestyles. Perhaps someday, if another global economic depression occurs, you will understand the true value of this knowledge and skill. That's why we at Peeper Pond Farm work hard to practice and preserve those skills for future generations.

Post 85: Extracting Liquid Gold from the Hives

July 23, 2018

    One of the farming operations we undertook at Peeper Pond Farm was raising honey bees (as discussed in many earlier posts). We acquired two colonies, one of Italian bees and another of Carniolans. We placed our hives at the far end of our small fruit tree orchard so that our bees could pollinate the apple and peach trees we planted there as they collected pollen to produce honey. Bees typically begin harvesting pollen for the coming winter when daytime temperatures warm into the mid- '50s and 60s and the spring wildflowers and trees begin to bloom. They collect pollen from the blooms, return it to their hive, convert it into honey, and store it in beeswax hive cells they have built and sealed for safe storage with a "cap." The honey they harvest during the spring and summer months will feed the colony during the long, cold, lifeless winter months.

    We managed our two bee colonies for a little over a year-and-a-half, until our bees were suddenly killed off in December 2017 by varroa mites that had invaded the hives. Varroa mites are tiny parasites that enter the hive via a host bee, then migrate into a brood cell when the host bee feeds its larvae. They then feed on the infected larvae as it matures and gradually spread through the hive when they emerge. They are one of many pests imported into America from Asia around 1960—a virtually unpreventable consequence (given the wide array of potential pests and diseases) of global trade. They are deadly to the bees and very difficult to exterminate. While there are a number of treatments that bee farmers can use, they tend to be quite expensive and they all pose some risk to the bees, which are very sensitive to chemicals and aggressive treatments. Many other bee farms throughout our Potomac Highlands region fell victim to varroa mites last winter, perhaps because of the prior warmer winter that allowed the mites to thrive. Although we could have rebuilt our hives this spring, we chose to wait for a year to see how the other bee farmers fared over the coming winter. It would be a major expense for us (living on a fixed retirement income) to order new bee colonies and the necessary varroa mite treatment, so we wanted to observe the larger bee farms and their treatment success before reinvesting. Besides, waiting for a year to rebuild our hives may allow the mites to die back naturally.

    This is the time of the season, when the spring and early summer blooms have expired, that make it possible for bee farmers (known in the industry as Apiarists) to harvest excess honey the bees have stored in their hives. Harvesting honey from the top supers (boxes) in a hive (honey supers) during this period allows the bees to replenish their winter food stores from the pollen produced by late summer blooms, including daisies, asters, goldenrod, wingstem and Queen Anne's lace. We had hoped to obtain our first honey harvest this month, but our run of bad luck during 2017 left us without both our dairy and honey operations. Instead, we used our time to help our nearby friends and neighbors, Jim and Donna Boyd, as they harvested honey from their rebuilt hives. Only a couple of their original colonies managed to survive the varroa mite onslaught, so honey production for them was very light this season.

Jim and Donna own and operate Middle Mountain Apiary from their home near the summit of Middle Mountain and a commercial building they bought on South Mill Creek Road in Petersburg. Jim is an experienced Apiarist who sells bee farming equipment in addition to raising about 25 hives of bees. We bought our colonies and most of our own equipment from him in 2016, and he taught me most of what I have learned about raising bees. So, when Jim invited Barb and me (along with some of their other friends) to help him with his honey extraction again this season, we eagerly agreed.

When we arrived yesterday (July 22) at their beautiful Middle Mountain home, they had already removed all of the honey supers they could harvest from their rebuilt colonies this year. Although they harvested between fifteen and twenty supers last year, their new hives produced only about five supers this season. Even within the honey supers they were able to harvest, many of the frames were only partially filled with honey. It was a very poor harvest for him, even though we had abundant rainfall and decent blooms.

The first step in the harvesting process is to remove the frames, one by one, from each super (a rectangular box frame in which the individual frames are hung) and remove the white beeswax storage 'caps' the bees created to seal each cell once they were filled with honey. This is done by holding each frame over a large bucket or container and scraping along the honeycombed sides of the frame to remove the caps. The caps can be opened or removed using either a simple carving knife, a capping scratcher with a row of sharp prongs or an electrically heated knife. The beeswax caps are collected on a mesh screen mounted on the container that allows any honey incidentally removed with the caps to drain off the scrapings and into the container to be recovered later. The caps can eventually be used to make beeswax candles.

Once all the honey cells on both sides of a frame are fully opened, the frame is placed into the cylindrical drum of an extractor. When the extractor drum is loaded with frames, it is sealed and rotated, either by a hand rank (as our own extractor is designed) or by an electric motor (as Jim's larger commercial extractor is designed). The centrifugal force created by the rotating extractor drum removes the honey from the cells onto the sides of the drum, where it gradually drains to the bottom.

The emptied frames are then removed from the extractor and the honey drained into a bucket, where it is further strained to remove any debris. The honey is then stored in jars for sale or consumption. The beeswax scrapings can be heated so that the pure wax can be removed and used to make candles and other useful items. This is how candles and honey (a natural cooking sweetener) were made by all of our early ancestors. The honey you buy in a store is manufactured by the same general process, only at an industrial scale by larger machines.

Hopefully, in some future year, we can bring a couple of bee colonies back to Peeper Pond Farm. Harvesting honey in this way is a time-honored practice and an essential and integral component of our desired educational homesteading operation. Raising bees has been made very difficult these days, due to increased pesticide use and the introduction of pests and diseases from other continents through global trade. You must always bear in mind that *both* of these contamination sources must be addressed in order to encourage the healthy recovery of honey bees. It is the cumulative growth of these threats that causes colony collapse, not just one or the other. Simply encouraging people to raise bees or plant more pollinators may be a good thing, but it won't ensure bee survival. Those approaches only treat the symptom, not the root causes.

The situation that bees face today is one of many unintended consequences of our modern, complex, global economy that I feel best illustrates the intrinsic benefits of our traditional lifestyle skills and folkways. We may need our massive global economy, technology and industrial complex to sustain and fuel our exponential global population growth, but if by satisfying that growth-induced need we ultimately destroy the environment that supports us, we will eventually cause our own extinction. That will be the hardest final lesson we will all inevitably learn.

Post 86: Our Deer Hunter

July 26, 2018

    Our new cat, Calli has some interesting traits. Top among them is her hunting talent which includes, as we have observed on several occasions, chasing deer. Calli and I usually awake early, usually sometime around 5:00 AM. This is the time of the day when herds of deer, sometimes numbering more than ten, but usually around four at a time, casually graze their way across our field on their way back into the dense forest on Cave Mountain. Sometime in early May, Calli, who had just developed her hunting skills catching field mice and juvenile bunnies, began to take a great interest in the deer as they strolled across her royal domain. I guess she considered them the ultimate prey to catch. After all, what housecat wouldn't thoroughly enjoy a deer feast? Several times we watched her exercise her youthful abandon by scrambling off the porch to stalk them in the tall, dense grass in our field. After a few moments, we would see the deer suddenly look up, sensing her approach, turn and begin moving determinedly towards the ravine uncertain of where or what she was. Once she had them on the move, Calli would bound after them, leaping through the grass and scaring the departing deer into a desperate escape. I once watched her chase four deer up the gravel road that fronts our property until she was nearly out of sight. Although she hasn't caught one, we realized that she fancies herself to be a ferocious deer hunter, as I first noted in my May 30, 2018 post entitled, *Calli's Catch*.

    Reality finally caught up with Calli's deer hunting aspirations yesterday morning, when a lone year-old doe invaded our vegetable garden around 5:45 AM, just as daylight began to stir the dew into a gentle, hazy ground fog. As has become our early morning routine, I let Calli out onto our front porch after she vigorously devoured her breakfast. I watched her briefly as she leapt onto her favorite front porch observation perch—our gas grill. From there, she surveys our hayfield and the vegetable garden carefully deciding which direction she will take to begin her morning ritual hunting safari. Although the morning light was still too feeble for me to see clearly, I noticed three dark, indefinite shapes just beyond the edge of the yard area that I mow, which I presumed to be two adult deer and a fawn. I noticed that Calli's gaze was riveted on them. I fully expected her to attack, but I was working on the computer at the time so I returned to the house fully expecting her to chase them back into the woods.

    However, after only five minutes or so, I noticed that she was peering in at me through the porch screen door. Calli usually likes to stay outside for at least half an hour before deciding to come back in briefly for some attention from me or to nibble on some dry food. I thought her desire to come back into the house was a little uncharacteristic for her, but she seemed quite eager to do so. I looked out into the field, but couldn't see the deer, so I figured she was satisfied that she had chased them away.

After receiving some of my attention and chomping down three or four crunchies from her bowl, Calli parked herself in front of the screen door to signal she was ready to go out again. I let her out and went back on the porch to check the low temperature for the day. It a very comfortable 62 degrees and wisps of fog were drifting along the field. The morning light was stronger then and I quickly noticed that the three deer had not run away but had migrated to the edge of the garden fence. I could now clearly see that there was a four-point buck accompanied by an adult doe and her spotted fawn. As I stood there on the porch, the doe determinedly jumped over the fence into the garden. I reacted immediately by waving my arms and yelling at them to get out of the garden, as I descended the steps and walked towards the garden. The doe responded promptly by jumping out of the garden. Then, perceiving my threat, the three deer bounded away with their white tails wagging behind them.

I was surprised to realize that Calli had not done her job to protect our garden. After all, she hadn't shown any fear of deer and typically spends a good part of her day playing and hunting for rabbits in the garden, so I fully expected her to protect it. I watched the deer race up the road and was about to turn away when I noticed some movement between the first two rows of tomato bushes. There, looking up at me, stood a yearling doe chomping on a green tomato it had just ripped off a bush. I was amazed to see that I had not also scared it off with all my commotions. The deer just continued to chew on the tomato as I studied it. This particular deer is one that I recognized having seen before.

Late last fall, sometime around October or November, I had seen a mature doe and her fawn feeding in our field most evenings. They were the only two deer that I saw regularly on our farm that season. I noticed that the doe would leave her fawn in our field in an area adjacent to the goat pen before strolling into the woods that began along our ravine. She would leave the doe there for at least an hour or more before I would notice that it too had disappeared. Around the time that fall transitioned into the winter, I noticed that the fawn seemed to be alone for longer periods of time. Eventually, I realized that its mother wasn't around, either having been killed during the hunting season or struck by a vehicle on the highway that runs down the valley a third of a mile from our house. We often see road-kill deer on our travels along the highway to and from Petersburg and Franklin.

I kept a vigil on the lone fawn fully expecting it would not survive the winter. As noted in my periodic website posts, the winter was especially cold and windy but rather dry with very little snowfall. I guess the lack of significant snow cover was the most critical factor that determined the fawn's winter fate. I continued to see the lone fawn periodically throughout the winter, as it often bedded down on the edge of our field where its mother had last left it before her final disappearance. Apparently, it managed to find enough dried grass and nuts to forage during the long periods of bare ground. When spring finally decided to return, so did the fawn, now a spotless doe. I believe it was that lone fawn that stared back at me from our garden, which would explain why I didn't see it with the other three deer I had chased away and why it did not leave with them.

Since the doe didn't leave, I decided I needed to go into the garden and convince it to leave before it devoured all of Barb's prized tomatoes. I watched it as I opened the metal gate, which usually makes enough noise when we swing it open to be heard from neighboring houses. Even that wasn't enough to disturb the doe, which continued to chew on its tomato as it casually watched me enter the garden. I continued to walk steadfastly towards the deer waving my arms as I instructed it to leave. When I got within about fifteen feet of it (at the end of the tomato row), I stopped, puzzled by its lack of fear. At this point, I became curious to see how close I could get to it. I stopped trying to frighten it and just began to approach it very slowly.

When I was a child, the deer herd was so low in my area that we rarely saw any deer, and any that we did see were so frightened by the sight of people that we never could get very close. Deer are more abundant here and many of them are used to seeing people, but I had never been this close to a wild deer in my life. The doe seemed completely unmoved by my proximity as I closed to within three feet of it. By now, it was swallowing the last bits of the tomato it was eating. Our eyes met as I extended my hand slowly towards it. I held my hand out to within a foot of its nose. I was close enough to see its nostrils flare slightly and the barrel of its chest expand and contract as it breathed. Yet, throughout my approach, it remained fixed in its position watching me with what appeared to be more curiosity than fear. As I stared into its eyes and stood with my hand extended, it cocked its head giving me the sense that it was trying to decide whether or not to sniff my outstretched fingertips. After a few seconds of thought, it casually twisted its head away from me and began to stroll down the tomato row away from me. I looked behind me back towards the porch and saw Calli creeping down the steps towards me. Perhaps the sight of the ferocious feline deer hunter convinced the doe it was now outnumbered. Whatever its actual thoughts were, I knew it wasn't the least bit intimidated by me alone. I followed the doe from behind to keep it moving towards the back fence, over which it eventually leapt. Throughout our garden walk, it stopped a few times to look back at me as if to make sure I was still following along. I never felt any fear from it, and it reminded me of all the times as a child that I followed our cows up the hill behind our barn to close the fence to their pen.

When the doe was outside the garden, I realized that I was missing a great opportunity to take a close-up picture of a deer. I decided to walk back into the house and retrieve our cell phone. In the process I called Barb to come with me and see this deer. When I emerged again from the house, the deer was still outside the garden, but was walking along the driveway *towards*—not away—from the house. I began to feel that the doe, having been so young when it was abandoned, eventually came to accept our farm as its home and felt more secure here than it did in the woods. The deer walked the full length of the fence along our driveway, then turned right and passed between the house and the garden. By now, Calli was in her path, and I watched as the doe took a curious interest in her and approached. Before I could wake the phone up and get the camera active, the deer had extended her head towards Calli to take a sniff, causing Calli to recoil and back away. Our deer hunter suddenly felt fear by the unexpected approach of a fearless doe. I did eventually manage to capture a few pictures of Calli and the deer, and Barb had an opportunity to get within about eight feet of it when it was walking up the driveway. After Calli backed away, the doe jumped back into the garden, and this time, I scared it out, and it ran across our field to the east, eventually disappearing into the ravine near the spot where it had been left so many times by its mother.

I have no idea what long term affect this strange experience will have on Calli's deer chasing career. When I let her out on the porch early this morning, she again jumped onto the gas grill and began her survey of the wild back yard. I saw no deer at the time, but she remained vigilant for some time. About a half hour later, at 5:50 AM, I looked out the window and saw the lone doe walking through the field towards the garden. Calli was nowhere to be seen at the time. I walked out onto the yard and down the side of the garden fence, intercepting the doe before it could get to the garden. It stared at me again with recognition, before it decided to simply walk away. I watched as it crossed the driveway and headed for Cave Mountain, having approached within ten feet of it. I don't know if I could ever touch it, but perhaps, after more close encounters, its curiosity will get the best of it, and it will sniff my hand—that is, assuming that Calli won't recover her deer hunter instinct and/or I won't be forced to chase it out of our garden again. Nevertheless, I will never forget my first close encounter with a wild deer that appears to have adopted our Peeper Pond Farm as its home.

Post 87: 2018 Tri-County Fair

August 2, 2018

After a brief three-week period of predominantly dry and sunny weather, we have entered into another period of sullen, fog-laden, rainy days. For most residents of our area, that weather is the traditional harbinger of the Tri-County Fair in Petersburg. It's hard to find a person here who doesn't say, "It always rains during the fair." That is certainly true during our own experience here. Nevertheless, dull and gloomy weather never dampens the spirit of those who attend and enjoy the fair.

It would be an understatement to say that the annual Tri-County fair is one of the biggest social events of the year in Petersburg. Even so, it amazes us to realize the number of festive events that Petersburg (a city of 2,500 people) manages to conduct each year. The city has three major parades for the Fourth of July, the Tri-County Fair and Christmas. In addition, Petersburg manages to have two public Christmas lighting displays, a Community Chorus, numerous stage performances at the Landes Theater, a Spring Mountain Festival, the summer-time Grant County Farmer's Market, and an impressive July Fourth festival and fireworks display. This list doesn't include a wide array of church socials and smaller celebrations sprinkled throughout the year. Barb and I have lived in many rural areas throughout our 27 years of marriage, and we can comfortably assert that we have not seen another community its size that can match Petersburg's ability to celebrate its community spirit. However, its small-town neighbors in Moorefield and Franklin certainly give it a run for the money. I guess you would say it's just a way of life here in the Potomac Highlands of West Virginia.

Since the Tri-County Fair encompasses all three adjoining counties (Grant, Hardy and Pendleton), it's only fitting that it would be one of the major events of the year. Counties that jealously divide their high school football loyalties during the fall manage to put those differences aside to celebrate their shared rural heritage at the fair. It is not uncommon to meet many friends and acquaintances from all three counties during a leisurely stroll through the fairgrounds. One of our friends, who was manning the WELD radio booth, even wondered why he didn't see us at the fair on Tuesday evening. For Barb and I, this year's fair was an even bigger event. For the first time since we were married, we were active participants in the fair. We entered a total of eleven different exhibits to highlight our Peeper Pond Farm products, including vegetables from our garden, canned goods, baked goods and Barb's quilt products. Although Barb was raised in a city and never participated in a fair, it was the first time I entered any exhibits in more than 30 years. Having joined the Petersburg Lion's Club earlier this year, Barb and I also volunteered to work three shifts at the Lion's Club food booth on Wednesday, Thursday and Saturday. Finally, I also served as a Pendleton County judge for the fair parade floats and bands. It has been a rewarding and fun experience for both of us.

Our Peeper Pond Farm exhibits were surprisingly well received. Of the eleven exhibits we submitted, six won ribbons. Our Early Brite tomatoes were awarded a Sweepstakes Ribbon. We felt that the tomatoes we raise in our vegetable garden were of good quality, and they are always our most popular item at the Grant County Farmer's Market, but the high praise we received from the judges really took us by surprise. Since we are not native to the area, have no other family who live here and are not broadly known (which is why we decided to enter so many exhibits—to increase public awareness of our farm and products), we certainly can't be considered inside favorites.

Other vegetable exhibits we entered that won ribbons include carrots and canned red cabbage (which won first place blue ribbons) and our banana peepers, which received a white ribbon (third place). The other food exhibits we entered, green peppers, green beans, banana bread, sourdough bread and canned tomato sauce, were not awarded any ribbons.

However, both of Barb's quilt entries won ribbons. Her Hot Toddy table runner received a first-place blue ribbon, and her Carpenter's Wheel lap quilt received a second-place red ribbon. We have displayed both of these quilt products at our Grant County Farmer's Market booth. One of our farmer's market patrons so appreciated her Carpenter's Wheel lap quilt, that he ordered from her a personalized variation of it as a Christmas gift.

The fair parade is the biggest civic event of the Tri-County Fair. As a Pendleton County judge for the parade, I had an opportunity to view it from a good vantage point. From our reviewing stand on the portico of the First Baptist Church, we watched the parade pass by for an hour and a half! It would have been even longer, but the drenching storm that spanned the final hour before the parade caused three high school marching bands and several floats to drop out. Only the Petersburg High School Marching Band braved the elements and led the parade, making them the obvious choice for an award, if for no other reason than their conviction and spirit. Although several participants withdrew before the parade began, resulting in numerous unofficial rumors that the parade was being canceled, we enjoyed viewing a number of commercial and civic floats, antique cars and tractors, fire trucks and walking entourages representing many local groups and fair sponsors. The judge's award was given to the Sons of Confederate Veterans for their beautifully and meticulously appointed McNeill's Rangers float, complete with a cannon, period costumes and muskets.

Fortunately, the rain abated just as the fair procession began, allowing the children lining the streets to turn their umbrellas upside down to serve as candy catchers for the parade participants to toss their wrapped treats into. One ecstatic, festively dressed 4-5-year-old girl was so proud of the plastic grocery store bag of candy she collected that she had to plunk it down on our judges table to show us how much candy she got. I smiled and told her that it might just last her until Halloween and, after catching her breath, she replied with a smile, "I sure hope so." It's just too bad there wasn't a judge's award for the cutest kid. She would have walked away with that, too.

I hope all of us who attend the Tri-County fair can feel as pleased and happy as that young girl did. If so, I'll simply hope that the good feeling we take away from it will last until next year, when we can all join together and celebrate the proud spirit and heritage of our rural community again. If you should be reading this post today, you still have a chance to be a part of it all. The Tri-County Fair will continue through this Saturday night, August 4.

Post 88: The Romaine Tenney Legacy

August 7, 2018

    We are experiencing another brief hot and humid period here at Peeper Pond Farm, so Barb and I decided to seek refuge yesterday (Monday, August 6) at a higher and cooler elevation—Skyline Drive at nearby Shenandoah National Park. I actually had another good reason to make this trip. I learned recently that a series of memorial monuments (in the shape of solitary pioneer stone chimneys) are being erected to recognize all of the families who were forced to leave their homes and land for the construction of Shenandoah National Park. I was very encouraged to hear that, nearly 80 years after they were evicted from their ancestral lands, their tremendous sacrifices would receive the recognition and honor they deserve. I should note that the National Park Service prefers the word "displaced," but it is sadly inappropriate to apply that term to those who were removed against their will. After all, I'm talking about the same government that called the Trail of Tears Cherokee removal a "relocation."

    I call their forced removal tremendous sacrifices because the "just compensation" they received did not recognize the intrinsic value of the pain they experienced by the taking of the land they cherished and the loss of the self-reliant lifestyle they obtained from it. All they received was the price that the land was worth to a prospective buyer—a price that was greatly diminished by the discriminatory negative stereotypes that had been applied to them by a society that viewed them and their way of living as simple, regressive, hostile and uncouth. Viewed from that perspective, the forced eviction from the land where their ancestors lived and were buried was for their own best interest. Just think of all the advantages they would receive by a forced assimilation into the outside modern world. They could take a bath to become more presentable; they could get an education that would make them smarter and more useful to society; they could get a job and earn money to pay for the replacement homes they had to buy, and they would learn how to function in a modern, fast-paced, sophisticated society that would gradually turn them into upstanding citizens in the eyes of the people who had judged them. With all those benefits awaiting them, why should anyone care about their forced separation from their own circle of friends and relatives, the loss of their connection to the land and abundant natural resources that allowed them to live the way they desired, the fear of a forced adjustment to a vastly different way of living and society that they had no desire to join, and the scorn they would continue to face more immediately from the outside world that now lived next door? These are the impacts they were forced to bear and for which they were not justly compensated, because no one cared to view them as different people who, in many even if not all cases, chose to live that way for generations.

I hear many people today in our highly politicized society refer to themselves and their values as "inclusive, enlightened and sensitive." As someone who was raised in a different social and economic setting that more closely resembled a self-reliant lifestyle, I strongly agree that those are respectable values. They are wholly consistent with my own core values which I internalized from my upbringing on our family dairy farm. However, I also recognize that those values are merely good descriptive words if they are not backed by the actions that give the words value, substance and integrity. The word "inclusive" means "not excluding any section of society or any party involved in something." I contend that those people who desire and aspire to live self-reliantly are a party involved in a free lifestyle choice that, while different in nature from the modern technology- and money-driven lifestyle that most people live today, should not be viewed as inferior or disreputable. They did not request or seek pity or support from others. Many people who live that way possess lifestyle skills that would give them a superior ability to survive and maintain their standard of living in the event that our modern economy should fail. To look down on that valid lifestyle choice would not bring legitimacy to any people who call themselves inclusive, enlightened, or sensitive. Yet, I know many people today who do and then illegitimately lay claim to those values. Unfortunately, for many self-reliant and poor citizens of our country, the monetary value of the land they own is decided exclusively from that paternal and condescending perspective—as it was for the people forced to leave their land so that the rest of society could have a new playground and for Romaine Tenney who was forced to leave his land for an Interstate highway interchange.

The story of Romaine Tenney is the reason why I was so glad to hear about the new monuments. I first learned of him during my childhood from my father, who was acquainted with him during the four years in the early 1960s when their lives overlapped. They weren't close friends, but our family farm was only five miles by road from Romaine's farm, and they eventually became acquainted with each other. Perhaps they didn't have time to establish a longstanding relationship, but my father understood him and held him in high esteem.

My father was not someone most people would consider to be emotional. He always faced the cold, hard realities of life with steadfast determination, dignity, and self-control. I now realize and admit that I internalized those characteristics from him. However, I recall many times when my father would tell Romaine Tenney's tragic story, and it would bring a tear to his eye, as he would struggle to maintain his composure. That always caught my attention, and it made the story something that would influence my thinking about the forces that took his heritage and homestead away, as I faced my own compelled transition into the outside world.

Although the government did not force me to leave the farm that raised me, my adoptive parents did by repeatedly instructing us not to aspire to live as we did and that our only futures were based in the outside modern world that we didn't really understand. Maybe I was not raised in my adopted home of West Virginia, but like many natives, I came to know what it was like to feel ashamed of my upbringing by the humor my fellow college students found in my accent, manner of speaking, rural behavioral characteristics and the very different stories I had to tell of my upbringing. Many of my college friends and acquaintances simply didn't believe the stories I told of how we lived. Society didn't feel very inclusive or accepting to me then until I learned how to recreate myself in their accepted way of being. I hope that experience earns me some understanding and acceptance from native West Virginians. Perhaps it, along with my 30-year professional planning career, also gives me a more balanced and credible perspective from which to discuss the issue of private property rights and public land takings. For that is the core issue that unites the new Shenandoah eviction monuments with Romaine Tenney. I hope you will indulge me while I explain his story to you. A very sensitive and more detailed account of his life can be found in the March/April 2013 issue of *Yankee* magazine. That article serves as the source for the details of his life that I will recount below, some of which I had forgotten over the years, and some of which I never knew.

Romaine Tenney was born and raised on a 90-acre dairy farm in the Weathersfield, Vermont village of Ascutney that his father purchased in April 1892. Romaine was the only child in a family of nine that remained on the farm as an adult to continue the family's dairy operation. He never married and eventually operated the farm alone without any modern conveniences. He milked his herd of 25-50 cows by hand, worked his fields with two teams of horses, mowed his yard with a scythe, lived without electricity, and owned no car or truck. If he needed to make a trip into town, he either walked five or so miles across the Connecticut River to the City of Claremont, hitched a ride along the way, or scheduled a ride with one of two brothers who lived in Claremont. He lived his own life in his own way and never changed his clocks for daylight savings time because it just didn't matter to him or his cows. He had a lean but muscular build honed from his years of manual farm work. While Romaine's lifestyle would seem difficult and reclusive by today's standard, he enjoyed it immensely and always openly greeted strangers and friends with an engaging and sincere smile of contentment. When one of his neighbors, concerned about his hand-milking difficulties caused by advancing arthritis, helped him install electrical service to his barn for milking machines, he soon had it removed because he preferred milking by hand. His land and animals were close to him because they were the pillars that supported his lifestyle. He simply chose to live as he did.

Romaine's life was fine and fulfilling until one day in the early 1960s, when a survey crew charting the path for Interstate 91 approached his property. The State of Vermont had tried to purchase his house for $10,600, but he refused to sell. Eventually, the state condemned his property and initiated eminent domain proceedings against him. (Eminent domain is a legal process by which private property can be taken without the owner's consent for a "public use" for "just compensation" as determined by the courts.) At his condemnation trial, a jury increased the state's purchase price by $3,000, and he was told he would have to leave his farm by April 1, 1964. He never complied and only stated repeatedly that he wasn't leaving his land—even to friends who had offered to assist him.

A standoff resulted that lasted more than five months until September 11, 1964, one week after Romaine's 64th birthday. That day, the local Sheriff arrived at his door with a court order to evict him. As Romaine watched solemnly from a side porch on the house, the Sheriff's deputies began to remove his personal belongings from the horse barn and sheds and stacked them in piles underneath an elm tree. That was the last day anyone saw Romaine Tenney.

Just after midnight, Romaine turned his cows and horses free and set fire to the barn. He then barricaded himself inside the house and set it aflame. When the fire department responded around 3:00 AM, the house was engulfed in flames and the doors were nailed shut. The fire burned so hot that it melted the plastic emergency light on top of the fire chief's car that was parked about 80 feet away. There was nothing more anyone could do.

When the fire died down, they found the remains of Romaine's body underneath his bed with a rifle that had been fired. All assumed he had committed suicide while the house around him burned to the ground. Romaine had said quite firmly, "I was born here, and I will die here." He wasn't trying to prevent the highway from being built; he only wanted it to bypass his cherished family farm. However, the state refused to alter the highway's course to spare his property. It was a showdown that neither side won, even though Vermont was able to build the Interstate across his land. By doing so, Vermont inherited a legacy that it is loath to acknowledge even today. Vermont got her highway at the expense of a permanent scar on her reputation—a blemish that boldly proclaims the state's lack of compassion, empathy and understanding for a man whose land meant far more to him than it could ever comprehend.

The pain that ended Romain's life is not impossible to comprehend. It is a pain that has been expressed by countless other politically marginalized people who have faced a forced eviction from their family lands. Those who were forcibly removed to make way for Shenandoah National Park and the Skyline Drive understood that pain. Their personal sacrifices in the face of "progress" were no different. Of the roughly 465 families living in the purchase boundaries of the proposed park—many of whom were removed by force—only fourteen were eventually given the right to live out their remaining lives on their ancestral lands. The last one to pass away was Annie Shank in 1979.

We rightly extoll and honor the sacrifices made by our nation's veterans and reward them with many forms of public assistance. Yet, when people stand gallantly and fearlessly in the path of "progress," our society labels them as regressives and proceeds to push them aside without regret. Something in that dichotomy seems ironic and inconsiderate to me. That's why I was eager to see the new monuments and praise the National Park Service for finally recognizing these great sacrifices. However, as we drove along the parkway, we struggled to find a park employee who could tell us where to find them. Eventually, we learned that the National Park Service had no role in building them and none of them have been placed on National Park property. They are being designed and built by the Blue Ridge Committee for Shenandoah Park Relations – a committee founded by Rockingham County, VA. More's the pity.

We eventually found one of the monuments built in Ed Good Memorial Park in the Town of Stanley. It stands starkly before the 4,051-foot Hawkbill Mountain, the highest point in Shenandoah National Park. Separated from the National Park, but visible to it—perhaps appropriately. After all, a government that refuses to truly understand and acknowledge the sacrifices made by *all* of its people certainly doesn't deserve any credit for honoring them. It is the counties that work on their own to memorialize them that do.

Before closing this post, I wish to clarify my personal and professional stance on the topic of Eminent Domain. I fully understand and agree that our country would not survive if there was no legal process by which major public projects— that benefit everyone—could move forward. However, that legal process should not work to the detriment of people who chose to live self-reliantly and, in doing so, have a special attachment to their land and lifestyle without due consideration for their sacrifices. I see nothing in the term "just compensation" that should not embrace and reflect the deeper intrinsic attachment to the land that self-reliant people hold simply because they are a poor and politically marginalized segment of our society. That is my measure of a truly empathic, sensitive, and inclusive government, and I tried hard to be sensitive to those concerns throughout my 30-year planning career. Whenever a community of people must be removed to make way for an essential public project, every effort should be made to understand, accommodate, and, if no other alternative remains, replace the essential living conditions and needs of its citizens. After all, we would do no less for our veterans. Were the sacrifices requested of Romaine Tenney and the hundreds of self-reliant families removed to make way for Shenandoah National Park any less significant? They all faced losing their land, their heritage, their way of life, and in some cases, their community of friends and family. I believe we should expect more from a government established by the people to protect and respect their fundamental freedoms. In my view, there is ample room for improvement. If you can agree with me, I hope you will always remember the story of Romaine Tenney.

Author's Update: As of the publication of this book, I am pleased to note that there have been some new developments regarding the preservation of Romaine Tenney's legacy. In 2019, VTRANS, the Vermont Agency of Transportation, announced that an iconic maple tree that prominently appears in historic photos of Romaine Tenney's farmhouse and still stands adjacent to the Exit 8 park and ride lot was dying and in need of removal. A group of descendants and supporters who remember Romaine and the sacrifices he made to protect his family farm organized to oppose the tree removal. In response to the outcry, VTRANS officials conducted a public meeting in Ascutney, VT on October 29 to determine how best to memorialize Romaine Tenney. The attending citizens insisted that only a portion of the tree was dying and that its health should be re-evaluated. VTRANS has agreed to undertake that re-assessment and to explore options for a fitting and lasting memorial, but the outcome of that work has not been determined. It is at least reassuring that the memory of Romaine Tenney remains alive some 55 years after he sacrificed his life. It is my eternal hope (although my expectations are far more tempered) that the State of Vermont will finally acknowledge publicly that it made a terrible and fatal error of judgement in its zeal to construct Interstate 91 and will take appropriate measures to guaranty the public that its work on future public projects will be more sensitive and respectful to the property rights of multi-generational, self-reliant landowners and their special way of living.

Post 89: Winnowing It All Down

August 8, 2018

This post is the third in a series discussing our adventures helping Jeff & Amanda Barger harvest and process an experimental plot of wheat into flour the traditional way—using traditional hand tools and equipment. This process requires a number of separate steps completed over a long period of time. The next segment in the series is Post 99: Grinding Wheat.

Previous posts in this series:

Post 81: Reaping Wheat – A Shocking Experience (July 5, 2018)

Post 84: Bringing in the Sheaves (July 20, 2018)

It was a sunny, warm and humid morning on Tuesday, August 7, when we found ourselves again at Jeff and Amanda's North Mill Creek Road farm to help winnow the wheat we had helped them harvest. Once again, their friends and family had assembled to participate in the effort. During our first visit, we had reaped (harvested) the wheat crop and stacked it into shocks to finish drying in the field. On our last visit, we removed the shocks and flailed (beat) the wheat sheaves to remove the husks containing the tiny wheat seeds from the stems and stored the seeds in cloth sacks to dry further. This drying period allowed the husks to open so that the seeds could fall out. The next stage in the harvesting process is to separate (winnow) the dried husks (chaff) from the seeds.

Our work for this step in the process would be accomplished using an antique winnowing machine called a "fanning mill" that was first acquired and used by Amanda's great-grandfather. Jeff had been restoring it to operating condition while the wheat was drying. The wooden mill stands nearly four feet tall and has a square hopper at the top into which the wheat is loaded. The operator turns a crank on one side which spins a number of wooden blades inside the machine to generate a breeze that blows the chaff away from the seeds as they fall into the device. The fan blows the seeds and chaff onto a series of mesh screens with openings small enough to allow the seeds to fall through, but not the chaff. These screens sway from side to side as the crank is turned to help shake loose the chaff, which is light enough to be fanned away from the mill. Once the bare seeds drop through the screens, they slide into a removable wooden bin at the base of the machine.

The fanning mill is just one design of many different winnowing machines that were built during the early years of advanced farming mechanization in the nineteenth century. Prior to the invention of these winnowing devices, the wheat hulls would be hand-tossed into the air from a pan on a windy day so that the prevailing breeze would blow away the chaff and the seeds would fall back into the pan. The fanning mill was a speedier and more efficient way to winnow large volumes of wheat.

The fanning mill worked quite well for its advanced age. It squeaked and groaned as we cranked it and blew a blizzard of chaff into the air from the back of the machine. A close examination of the seeds in the collection bin indicated that it effectively removed between forty and sixty percent of the chaff. We decided that our extended bout of humid weather prevented the husks from drying completely, which is why the mill was unable to blow more of the chaff away. As a result, we poured the winnowed seeds back into the cloth sacks so they could be hung to dry further, then winnowed again before we begin the next stage in the process.

The next step in the harvesting process will be to grind the winnowed wheat seeds into flour that can be used to bake a loaf of bread. During the early stages of the project, we found it difficult to judge how much flour the wheat would produce. It now appears that we will be able to make somewhere between ten and fifteen pounds of flour when all the work is done. That's enough flour to make many loaves of bread, as well as some cookies, cakes and pies—ample delectable rewards for our efforts. We hope you'll continue following our exploits as we finish processing Jeff and Amanda's wheat crop the old-fashioned way.

Post 90: Our Abandoned Doe Returns

August 10, 2018

When we built our farm buildings—garage, goat barn and garden shed—we placed them all close to the house (within twenty feet) so that they would be easily accessible in bad weather, especially the deep snowfalls we can get. To build them on the same level, we had to cut into the highest point on our property, leaving a fairly short but steep bank that is about four feet high. Barb did not like the bare bank, so she has been scattering native wildflower seeds across it, and has deliberately planted some phlox, purple coneflowers, costmary and lantana. Now the bank is bearing a wildflower garden with cosmos, Queen Anne's lace, daisies, chicory, black-eyed susans, and any number of other wildflowers that bloom periodically throughout the season. Our cat, Calli, likes to hunt among the flowers and weeds searching for bunnies, grasshoppers and crickets that live and feed among the plants. This morning, she was treated to some bigger game.

In my July 27, 2018 post, "Our Deer Hunter", I introduced you to a yearling doe who was abandoned by her mother on our farm this past fall. When her mother disappeared, she was a baby fawn still bearing all her spots. We were surprised that she managed to survive the winter alone in our woods, probably because there was so little snowfall over most of the winter allowing her to feed on all the nuts, grass and bark that she could find on our 12.5-acre farm. My son, Michael, said we should adopt her, but I don't think we have to. I think she has adopted our farm as her home. She lives in the woods and the ravine that bisects our farm during the day and feeds in our field during the nights. She has become a frequent sunrise visitor to our field and vegetable garden. Peeper Pond Farm has become her home, and she is less afraid of us than she appears to be of the deep forest that flanks Cave Mountain. We have ushered her out of our garden a couple of times, but we can't seem to frighten her away.

When I let Calli out this morning, she hadn't touched her breakfast meal. She was quite adamant about going outdoors first, which is very unusual. I thought she might be ill, so I kept an eye on her through the windows. I let her out onto the front porch and watched her determinedly trot down the stairs and towards the driveway on the opposite side of the house. She stopped briefly in the driveway at the corner of the house and then began to walk hesitantly along the side of the house towards the garage where Barb's wildflower garden is located. I thought she was preparing to chase a rabbit that has been frequenting the wildflowers for a morning meal, so I grabbed the phone thinking it would be a good opportunity for a picture and slowly opened the main entrance door and stepped out onto the porch behind her to watch the scene.

To my surprise, it wasn't a bunny she was after; it was our abandoned doe. She was standing there beside the garage chomping greedily on some succulent plants she had found there. What was even more unusual about it was that it was 7:45 AM and the sun had been up for a full hour. No deer has ever approached so close to our house before during broad daylight! Yet, there she was, standing there casually eating her breakfast, staring unphased at Calli and me as though we were the curiosity. I activated the cell phone camera and slowly approached her, as I have done several times before. The doe never flinched, but watched me with interest. When I got within eight feet of her, I raised the camera and took a picture of her. She gave me a distinctly inquisitive look, but still didn't flinch. I extended my hand and began to approach her, when the doe swung her head slowly to my side. I then realized that Calli was also approaching her and was about two feet to my right.

The doe apparently began to feel uncomfortable with both of us approaching her at the same time, so she backed a few steps away from us, but continued to stand her ground. I then knelt down onto the driveway to present less of a threat. However, Calli continued to approach the doe. Soon, the doe lowered her head and started to slowly approach Calli. Suddenly, they both froze with their eyes fixed on one another, trying to decide which of them should make the first move. Calli was within one foot of the doe's nose. They contemplated one another for a few seconds until the doe twitched her white tail. At that moment, Calli charged at her and the doe jumped back in surprise and darted back about fifteen feet from her, then turned back to see if Calli was pursuing.

Calli was initially surprised by the doe's quick retreat and had stopped briefly in her tracks until the doe stopped retreating. Then, Calli began to walk towards her again. This time, Calli didn't make a direct approach. She moved slowly to the left and began to walk across the doe's path, as though she was trying to corral her or communicate that she wasn't allowed in Calli's wildflower garden. As usual, the doe just contentedly watched Calli make her statement with a cold indifference. I guess this made Calli somewhat disappointed, so she again charged the doe, eventually chasing her back into the woods along the ravine. Having satisfied herself that the doe finally understood her message, Calli turned around and proudly strolled back to me for some attention with her tail raised high in victory.

I was able to take a number of close-up pictures of the scene. I wish I could have filmed a video clip, but the video function involves a one or two second delay that made it hard to capture what I wanted to film. However, I did take a total of five still photos at various moments, all of which I have placed on our website.

Our resident doe is quite curious about us, despite the fact that she isn't tame. I guess that the doe imprinted with our property when her mother left her at the end of our field before disappearing. Since then, the fawn learned how to survive on her own while waiting patiently, but fruitlessly, for her mother to return. We never posed a threat to her during the many times she saw us in the distance and has, perhaps, accepted us as guardians rather than a threat. Whenever we have approached her, she has looked at us with casual interest or fascination rather than fear. If anything has startled her, it has been Calli's efforts to chase her away. Even so, Calli has never growled at her or displayed threatening behavior when the doe has approached her. In fact, each time the deer has approached Calli, she has backed away until she senses that doe isn't threatening her. Then, she will charge at the doe to see if she can scare it. When the doe retreats, Calli will chase her for a short distance, then check to see if she has sufficiently established her superiority. It may just be a game she plays with the deer, but it always looks as though she is trying to hunt them.

One of our friends told us that deer often fear cats, which might explain her apparent success. Deer can be rather flighty, but it's hard for me to believe that such a relatively large animal would have reason to be frightened by a housecat. Calli is still a very playful kitten and not yet a full year old. We still call her our Deer Hunter, anyway. I'm sure she's quite proud of her success.

As for the doe, I find myself intrigued by her lack of fear of us. Both Barb and I have approached her several times, and she appears to be as curious about us as we are of her. Is it possible that she was abandoned so young that she never learned to fear humans? Has she seen us enough times from our field that we have become familiar to her so she doesn't perceive us as a potential threat? She has never raced away from me even though I have tried to frighten her out of our garden twice. Each time she has left, but only with casual indifference, not with fear. It appears that we may have taught her to stay out of the garden, because she hasn't invaded it since the last time I convinced her to leave. However, she has appeared in other locations and still allows me to get close to her with no fear. I find myself curious to know if she would sniff my extended hand someday or allow me to touch her. I have a friend who operates a deer farm, which might eventually be a better home for her, if she lacks the natural fear she should have of us and other potential threats. It will probably be some time before I know for certain how accepting she truly is of us, but I will continue to test her apparent patience. I will be sure to let you know if and when our resident Peeper Pond Farm doe finally decides what to make of us. Until then, the doe will remain one of the most memorable natural curiosities of our life here at Peeper Pond Farm.

Post 91: A Dairy Kind of Day

August 16, 2018

Barb and I have been so busy during the past three weeks that it's desperately hard for me to remember what we did recently or what day it is today. We've been working in our garden, volunteering to work at the Lion's Club food booth during the Tri-County Fair, mowing our yards, attending local meetings, helping the Barger's process their wheat crop and selling our products at the Grant County Farmer's Market. When we get this busy, it's hard to find time to just stop and think. Actually, that's not a bad thing for me right now. You see, this period of time last year was very difficult for me. Our old cat, Ninny, died on July 20 last year, followed in quick succession by the death of one of our original goat kids, Gertie on August 1, and the sale of our remaining dairy goat herd on August 5. It all happened so quickly that I didn't have time to comprehend it all until our farm became silent and the dust settled. The only consolation I got from it was that our first original goat kid, Essie, lives at a farm that is only three miles from us at the entrance to Smoke Hole Canyon, and I have been able to visit her at least once every month since we bade her farewell. I still miss her today as much or more than I did the day I sold her, and the pain of the regret I've lived with since then remains fresh in my conscience. Knowing that we had no choice at that time gives me no solace.

Those feelings were refreshed yesterday as we made our annual pilgrimage to the State Fair of West Virginia near Lewisburg. While there, we visited both the 4-H and FFA exhibits at the Youth Building, the West Virginia Country Store in the Department of Agriculture building, the farm and home exhibits at the West Virginia Building, and all the dairy goat and cow livestock. We were surprised to find two Pendleton County farm products displayed in the Country Store—Swilled Dog hard cider produced in Franklin and Mark and Sarah Kimble's maple syrup. They live along Mozer Road up Brushy Run Hollow only two miles from our farm. We look up that hollow from our porch. The day was sunny and fair with moderate summer temperatures and the crowd was light, making it comfortable to just stroll around the fairgrounds and truly savor the sights and sounds. In the eight or so years we have attended the State Fair, we've never had a more pleasant experience. It was so relaxing, in fact, that it gave me time and reason to think back about my childhood on our family dairy farm and the retirement dairy goat operation we lost one year ago.

As we toured the 4-H and FFA exhibits in the Youth Building, my mind traveled back in time to my childhood membership in those rural clubs. I participated in our local 4-H club for five years during my early childhood. I remember receiving my five-year pin and attaching the prior year bars to it that I was awarded for each of my first four years of participation. My adoptive mother was a 4-H instructor for many classes covering crafts and home economics. I remember attending one of her craft classes, where I made several Christmas ornaments, some of which involved placing colored crystals into metal forms, and then baking the forms until the crystals melted into plastic panes that would glow like tiny stained-glass windows on the tree when hung in front of Christmas lights. We still have the crystal bell and Christmas stocking ornaments that I made and hang them on our tree each year. She also taught us how to take standard styrofoam coffee cups and melt them down (shrink them) into pilgrim hats by heating them in the oven. I also remember taking a small engine class, a photography class, a knot-tying class and a baking class (also taught by my mother, of course).

My high school participation in the FFA (Future Farmers of America) ran until I was a sophomore. I also took a course in soil science that year. At the time, I was still trying to convince my adoptive father that I was capable of farming, but it was futile. I was an FFA member for only a year-and-a-half, but I managed to sell enough oranges, grapefruit and nectarines to earn the prized denim jacket boldly displaying the blue and gold FFA seal. I actually enjoyed the FFA club more than I had anticipated. In fact, I can confidently say it was the *only* experience I enjoyed in my four years of high school. Once I graduated from high school, I went away to college to begin my compelled transition into the modern, outside world, where I would learn to live and work for the next 36 years.

I don't know how others who have made that intimidating transition felt about it, but I remember being scared and made to feel ashamed of my rural upbringing. I wasn't even sure I could gain enough acceptance from people who lived vastly different lives and lifestyles to be successful. I spent a lot of time with a college friend and roommate, Greg, who was raised in suburban Boston by his father, who had built and was the president of his own successful business. Greg dragged me to movies, a live theatrical performance, and an opera (*Aida*) which I could not understand and during which I eventually fell asleep. Much of the cultural exposure I gained seemed stuffy and "above my station" to me. However, through my long-time college and post-college friendship with him, I learned how to redesign myself, including my behavior and manner of speaking, to live effectively in the outside world.

However, as my professional career evolved, I eventually learned that, regardless of the values that modern society proclaims for itself, the daily workings of life in the outside world was rarely governed by them. I struggled to decide if I needed to just abandon the core values I learned from my childhood (because they seemed so outdated, chided and irrelevant) or to speak out against the abuses of those values I often witnessed (which might have threatened the standard of living that I worked hard to achieve for my wife and son and now depended upon). These occasional moral inconsistencies and the fundamental dependency on money that our modern lifestyle of convenience demanded made life feel unreal to me; like a Halloween costume party that never seemed to end. Did I really have to change everything I was to fit in? My outside-world life was so fundamentally different to the self-reliant farm life I had lived as a child that it seemed like the farming world I once knew had ended, even though I spent most of my professional career living in and working for rural and small communities. The disillusionment I felt after working a 30-year professional career eventually led me to pursue our recently abandoned dairy goat operation in retirement.

These thoughts and memories once again filled my mind as we visited the livestock barns to view the dairy cows and goats. We spent a lot of time visiting the dairy goat pens freely giving reassuring attention to all the does that were eager to accept it. As I scratched the heads and necks of the Oberhasli goats, I remembered all the times I spent caring for and working with our own goats— Essie, Gertie, Cara, Emerald and Lady. I especially remembered the times in their first few bottle-fed months that Essie and Gertie would playfully scamper and bounce around our goat pens, and how they loved to compete to be in control of the top of the rock pile and wooden cedar tree platform I built for them. It all made the loss I felt for them fresh and overwhelming, as though the enormous barrier of time between my childhood and our recent farming life had all but vanished. All in all, it was a dairy kind of day where the struggles and inconsistencies of the life I lived in the outside world disappeared, and I could enjoy once again the simple pleasures of farm life, even as I had to deal with my regrets over the gradual loss of that innocence, swept away by time and change, like a receding tide.

We tried to stay for the dairy goat show, but it was delayed too long (over an hour) by the Charolaise cow judging, and we eventually had to leave for the long drive home. I hope that my thoughts and memories about farm life and my eventual transition into the outside world—as I've expressed in this and many other posts I have written for our farm website—will be familiar to some of our followers. Only those who have lived both of these lifestyles will truly understand how difficult that transition can be, and how much of our traditional heritage—which we *all* share at some point in the past—we have lost to time and change. They say that nothing is lost as long as we remember. I guess I can't casually accept that thought because so many of the memories I recall can be truly understood only from experience, which most people today have never had and will never have the chance to know. That thought recalls in my mind the lyrics to Jamie Johnson's wonderful song, *In Color.* Those old black and white photographs of life in the past never seem to capture and convey all the nuances and richness of life that really should be seen and lived in color. I hope I can find the time to enjoy more dairy-kind-of-days as I live out the rest of my life here at Peeper Pond Farm. Despite the sorrow those mellow memories can often bring, they best capture the true fullness of a life well lived to me. I think we'll go to visit Essie this afternoon to let her know that she is not and will not be forgotten.

Post 92: Family Gathering

August 27, 2018

    Summer (Memorial Day – Labor Day) is the traditional time in West Virginia for family reunions. In our state, these gatherings tend to be very large, spanning multiple generations and including distant relatives, with family members often traveling great distances to attend. Here in Pendleton County, the largest annual event may be the Alt-Kimble family reunion, now celebrating its 84th gathering, which is held at the Old Judy Church about three miles north of our farm, near the Grant/Pendleton county line. This reunion is so large that it includes a church service, bluegrass band performances and guest speakers. Even non-family members routinely attend. This year, Barb and I were invited to attend, even though we are not related in any way to the Alts or Kimbles, although we have become good friends with several of their distant relatives.

    This year, one of the scheduled guest speakers was WV Delegate Bill Hamilton, who is now running to become our State Senator. I needed to speak with him about my effort to pass a bill that will allow direct farm-to-consumer sales of unprocessed farm-fresh milk. At this point in the election season, he has no formal opposition for that seat, so I hope to gain his support for that initiative. This gave me an added incentive to attend, but as it turned out, he was unable to be there.

    I did, however, get an opportunity to meet Estyl Curtis Shreve, who was a long-time Pendleton County Sheriff from the Smoke Hole community. His brother, Dona Barton Shreve, wrote a trilogy of books detailing his childhood experiences and many interesting, colorful stories and legends about Smoke Hole that define its heritage and special character. I have referenced some of those stories in my previous posts. One of the three books features stories about Estyl's experiences as the County Sheriff, and I had been interested in getting his signature on that book for more than a decade. At 96 years of age (he will turn 97 in October), he was the oldest person attending the reunion. I truly enjoyed the opportunity I had to sit down with him and share some of our personal memories. Despite his advancing age, Estyl's memories remain sharp and vivid, and he carries himself with great dignity. I was honored to get his signature on the book, which, ironically and coincidently, I just happened to be rereading at the time.

    This was the second time in my life that I had an opportunity to listen to and talk with a 90+ year old person at a family reunion. During my childhood on our family farm in New Hampshire, I attended a number of my father's Hill-Courier family reunions in Belmont, NH. The Hills were his mother's immediate family and her oldest brother attended once in 1970 or '71. At that time, he was 94 or 96 years old (I forget which), having been born only a decade or so after the Civil War. Two of his uncles had fought in the war, and he recounted tales of their exploits and his life experiences throughout the late nineteenth century. Having lived most of his life deep in the mountains of northern New Hampshire, he had a very traditional manner of speaking that included words and phrases that we struggled at times to understand as the stories flowed from him. I recall his memories of hunting in the White Mountains where "wildcats" still roamed (which I now know to have been an exaggeration) and of the first "horseless carriage" he ever saw and how it spooked his horse as it passed by. Like most multi-generational mountain patriarchs I have known, he was a spell-binding story teller who mesmerized us by the way he told his tales. Although we attended a number of the annual Hill reunions, I remember that one best because very few children ever attended them (most of my father's extended family had no children), so we were often bored with the affairs. At that time, we were told that children were to be seen, not heard, so any stories that could be told in an engaging and entertaining way stood out in our minds.

At this year's Alt-Kimble reunion, we also had an opportunity to see the Old Judy Church, which was built in 1848. During the church's early years, the Pendleton County line was located about three or more miles north of where it is today. It was the first church built in Pendleton County, and although it has been substantially rehabilitated over the years, it still retains its chinked log construction. A close inspection of the large white pine logs clearly revealed the adz marks made when they were first hand-hewed. The walls of the church were also adorned with pictures of family members and memorable events in the past, such as the historic flood of 1949 and the first train to arrive in Petersburg.

It was a pleasant day for the reunion and everyone appeared to enjoy the festivities. It certainly captured the spirit of family fellowship and loyalty that so gracefully frames traditional life in the mountains and hollows of wild and wonderful West Virginia. In all honesty, we had a far better time at the Alt-Kimble reunion than I ever had at the old Hill-Courier family reunions.

I'd also like to use this post to give you a brief update on some of my previous website posts from this summer. In my August 2 post regarding the 2018 Tri-County fair, I announced that we had won ribbons for six of the eleven produce and product exhibits we entered. However, earlier last week, we received a check for the awards we earned, and it was a little more than we had estimated. As it turns out, two more of our exhibits (my banana bread and Barb's sourdough bread) also won second and third place ribbons, respectively.

To our surprise, we actually won eight ribbons from our eleven entries, not six as I had reported in my original post. Not too shabby for our first participation in the Tri-County fair.

Also, as I informed you earlier, we have been appearing at the Grant County Farmer's Market most Saturday mornings since June 30 to sell some of the fresh vegetables we have harvested from our garden. Although the weather this year has been challenging, with all the excessive rains, high humidity and limited sunshine, our garden produced well and we managed to set some new record proceeds levels. However, after a total of seven appearances, many of our vegetables have been exhausted (including cabbage, squash, pumpkins, cucumbers, broccoli and corn), so we don't feel our remaining garden production will support continued appearances. It appears that our last regular farmer's market sale for the season was on August 25. We will now be working to store and preserve what little our garden has left to offer in preparation for the coming winter.

As for the weather conditions during this growing season that I discussed in several earlier posts, the excessive rains we experienced this spring have continued throughout the summer. We received higher than average rainfall totals in both July and August, with every month since April producing two or more days with rainfall totals in excess of an inch. We have received a total of 8.08 inches of rain in August (for which the 30-year average rainfall is only 3.54 inches) and more rain is forecast over the final four days. July and August also plagued us with high humidity levels, even though our highest temperature reading so far this summer has topped out at 92 degrees on June 18, July 4 and July 14. If that high temperature holds through the rest of August and all of September, it will be one of the coolest yearly maximum temperatures we have seen over the past decade. I think the cloudy skies that have accompanied the endless days of high relative humidity have helped keep most of the daily high temperatures below 90 degrees. If we're lucky enough to deserve some dry and frosty nights in early fall, we should be able to enjoy some spectacular fall foliage this year. I don't know about you, but I think we deserve it. As for winter, I have no idea what to expect from it.

That's how we stand today at Peeper Pond Farm. As always, we wish you and yours the best of what life has to offer. We hope you'll continue to follow our adventures.

Post 93: An Ode to Fall

September 7, 2018

    This summer has given us many torrid and sultry days. The excessive rains that began in the spring and continued throughout the summer have kept the soil so saturated with moisture that it is stirred into a dense ground fog by the rising sun that gradually dissolves and hangs oppressively in the air throughout the day before returning to the ground at the end of the day as an evening thunderstorm or a heavy dew. This daily summer pattern is familiar to us from all the years we spent living in Georgia and Alabama between 1991 and 2004. Every time that a front has swept through, enticing us with a brief reprieve of refreshing dry air and cool nights, the heat and humidity returns and dampens our hopes for a lasting relief. In all honesty, the heat itself has not been extreme, as the highest temperature of the year (thus far) has been 93 degrees on August 29, but the intense humidity combined with numerous daytime highs between 86 and 92 degrees has made it very uncomfortable to work outdoors. There is little relief from the heat after sunset, as our morning low temperatures have not dipped below 63 degrees since August 26. What cooling we have received after sunset only serves to make the air feel even more dank and humid than it was during the heat of the day. Yet, as we work our way into the month of September, we relish the knowledge that this oppressive summer weather pattern will invariably change for the better.

    That confidence is bolstered by the changes we see emerging across our landscape. The summer flowers have gradually faded away and are being replaced by the early golden autumn blooms of wingstem and goldenrod. The summer weeds are dying back as evidenced by the growing prevalence of brown and wilted stems along the roadsides. Even the droning sounds of the cicadas and katydids are fading away despite the lingering heat. The daylight hours are waning rapidly now, and each night becomes noticeably longer than the last. Our memories of these changes tell us that the weather can only resist them for so long. Fall is certainly on the horizon.

    I was thinking about this yesterday morning, as I sat on our front porch admiring a truly beautiful sunrise. I realized that we would have a pretty sunrise when I noticed an orange glow building low on the horizon over Middle Mountain. The air was still and the sky was dotted with dark, thin morning clouds. After a few moments, the sunlight began to decorate the edges of those clouds with a soft, rosy tint, and the dark background sky began to assume a subtle shade of aquamarine. As the sun approached the horizon, I could see its golden glow reflected on the leading edges of the most distant clouds over the mountain. It was a peaceful and reassuring scene that boldly proclaimed better days are on the way. I look forward to cooler, refreshing nights and a vibrant, colorful fall foliage season.

Our summer chores here at Peeper Pond Farm are also changing. Our vegetable garden is dying back, and we have begun removing many of the plants we sowed. Much of our bounty has been canned or frozen for the winter. We look forward to making some fresh homemade cider for the winter. Lawn mowing is the only summer task that remains. Once the heat and humidity finally break, we will begin our routine fall chores in preparation for the cold and snow of winter. We really don't know what to expect for winter this year, but as usual, we will prepare for the worst. Aside from ordering a refill of our LP gas tank, we have already acquired and stored all the heating fuel we will need for the coming winter season. No matter what happens or how hard the wind blows, we know that our house will remain warm and cozy.

By the way, our resident deer, which we named, Peeper, has disappeared. We haven't seen her for at least three consecutive weeks. Even Calli has stopped watching for her to emerge from the ravine in the mornings. Perhaps she was struck by a car. We have no idea of where she has gone or why, but we hope that she is off seeking a mate for the fall. Maybe she is finally asserting her adult independence and no longer needs the security of her childhood home on our farm. All we can do is wish her well. It is the same wish that I have for you, our loyal readers. Happy autumn from all of us here at Peeper Pond Farm.

Post 94: Smithsonian

September 9, 2018

I saw a recent television news segment highlighting a special farming exhibit at the Smithsonian National Museum of American History in Washington, DC. The story stated that the exhibit was being displayed to celebrate the 100th anniversary of John Deere's successful Waterloo Boy tractor, which the company first acquired in 1918. The company and the John Deere trademark name are much older. It began manufacturing operations in 1837 with its pioneering plow and an assortment of farming hand tools. The company started experimenting with and producing tractors in 1912, but its tractor line did not begin to enjoy widespread popularity until the introduction of the Waterloo Boy. As those of you who have read my thoughts about the history and evolution of farming in my previous website posts know, I feel it is about time that the importance of agriculture to our American society is given greater attention. This was a special exhibit I had to see for myself.

Admittedly, I was not excited about making another trip to Washington, DC. It is a three-hour drive from our farm just to reach the Fairfax, VA transit station at the western edge of the Metro Orange Line. To add insult to injury, not only have the Metro transit fares increased (which I anticipated), but they now charge a fee for weekend parking at the station and an additional fee for the fare card. Both of these were free the last time we used the system more than two years ago. The attendant at the station told us that the new fare card charge was for the plastic card they have introduced. He said that the paper cards were eliminated to "save the trees." So, in the established tradition of our society's hysteria-driven rush to a solution, the system now charges its patrons an additional fee for an allegedly "environmentally friendly" fare card made from a petroleum-based product. Oh, Admiral Farragut, I wish you had never uttered your immortal words, "Damn the torpedoes; full steam ahead!" Will we ever again learn to think critically before reacting?

However, we had already decided to abandon sensibility by going back to Washington in the first place, so we pressed on to our destination, the Museum of American History at the National Mall. Fortunately, the damp and unseasonably cool weather, along with the recent ending of the official summer tourist season combined to grant us uncrowded trains and a low turnout at the museum. Having heard that the agriculture display was a "special exhibit," I asked a museum attendant where I could find it. After a small group consultation (two of them did not appear to know what I was talking about), I was told I could find it in the west wing of the museum's first (ground) floor.

The 1918 Waterloo Boy tractor was not difficult to find, with its trademark bright green and yellow paint, but it seemed to stand alone. The rest of the supporting "agricultural" displays were scattered throughout a broader exhibit detailing the evolution of our national economy. While it wasn't an inappropriate place to educate the public on how the growth and evolution of agriculture influenced our modern economy, it hardly seemed like a special tribute to that story.

The overall display included a second antique Fordson tractor, a small-scale model of the 1794 cotton gin, an interactive computer display that allowed participants to understand the thought process and choices a farmer must consider to successfully operate a modern farm, and scattered tidbits of information detailing how the agriculture industry has achieved great increases in productivity from a declining workforce. These are points I have made in some of my past website posts and writings.

I did find a display that explained how the introduction of the tractor contributed to farm productivity. Although a tractor allows a farmer to cultivate and harvest more land faster and easier than using work horses, the farmer also benefits from reduced "fuel" costs—a tractor requires fuel only when it is being used, where a team of horses must be fed constantly whether or not they are working—while making more land available for production (instead of dedicating it to grow food for horses). The competition to produce more food at a lower cost drove farmers to modernize their farm operations with tractors and other advanced equipment. These points, as well as the nation's transition from a predominantly rural to a predominantly urban population, were clearly explained, although one has to search for the information in the larger exhibit.

However, I noticed that some important aspects of the evolution of modern farming were not clearly discussed or were simply overlooked. For instance, I found no discussion of how these technological innovations allowed the most profitable farms to expand in size and scale, while the smaller, less profitable family farms slowly disappeared. The increased productivity from industrial farms, combined with the evolution of modern food processing industries, provided more food for consumers at lower costs, which contributed to the gradual demise of non-commercial, individual family farming activities, such as milking a cow, raising a hog and planting gardens. Why do all that work when you can afford to buy all the food you need from a store? It is during this transitional era that raising children became an increasing cost to the family and a less necessary source of supporting labor.

In my view, the full story of how advances in farm technology and mechanization helped fundamentally change American society is muddled when these other related trends are not explained or discussed. They help us understand why and how we have produced an industrialized food processing industry and why so many people today do not understand where their food comes from. They also explain why so many small family farm operations have disappeared and why farmers and farm issues are so politically marginalized or misunderstood in our society. In that sense, I feel the Smithsonian's agriculture exhibits fail to capture the true scope of today's farming crisis. Acknowledging the role that agricultural modernization played in building our nation is an important first step. Unfortunately, it doesn't go far enough to help the public understand why farmers struggle to produce the food our increasingly urban society needs. Perhaps they should consider adding a new dedicated farming museum to their collection. Until then, I'll just have to keep discussing these obscure issues. I'm just relieved to be back home at Peeper Pond Farm.

Post 95: A Mist Opportunity

September 12, 2018

We continue to experience Seattle weather here at Peeper Pond Farm. Another front has draped itself across our mountains feeding us a daily dose of rainfall. Today will be the sixth day in a row it has rained and the sun has been hidden by low clouds and fog. It began on September 7 when we received 1.43 inches of rain. During each of the following days, we received 0.78 inches, 1.12 inches, 0.56 inches and 0.31 inches. When I awoke this morning to another fog-shrouded daybreak, I discovered another 0.38 inches in our rain gauge and we are expecting more in the afternoon. As of the morning of September 12, we have received a total of 4.92 inches of rainfall this month, while the 30-year average for the entire month in nearby Upper Tract is only 3.15 inches. That brings our total cumulative rainfall since April 1 (the day I set out our rain gauge for the season) to 45.61 inches. This compares to the 30-year average for Upper Tract over a full year of 35.33 inches. In less than five-and-a-half months, we have received just over ten inches more rain than would occur in an average full year.

Consider that we are still waiting to see what Hurricane Florence will drop on us after it comes ashore in the Carolinas and you can see why we loudly proclaim we've had enough rain for a while! Nature needs to understand that the *last* thing a drowning person needs is another glass of water. We desperately need a chance to dry out and clean up from all the mudslides, downed trees and accumulated flood debris. It's bad enough that I can't find a good time to mow the grass, which has grown relentlessly all summer long.

Although we are in our sixth consecutive day with no sunshine, I can't say that we have been completely deprived of the natural beauty that surrounds us. The dense fog that settles across our mountains and hollows has a beauty all its own. I was sitting on the porch this morning, watching it creep through the forests and drift down Brushy Run Hollow. It's the one opportunity we get to watch up close as a cloud grows and drifts across the land. I've watched the mist fall and collect on the grass in tiny droplets that cling to every blade, leaf and wildflower petal in our field. I have also consoled Calli many times when she races to visit me on the porch from her hunting forays, drenched from nose to tail and the top of her back to the soles of her feet and seeking a brief respite to clean the accumulated water off her fur. I also enjoy hearing the steady rush of water in our ravine as it cascades down from Cave Mountain, accompanied by a chorus of tree frogs. Each occasional storm announces its approach by the soft, swelling patter of raindrops on the forest leaves and boldly proclaims its power with a rumble of thunder that echoes endlessly along the valley. It's a pleasure to watch rippling curtains of rainfall tumble down from a distant shower as it slowly creeps across the landscape. Many times this summer, we have enjoyed full double rainbows spread out across our mountain view.

These are but a few of the sensual delights that rainy weather can bring. Even though every opportunity for mist is another missed opportunity for sun, our rural Pendleton County mountain landscape displays a beauty all its own that we never cease to enjoy and appreciate. How many of you take the time to truly enjoy the natural beauty of your own home, and how many of you get the opportunity to live in a place that abounds in such natural beauty as we experience daily here at Peeper Pond Farm? Trust me when I say it's the best cure for a rainy day—even for a bunch of them.

Post 96: The Siege of Fort Seybert

September 18, 2018

Our extended stretch of cloudy and rainy weather continued yesterday, as the remains of Hurricane Florence swept through our area. We received our third day this month with one or more inches of rainfall, with a total of 1.05 inches from the storm. Through September 17, we have received a total of 6.45 inches of rainfall as compared to a 30-year average of 3.15 inches for the month. Regardless of what we receive over the rest of the month, September is already the sixth consecutive month in which we have received twice or more the average amount of rainfall.

What has made it worse has been the high humidity levels we have experienced for the past two months and the nearly continuous eleven-day stretch (beginning on September 7) with no sunshine, except for some brief periods in the afternoons of September 13 and 17. We have had dense fog and drizzle most mornings and measurable rainfall on every day of the stretch, including three days with one or more inches of accumulation. It was during this soggy period that we attended and participated in the 50th Treasure Mountain Festival—Pendleton County's biggest annual event.

Although we have attended the prior eleven festivals, this was the first one in which we actively participated. Barb worked with the Sew and Sews Quilt Guild of Pendleton County to host the fair's annual Quilt Show, in which many of her quilt products were displayed. The table runner and lap quilt that won first and second place ribbons (respectively) at the Tri-County Fair earlier this summer also won first and third place ribbons at the Quilt Show—a very pleasant surprise for her. Also, this year, we attended (for the first time) the annual restaging of the April 28, 1758 siege and burning of Fort Seybert. This is the historic event for which the Treasure Mountain Festival was named.

The construction of Fort Seybert in eastern Pendleton County was commissioned in 1755 by George Washington after the fateful loss of the colonial invasion of Fort Duchesne (later Fort Pitt) to remove French forces that had become established in present day Pittsburgh, PA. The battle ignited the French and Indian War (1755-1763) which threatened to halt and repulse British colonial expansion into the Allegheny Mountains. The Shawnee and Delaware Indian Tribes, who opposed the gradual movement of pioneer settlers into their favored sacred hunting grounds, joined forces with the French to drive the colonial American settlers back to their original territorial boundaries east of the Alleghenies.

One of the more significant skirmishes that framed the early years of the war was the 1758 attack and burning of Forts Upper Tract and Seybert in Pendleton County, which also resulted in the brutal massacre of most of the settlers who sought refuge in those forts. The attack by thirty or so Shawnee and Delaware Indians was led by Chief Killbuck, who was seeking vengeance for prior alleged offenses by prominent British settlers, including Thomas Cresap. The Indians had attacked and burned Fort Upper Tract, killing all of its inhabitants, just days before arriving at Fort Seybert on April 22. Uncertain of how many forces were garrisoned at the fort and realizing their closing proximity to Colonial support forces, the Indians quietly surrounded the fort in the early morning fog. Unbeknownst to the Indians, a large party of the fort's defenders had recently headed east over Shenandoah Mountain to secure provisions. When two of the settlers (a man and woman) emerged from the fort, the Indians quickly subdued and captured them, but in so doing made the occupants aware of their presence.

This incident touched off rounds of periodic gunfire as the settlers defended the fort. One of Killbuck's war party was seriously injured, and his survival remained in question throughout the battle. Realizing that his success was not assured, Killbuck offered surrender terms to the settlers, promising that if they abandoned the fort their lives would be spared. Since the fort's complement was reduced, the settlers agreed to Killbuck's terms and surrendered the fort— although two of the defenders lagged behind. This led to a period of mutual distrust that caused confusion on the part of both the invaders and the settlers. Eventually, the invaders decided to kill some of the settlers. As the settlers were being separated into two parties (one that would be spared while the other would be killed), some of the settlers managed to escape, which ensured the story would be known and raised fears by the Indians that they would soon be pursued by Colonial forces. The Indians then killed the doomed group of settlers with their tomahawks and set fire to the fort. After burning the fort, they marched the surviving settlers to the west, over the mountains, to evade pursuit.

In the process of invading the fort, legend states that the Indians took all the settlers' valuables and stored them in a large iron cook-pot to carry them on their journey back to their Ohio homelands. The pot was suspended on a pole and carried by two of the warriors as they trudged up the steep mountains. The heavy weight of the pot laden with their plunder caused the Indians carrying it to repeatedly fall behind. To quicken their pace and avoid capture, they decided to bury the treasure along the way and retrieve it later when it would be safer to carry it. Little did they know that this would be the last time the Indians would travel into Pendleton County, so the treasure was never retrieved. Although many attempts have been made to retrace the war party's path, the buried treasure from Fort Seybert has never been found. Thus, the legend of Treasure Mountain was born.

We enjoyed the mock performance of the legendary siege and burning of Fort Seybert. It was a fitting celebratory climax to the annual Treasure Mountain Festival. We were surprised by the large crowd in attendance despite the inclement weather and periodic showers. We only hope that the battle and the passing of Hurricane Florence will clear the air in our area and herald the return of sunshine and dry weather to Pendleton County. We truly need a break from the gloom.

Post 97: Emerging from the Fog

September 30, 2018

    Now that September is effectively over, I wanted to let you know where we stand with our excessive rainfall season. We finished the month with 9.33 inches making it the fourth month in the past six to top nine inches of rain. Our 30-year monthly average for nearby Upper Tract is 3.15 inches. In the six months that have passed since April 1, we have received 50.02 inches of rain at our farm, which compares to a 30-year *annual* average (for a full twelve months) of 35.33 inches. This is a tremendous amount of rain for a full year, much less for only half a year.

    September 27 was the 18th of the preceding 21 days that we had received measurable rainfall. Most of those days were cloudy with dense, heavy fog that clung to our mountains almost every morning. For the first time this month, the last three days of the month have been mostly sunny with cool, dry air. Despite this extended dry period, most of our rivers and creeks are running full just draining our mountains and hills of all the accumulated rainfall. Still, it was a pleasure to watch the fog lift from the mountains at sunrise on September 28 and to again see the high ridgelines that had been obscured by the clouds for weeks. The cool, dry weather over the past three days, with highs in the mid-70s and lows in the upper 40s and low 50s, has given us a welcome opportunity to open the windows and air out the house. We will need more than a week more of this weather to dry out the saturated topsoil, which squishes under our feet when we walk in the yard.

    It has been a wet and muggy summer that we will remember for many years to come. Even our hummingbirds stayed a few days later than usual, probably because they couldn't tell from the temperatures and changing sun angle that the time has passed for their annual fall migration. It has been a long time since we have seen the stars at night or the sun during the day. I know that Seattle is a popular place to live, but I hope they won't mind taking their weather back. We've tried it out this summer and decided that it's not that popular with us. Unfortunately, it appears that the arrival of true fall weather will not deliver the brilliant fall foliage we usually enjoy. The supersaturated soil has stressed many of the deciduous trees, which are dropping exhausted brown and dried leaves early. Our landscape is drowning and even the grass has lost its brilliant green luster. The landscape can enjoy only so much rain in one season.

    The big question everyone is asking now is what we can expect for winter. We've had two straight winter seasons with below average snowfalls. If the precipitation we've received this summer could be converted to snow, it would amount to nearly 500 inches. I certainly hope I don't have to shovel that much this winter.

Post 98: Passing on the Tradition

October 14, 2018

    Back forty or more years ago in time when I was growing up on a small family dairy farm, I lived a lifestyle that was another generation older for that point in time. Although that way of living seems today as though it's been dead for a generation or more, many aspects of it live on today in the Potomac Highlands region of West Virginia. That's why we chose to retire here. It feels right to live out my old age in a place that surrounds me with people who understand that lifestyle and still honor certain aspects of it. No one wants to die thinking he or she is the last person in the world who remembers the things that were special to them in their childhood. There's just no dignity in that. Many of those memories remain fresh in my mind, and it just doesn't seem possible that they could be so far in the past and rejected by a society that acts as though it has no living memory of anything that happened more than two computer generations ago. I suspect some of you reading this post understand how I feel.

    One of those old memories that always comes to mind when the first cold, crisp fall breeze arrives is apple picking. Our family would spend a day picking fresh MacIntosh apples in a small commercial orchard less than a mile from our house, behind the old two-room Farwell School. All of us kids would scramble up the apple trees to see who could pick the highest apple. If one of us fell in the attempt, we just dusted ourselves off and climbed another tree. The game rules did not allow for any crying. It was a time when simple things like that were a fun and memorable break from the daily chores that drove our life on the farm. I can even remember when kids attending the school proved their metal by climbing up the rear stone wall of the building during recess to jump over the fence and steal some apples without getting caught by the teachers.

    We visited that old orchard for several years before it was abandoned and sold. Then, for a few subsequent years, we visited a local water-powered cider mill to buy a few gallons of fresh apple cider. I found that trip to be even more exciting than the orchard. The sounds of that mill would capture my attention and remain ingrained in my mind. There was the splashing sound of water tumbling over the waterwheel that powered the mill, the clattering and clacking noise made by the large wooden pegs and gears that drove the big fruit press, and the groans made by the old timber axles that drove the press. While these sounds were quite loud, they weren't offensive to the ear. For me, they fueled a sense of awe and wonder to learn how it all worked. However, it was the overwhelming scent of the antique wood soaked with apple juice that stands out most clearly in my mind. We always found the cider to be affordable for our budget, probably because it was not always the primary source of income for the mill. Most of those old mills made far more money producing applejack – a highly fermented form of apple wine that was often referred to then as New England or New Hampshire moonshine.

While I no longer have access to a cider mill, I decided to buy a fruit press for our retirement farm operation so we could make our own fresh apple cider each fall. We had planted a small orchard of apple trees to provide a source of apples, but our trees have struggled to produce useful fruit because of the red cedar blight that we cannot control. Instead, we purchase apple culls and drops from a Mennonite fruit farm in nearby Rockingham County, Virginia. These apples are fine (and less expensive) for producing cider, even though they have bruises and blemishes that make them less commercially desirable for city customers seeking fresh apples for eating or baking. We simply cut out the blemishes and run them through our hand-operated fruit grinder and press to produce the cider we desire to make.

This year, we decided to share the cider-making experience with some of our local friends, Bonnie and Wayne Ours and Dale and Merrily Carroll (who now own our first dairy goat kid, Essie). We also invited Marina Barnett, the WHSV-TV reporter who filmed the news segment about our dairy issues, to join us. During the filming, she expressed an interest in learning how we make our cider, and I jumped at the chance to encourage a member of the younger generation to learn this simple traditional lifestyle skill.

We all gathered here at Peeper Pond Farm yesterday morning to process three forty-pound boxes of apples into nearly six gallons of fresh cider. The air was as cool and breezy, just as I recalled from my childhood days of apple picking. I explained the process to Marina and showed her how the press worked. We then began cutting up the apples, crushing them into pulp, and pressing the pulp into cider. Marina eagerly participated in all aspects of the process as we all took turns operating the fruit press. Throughout the process, we shared stories and laughed freely at our blunders. After two hours of work making the cider, we enjoyed a warm meal of soup and grilled cheese sandwiches. I can honestly report that a good time was had by all. After all the conversations we shared about the traditional ways of living, Marina decided she wanted to return again and learn how we make goat milk soap. We are looking forward to her next visit and hope we can find other ways to share our knowledge of the "old ways."

Passing on these time-honored lifestyle folkways to the next generation was one of our primary aspirations for our retirement homestead farm operation here at Peeper Pond Farm. We feel honored by Marina's interest in learning them and giving them relevance in the twenty-first century. Many may feel that these practices are outdated or a waste of time, but to us they are a cherished tradition that helps us understand how our ancestors lived and where the basic products we consume come from. When you stop to think about it, most of us are less than four generations removed from ancestors who knew these skills and made these products for themselves. That makes them part of our shared cultural heritage. With all the interest in genealogical research, isn't it as important to understand how our ancestors lived as it is to know who they were? Doesn't our human curiosity extend that far? We hope you'll want to learn these experiences for yourself and realize the value of self-reliance. If the interest captures your imagination, please consider giving us a call. You'll find us eager to satisfy your interest, and who knows, perhaps you'll also discover what fun the adventure can be.

Post 99: Grinding Wheat

October 22, 2018

This post is the fourth in a series discussing our adventures helping Jeff & Amanda Barger harvest and process an experimental plot of wheat into flour the traditional way—using traditional hand tools and equipment. This process requires a number of separate steps completed over a long period of time. The next and final segment in the series is Post 100: Baking Homemade Wheat Bread.

Previous posts in this series:

Post 81: Reaping Wheat – A Shocking Experience (July 5, 2018)

Post 84: Bringing in the Sheaves (July 20, 2018)

Post 89: Winnowing It All Down (August 8, 2018)

One of the oldest structures I recall from the family dairy farm where I was raised was the "corn shed." It was a small, square shed—approximately twenty feet wide by twenty feet long—built upon a cut stone foundation. The foundation stones were simply and precisely stacked, not mortared into place. The framing for the shed consisted of four-by-four-inch, hand-hewn timbers connected by mortise and tenon joints with wooden pegs. Each peg had squared tapers that were driven into round holes for extra strength. The exterior planks were all mounted up and down lengthwise on the framing, instead of side to side. It was an impressive marvel of pioneer hand construction that stood for nearly 200 years before it finally collapsed under a heavy winter snow load.

I don't believe it was always called a corn shed, but it had probably served in that capacity for 50 years before my parents bought it with the farm in 1960. The more modern name for the shed was likely given to it when a small, hand-operated corn mill was installed in the center of the building. We never knew how old it was, but it probably dated back to the turn of the century. As I remember, it stood about four feet tall, topped by a square wooden hopper. The internal grinding components were completely enclosed in a wooden frame (about three feet deep by three feet wide), so we couldn't see its inner workings. At the base of the mill was a wooden chute that dispensed the ground corn meal into a receiving bowl. A large hand crank was mounted on one side of the device. Aside from the legs upon which it stood, the crank was the only other visible metal component. It was shaped like a steering wheel with four slightly curved spokes and a heavy wooden handle bolted to it. What painted labeling we found on the front of the mill had faded and worn so much over time that it was no longer legible. We tried to crank it a number of times over the years, but its inner gears and grinding components had degraded or worn to the point that the crank was frozen in place. Since we knew nothing about its operation and we had no need to use it, we just left it alone and filled the rest of the shed around it with an assortment of tools, tubs of nails and fencing staples, burlap grain sacks, spare construction materials and other miscellaneous farm implements, until it eventually collapsed.

Although I never saw the corn mill operate or learned how it was constructed, we used a very similar milling device on Saturday, October 20, 2018 to grind Jeff and Amanda Barger's summer wheat crop. The Bargers bought the portable mill from a farm in central West Virginia and restored it to what we all hoped would be a stable operating condition. The mill was well worn by decades of use. The wooden hopper at the top was missing, but we were able to scoop the wheat grain into a hole in the center of the top grinding stone. The missing hopper would have funneled the grain into that hole. The grinding face of each mill stone showed significant wear, and several of the cut channels that conveyed the wheat grains between the stones had worn nearly smooth, but Jeff felt it would be okay for the small volume of wheat we needed to grind. Jeff had mounted two wooden skids on the base of the mill and reinforced its framing, but it was clear that it was in an overall weak condition.

The first step in operating it was to connect it to a tractor. A wooden drum at the base of the bottom grinding stone was connected to a tractor flywheel (a metal drum that was powered directly by the tractor's engine) using a long, heavy leather belt. The most critical issue was to make sure that the tractor flywheel was properly aligned with and at the same elevation as the drum at the base of the mill. If it isn't aligned properly, the belt will gradually work its way off the drum or flywheel as it operates. We struggled to get the tractor position, angle and level correct so that the belt would remain in place during operation. After at least an hour of trial and error (and a lot of kibitzing), we managed to get the alignment close enough to safely operate the mill.

Once the tractor engine was able to get the bottom mill stone rotating to grind the grain, we had to adjust the level of the bottom stone so that it would effectively grind the grain. This required a few small adjustments as we began loading grain into the mill. The next problem we encountered was the prevailing wind. Although the air was dry with outdoor temperatures of 55-60 degrees (quite typical for this time of the year), we had to fight against some blustery winds ranging between ten and twenty miles per hour that blew some of the finely ground grain away as it discharged from the back side of the mill. Most of the fine flour we could produce was too light to fall into the bowl we used to catch the output, leaving behind the larger grit that the mill stones were unable to completely reduce to powder. We tried grinding the wheat twice, but were unable to get all of it thoroughly reduced to flour. The age and wear on the mill had reduced its grinding efficiency, and we could not prevent the winds from blowing away the most finely ground flour it could produce. We eventually decided that the product we obtained from the mill would need to be ground further using a smaller hand-operated mill inside the house to finish the milling process.

Despite the difficulties we faced, we all enjoyed the experience. Our gathering numbered about a dozen neighbors and friends, all of whom helped with various aspects of the milling process and/or prepared food for the evening pot luck buffet meal we shared. The spirit of comradery and fellowship that we shared through our work made the job more pleasant and enjoyable. Some of us had not met before, but we were all exchanging stories and laughs well before we sat down for the evening meal. It was another reminder that self-reliant living does not require working in isolation. As the Amish experience has documented over generations of determined separation from the modern world, nothing builds a stronger community spirit and social cohesion better than shared values and hard work.

Our cooperative efforts to process a plot of wheat into flour the "old-fashioned way," using manual labor and technology at least 100 years old taught us that working closely together in achieving a common goal is a compelling social binding force that modern high-tech social media lacks. (It also reminded us why farmers needed large families to share the workload.) Working cooperatively in the face of a difficult task forges strong social bonds that build interpersonal understanding and companionship that is completely lost in a faceless e-mail or text message from a person you've never seen or met. It is interesting to note that, while practicing self-reliant living, we were actually building a small community of people who share those basic lifestyle values. The memories we gained through that community effort will last us a lifetime—ore that, for some of us, may last almost as long as the historic practices we used to complete our work. In a fitting celebration of those time-honored old ways, we concluded our meal with an impromptu bluegrass music sing-along. As we at Peeper Pond Farm insist, the old ways of living are not necessarily wrong simply because they are considered outdated by modern conveniences. A simple comparison of the strong social cohesion that exists in today's Amish society with that of our modern, politically divided, technology-driven urban society will certainly make that point clear.

Once Amanda and Jeff have finished grinding the wheat into flour, they will give us some to use in making a loaf of homemade bread. That will be the fifth and final step in the process. If the weather is cold enough at that time, we will even bake it in our own wood cookstove, which will allow us to complete the process using technology that is at least 100 years old. We hope you'll continue to follow our farm website posts to learn the success of our effort.

Post 100: Baking Homemade Wheat Bread

November 5, 2018

This post is the fifth and final post in a series discussing our adventures helping Jeff & Amanda Barger harvest and process an experimental plot of wheat into flour the traditional way—using traditional hand tools and equipment. This process requires a number of separate steps completed over a long period of time.

<u>Previous posts in this series</u>:

Post 81: Reaping Wheat – A Shocking Experience (July 5, 2018)

Post 84: Bringing in the Sheaves (July 20, 2018)

Post 89: Winnowing It All Down (August 8, 2018)

Post 99: Grinding Wheat (October 22, 2018)

Few people I know today remember the story of "The Little Red Hen." According to this old-time children's folk tale, a little red hen finds a grain of wheat, which inspires her to plant, harvest and grind some wheat into flour to make a loaf of delicious homemade bread. Realizing this to be a long and laborious process, the hen asks for help from other animals that share the barnyard with her, including a dog, a cat and a duck. All of them refuse to help with the hard work, so the little red hen does it all by herself. When the hen finally bakes the bread and is ready to eat it, she asked each of them if they wished to join her. With all the hard work done, each of the animals eagerly wanted to share the bread with her. However, the little red hen denied them a share of the bread, because they had done nothing to help her with the work when asked to do so. The moral of the story is that those who wish to enjoy the fruits of hard work should be willing to offer their help to produce it. This is one of the core values of traditional living that I learned growing up on our family dairy farm.

This is why Barb and I were eager to help Jeff and Amanda Barger harvest and process their experimental wheat crop to experience and learn the process with manual abor and traditional practices and equipment commonly used 100 years ago. We participated in a community effort with like-minded friends and neighbors throughout the summer and fall to harvest, flail, winnow and mill the wheat into a coarse grain. We shared in the labor and enjoyed the time we spent together at each stage of the process. In appreciation for our help, the Bargers graciously shared with us a portion of the wheat grain we all produced.

Four months to the day after we first harvested the wheat crop, we were finally ready to make a loaf of wheat bread from the grain we received from them. Before making the bread, we decided to see if we could grind down the coarse grain we received into a finer product. On October 29, I took our share of the wheat and sifted it a final time using a standard wire mesh strainer to remove the largest grains and as much of the remaining chaff and hulls as I could. I then used our hand-cranked grain mill to further grind the coarsest residual grain. After grinding it twice through the mill and a third time using a mini food processor, I managed to reduce the grain to the general consistency of a fine beach sand with some flour mixed in. In terms of coarseness, I consider the resulting grain to be the consistency of middling—somewhere between cracked wheat and flour. I simply lacked the equipment necessary to effectively grind it all down to a fine flour. However, after reviewing a number of recipes for wheat bread, we determined that our middling wheat was sufficiently fine to use in making bread if we soaked it before mixing it into the bread dough.

Having achieved a useful product, Barb made the bread dough on November 5, and we baked our first loaf of homemade wheat bread. We have enough remaining grain to use in making many more loaves of bread, so we stored it in our chest freezer to preserve it for future use. Barb allowed plenty of time for the dough to rise, given the density of the grain we were using. We wanted to make sure that the bread would be as light as possible.

We wanted to bake the bread in our wood cookstove, but the temperatures have been too warm lately to fire up the stove. Even on the coldest days of winter (when the outdoor temperatures remain below freezing), our wood cookstove can heat the entire house to nearly 80 degrees. With the daytime temperatures now hovering in the mid-50s, it didn't seem wise to bake the bread in the wood stove. However, our gas range is a technology that would have been available roughly 100 years ago, so we still managed to honor our guiding principle—to produce a loaf of bread from standing wheat using only manual labor and equipment that was available 100 years ago.

The loaf of wheat bread that we baked turned out well. The consistency was perfect (not too dense), and it tasted the way homemade wheat bread should taste. Yes, it was a lesson in making bread the hard way, but the community spirit and personal satisfaction we enjoyed along the way made it all well worth the effort. The effort reinforced what we already knew, homegrown food always tastes best. Now we have a half gallon of natural wheat grain to use in future baking projects. It is a benefit that we will enjoy over many more meals.

While we can't share the fruits of our labor directly with you, I hope this series of website posts will entice you to consider using the old ways to serve your own basic needs. The satisfaction you will gain from your own efforts will help you better appreciate the value of a natural and simple lifestyle—the kind your ancestors once lived. That is what we hope the stories of our life here at Peeper Pond Farm will ultimately mean to you.

Post 101: Our Diminishing Farmlands

November 8, 2018

The only periodic magazine I now subscribe to is *Small Farmer's Journal*, which is published in Sisters, Oregon. It is a wonderful publication that extols and discusses (as we try to do here at Peeper Pond Farm) historically traditional methods of farming for small farm operations. Although it is only published quarterly, I eagerly await and enjoy reading the stories, subscriber letters and instructional/research articles contained in each issue. Although I could devour the contents in a day, I try to read a little at a time, judiciously spreading it out over weeks after the arrival of each magazine.

The latest issue I received (Volume 42, Number I – the 165th Edition), contains an interesting compendium of subscriber letters discussing a standing issue—our rapidly diminishing farmland resources. It is entitled, *"We Need a Stay of Execution for Farmland…until farmland preservation gets figured out."* The discussion was triggered by some alarming statistics recently released by the American Farmland Trust that documents the dramatic loss of 31 million acres of American farmland between 1992 and 2012. That amount of farmland is roughly equivalent to all of the available farmland in the State of Iowa. Of the farmland acres that were lost over that twenty-year period, roughly one-third of it rated among the best (and presumably most productive) farmland in the nation, and 59 percent of the total loss was attributed to development encroachment from expanding urban areas.

Having witnessed first-hand the dramatic loss of small family dairy farm operations over the past 35 years (an issue I have discussed extensively in previous website posts), I read all the subscriber's perspectives with great interest. All of them, like me, are appalled by and concerned about these trends. In my mind, there is no question that we need to find a way to make farming more profitable for farmers, and I initially thought that would be the central focus of the debate. Two of the contributors (Klaus Karbaumer and Lynn Miller) noted a significant contributing problem—the appalling lack of a meaningful retirement program for farmers, many of whom have little savings or income to support themselves when they become too old to continue farming. I would also add the need for affordable health benefits and liability insurance, because small farms generate very low profits and incomes to support and protect the farmer and his/her family. Since nearly all land is valued more highly for its non-farm development potential than for its agricultural productivity, farmers are often forced to sell their land to pay for expensive operations, treatments, and law suits—and then later, for retirement (assuming they can survive all the other routine farming risks).

Although the new Affordable Health Care act has helped make "basic" health insurance more affordable, I would contend it does very little (if anything) to control or cap the spiraling *cost* of health care services and pharmaceuticals, much of which must be borne by the consumer in the form of co-payments, deductibles and other out-of-pocket expenses not covered by the most affordable insurance policies. Remember, farming is a dangerous, high-risk operation that increases the potential cost of basic health and liability insurance for farmers. Public tax subsidies to offset or reduce personal health insurance premium costs may ultimately fail to ensure that they are truly affordable, if they can't effectively bring spiraling health care costs into a more reasonable balance with the public's ability to afford them. The public will invariably absorb those future costs either in the form of higher taxes to cover policy subsidies, higher co-payments or deductibles, or reduced coverage. Ironically, it is a similar imbalance between agricultural production and the urban development value of farmland that the contributors desire desperately to reverse.

I would also point out that one big reason for the growing (pun intended) disparity between the development and agricultural value of land is our ability to make each available acre of farmland more and more productive through technological advances and bio-engineering. The farmer's monetary cost to employ those high-tech advances also drives the trend towards larger and larger industrial farm operations, in order to generate the higher production profit margins needed to finance those improvements. Small farmers have very limited access to capital, and their profit margins are too low to justify the investment costs. Therefore, the smallest farm operations (especially those closest to growing or expanding urban centers) are the most likely to be lost to development, unless they are close and suitable enough to the biggest operations that they can be acquired and absorbed into the neighboring monster farm that is more solvent. This trend has been especially damaging to the dairy sector.

Another commenter, Shannon Berteau, suggested that "with the increasing droves of people sheltering in cities over the last decade [presumably including their suburbs, which, for most large urban areas, are the front line for urban encroachment on farmlands], city planners should be scrambling to secure [vulnerable farmland] acreage within close proximities to feed their masses." While his observation seems, at face value, to be a sensible way to relieve the pressures of development encroachment, it overlooks the fact that the farmlands that would be most valuable to cities and their suburbs are not typically located within their corporate boundaries. As a former city and regional planner, I know that municipal annexation powers are limited by law in most states, and the best farmlands outside corporate boundaries to protect from development aren't usually made available for municipal annexation until they have already been sold to developers who are seeking access to urban utilities or services to increase their land's development value and potential. The zoning laws that prescribe or control development potential in cities cannot, in most states, be legally applied to lands outside the city's boundaries. Therefore, city planners in many states don't have the authority to effectively protect those hinterland farms from development.

You also need to understand that cities and towns are inherently expensive to operate and maintain. They require significant ongoing public investments in utilities, roads and public services to satisfy the basic needs of a dense urban population. Therefore, landowner taxes are usually higher in cities than they are in rural areas. Farmers can't afford the extra taxes they would incur to be incorporated by a city, so they usually resist any municipal annexation effort. That's the most common reason why annexation of farmland is sought only when the owner is ready to take it out of agricultural production. What's more, the higher property taxes that cities impose may have the unintended effect of making the cost of farming even less affordable for the farms they annex—thereby creating an added potential for farm failure or farmland conversion. For these reasons, Shannon's suggestion is not as workable from a practical perspective as it may seem at first blush.

Overall, the general consensus of all the contributors to the discussion was that the greatest ongoing threat to future farmland loss is the basic profit motive and nature of our free market system. Most of the writers condemn our economy for its failure to value farmland and farm production as highly as it does alternative development options. I admit that's a problem, but I must also admit that our economic system has spawned agricultural innovations and advances that have increased food production to the level that we can affordably feed ourselves and many other nations that are not able to do so on their own—and to do so effectively on less and less farmland. Admittedly, I noted earlier in this post that those technological advances have driven the rise of mega-farms which has contributed to the loss of small family farms. However, I can't, as the other contributors apparently do, simply overlook or ignore the significant benefits those advancements have bestowed on other nations, especially those populations that might face increased starvation without it. I also can't point to any other alternative political or economic system existing in the world today that has achieved anything close to the level of agricultural productivity as our own free market system, even despite the imperfections I can find in it. I have even noted in earlier posts (please see my February 17, 2018 post entitled, "What the Reaper Sowed," and my September 9, 2018 post entitled, "Smithsonian") that those technological advances in agricultural productivity made it possible for cities and urban centers to emerge because they freed many people to pursue other lines of work instead of having to grow their own food for themselves. If we never enjoyed any of the advances in agricultural productivity our economic system created, we might not be able to feed the urban population we have today or we might lose even more of our land resources to house the population than we do today.

I don't deny that our economy and its vitality depend greatly on access to abundant, low-cost natural resources that can be exploited for profit. My own State of West Virginia remains one of the best examples of the ravages, both physical and social, that can occur when outside interests exploit natural resources and remove the wealth they create. However, I really find it difficult to lay the full blame of the loss of our farmland exclusively on the negative consequences and social inequities that often arise from capitalism. After all, a significant percentage of the farmland we have lost in West Virginia has resulted not from over-development and urban sprawl, but from the gradual conversion of farmland to forestland due to farm failures, the lack of a next generation to continue farming, and rural population decline.

Unlike other states, West Virginia has very little flat land for farming, so our agricultural base depends on small family farms, which struggle to compete with larger commercial operations. That, too, is a problem influenced by competitive economics, but it is not a problem that is unique to our country and our economic system. In fact, many of the economic problems that farmers face today are shared by farmers in other countries, some of which do not operate under the same free market economy that we practice. Every issue and every economic system will have benefits and costs depending on how you choose to look at it or whose perspective you view it from. The same can be said for every political and economic system that exists today, even though none of them seem to offer an ideal or practical solution to the core problem the contributors debate—how to save farmland from excessive development over long periods of time. I also don't pretend to have a solution for it, primarily because I think all the contributors have overlooked an even broader issue that must be addressed before any effective long-term solution to farmland loss can be devised.

I feel that farmland loss has become increasingly important to us all because of our exploding population growth—an issue that I did not see mentioned in the article. It drives our growing needs for *both* developable land and food. According to my 2015 World Almanac, the world's human population has grown from 2.557 billion in 1950 to 4.088 billion in 1975 to 6.090 billion in 2000 and was recently estimated to be 7.176 billion in 2014. That tells me that the number of mouths we ultimately need to house, employ and feed has nearly tripled since 1950. While I agree that we do have choices we can make in how we house and employ those masses, those choices will only buy us some time without effectively addressing the 900-pound gorilla hiding in the room. It would be a temporary solution, akin to loosening your belt to control a weight problem. No matter what happens to any individual country, we need to recognize that we live on a planet that has limited resources to sustain us all. There is, and will always be, a practical limit to how many people any country or our planet can support.

We sometimes forget that the survival of our species is subject to the exact same limitations (and ultimate fate) as any of the prior 99 percent of all species that have lived on this planet and are now extinct. Overpopulation and the environmental stresses eventually caused by it, has been a critical factor in the vast majority of those prior extinctions. If we need a human example to remind us of that, consider the extinction of the culture that existed on Easter Island. They weren't killed off by the excesses of capitalism or, for that matter, any alternative socio-economic system. They first trapped themselves on the island by consuming all of their forest resources (so they couldn't build any boats) and then gradually starved to death as their population exceeded their island's ability to feed them. When you consider the pattern and trend in human population growth, we all face the same ultimate fate regardless of whether or not we can fix our current economic system or transition to a different one that can effectively stop the loss of farmland to development.

Viewed from this perspective, the stress imposed on our agricultural system and economy by farmland loss is as much a symptom of the larger population growth problem than it is the problem itself. I will also point out that *none* of the various political or economic systems that exist in the world today has successfully controlled or even effectively managed population growth-- including China, which remains the only one I know that has actively tried to do so. Perhaps the biggest reasons why nations find it such a difficult problem to control is because humans possess a natural, innate drive to reproduce (as do *all* species), and any success gained by reversing population growth would have a corresponding negative impact on the economy that sustains us, *regardless* of what form of government you would choose to have. You simply can't alter one fundamental variable of economic vitality without affecting the others.

If I had to give you a simple analogy for what I'm trying to say about the issues debated in the recent *Small Farmer's Journal* article, I would say the following. It's fine to conduct a back-seat conversation on a complex issue like farmland loss, as long as in doing so, you don't get so distracted by the details that you forget to hit the brakes before the car plunges over the cliff. I believe there is a much more basic and fundamental concern that we need to face before we can hope to solve the subsequent problem of farmland loss—one that challenges our fundamental ability to feed ourselves regardless of how many acres of farmland we have to protect. If we can't find the courage or consensus to address the core issue of overpopulation, all the others may eventually become moot. What's good fodder for discussion will not fill a starving belly.

For what it's worth, I will say that I simply believe that we humans, like every other species that has become extinct before us, will ultimately face our own extinction. Ask any astronomer—if we don't do it to ourselves, the sun will eventually do it for us. After all, no matter how you choose to deal with it, death is an unavoidable aspect of life itself. We may have a greater intellect than any other species, but that alone is no guarantee that we can overcome the most fundamental realities of life itself. It may not be a happy or optimistic ending to this post, but it may be the most realistic one I can give you. As one who has worked as a farmer, I understand and accept the need to face reality on its own terms, not on mine.

Post 102: Early Winter Snow Cover

November 16, 2018

During my childhood, winter always came early to our New Hampshire dairy farm. The first snowfall (usually nothing more than flurries) would always occur in October and the first storm that would blanket the ground with snow would arrive in November. Sometime during the first week of December, we would receive the first snowstorm that would completely cover the ground and with the help of subsequent snowfalls, keep it covered over until it all melted away in late March or (more often) early April. Winters were always white and bitterly cold throughout my childhood, with the sole exception of the final winter before I left home for college, when we had our first "green" Christmas in many decades. I should admit, according to my adoptive mother and father who lived all their lives in the state, winters in New Hampshire tended to be snowier and colder during the 1970s than they were in *both* earlier and later decades.

Yesterday, we received our earliest measurable snowfall since we moved to West Virginia in 2008. It began with a mix of snow, sleet and rain early in the morning on November 15 and changed to heavy, wet snow when the temperature slid below freezing around sunrise. It snowed most of the day, then changed back to a mix of snow and sleet before ending after dark. Even though the ground was not frozen, it left us with a fresh, crusty 3.5-inch snow cover. Last winter, we didn't receive that much *total* snowfall until February 17! The only other time we had a storm that dropped a measurable amount of snow in November was on November 26, 2014—the day before we celebrated our first Thanksgiving in our newly constructed home here at Peeper Pond Farm. That storm dropped a total of eleven inches on us, and Barb and Michael had to trudge through it to get to the house when they arrived on Thanksgiving morning because our 350-foot driveway was not cleared.

Everyone knew yesterday's snowstorm was coming earlier in the week and had adequate time to prepare for it. That is, everyone except the State Highway Department, which had not pretreated any of the roads (as has become the custom over the past decade). From our living room, which looks down onto a big, sweeping curve on U.S. Highway 220, we watched the morning traffic crawl tentatively along the snow-covered road. As for us, I lit our wood cookstove for the first time this season, and we spent the day indoors. While I sifted and ground a second gallon of coarsely ground wheat from Jeff and Amanda Barger's farm, Barb did a lot of cooking and baking using our wood stove and oven. She made a batch of pepperoni rolls (a traditional West Virginia staple), a large pot of Rigatoni sauce and a pizza from scratch.

Calli tried to go outdoors several times throughout the day but never made it off our big front porch. She has never dealt with snow, as she was too young last winter for us to feel comfortable letting her outdoors on her own. She studied it carefully many times, but lacked the courage to venture out into it until after the storm ended this morning. The final round of sleet that fell during the night left a one-quarter-inch-thick crust on the snow cover that was strong enough to support her weight, most of the time. She spent the rest of the day indoors with us just lounging lazily on a cedar chest in the spare bedroom that also serves as Barb's quilting room. The chest was covered with fabric scraps and batting from current projects that Calli found irresistible as a refuge from the snow and cold.

By the time daylight returned to our landscape this morning, we were treated to a beautiful postcard winter scene capped by a fresh, untrodden blanket of windswept snow. Now that all the leaves have fallen, Wilson Chapel stands out starkly on Jake Hill, and Brushy Run Hollow proudly displays her new majestic, white coat framed by the delicate skeletons of bare trees. It's hard to know if the warmth I feel as I survey the landscape is evoked as much by the embracing heat of the wood stove as it is by the stunning beauty of the scene. All I can say for certain is that winter here at Peeper Pond Farm is off to a beautiful start.

Post 103: Natural Bridge

November 24, 2018

According to legend, many years (perhaps centuries) before European discovery of the Americas, a small band of Monacan Indians was racing through a deep, dark, mountainous forest of giant trees trying to evade a much larger band of warriors from a neighboring enemy tribe. They were retreating west and to the north of a mighty river that is known today as the James in west-central Virginia, motivated by the knowledge that capture by their pursuers would result in the death of their braves and elders and the forced adoption or rape of their women and children. Desperately, they scrambled over boulders and downed trees scattered along their path unsure of when their enemies would overtake them.

Eventually, their flight was halted by a deep, precipitous gorge that sliced across their path. The chasm was too steep to descend and far too wide to leap across. There was no visible way to circumvent the great ravine. The women huddled in fear around their children, as they trembled and wept in anticipation of the terrifying threat they knew was rapidly closing in on them. There seemed no way to escape their ultimate fate, and it appeared that all was lost.

Exhausted from the relentless chase, they knelt together at the rim of the gorge and prayed to the Great Spirit to spare them from the horrors of their impending doom. As they opened their eyes, they were stunned to behold a narrow bridge of land spanning the gorge before them. With joy in the knowledge that the Great Spirit had granted them salvation, the band scrambled across the bridge and prepared themselves for the impending arrival of their enemies. The women and children sought safety in the nearby woods while the braves staged themselves at the far side of the land bridge to defend it. When their enemies finally arrived at the narrow land bridge, they were unable to form an effective offensive line to cross it. After a ferocious battle, the small band of Monacan braves were able to defeat the larger opposing force and forced it to retreat.

It is uncertain if the legend I just recounted originated with the Monacan Indians or the European settlers, who eventually took possession of their ancestral lands. What I can say is that, legend or not, the narrow natural bridge of land that spans the Cedar Creek gorge is one of the most impressive natural features of the Great Valley between the Blue Ridge and Allegheny Mountain ranges. That is why we decided to visit again, yesterday.

For a period of time after its discovery, Natural Bridge was considered—along with Niagara Falls—to be one of the choicest and grandest natural features to visit in America. At 215 feet above the creek and 90 feet in length, Natural Bridge has been respected as a truly sacred place by all who have owned it, but none more sensitively than Thomas Jefferson, who purchased it from King George III of England in 1774 and owned it for much of his adult life. Imagine how unlikely his lengthy stewardship of Natural Bridge would have been if he had waited only two more years to petition the King to buy it. The value of land is not simply determined by location, location, location—as most realtors will say. It is also greatly affected by timing.

Long after Jefferson's ownership of Natural Bridge, the celebrated natural feature was developed for tourism by an entrepreneur who devised and built a cage that could be raised and lowered by a winch from the adjoining Pulpit Rock column so visitors could admire the grandeur of the arch as they descended slowly and securely to Cedar Creek at its base. The hoist system operated during the Civil War, when passing soldiers from both the North and South would detour from their movements up and down the valley to see the spectacle.

Many visitors throughout the centuries have been inspired to inscribe their initials in the rock walls of the arch. Another Natural Bridge legend recounts that George Washington was part of a team that surveyed the bridge in 1750. State Park interpreters point to an inscription with the letters "GW" about 25 feet up the rock face on the west side of the creek that Washington himself allegedly chiseled into the rock. We were also told a story that George Washington, who had a strong throwing arm, threw either a coin or a rock onto the top of the bridge from the creek below. Unfortunately, the Natural Bridge Hotel has no registry record to show that he slept there, despite the fact that Washington is alleged to have slept in most historic homes throughout the region. Thank heavens there are no cherry trees at Natural Bridge—or is it possible that there were some *before* 1750?

According to the State Park docent who led our tour, how Natural Bridge came into being has not been determined definitively. However, if you carefully study the opposing cliff walls on both sides of the creek and the spanning arch, you will see that, as the walls get higher, they curve gradually inward towards the creek. This strongly suggests that the narrow bridge we see today was much wider in the past and, over geologic periods of time, may have once formed a tunnel or cave that Cedar Creek passed through on its path to the James River. Since the gorge is composed of limestone rock, it erodes over time as groundwater seeps through it. As we were standing below the bridge admiring its beauty, water was dripping through it onto the path around us. Eventually, groundwater seepage, as well as seasonal freeze and thaw over time, will erode the limestone base of the bridge, and it will collapse into the creek—in much the same way as the rest of the ancient rock tunnel or cavern that preceded it. The Commonwealth of Virginia obviously agrees with this assessment, because they are now working to relocate U.S. Route 11 (the Wilderness Highway), which was built along the top of the bridge nearly 100 years ago. They are concerned that traffic impacts over time may impact or accelerate the natural degradation of the limestone arch.

There are many other rivers in our region that either begin in caves or even pass through them. In Hardy County, WV, Lost River disappears into a mountain and emerges on the other side as the Cacapon River before it empties into the Potomac. The Sinks of Gandy, another WV natural landmark in our area that I introduced in my June 20, 2018 post on this website, was carved by Gandy Creek which passes through it on its descent from the summit of Cunningham Knob, is another prime example. It is only natural to conclude that the great stone bridge is the remains of a similar cavernous tunnel.

Regardless of how it formed or what human events really occurred there, Virginia's Natural Bridge is truly an amazing sight to behold. It is a majestic and inspiring reminder of how diverse and unique the ancient Appalachian Mountain environment truly is. However, as I have explained in this post, the feature is as important to the cultural heritage of our area as it is a geologic wonder. Natural Bridge State Park is located about 2.5 hours south of Peeper Pond Farm along Interstate 81 and U.S. Route 11—at least until Virginia decides where it will relocate U.S. Route 11. We also hope that all of our loyal readers had a very happy (and delicious) Thanksgiving.

Post 104: Meet Our New Official Peeper Pond Farm Meteorologist

December 4, 2018

I awoke this morning to another early winter snowfall that coated the ground, rooftops and the pine and cedar trees with a fluffy white blanket of snow. It was beautiful to watch small globs of snow fall from the cedar boughs as they shivered in the gentle breeze. From what we've experienced since the beginning of fall, we may receive a lot of snow this season.

As I noted in my earlier posts this spring and summer, we have already received a lot of rain this year, and we now face the possibility of a snowy and cold winter. Since weather conditions have a significant bearing on the success or failure of our farming ventures, we (and other farmers in our area) really need a reliable way to track and forecast our changing weather patterns. To date, I have used the old weather sayings I learned from my childhood farming experiences, which I have recounted in several past posts on our website. They have been helpful, but I could really use some additional help.

Weather forecasting has become much more complicated than it was when I was growing up. Since the 1960s, we have launched geostationary satellites to track and study active weather systems, built supercomputers to analyze mountains of complex weather data, and devised sophisticated computer models to predict weather patterns. The result of all these technological advances in weather forecasting is that the reliability of the three-day weather forecast that we used to guide our farming when I was a child is now marginally more reliable today. From what I'm repeatedly told, we seem to know with a much higher degree of confidence how the weather will be in the next 50 years (and exactly what we need to do to fix it) than we are able to accurately predict tomorrow's weather. Sometimes, I have to wonder if today's meteorologists would benefit from more windows in their offices. It all makes me think we may need to do a better job of reconciling our sophisticated computer models—and their basic underlying assumptions—so that they will more reliably and accurately predict tomorrow's weather. Complex systems influenced by multiple independent variables are inherently difficult to reliably model.

I have studied meteorology over the years, but I am not a certified meteorologist. I know many people who will assert that I'm certifiable, but that's an important step shy of being certified as a professional meteorologist. I learned that my biological grandfather understood this distinction. He used to say that he went all the way through high school. Unfortunately, he was unable to obtain a diploma by demonstrating that he could successfully pass in through the front door and out the back door. Perhaps my understanding of basic meteorology is a little more substantial than that, but I must admit I am not a professional. This is why I decided I needed some help from someone with a better basic understanding of the typical weather conditions in our area.

After careful consideration, we have decided to appoint our new housecat, Calli, as our official Peeper Pond Farm meteorologist. Although she also has no professional credentials, she has an extensive understanding of our local weather conditions and has proven to be very honest, objective and reliable in reporting weather conditions to us. For example, Calli correctly reported that it was snowing this morning—even though it was totally dark when she left the house. In fact, it was so dark this morning that I was unable to see anything beyond the porch railing. However, Calli bravely faced the unseen elements and, when she returned only ten minutes later, I could clearly see snowflakes all along her back. Her weather reporting acumen was equally reliable during the summer. After only a few minutes outside on a rainy day, she would return to the house soaked from the top of her head to the tip of her tail. If there was a heavy dew, but no active rainfall, only her paws and legs would be wet. Whenever it is windy outside, she returns to the house with her fur fluffed up. She is so incredibly perceptive about the weather that she refuses to go outside when it is bitterly cold. Imagine that. She doesn't even have to leave the house to accurately tell us how cold it is! We have even noticed that the colder it is outside, the less time she spends outdoors. When the weather is sunny and warm, she spends a lot more time outside. When the weather becomes hot and humid, she will seek out a shady area and rest a lot or come indoors and stretch out on the cool hardwood floor for a while.

Although I have daily access to weather reports from certified meteorologists at the National Weather Service, WHSV-TV in Harrisonburg, VA, and West Virginia Metro News, I simply can't obtain as much reliable and accurate information on current weather conditions than I get from our cat, Calli. When she told me that it was snowing before sunrise this morning, our local weather radio forecast was calling for a 70 percent chance of snow. We ended up receiving a half inch of snow over the next hour. Who needs certified meteorologists when you can obtain such consistently reliable and unbiased weather reports from your own cat? Consequently, I made the only logical selection available to me.

By the way, Calli is happy to serve as our official meteorologist for free—as long as we feed her regularly and give her a warm, dry refuge from all the bad weather she has to report. Even though Calli is only a cat, she clearly understands that the value of your work is not measured by how much money you are paid but how well you do the job. From my perspective, that's not just a measure of how valuable an employee you are, but also of how much personal integrity you have.

We hope you'll join us in congratulating Calli for earning this important, responsible position here at Peeper Pond Farm. Now if I can only convince her to stop chasing the deer.

Post 105: Another Good Drenching

December 15, 2018

Once again, our rainfall saga continues. During the past 24 hours (ending at 4:00 PM on December 15), we received a total of 2.12 inches of rainfall here at Peeper Pond Farm. That just happens to be the 30-year average for the month in Upper Tract, about five miles south of our farm. So far this December (at the middle of the month) we have recorded 2.46 inches of rain with more forecasted to fall tomorrow and yet again before Christmas day. Nevertheless, December has become the ninth consecutive month of rainfall this year in excess of the 30-year average. Today actually marks the first day on which more than one inch of rain has fallen at our farm since September 27. We thought we were beginning to get lucky in that regard, even though the monthly total rainfall in both October and November still exceeded the 30-year averages. As of today, our cumulative total rainfall since April 1 has been 60.19 inches—which is 24.86 inches above the 30-year average for an *entire* year, and I don't even have rainfall records for the first three months!

According to the meteorological staff at WHSV-TV in Harrisonburg (which has also recorded about 60 inches of rain thus far in 2018), this year is running shy of the rainiest year in recorded history. Apparently, Harrisonburg received more total rainfall in 1996 and in 1886, when the all-time annual record of just over 68 inches of rain fell. Irrespective of whether we set a new rainfall record this year or not, this soggy, humid year will be long remembered in our area. We witnessed a number of floods, mudslides and road washouts throughout our region. Local farmers struggled to grow healthy vegetables and to harvest their hay crops. Rotting, moldy hay bales can be seen abandoned in two small creek-side fields just down the highway from our farm. We lost all of our pumpkins and a significant amount of our butternut squash and cucumber crops to white mold and rot because we could not harvest them early enough with all the frequent rains. Mowing our yards was a constant struggle to find dry days to mow when the ground was not too soggy. We experienced frequent foggy days that became torrid during the heat of the day. Colorful fall foliage was hard to find and spotty at best. Many trees and shrubs were stressed from the persistent struggle to draw sufficient oxygen from the supersaturated soil, thereby causing them to lose their leaves early. All in all, 2018 will be remembered as a dreary, soggy year.

There's just not much more I can say about it. I have seen no convincing evidence that the weather is something we can effectively control or regulate.

Remember all the unfulfilled promises of cloud-seeding back in the 1970s? Of course, that history is centuries removed from the minds of the average citizen in the twenty-first century. We'll just wish each of you a Merry Christmas and a drier New Year in 2019. I just wish I could wrap it up in pretty paper and place it under the tree.

Post 106: Happy New Year

January 4, 2019

    Here at Peeper Pond Farm, 2019 swept in on the back of strong winds ranging from about ten to thirty miles per hour. At least the new year began on a warm note. The high temperature of 63 degrees on New Year's Day occurred around 1:30 AM and decreased slowly throughout the day. Heavy clouds ruled the sky, offering only brief breaks of sunshine. Unfortunately, the year did not begin without some rainfall. We received 0.04 inches of rain as the warm front whisked through during the early morning hours. We hope the fierce start to the new year will bring a decided change to all the wet weather we experienced in 2018.

    After discussing the rainy, humid weather that we received last year so often in my farm website posts, I thought I should wrap it up with some final figures. We ended the month of December with a total of 5.89 inches, which was nearly triple the thirty-year average of 2.12 inches. Since April 1, 2018 (when I began tracking rainfall in 2018), we recorded a total of 63.62 inches of rain. The corresponding thirty-year average annual rainfall for Upper Tract is 35.33 inches. Although I did not have my rain gauge out during the first three months of the year (because of all the cold weather), I doubt that we received more than three additional inches of precipitation because we didn't receive any significant snowfall until mid-March when our extended dry period began to end. Boy, did it ever end in a big way.

    Although I don't have access to any longer-term historic weather data in our immediate rural area, the City of Harrisonburg, VA (52 miles and two river valleys to our east) recorded 63.69 inches, the highest rainfall total of the year since its all-time high of 68.37 inches set in 1886. In an average year, Harrisonburg experiences 117 days of rainfall. They received 153 rainy days in 2018. Although you have to realize that microclimates in our rugged, mountainous region create significant variations in weather over short distances, it was clearly an excessively wet year throughout our Allegheny Highlands region. Our ground remains saturated with standing water in many areas. We could actually benefit from all the dry weather we received over the six months immediately preceding our rainfall deluge. We hope spring planting conditions will improve significantly before the growing season begins sometime in May.

    At least 2019 is beginning on one good note. I have been talking to our state legislative delegation about the draft bill I have written to reopen direct farm-to-consumer unprocessed milk sales in West Virginia, and one of our local

Senators has expressed an interest (not necessarily a promise) in introducing the bill this coming session. I am still speaking with state officials and our legislators to finalize the language of the draft bill to help facilitate its passage. You can never be certain what changes will be made to any draft bill after it is introduced for consideration, so I have made extensive efforts to obtain comments from small dairy farm operators, health professionals and other affected interests over the past year. I am hopeful that this bill will be considered for adoption during either the 2019 or 2020 legislative sessions. The verdict on that issue is still uncertain. To improve the chances for introduction, I am also working on building a coalition of supporters to testify for the bill and encourage a broader legislative delegation to support it. One of our new coalition members has offered to build a website and Facebook page for the initiative, which I hope to introduce to you within the next couple of months. Please watch for them to be posted.

    Whatever the old year gave you, I wish one and all a happier and more prosperous new year in 2019. Thanks again for your loyal support of our farm website in 2018.

Post 107: Defending Sales of Farm Fresh Raw Milk

January 14, 2019

    Ever since financial constraints forced the sale of our dairy goat herd on August 5, 2017, I have been working to write a draft bill to end West Virginia's lingering legal prohibition on direct farm-to-consumer sales of unprocessed (raw) milk. This law is the most significant impediment to our financial success. I have discussed the language of my bill with both cow and goat dairy farmers from around the state and representatives of the West Virginia Raw Milk Board of Directors to solicit comments that will make the bill work for the smallest dairy operators. I have discussed our effort publicly on local television and radio stations and before any group that would listen. I even met with State officials and legislators to discuss the bill and seek support. Now we have a real chance to make some important progress on this initiative. Unfortunately, it means that the political battle for its fate is about to begin. I apologize for the length of this post, but it is necessary to fully address all of the critical issues that we may face during the adoption process.

    I received a welcome telephone call on Saturday, January 12 from Pendleton County House Delegate, Isaac Sponaugle, a prominent Franklin attorney. He called to tell me that he has submitted my draft bill for legal review prior to legislative action, after which he will introduce it for consideration during the 2019 Legislative Session. I also have the support of a prominent State Senator to back this bill. This is the big step we have worked for over the past seventeen months, and we greatly appreciate Delegate Sponaugle's courage and willingness to support its adoption. I call it courage, because the prior legislative effort to reverse this prohibition was fought over a seven-year period and resulted in a compromise "Herd Share" bill that allows dairy farmers the option to "sell" a share of their herd to prospective customers in exchange for some of the milk they produce. While it does allow a veiled opportunity for raw milk to be sold, it is not an ideal solution that works for all small farm operations—especially for small dairy goat farms. My reasons for saying this have been discussed in prior posts on this website, most recently in my June 28, 2018 post entitled, "WHSV Tells Our Story."

    This means that the political struggle for its adoption will soon begin. I certainly can't guarantee success, as history has shown it could be a hard and bitter fight. I'm afraid I am not a fan of twenty-first century politics as I have seen and experienced it. I have seen many recent political wars fought through intimidation, fear and anger. The intense emotions these tactics raise are carefully courted and cultivated to make the public suspend careful, critical thinking and make snap decisions based largely on bold leaps of faith or their broader political allegiances. It may be the primary reason why politics today are so divided, and politicians find it so difficult to sort out fact from fiction or to tackle the most controversial issues. While our access to data is much greater today than it was in the last century, our ability to comprehend what it all *really* means—rather than just what its proponents *say* it means—is not easy. I have always heard it said that statistics don't lie, but they can be used to spread lies. That is a universal, common-sense truth. I would add a corollary to that statement. That those who seek to lie using statistics find it easier to do so by using intimidation, fear and anger.

In order to make sound, objective decisions, we all must be responsible for applying critical thinking skills to challenge the information we are routinely fed. If we want the freedom to choose how we conduct our personal lives, we *must* assume the responsibility to understand why others are motivated to influence our choices, what the various consequences (both intended and unintended) of our choices will be, and what information we should use as a basis for our choices. This line of thinking is where the age-old saying, "caveat emptor" (buyer beware) comes from. If you don't wish to assume those three basic responsibilities, you will either make bad decisions or you will abandon your freedom to choose what you will do in favor of what someone else says you should do. I don't think I can explain it any simpler than that. I believe that my primary job during the adoption process is to encourage our legislators to think critically and objectively about what they will be told by *both* sides of the issue. I have no fear of that.

I believe that the final outcome of our bill will hinge on two primary sources of opposition. The first will come from large commercial dairy and dairy processor interests, backed by the Dairy Council and Farm Bureau. It seems strange that some dairy interests would be motivated to oppose a bill designed to relieve dairy farmers from excessively onerous regulations, but it is surprisingly easy to understand. Many commercial dairy interests initially fear that allowing sales of raw milk to the public will unleash a wave of pathogen-borne illnesses that would tarnish the public image of milk. I will address that concern later in this post. To understand other commercial dairy concerns, you need to "follow the money" in the dairy sector.

Over the past fifty years, all dairy farmers have struggled to finance their operations. As direct farm-to-customer sales of milk, cheese and butter were eliminated by the laws we seek to change, farmers became increasingly dependent on dairy processing plants to buy, pasteurize and process their milk for sale. Their only alternative was to build their own milk processing facilities, which some large, wealthy operations did. In the latter half of the twentieth century, periodic milk gluts emerged during this regulatory market transition, making it increasingly difficult for small farms to earn a living wage from the milk they could produce. These family farms (like ours) were unable to buy additional land to support a larger herd or to afford to hire the additional outside labor needed to milk and feed them.

Many farmers worked to improve the milk productivity of their herds through selective breeding, bioengineering, adopting advanced milking and farming technologies, and switching to special feed and supplements specifically formulated (engineered) to increase milk production. Of course, the application of these strategies also increased the cost of production. Gradually over time, the smallest farmers were simply forced out of business because they couldn't finance the cost. However, some farms grew into larger and larger operations, which made them more profitable because they could absorb the increasing operating costs through increased milk production. These farms expanded their operations by buying cows and land from the surrounding smaller failed farms and by redesigning their farms with new technologies and equipment that allowed them to keep more cows on less land. Over time, the milk produced by the growing mega-farms increased the competitive market pressures on the remaining small farms, resulting in a rapidly expanding and self-reinforcing trend towards bigger and bigger industrial-scale dairy farms.

According to a 2016 USDA Report, Changing Structure, Financial Risks and Government Policy for the U.S. Dairy Industry (Economic Research Report 205), which documents this dramatic trend, the median herd size of dairy farms nationally has increased from 80 cows in 1987 (two years after the whole herd buyout program was implemented) to 570 in 1997 and 900 in 2012. The largest single dairy farm documented in the report (located in Oregon) milks 32,000 cows on 39,000 acres. Small family farms clearly can't compete with huge industrial-scale dairies, so they have disappeared over time in waves of failures driven by periodic milk gluts and the anemic market prices paid by the dairy processors. This transition in our local area became complete in December 2017 when the last family owned and operated commercial dairy farm in the tri-county area of Grant, Hardy and Pendleton was forced to sell its herd because the milk hauler refused to transport its milk to the processing plant. Since the rugged landscape of West Virginia is not capable of supporting giant, modern industrial-scale dairy operations, there is no economically viable way, under our current laws, to revive the industry through new start-up small dairy operations. However, a few large commercial dairy farms remain in other parts of the state.

These are the dairy farmers who may not support our bill because they don't want to encourage milk competition from smaller farms who do not have to absorb the production costs of the current Grade-A Dairy rules. They may be joined by the Farm Bureau (of which they are important members) and the milk processors, who don't want any competition for retail milk sales. Ironically, the threat they perceive is greatly exaggerated, and I can tell you why.

Our proposed bill places limitations on the daily amount of unprocessed milk or milk products that can be sold from a farm. These limits effectively prevent any raw milk producer from becoming a large operation, just as they would prevent any of the largest producers from fully converting to a raw milk operation. This ensures that only small, West Virginia-sized family raw milk dairy farms could be created, which best fit the landscape and available land resources of our Allegheny Highlands region. The potential sales volume is also limited because the emerging consumer market for unprocessed, raw milk is also constrained. It is driven by a small, but growing number of people who desire unprocessed foods because they want to buy natural and organically grown foods and have concerns about the potential health effects of genetic engineering and artificial additives on the quality of processed foods. Many of them are moving into West Virginia from surrounding cities and urbanized areas in search of a healthier rural lifestyle and alternatives to store-bought foods. Our local farmer's market serves a number of these consumers. As a result, they are not actively seeking to buy milk produced by the large commercial dairy farms and milk processors. Furthermore, the large commercial farms, which are tailored to serve the processed milk market, cannot by law directly serve that highly specialized market. The only question is whether we will allow them to purchase it in West Virginia or they will have to go one of the other 31 states (one of which is neighboring Pennsylvania) that permit such sales.

I would suggest that their opposition is based on a false sense of competition because any small dairy operations created by our proposed bill would serve a different and inherently separate specialty milk market. Our proposed bill could only affect the processed milk market if they are denied the option to purchase the unprocessed milk they desire and are subsequently forced to buy store-bought milk. Since raw milk can be sold in the way we propose in 31 other states (including Pennsylvania), retaining the current regulatory advantage the biggest farms enjoy may only have the unintended effect of discouraging some people from moving to West Virginia. Our bill would not change the current Herd Shares law; it would only provide another option for the smallest diary operations to enjoy the same privileges conveyed to some farmers by the Herd Shares program. The legitimate question this opposition raises is not what effect our bill would have on the state's remaining dairies, but whether the state will effectively serve the specialized market choices of an emerging group of informed consumers. Which scenario do you feel would help expand and diversify the current agricultural economy in West Virginia?

The second, and perhaps strongest, source of opposition will come from public health officials and their supporters (which currently includes the Farm Bureau). This vocal, entrenched and politically powerful group fears the public sale of raw milk because they perceive it to be an "elixir of death," as explained in my July 28, 2018 post. The basic thrust of their opposition is that raw milk contains a number of bacteria and pathogens that can cause illness and death in humans, and that milk can *only* be made safe to consume through pasteurization. They will freely provide reams of health statistics to document the pathogens that can exist in milk and the illnesses and deaths those pathogens cause each year. They will even provide data specific to illnesses and deaths resulting from consumption of raw milk. From this body of statistics, they will implore everyone to conclude that raw milk is a deadly risk and permitting its sale to the public will unleash a Pandora's box of pathogens, including the potential for deadly and drug-resistant superbugs, on an unsuspecting, vulnerable public. Of course, they will only arrive at these conclusions after they have bewildered the audience with an exhaustive techno-babble presentation that would challenge any layman's attention span and fan the germophobic fears that are so prevalent in society today. I say this because I've heard it all a number of times before. It's an old, but very well practiced and polished strategy that has served them well for many years.

The basic premise behind this opposition strategy is that you can win an argument by introducing more pounds of data and statistics than the opposition. Lawyers routinely use this sleight of hand in responding to discovery requests. However, I believe that a few ounces of critical thinking can outwit one hundred pounds of data. You simply have to be concerned enough about the issue to ask the critical questions. All data and statistics have certain qualifications (often denoted by asterisks and small print) that can greatly affect its relevance and accuracy in supporting the position built from it. You simply have to find the critical holes in the data.

The argument that health officials typically use is very convincing because it is based on a basic valid point. Can the bacteria and pathogens in raw milk cause illness and death in humans? Yes, of course they can and do. The problem with their argument is that they want to end the discussion on that point. However, health statistics will also show that the same bacteria and pathogens in raw milk that can cause human illness and death can be found in pasteurized, USDA inspected milk products. In fact, more people die on average each year from bacteria and pathogens consumed from store bought milk and milk products than they do from raw milk consumption. The unfortunate truth regarding this issue is that we all will die—some of us from auto accidents, cancer and food-borne pathogens. However, when you view all the causes of human death and illness, you will find many more people will die from auto accidents and cancer than from raw milk consumption. The big difference I see is that West Virginia law does not try to protect you from auto accidents and cancer deaths by making it illegal for a retailer to sell a car or a package of cigarettes or conversely, for you to purchase a car or a package of cigarettes, *despite* the well-documented risk to your health. It does, however, expressly prohibit a farmer from selling (and you from buying) raw milk. This is one basic reason why I contend that the current prohibition on raw milk sales may be unreasonably excessive to the actual health threat.

Statistics may show that raw milk represents a potential health risk, but that risk must be viewed in its proper perspective. Another fact that health officials conveniently forget to admit in their public statements is that they can never guarantee that *any* food product, whether processed, unprocessed, or inspected will not cause human illness or death. They will just allow you to assume that. How many processed food recalls do you hear about each year?

Although I freely admit that raw milk *can* contain potentially harmful pathogens, I will also contend that the level of pathogens can be held within reasonable safe consumption limits, if the farmer follows all of the specific best sanitary milking and milk handling standards required by our proposed bill. Furthermore, our bill requires that all raw milk dairy producers offer a tour of their farm to all potential consumers to demonstrate and explain how they comply with all required sanitary milking and milk handling requirements. This provision provides some confidence that the consumer is informed about what he/she is buying and that the farmer understands and complies with the law. I will freely admit that some farmers will flout the law and sell their milk to unsuspecting customers. That has been occurring for years and will continue to do so even if our bill is rejected. That's also true of all other laws. The mere fact that some people willingly violate any law that we pass is not a compelling reason to reject it. Otherwise, that would be a compelling reason to abandon all speed limit laws, given the number of people who casually violate them. All I or anyone else (for that matter) can do to effectively promote public safety is to impose *rational* rules that are conducive to safe sales and grant consumers the right to know how their milk was produced. Can we trust *informed* consumers to make the right choices for themselves? Why else would we require such strict labeling requirements on all food products? Raw milk advocates only seek the same opportunity to sell their products.

The data and statistics that public health officials use to document incidents of human illnesses and deaths resulting from raw milk consumption also should be carefully critiqued. Many of the incidents they cite may have been "reported," but not "confirmed." Incidents of raw milk illnesses or deaths that were reported may not have been definitively confirmed to have been caused by the milk. Occasionally, raw milk producers have been blamed for causing illnesses when only one of their customers reported an illness, even though the milk came from a batch that did not cause an illness among their other customers. In such cases, the source of contamination may not have been the raw milk or it may have entered the milk only *after* it was purchased. I would also want to know if a farmer in another state who sold raw milk that was confirmed to be contaminated was following all of the best sanitary milking and milk handling standards required by our bill. If not, then that incident may not be relevant in deciding the merits of our proposed bill, even if that farmer was in full compliance with the applicable laws in his/her own state.

It is always important to know if a confirmed illness was caused by the milk producer or the consumer's incidental mishandling of the milk *after* it was purchased. Many people today are so far removed from any practical experience in the safe handling and storage of raw milk that they may casually treat it like pasteurized milk. However, the pathogens in raw milk will multiply if its temperature is not maintained at about 35-40 degrees Fahrenheit. You can't casually leave raw milk sitting out on a table or kitchen counter as long as you can with pasteurized milk. Raw milk also has a shorter safe shelf life for that reason. Our proposed bill requires all raw milk producers to give each customer a detailed list of safe milk storage and handling instructions to ensure that the customer understands his/her responsibilities to keep the raw milk safe for them to consume after the purchase.

I contend that the fear of so-called "superbugs" and pathogens that health officials often discuss is also grossly excessive to the actual threat. Although these deadly germs and bacteria do exist, they are not typically found in the milk of dairy animals. Sure, many of their less-deadly precursors, such as e-coli, listeria, salmonella and other potentially "bad" bacteria, can be found naturally in milk at low levels that are not immediately dangerous. Raw milk also contains antibodies from the dairy animal's blood stream that, over initial brief periods of refrigerated storage time, combat and reduce pathogen levels. Some of the same bacteria and pathogens in raw milk that can cause illnesses already exist in our bodies. These bacteria occur naturally and, at the low levels that they occur in impurity-free fresh milk, help us build antibodies that strengthen our natural immune systems and resistance to them at an early age.

All mammals have natural immunity systems that help protect us from the germs and bacteria we routinely encounter in the course of our daily lives. They produce the antibodies that help kill the invading germs, diseases and bacteria that cause illnesses and death. Those individuals with the strongest immune systems are among the healthiest people in society. If your immune system is underdeveloped or weakened by disease or age, your threat of illness is greatly enhanced. Most people understand this, as it is common knowledge. Health officials insist that milk be pasteurized (heated to a specific temperature over a specific length of time) prior to consumption to kill any bad pathogens (originally bovine tuberculosis) that may be in the milk. I agree that it can make milk *potentially* safer to drink. However, in making their argument against the sale of unpasteurized milk, public officials conveniently fail to acknowledge a number of other pertinent facts that should be considered.

First of all, pasteurization is an indiscriminate killer. It not only kills the potentially bad bacteria; it also kills the potentially good bacteria that exists naturally in milk we need to help build stronger bodies. In fact, even the presence of bad bacteria in milk can help strengthen human immune systems to reduce the threat of future illnesses. By preventing gentle exposure of our immune systems to these bad pathogens through pasteurization, we are shielding them from the low-level exposure they need to make us stronger. This is why milk is the first and most basic food consumed by all mammals, from the smallest shrew to the biggest elephant or whale. It contains all the most essential nutrients, proteins, vitamins and other elements that our bodies need for healthy growth. Many of the diseases we face today from weakened immune systems could be caused by our determined efforts to avoid natural childhood exposure to bad pathogens and bacteria. Our growing fear of exposure to bad germs and bacteria is also causing people to over-use antibiotic and antiseptic treatments to the point that we damage our flesh (specifically from over-use of hand sanitizers) and cause the pathogens to become resistant to treatment.

As I said, the newest virulent and deadly superbugs that public officials fear most simply do not occur naturally in dairy animals. If they did, they would kill the animals as quickly as they do the humans who contract them. They actually arise from our efforts to kill their less deadly ancestors. The second fact public health officials do not advertise is that our efforts to create stronger and stronger antibiotics to kill the most basic and common germs and bacteria actually cause them to mutate quickly into stronger and more deadly germs and bacteria. These pathogens are very simple organisms that have no immune systems, as do more complex creatures like humans. Their defense mechanism to ensure their survival against the things that threaten them is their very short lifespans and rapid reproduction rates. Virtually all of them create multiple generations of themselves in a single day. With that rate of reproduction, they are capable of mutating rapidly into stronger (and inherently more deadly or resistant to treatment) forms at a much faster rate than we can develop new and stronger antibiotics to kill them. Therefore, it is the overuse of antibiotic treatments, as well as excessive use of sanitizing agents to clean food processing equipment, that can cause superbugs to get into the foods we produce and eat—including milk. In fact, you are far more likely to contract a flesh-eating bacteria or super staph infection at a hospital, the most highly sanitized environment that most people typically visit, than you ever would by drinking raw milk.

As I learned how these deadly superbugs have emerged, I decided to call the process, "inverse engineering." What I mean when I use that term it is that all of our determined efforts to develop drugs to kill bacteria that could cause human illness only makes the bacteria mutate into more drug resistant and deadlier forms. We are not *intending* to make them stronger, but we are getting the "inverse result" because of their nature. Thus, our efforts to impose increasingly stricter sanitization in milk production, handling and processing can have the potentially inverse effect of increasing the public health threat from the mutated end product. The same can, under the right circumstances, be true of some preventative treatments and vaccinations given to dairy animals. This effect should be studied more carefully and specifically by health officials before they casually conclude that unprocessed milk represents an elixir of death.

As a society, we essentially have two choices. We can either continue to feed our current frenzied germophobic fears by desperately working to create stronger and stronger antibiotics and drugs to kill off deadly superbugs before they kill us, or we can find better ways to strengthen our natural immune systems to protect us from the less deadly pathogens recognizing that a small number of us could become ill or die, but that we may avoid a superbug apocalypse. Our opponents choose the former course. We endorse and try to practice the latter. If you wish to have a choice, I encourage you to think about it carefully and quickly, before public health officials and the pharmaceutical companies make that choice for us.

The vast majority of all people seeking to buy raw milk fully understand what I have said about it. They want to buy it as part of a lifestyle choice that they have determined to be healthier than can be achieved by consumption of processed store-bought foods. They want to know where their food came from. They have done their homework and accept the potential health risks from their informed choice. Our bill responds to their interest and concerns. It poses no threat to the current Herd Shares bill, large commercial dairy producers, or milk processors. What, then, is the *legitimate* reason to deny its adoption? Please think carefully about this issue and, as I have suggested, apply a healthy dose of critical thinking to the arguments against it. I have tried to be rational and fair in defending my position. I urge you to do the research yourself, if you need to be further convinced. Regardless of what you think about my reasons for defending sales of raw milk, I ask you to consider why *we* are urging you to use critical thinking in making your decision, not our opponents.

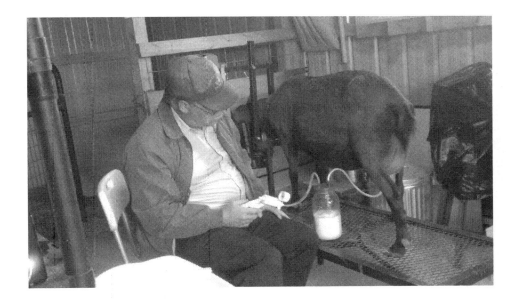

Post 108: Our Dairy Bill Has Been Introduced!

January 25, 2019

It took the 2017 failure of our retirement dairy goat operation and an additional seventeen months of research, hard work and public advocacy, but it all paid off yesterday when Delegate Isaac Sponaugle formally introduced our WV Farm Fresh Raw Milk Act bill for consideration in this 2019 Legislative Session. I wish to extend our greatest appreciation to Delegate Sponaugle for having the courage to introduce our bill and to Delegates John Hott, Scott Cadle, Daryl Cowles and Pat McGeehan for agreeing to co-sponsor the bill, which ensures that we have bi-partisan support for it in the House of Representatives. I am eager to work with each of them to prove that their confidence in the design of this bill will not be misplaced.

We now have a chance to repeal the lingering legal remnants of West Virginia's outright prohibition on direct farmer-to-consumer unprocessed milk sales. As I noted in my previous January 14 website post, the drive and battle for adoption has only just begun. Now we must survive potential committee meetings, deliberations with public officials and opponents and legislative action in both houses, before we will know the outcome of this process. We are actively building a groundswell of support for it, as can be seen in the public comments attached to our January 14 website post. The last drive to change the law spanned seven consecutive legislative sessions, so we can't even be confident that we will have a decision this year. However, the group of supporters we will bring to the table may be more thoroughly informed of the issues and capable of firmly defending our position than was present for the prior debate. All we know for certain is that we must persevere whatever the process may dictate. As any farmer will tell you, hard work does not guarantee success in farming, but you certainly cannot succeed without it.

While I have outlined a very rational, documented defense of the bill, I want all our followers to remember that there are other less tangible reasons to support our effort. Dairy farming once had a very visible footprint on the West Virginia landscape. Small, family-owned and operated dairy farms with herds of fifty or fewer cows could be seen clinging to the river valleys throughout the state. Even today, I can take you on a tour along the South Branch River valley in Pendleton, Grant and Hardy Counties and show you the deteriorating remains of more than fifty dairy barns that are among the most recognizable and photographed landmarks of our rural environments. The last of them, the multi-generational Keller Farm ceased commercial operation in December 2017, only months after our own start-up dairy goat operation was abandoned.

Dairy farming is more than a job. For all who lived it, it was a lifestyle choice—one that forged and reflected West Virginia's traditional self-reliant lifestyle folkways and values. West Virginia and her people have been stereotyped, exploited and marginalized by outsiders before she became the 35th state. Few have made the effort to truly understand that our state represents one of the last vestigial remains of a time-honored way of life that will *always* be an important part of our shared heritage. You don't have to trace any genealogy back more than 100 years to discover ancestral links to someone who farmed. It is a part of *your* own heritage, regardless of who you are. No casual attempt to rewrite history or to avert one's eyes can ever purge our national heritage of it. However, we only need to open our eyes and acknowledge it to realize that it is an important element of our national identity and values. While you may not have lived that lifestyle for yourself, you cannot deny that you have much to learn from it. Our legislative effort is one way that you can honor that heritage and demand that it should not be allowed to die. Small family dairy farms cannot be successfully operated under our current laws and regulations. It is those laws and regulations that have driven the dairy industry into the mechanized mega-farms that dominate it today.

West Virginia needs small, start-up dairies to give that lifestyle a meaningful presence or our landscape. It is also the only way that an emerging market of consumers who desire farm fresh, unprocessed foods can be served in our state. These people understand the issues surrounding their food choices and want to know where and how their food is produced. They seek a natural and healthy alternative to store-bought packaged foods. We hope you can value their informed consumer choices and your own family heritage enough to support our bill and, in doing so, help preserve and promote our traditional rural landscape in West Virginia. The choice is yours, at least until the last of it disappears forever. That is what we proudly and firmly stand for here at Peeper Pond Farm.

Post 109: Calli's Pink Leg

January 30, 2019

    The coldest weather of this young year is sweeping into our area this morning, bringing with it fierce northwest winds and intense snow squalls. Our overnight lows are expected to drop slightly below zero (-1° to -5°) with windchills of 15°-25° below zero. Our previous coldest morning low this month was +4° on January 22. In our area the average coldest temperatures of the year usually range between +5° and -5°, so it appears we will be right on the mark again in 2019 for the fifth consecutive year. It has certainly been cold enough over the past week to make us more than happy to stay indoors where we can bask in the warmth of our wood cookstove and pellet stove. That works for Barb and me, but Calli is spending all of her time window dreaming about the time when she can go outdoors again.

    Calli has been sentenced to remain indoors by her vet, Dr. William Kittleberger of the Mill Creek Animal Hospital in Petersburg, as we try to rid her of a Pasteurella infection in one of the bones of her left rear foot. She contracted the infection from a bite that punctured one of her bones. We noticed that she was spending a lot of time licking the initial wound about a month ago, but we soon noticed additional lesions forming on her leg. We took her to the vet's office on January 9 to determine what was causing the open sores on her leg. After taking some x-rays of the leg, he found the bone puncture and obvious signs of infection in the bone. We took her back to see him on January 17 so he could open the wound and obtain some cultures of the infection to determine the cause. He then put a pink cast on her leg and gave her a prescription to begin treating the infection. She had to wear the cast until he removed it on January 25. She was ordered to remain indoors after her surgery until we can get the infection under control.

    Calli did not know what to do about the cast for the eight days that she wore it. I think she blamed it for her banishment from the outdoors, where she loves to spend nearly all of her daylight hours regardless of the weather. Calli chewed on it frequently and flicked her foot in a futile effort to shed it. It was bad enough to be sentenced to spend her days indoors, but the added embarrassment of the pink cast she was forced to wear was almost more than she could bear. After it was removed on January 25, she began to relax, and she found it easier to accept her ongoing incarceration. However, she was fascinated by the sudden loss of fur on her leg. She can be glad she didn't have to wear a body cast.

Having lost the annoying pink cast, Calli has resumed many of her former indoor antics and hijinks she performed during her kitten period, including trying to jump through our dining room window to catch goldfinches at the sock feeder, chasing her jingle balls around the house, and curling up in front of the front porch door with a stuffed toy of her choice. Her current favorites include a fluffy yellow mouse that looks more like a baby hedgehog and a catnip-filled mouse that Barb made for her this past Christmas. Her only disappointment came when she realized she had grown too big to fit inside one of Barb's shoes.

Although Calli is gradually resigning herself to her indoor life, she doesn't realize that it is only temporary. If her current treatments appear to be effective at her next scheduled visit on February 4, Dr. Kittleberger may clear her to resume her outdoor activities. Since the weather is forecasted to be much warmer then, I wouldn't want to be standing in her way when we open the door for her for the first time in more than two weeks. That could be cause for another hospital trip (for one of us), only I can assure you it won't be to the animal hospital.

Post 110: Shanksville

February 1, 2019

If you study a map of Pennsylvania, you may have a difficult time finding the tiny village of Shanksville. With an estimated population of about 225 people, it isn't what you would call a bustling town. Although it was first laid out in 1829, it did not merit serious attention from the rest of America until September 11, 2001. On that fateful day, United Airlines Flight 93, which had been hijacked by four Al Qaeda suicide terrorists, crashed into a nearby reclaimed mine site killing all 40 civilian passengers and crew. It was the only one of four hijacked aircraft that failed to reach its intended destination, which was the U.S. Capitol building in Washington, DC. That was the day and event that brought Shanksville, PA to the attention of every American.

Because its scheduled departure time was delayed, the passengers of Flight 93 had an opportunity to learn what was happening and collectively decided to risk their own lives in a desperate attempt to seize control of the aircraft from the hijackers. They stormed the cockpit and managed to convince the terrorists that their control of the plane was in jeopardy. On-flight voice recorders captured the hijackers' decision to intentionally crash the plane because they knew they couldn't complete their vile mission. When the plane finally hit the ground at full speed, it left a relatively small impact crater and a debris field that covered a linear mile of ground along the flight path. All aboard were killed instantly.

We had discussed visiting the Flight 93 memorial that was eventually built on the site a number of times, but we didn't actually do it until this past Monday, January 25. The monument was reopened that day after a recent partial government shutdown. We visited the 93-foot-tall memorial tower, with its carillon of wind chimes that represent the muffled voices of the 40 brave civilians who died in the crash. We also toured the visitors center with its videos and recordings of the events of that day and a wall of pictures of the victims. The starkness of the buildings and memorial tower epitomizes the utter shock that captured the nation's attention that day and the dramatic changes that the event eventually brought to our daily lives.

Those of us who lived through that incident remember exactly what we were doing when they learned of these unfolding events. We were living in the Anniston/Oxford, AL area at the time, and I remember hearing that a plane had crashed into one of the World Trade Center towers as I walked towards my office from my car after driving in to work. My wife was working for a nearby Credit Union that served employees and service men and women who worked at the Anniston Ordinance Depot. My first thought was that the crash was some kind of crazy accident, and the pilot would be to blame. However, as time passed, we all learned the truth that it was an organized terrorist attack on our nation, and it cost the lives of nearly 3,000 innocent people.

I guess all of us think about that day and event whenever it is mentioned. Many people probably recall personal friends and family who lost their lives. Although the incident still occasionally haunts my mind, it's not because I lost any friends or relatives. It's because of the car I was trying to sell at that time. That car represents my only potential link to the September 11 terrorist attacks. It is a strange story indeed, so I will explain it to you.

In the month prior to the September 11 attack, Barb and I decided to sell a 1994 Mazda Protégé that we had been driving. The car's mileage had reached a point where we could receive the best resale value for the use we had obtained from it. To minimize the cost of buying a new replacement car, I decided that we would try to sell it ourselves, so that we would receive the full resale value and could approach the car dealership with a significant cash down-payment rather than a trade-in. We felt we could work a better deal on the price of a new car that way. To further minimize our cost for a new car, we decided to buy it in September, when we could get a good deal on a prior year (2001) model the dealer would be motivated to sell to make way for the new 2002 model cars. That's why we were trying to sell our Mazda at that point in time.

I decided to list the Mazda on the Internet, as it was a brand of car that would garner a lot of attention from prospective buyers. Barb, who was working in the banking field at that time, researched the Blue Book value and determined that it was worth $2,800. I listed it at that price to ensure a quick sale. As it turned out, I received a call from an interested buyer the next morning, which was a Saturday. Unfortunately, I don't remember the exact date, because it wouldn't stand out in my mind until the days following September 11.

The person who inquired about the car was living in the Atlanta area, which was a 90-mile drive via Interstate 20 to our home in Oxford, AL. I had a difficult time understanding what he was saying because he was speaking with a very thick accent that I recognized as Middle-Eastern. (I had an undergraduate college friend who was born in Iraq, so I was acquainted with the regional accent.) He asked if he could see the car that day, so I gave him driving directions to our home. He arrived early that afternoon in a rental car with three "friends." They were all roughly the same age and of Middle-Eastern descent. I showed them the car I had to sell, and one of them climbed into it and studied the interior. I had recently washed and cleaned it, so it appeared to be in very good condition. The four men conversed with each other in Arabic as I watched them.

After about fifteen minutes of discussion, one of them turned to me and said they wanted to buy it, if I would accept $2,000 in cash for it. He produced from his front pocket a wad of $100 bills, which he unfolded and fanned before me. This took me by surprise and I replied, "Don't you at least want to test drive it?" He smiled at me, then looked at his friends, each of whom were looking at each other as if they were surprised that I didn't immediately accept their offer. The man with the money turned back to me and said, "Sure, that would be fine."

I then climbed into the middle of the back seat as all four of them got into the car with me. I gave the money man the key, and he started the car. I gave him directions as we drove down the hill from our house onto U.S. Route 78, which he drove along for a couple of miles before turning around and returning to the house. After the tour, he reiterated his cash offer and once again drew the wad of bills from his pocket. They all stared at me as I thought for a moment of what to say. He was offering me cash, but it was $800 less than we had hoped we could get for it. I told him that the book value was $2,800, and that I would appreciate a little more for it. He said that was all he had to offer, and that he was ready to buy it now. We negotiated a little more, but I finally told him I'd rather wait a little while to see if I could get a better offer. After all, it had only been listed for one day.

I asked for his telephone number in case I later decided to accept his offer, but he refused to give it to me. He said he would look for another car. He then collected his friends and they drove away in their rental car. That was the last I saw them or heard from them. I eventually sold the car a couple of weeks later to a local nurse who agreed to pay me $2,500 for it. We then went to a dealer and bought a 2001 Chevy Malibu, which I drove to work on the morning of September 11, 2001.

However, in the weeks following the September 11 attack, I saw news stories documenting that some of the Al Qaeda terrorists had been staying in the Atlanta area within the final months before the attack. One of them was Mohammed Atta, one of the ringleaders in planning the coordinated attack. He and one of his cohorts were taking practice flights at a local airport. After hearing these stories in the news, I began to think back to the day the group of four Middle-Eastern men tried to buy my car. Although I never knew their names and could never recognize their faces, I had to wonder if I might have sold my car to some of the terrorists who carried out that brazen, despicable act. That lingering thought, which came to mind every time I have heard the event discussed, was my strongest motivation to visit the Flight 93 Memorial. I guess I'll always wonder if my car might have been one of many tools that supported them and their activities. However, it always reminds me of how small the world can become, and how even the smallest incidents can have huge consequences and ramifications. That's probably a good thing for all of us to think about from time to time.

This remains my only potential link to the September 11 attacks.

Post 111: Imagine

February 3, 2019

    Most of the website posts I write are inspired by events that occur on our farm or the places we visit. However, every once in a while, an idea for a new post just comes to mind. This is one of those posts. It also differs from my standard posts because it will be a post without pictures. Now I know my readers have asked me to include pictures, but I want to see if I can encourage you to picture in your mind the thoughts I want to express. Many people who know me and read my writings have said, "You write so similar to the way you talk that I can actually hear your voice as I read it." I guess I just say and write what's on my mind. When it comes to painful thoughts, I usually find I can express them more comfortably in my writings than I can in spoken words. Maybe it's because I can choose my words more carefully when I write and edit them before they are seen by anyone else. Now, with your polite indulgence, I'd like to put it to the test. Can I get you to visualize in your mind what I'm writing about? Can I express my thoughts clearly enough in words that you can visualize it too? Let's see about that. I'll be interested to know what you think, so please feel free to submit your comments on this post.

    I'd like to take your mind on a visit to a very different time and place. It's a place and lifestyle that I remember clearly from my past, but is very hard to find today. Oh, to be sure, remnants of it remain, but you have to look hard for it. Some people stumble across it in their travels without even realizing or appreciating what it was. As I've said in many prior posts, it is part of the ancestral heritage of *every* living person today. It is only a question of how many generations back you have to go to find it, but I assure you, it's there. Now I'd like to help you understand it better in your own mind. It's easier than you might think, if you try.

    Imagine a place where people spend almost as much time outdoors as they do inside their homes. Most of them earn their living from outdoors work. Some work in the nearby fields and barns. They may be repairing a fence or building, tending some livestock, or driving a tractor. The unmistakable sounds of their activities catch your attention, reassuring you that you are not alone. These are people who work close to the land. It provides them with their income and the food they eat.

    This is also a place where children prefer to play outdoors. When you step outside your house, the air is filled with the sounds of children laughing and squealing with pleasure as they romp energetically around the yard. Perhaps they're playing a game of tag, cowboys and Indians, marbles, or jacks. Maybe they're competing with each other to see who can climb the highest into a large shade tree or they've commandeered the entire yard for a game of softball. When they're not actively playing, you may find them sitting together on a porch, engaged in quiet conversation. If you listen carefully, you can hear them talking, but you may not understand everything they're saying. You realize they're sharing their secret thoughts directly with each other, their minds dancing in a world that's all their own.

You hear almost no traffic on the main road, as only an occasional car or truck drives by. Even the sound of an airplane is so rare that it draws your attention when you hear it. The only other sounds you hear are the noises of nature—birds singing in a nearby tree, frogs croaking in a nearby pond, the occasional lowing of a cow, the neigh of a horse, or the cackling of a flock of chickens. Trees and rolling hills dominate the landscape, and the few houses, barns, silos, fences, weather-beaten sheds and open fields that you can see only enhance the picture.

The people who live in this place live and act very differently from those living in the city. They don't adorn the houses and properties with trappings of wealth, although they may decorate them festively for the holidays. They almost never lock their doors. They eat as many meals outdoors as they cook on a grill. They open their windows to let in fresh air in the summer, and they heat their homes in the winter with a wood stove or fireplace. You can tell that because you will see a neatly stacked pile of firewood in the warmer months and smoke rising from a chimney in the winter. On warm, summer evenings, the parents will gather on the front porch or go for a slow stroll along the road, greeting all their neighbors on the front porch as they pass. As the darkness of night descends, the children resume their play on the lawn, chasing fireflies and placing them in a jar. They're trying to see who can catch the most.

People greet you warmly when you stop to talk with them. They often wave at complete strangers when they pass by. Even if they may feel quietly reserved when first meeting strangers, they have no fear of them. Their smile is genuine and their manner of speaking is plain and easy to follow, even if they use some words that are not familiar to you. Their feelings show clearly on their faces. They reserve judgement of you until they get to know you. If they should say or do something that unintentionally offends or harms you, they are quick to apologize and eager to make amends. You can sense their shame and regret reflected in their facial expressions and the tone of their voice. They are honest and forthright when answering questions. Although they act and speak with great humility, they present themselves in an overall manner that conveys a comforting self-assurance and dignity. Their dedication to hard work and manual labor shows in the firmness of their handshake and the lines on their faces. Their casual presence and demeanor make it easy for you to feel comfortable in their presence. They go out of their way to make you feel comfortable in their home.

I wonder if you can visualize the people and places I'm describing. If you can, the image may seem quaint and idyllically or unrealistically nostalgic to you. You may judge it to be a sickly-sweet characterization of an outdated way of life that only served to mask the harsh realities and sordid behaviors that fester beneath the surface. It's true that we *all* have an inner self that we hide from public view and that, if revealed, would tarnish the carefully cultivated image we project of ourselves.

However, the people and places I described are more real than you might ultimately wish to think. I should know because I was raised in that environment. Even though our family relationships were often strained, we never let those personal conflicts interfere with the way we treated others. In fact, we sometimes found it easier to show greater respect for others than we displayed to each other. Mark Twain may have explained it best when he once observed that "Good breeding consists in concealing how much we think of ourselves and how little we think of the other person." This is a code of behavior that is often ignored by our modern, urban society, where everyone seems to say whatever they feel without regard to the feelings of others. To me, that might be a reason why the people and places I described may be difficult for some people to accept. Be careful how you judge what I've described. You may discover that it says more about your own lifestyle than the one I once lived.

It's hard for people who accept a very different code of behavior to understand and believe what I have to say about my traditional, rural upbringing. I faced that disbelief when I first started college, so it never surprises me. You don't have to be the best person you could be to be better than people will give you credit for. You also don't have to be the best person you could be to become a better person. What you do need to do to improve yourself is to think carefully about your core values and live by those that will bring greater honor and integrity to your life. You will find they are also the values that demonstrate the greatest respect and courtesy for others. I think this is a lesson our modern society would benefit greatly from. That's why I decided to write this post. Did I express my message clearly?

By the way, I should declare that any resemblance you may find in the theme of this post to the lyrics of a popular 1971 song by John Lennon is merely coincidental—as far as you know.

Post 112: Shame
February 14, 2019

While most of my website posts focus on traditional farming practices and our farm activities, I do try to discuss and explain the core values that serve as the foundation for traditional self-reliant living. If you want to understand how rural people think, you must first understand the core values upon which their perspective on life is based. I would like to offer this post as a contribution to that understanding.

In my most recent (February 3, 2019) post entitled "Imagine," I made an observation about the humble nature of rural behavior patterns that helped focus my thoughts on the subject for this post. In it, I wrote that rural people "*...reserve judgement of you until they get to know you. If they should say or do something that unintentionally offends or harms you, they are quick to apologize and eager to make amends. You can sense their shame and regret reflected in their facial expressions and the tone of their voice*." This behavior pattern is common among people who feel truly sorry for the offenses they may commit, whether unintentional or accidentally intentional. They feel a strong sense of shame for their actions that motivates them to apologize and make amends, even if only by altering their behavior or attitudes.

Whenever I interact with front-line customer service representatives for large businesses today, I find them eager to apologize for any inconveniences that their product or service may have caused. To me, that is a patronizing apology, because I know that they have no influence to ensure that the business will modify its behavior to prevent the infraction that caused my complaint from recurring. They just want me to feel better and perhaps defuse any anger I'm feeling that they may have to listen to, but have no power to address. While they might be able to feel some sense of shame that their employer caused harm to one of its consumers, they don't have to internalize it personally because they know they don't have any effective control over the business' operations. The fact that any shame they might feel for my problem does not reflect on their own self-image means that any apology they offer may be totally insincere. The knowledge that such apologies people get from big businesses and government are basically insincere is what contributes to the overall impression that modern society is cold, impersonal and unfeeling. I also see it as a consequence that the businesses and institutions driving our society today are simply too big to internalize any sincere concern or remorse for an individual.

I hear many news stories on the radio about people being harmed by "body-shaming." In essence, their self-image is being destroyed by people criticizing their appearance. While this is a form of bullying, which should bring a sense of shame to the offender, it is the victim who is internalizing the shame. As one who was a frequent target of bullying when I was young, I have come to learn that a positive self-image is *not* something that you can obtain from other people; it is something that you must be able to give yourself regardless of what other people think or say about you. As I see it, the core of the problem is that most people today will internalize personal shame from the criticism they receive, rather than the things they do to harm other people. If shame is something that can devastate a victim's self-image, it is reasonable to assume that it can be an effective deterrent to prevent people from being insensitive to others. The traditional rural people who raised me taught me to internalize shame (and guilt) for my actions if they harm someone else, not if someone else does something to me. That is one of the core values of traditional, self-reliant living that appears to have been forgotten today.

We seem to live in a society that is reluctant to punish people for harmful actions. Our legal system goes to great extent (and expense) to defend people who commit crimes, even when they are caught red-handed in the act or there are so many witnesses to the crime that there is no reason to question their guilt. More and more people protest against the death penalty as an inhumane form of punishment. There is no question that it can be if innocent people are executed, but we also have a serious problem or injustice to deal with if a convicted, unrepentant murderer is able to murder again. In states where the death penalty has been prohibited by law, the maximum sentence that can be issued is life in prison. However, I hear that Pope Francis now considers lifetime sentences to be inhumane. I don't wish to debate these issues in this post. It is our apparent inability to decide what form of punishment society should impose for transgressions against innocent, law-abiding citizens that I wish to address. In other words, how should society dissuade people from bad behavior that violates basic community standards of acceptable behavior?

I guess some people will never accept any form of punishment as an appropriate response to bad behavior. That might be fine if they are the only victims of crime. However, the lack of any punishment for acts of aggression toward others makes the innocent victim the only person who will ultimately be punished. Just go back to my earlier discussion of body-shaming to see how that will be the consequence. Can bullying be effectively controlled by demonstrating greater sensitivity and concern for the person who bullied rather than the person who was bullied?

What I'm trying to say is what will our society be if there is no effective way to *enforce* "NO?" One of the biggest issues being advanced today by the "Me Too" movement is the violation of sexual assault victims by people who won't accept "no" for an answer. Our law enforcement system has a hard time with that, because violating "no" does not become a prosecutable crime until the rejection has already been violated. It also has a difficult time convicting the criminal when there is no clear and documentable evidence that it is not just a he-said/she-said argument. Wouldn't our society function so much better if the criminals would simply accept "no" as an answer? If you do not want tough law enforcement or stiff penalties for violations, you need to find some way to ensure that people won't exercise their own liberties so selfishly that they can freely take advantage of or harm law-abiding citizens.

At this point, I'm sure you want to ask me what all this has to do with farming or traditional values. Has the cheese finally slipped off my cracker? Well, I'll answer that for you. You see, there is a segment of our society that does a very good job with that very issue. Although no segment of society is, or ever will be, free of criminal activity, there is one segment that has very low crime rates and does not use prison or the death penalty as a deterrent. It is the Amish. They don't believe in the "eye-for-an-eye" approach to justice, and they don't exact prosecutorial vengeance against known criminals. They won't even defend themselves with guns. What they will do, however, is punish an unrepentant person for violating their values of social decency by "shunning" them from their community. They find that their practice of "shunning" criminals is the best way to make the violator internalize some meaningful sense of shame for the crime he or she has committed. Of course, the fact that their social code also promotes strong values of civility and imposes great restraint on personal egos are contributing factors to their success.

Now, many people will not want to live by their specific values of social decency, but that is not the point I'm trying to make. The point is that they use "shunning" as an effective, non-violent tool to deter people from violating their basic values, regardless of what those values may be. If you wish to criticize this approach, then compare it to our modern law enforcement system and show me that it is less effective. It is certainly less expensive. Of course, this approach works better in the context of a small, rural society than it does in a big city, which is why I am using it as a way to show how traditional rural living can be fundamentally different from urban living and how it is based on different core values. Perhaps it shows why rural living and the strong core values it typically embraces can be a fundamentally better way to live. Can you see how my discussion of shame relates to traditional rural values? All I can say is, if you can't, what a crying shame that would be. Consider it fresh food for thought from Peeper Pond Farm to you.

Post 113: Mountain Music

February 25, 2019

 Traditional Appalachian Mountain lifestyles are based on a number of cultural pillars that form a solid foundation. These pillars include a strong devotion to family, deep-seated religious values, a determined independent spirit and a firm devotion to a cultural heritage. Most often, the devotion to a cultural heritage is forged through the art of story-telling and traditional music—predominantly mountain bluegrass. The earliest pioneer settlers of the Appalachian Mountains were poor immigrants seeking political and religious freedom. They often carried few possessions with them on their journeys, so they relied upon the art of story-telling and music to preserve their cultural heritage and pass it along to their children. This is why the lyrics of most traditional mountain bluegrass songs tell stories, many of which can be rather tragic tales. Nevertheless, they represent the trials and struggles of a people whose search for freedom led them to carve a self-reliant life out of a wild and untamed mountain wilderness. In this sense, the music, stories and legends of traditional Appalachian society represent a true American cultural heritage. This is another dimension of traditional folkways that we wish to help preserve through our ongoing efforts at Peeper Pond Farm.

 I must admit, my childhood farm upbringing in the northern Appalachian Mountains was not based in a tradition of music. My adoptive family tended to rely on story-telling to pass along the traditions. A number of them proved to be tall tales, to say the least. However, I did make some effort to learn how to play music. I took a year's worth of piano lessons when I was in second or third grade (I can't remember for certain), but I got bored with the rather mundane songs I was told to practice ad nauseum. I simply got tired of practicing songs I didn't like, so I just refused to practice them until the teacher gave up on me. My mother did eventually obtain a small electric organ that I later tried to play. The organ came with a card that was placed behind the keys with numbers on them that corresponded to the numbered notes on the sheet music that came with it. I learned to play a few of the songs, but couldn't transfer that knowledge to other songs that I would have preferred to play.

 When I was in fifth and sixth grades, I was encouraged to play a band instrument by our music teacher. My personal preference was to learn how to play a guitar, but that was not an instrument that you could choose to play in a marching band. I ended up trying to play the trumpet instead. That didn't last very long when my rather shrill efforts to practice at home met with disapproval from my parents and sisters. Even our cows occasionally complained, so I was soon outvoted.

During the early years of our marriage, Barb bought me a six-string guitar for Christmas in 1995. I tried to learn how to play it from an instructional book, but I never did grasp it well that way. I intended to get some lessons, but my busy overtime work schedule made it virtually impossible to make time for formal instruction. After a few years collecting dust, we sold the guitar in a yard sale. At that point, I just decided that music simply wasn't my forte. After all, my wife led me to believe that the only thing deadlier than my aim was my singing, so I eventually decided I couldn't take my music very far even if I could learn to play something.

Barb, on the other hand, does possess a decent alto singing voice and had learned how to play the piano as a child. She actually took formal lessons for ten years and can read sheet music. She inherited a spinet piano from her grandmother, which she would play once in a while, but it was never her passion. She preferred to sing and performed in a number of different choirs and choruses over the years. During the first two years of our retirement, she performed with the Petersburg, WV Community Chorus. Although we brought her piano with us on each of our professional working career moves, she decided to sell it before we retired to our Peeper Pond Farm home in 2017. It was just getting too big to carry with us at our age.

After we retired, our connection to traditional mountain music grew. Our local radio station, WELD-FM, plays a wide range of country and bluegrass music. We also started attending and participating in Jeff and Amanda Barger's occasional pot luck supper gatherings at their North Mill Creek homestead farm, each of which would culminate in an impromptu bluegrass sing-along performed by their friends and neighbors. We even attended a number of mountain bluegrass sessions at the nearby Landes Ruritan building about eight miles north of our farm. Throughout that time, I have learned a lot of wonderful traditional bluegrass songs that preserve the Appalachian story-telling heritage I have described.

Within our first year of retirement, we began to visit a number of local churches to find one that best suited our interests. After attending at least ten different church services, we finally settled on the Dorcus Baptist Church. The long-time pastor of that church, Steve Davis, is a man I greatly admire, and his light-hearted approach to sermons grounded in every-day life appealed to us.

Barb's only initial disappointment was that the church did not have a choir she could sing in. The congregation was rather small, so they only had a part-time piano player; most of the hymns were sung acapella with Steve Davis in the lead. Steve has a beautiful bass/baritone voice that would ensure him a second career as a professional singer if he ever decided to retire from preaching. He can also play the guitar, but not the piano. However, once I let word slip out that Barb could play the piano, the wheels began to turn in the congregation's collective mind. Eventually, she was "encouraged" to play for the weekly services, and she finally relented to them in August 2018. Since then, Barb has become the primary pianist for the church, a role she has grown to enjoy. The only problem was that we no longer had a piano at home, so she had to drive weekly to the church to practice—a twenty-six-mile round trip.

This past December, we decided to splurge and buy a relatively inexpensive electronic keyboard for her to use for practice at home. At the same time, I decided to try to learn how the play the Mountain Dulcimer. I often enjoyed listening to hammer dulcimer performances I encountered during my childhood, but found the instrument too expensive for yet another experiment in learning to play music. However, I soon learned that the Mountain Dulcimer is much easier to learn than most other instruments, and it was not very expensive to buy. I decided to give it a try and began a self-instruction effort to see how much I could learn.

During the month of December, I managed to learn how to play a total of six songs on my dulcimer. The first two simple songs, "Mary Had A Little Lamb" and "Twinkle, Twinkle Little Star", I learned how to play by video on the first day. From that starting point, I learned to play additional songs by ear—I still can't read sheet music. I learned how to play "Taps" and "Row, Row, Row Your Boat" within the next day. I then began to figure out how to play two traditional Christmas carols, which were far more complex. Within a few more days I had figured out how to play "Hark, the Herald Angels Sing" and "O' Little Town of Bethlehem" on my own. I began to learn a few other songs, but decided to concentrate on mastering my starting repertoire before trying to learn any new songs. My failing memory was making it harder to remember how to play each song when I tried to expand my vocabulary of songs. Now that I have convinced myself that I am capable of playing an instrument, I plan to take some formal lessons, assuming I can find an affordable instructor.

The Mountain Dulcimer is an American invention that is tied to traditional mountain music. It is shaped like a violin but strummed like a guitar. I purchased a four-string dulcimer, which has two melody strings (that are played together), a middle string and a bass string. Some older dulcimers tend to have only one melody string. The pitch of each string is changed as you play through the use of bridge frets, like a guitar. Each fret corresponds with a different note.

Although the musical range of a mountain dulcimer is more limited than other string instruments, I have found it easy to learn, which is a distinct advantage for a musical novice. I am hoping to learn how to read sheet music and play chords through formal instruction.

My ultimate goal is to sit on our front porch this summer and play traditional songs that have echoed through our mountains for generations. With any luck, I hope to invite Jeff and Amanda and many of our new friends to join us at Peeper Pond Farm for a pot-luck dinner and bluegrass sing-along as we have enjoyed at their home. I do promise that if I attempt any singing, it will be to myself. This is how we hope to help pass along the traditions that make our rural mountain life special and distinctly American.

Post 114: It's Snow Quiet Outside

March 6, 2019

We've had a lot of snowy days this year, but no really big snowstorm. The most we've received from any individual snowstorm this season was six inches on February 20. However, since the beginning of March, we have received 1.5 inches on the first, 2.5 inches on the third, and one inch on the fourth. We are expecting another one-to-two inches on March 8. This winter has brought a number of small, but measurable snowfalls and a lot of cold, blustery weather to accompany them. Our total snowfall for the winter season stands at 23.5 inches, which is only 1.5 inches away from our thirty-year seasonal average. It is the lack of any big ten-plus inch storms that is most perplexing. It seems that all areas around our little valley area have received at least one snowfall of twelve or more inches this year except us. That's okay, though, as we've had more than enough precipitation over the past year to last us for a while.

Winters in our area are a quiet and reflective time. Oh, we have our weekend "flush" of tourists driving through our area to enjoy the big ski area resorts (including Snowshoe, Canaan Valley and Timberline) from Washington, Baltimore and Richmond. However, most days, the hustle and bustle of economic activity is minimized by the cold and snowy weather. That's why I can really appreciate the small but frequent storms we've had. It creates such a picturesque winter scene across our landscape without making the roads so impassable or treacherous as to limit our essential travels. We have enjoyed periods of snow-draped trees, unbroken blankets of white across our fields, stark white ridgelines, and even the sparkle of sunlight across a mountain forest of bare trees with limbs coated in ice.

These are the visual pleasures of the winter season that add variety to our life at Peeper Pond Farm. I consider them to be candy for the eye. However, I also greatly appreciate the intense stillness and quiet I experience from our front porch during a gentle snowfall. Most times, as I stand on the porch, I can hear the constant sounds of the rural landscape around me. On any average day, we can hear dozens of varieties of bird song, the chirping of crickets, the lowing of cows, the neigh of a horse, the crowing of a rooster, or the whisper of a strong breeze sweeping down the faces of our mountain ridges. These are the typical natural sounds of quiet that can be quite deafening at times.

However, when a cold, winter snow settles in across our valley, all of these sounds simply disappear as the animals and wildlife hunker down and the breeze grows still. Only then do we experience the intense stillness of a storm that adds a sense of true peace and serenity to the scene. I appreciate these brief quiet times that allow you to focus on the natural beauty of the landscape that surrounds us. They gently wash away the stress and worry that so complicate our daily lives, as they provide a welcome sense of solace and relief in times of despair. In doing so, they refresh the soul and cleanse the mind. To me, that is the most pleasurable aspect of winter that I experience from the front porch of our home at Peeper Pond Farm. I hope you can take the time to experience it for yourself when a brief snowstorm stands in the way of your best-laid plans. We all need to enjoy the full measure of our lives—especially the quiet times when we can reflect on it all and put our lives into proper perspective. I know I find it as relaxing as it is peaceful.

Post 115: Turn, Turn, Turn

March 15, 2019

To everything there is a season, and a time to every purpose under heaven. This chapter of Ecclesiastes was always my adoptive grandfather's favorite passage from the Bible. He recited it to me so often when I was a child that whenever I heard The Byrd's musical rendition of it playing on the radio, I would announce, "They're playing Grandpa's song!" The ever-cycling patterns of life always brought him great joy.

Winter is now turning into spring here at Peeper Pond Farm. We faced a long, cold winter with temperatures persistently below average and frequent brutal winds with gusts that topped 60 MPH at the end of February damaging numerous farm buildings in our area. Our total snowfall now stands at our seasonal average of 25 inches, but we have not reached the end of the average snowfall season. We still have not received any snowstorm that dropped more than six inches, but virtually everyone around us has at some point earlier this season. Now we have reason to exult in the gradual transition to spring.

Yesterday, March 14, was the first day since November 1, 2018 that our high temperature surpassed 70 degrees—topping out at 72. Last winter was also very cold, but we recorded our first high temperature of 70 degrees or more on February 15, nearly a full month earlier. Our forecasted high for today is also about 70 degrees, after which a dry cold front will sweep through, returning us briefly to below average temperatures.

However, I awoke this morning to a rousing chorus of spring peepers from our signature farm pond. I could hear them calling as Calli burst through the door and raced off the porch to begin her early morning hunting routine in the pre-dawn darkness. She paused only briefly when she heard the sound of a nearby dog barking from an unfamiliar direction—something she knew wasn't right and realized she should heed. It is a very warm morning with a low temperature of 61 degrees and gusty breezes that carried the raucous mating calls from the pond to my appreciative ears. I had heard the first tenuous peeps from the reeds that hug the swampy shoreline when I followed Calli to the pond late yesterday afternoon. Now their song fills the air in celebration of the coming spring weather.

Over the past couple of weeks, we have noticed the return of the robins to our yard and the occasional songs of summer birds, as they sweep back into our hills and mountains to begin their annual summer migration. The birdsong was especially cheerful this morning. I sat on the porch yesterday and watched several buzzards gliding lazily on the breeze as they spiraled higher and higher into the sky prowling for small prey in the surrounding fields. Even Calli has been busy playfully hunting field mice roused from their winter hibernation chambers by the emerging warmth. Soon our own activities will change as we challenge our hibernating muscles to begin preparing our vegetable and herb garden for the annual spring planting ritual. However, we are still waiting for our crocuses and daffodils to bloom. I guess they want to see if the recent spring weather is going to last. After the winter we have experienced, I can't blame them.

Post 116: Missing the Mark

March 18, 2019

    Snow is falling this morning, as I write this post. It is a soft, gentle snowfall that has dusted all the rooftops and sprinkled a light coating of sugar on the grassy surfaces. The low clouds and subtle, snowy haze that accompanies it casts a grey pall across our mountain landscape, reinforcing the disappointment I feel in having to write this post. As I joyfully announced in my January 25 website post, our West Virginia Farm Fresh Raw Milk Act bill was introduced into the 2019 Legislative Session as House Bill 2643. The intent of the bill is to remove our state's final prohibition on unprocessed milk sales to allow consumer direct sales of fresh milk from small dairy farms. This is a goal I have been working to achieve since we sold our dairy goat herd in August 2017. We ultimately received active support for our legislative initiative from five House Delegates and one State Senator. Shortly after our bill was introduced into the House of Delegates, Senator Dave Sypolt introduced a concurrent bill (Senate Bill 471) into the Senate. However, the regular session of the West Virginia legislation ended on Saturday, March 10, and I subsequently learned that our bill was one of many that did not make it out of Committee before the deadline.

    To his credit, Senator Sypolt, who chairs the Senate Agriculture and Rural Development Committee, tried to introduce a concurrent study resolution that would have established a joint House/Senate task force to study the bill before the 2020 Legislative Session begins. Unfortunately, that resolution also did not pass. That was not an unexpected outcome given the intense opposition we face to gain adoption of this bill, as I have thoroughly discussed in previous website posts. We always knew that success would not come easy.

    While this means our bill will not be adopted in 2019, it does not mean it cannot be reintroduced next year. The last time a bill was introduced to open raw milk sales it took seven years of deliberation and reconsideration before the compromise Herd Shares bill was ultimately adopted in 2016. Even if it takes another three years to get our new bill adopted, it will have achieved swift passage by comparison. I am working with Senator Sypolt to discuss what our next move should be to improve its chances for passage the next time it is introduced.

    I remain determined to pursue adoption of our bill. The survival of a meaningful small, family dairy presence in our state ultimately depends upon it. I was raised by dairy farmers, and they are my people. I will not abandon them just because the path I must follow is difficult. As I've explained many times before, farmers know they are not guaranteed success from the hard work they do, but they also know that you can't expect to succeed if you are unwilling to work hard for it.

In the final analysis, we achieved a lot in our first year of determined work. We produced a draft bill that was in proper legal form for legislative introduction (without any paid, professional legal assistance), we built a solid core group of determined supporters representing a broad spectrum of interests, we managed to get a bi-partisan group of Delegates and Senators to introduce the bill, and we have prepared a strong argument and background data to defend it. We also managed to get attention from mainstream media outlets (newspapers, radio and television) for our initiative. We can be proud of those accomplishments.

I wish to extend our sincere appreciation to the elected officials who placed their confidence in our effort this year. They include, Delegate Isaac Sponaugle (who introduced our bill into the house), Senator Dave Sypolt (who introduced our bill into the Senate), and Delegates John Paul Hott, Scott Cadle, Daryl Cowles and Pat McGeehan, who courageously co-sponsored the House bill. I hope we can count on your continued support in 2020.

Now we must take the effort to the next level and work to secure support from more elected, state and advocacy group officials for our cause. We also hope to secure more vocal public support from average citizens who demand consumer-direct sales of farm fresh foods to support preserving this time-honored farming lifestyle before it becomes extinct in West Virginia. To that end, I am rewriting my 2017 Peeper Pond Farm Story manuscript into a new, expanded book, Country Life at Peeper Pond Farm, that I will seek to get published later this year. We will also make digital file copies of the book available for sale during our appearances at the Grant County Farmer's Market this year. I hope you will continue to follow our progress on this issue and will lend your enthusiastic support for it. If you would like to know what you can do to help, please contact us here at Peeper Pond Farm. Our contact information can be obtained from our farm website, www.peeperpondfarm.com.

Post 117: Indian Spring

March 29, 2019

    Our weather continues to warm over time with typical spring-time tussles between warm and cool periods. The exuberant calls of the spring peepers from our pond can be heard day and night. Red-wing blackbirds are nesting among the nine-tail reeds surrounding the pond, and their trilling calls from the neighboring cedar trees and power lines contribute to the auditory delight that harkens the true arrival of spring.

    When I was young, my adoptive father often said that you could tell when the early fickle whims of spring weather were winning the battle with winter after the first bout of "Indian spring" occurred. He was an old-time weather observer, and he understood the patterns of our local Connecticut River Valley climate intimately. Although I have never heard the term "Indian spring" mentioned in professional meteorology circles, it was a very real phenomenon to him, and I came to understand what he meant by it.

    Indian spring is considered to be the vernal counterpart of the more commonly recognized "Indian summer." As most people know, Indian summer refers to a stretch of three or more consecutive days of 70-plus degree high temperatures that occur after the first hard freeze of the fall. My father recognized that the same phenomenon often occurs in the spring, before the final hard freeze of the winter season that marks the beginning of the growing season. Whenever we would experience an early spring period of three or more consecutive days of 70-degree or higher temperatures, he would conclude that it was time to prepare the garden and plant the heartiest vegetables, including peas, broccoli, onions and cabbage. These plants can survive the remaining periodic frosts that occur in early spring, but become less frequent and harsh over time.

    In our local climate here at Peeper Pond Farm, the final spring freeze that marks the start of the growing season typically occurs sometime around May 15, but can occur as late as the first day of summer. We feel it is usually safe to plant our early corn seeds during the first week of May, as they will not sprout from the ground (making them vulnerable to frost damage) until after May 15. According to our current weather forecast, we are in the second of the first three-day period of 70+ degree temperatures of the year. Yesterday's high temperature was 71 degrees and as I am writing this post, our current temperature is 67 degrees. If the forecast is correct, we will experience our first "Indian spring" of the year tomorrow.

Having placed our confidence in the meteorologists, we are working to prepare our vegetable and herb gardens for the ritual spring planting. We have purchased our seeds, mapped out our garden plots, tested the pH of our soil, spread wood and pellet stove ashes in the planting areas that require amending, and begun tilling the soil to mix and loosen it for planting. With any luck, we will have planted all our early season vegetables before the end of the day tomorrow.

This is the most exciting time of the year when we can stretch our sleepy muscles and enjoy the scent of fresh spring air. It feels good to be spending more time outside after the long, cold winter. We don't know if you have experienced Indian spring where you live yet, but if you haven't, we hope it arrives soon. We wish everyone a wonderful and colorful spring, and we look forward to seeing all our friends at the Grant County Farmer's Market in Petersburg this summer, when we can finally share the bounty of our farm with you.

Post 118: Sew Many Pieces

April 1, 2019

To date, I (Dave) have been the author of all our website posts. However, there is one traditional folkway skill we practice that I am not qualified to discuss—the fine art of quilting. That is Barb's forte. Most recently, she was hired by a local attorney to replicate the hand-sewn "Pride of West Virginia" quilt that has been displayed in the Grant County Bank main office in downtown Petersburg for many years. Although she was raised a blue-collar city girl in Schenectady, New York, she had learned to appreciate quilting well before we met and decades before we decided to create Peeper Pond Farm. Recognizing that our traditional lifestyle skills training efforts would be incomplete if we did not address this subject, I will turn over my trusty pen to Barb so that she can explain how she came to cherish it and why it remains a valuable traditional living skill. Here is her story in her own words...

I began sewing during my elementary school days, a skill I learned from my mother. She made many of my early school clothes and taught me how it was done. At one point during my professional years, I had sewn probably half of the clothes in my closet. However, it was during my college days that my interest in quilting emerged, after seeing a crazy quilt that my roommate had made during our four-week Christmas holiday. I went so far as to cut squares from left over fabrics that I had, using all varieties of fabric (polyester, wool, corduroy, etc.) and patterns (plaids, prints, solids, etc.). Although cutting the squares was as far as I got, I learned a lot about the right fabric choices with that project! My next attempt during the early 1980s was much more successful, and, in fact, that quilt covers the twin bed in my sewing area today. My interest in quilting has been sporadic over the years, but is now almost overwhelming. Ask Dave – whenever we make plans to visit a new community, all I want to know is if there is a quilt store in the area. However, I have made nearly 25 quilts, ranging from lap size to king size, five baby quilts, five quilts in honor of our local veterans, Christmas tree skirts, countless pot holders and table runners, and three wall hangings during those years. Am I an expert? Not by a long shot, but I know enough to be dangerous, and some of my pieces have won ribbons at the local county fairs.

Quilting is an art form that had its beginnings in Medieval Europe and Asia. Patchwork quilting, as we know it today, is mostly an American craft born more from need than anything else. Patches of fabric cut from old, worn or outgrown clothing, or feed and flour sacks were stitched together in a pleasing pattern such as the traditional patterns of Nine-Patch, Rail Fence, Ohio Star, Windmill, Bear Paw, Hour Glass and Carpenter's Wheel. They were then layered with some form of batting, probably an old blanket and another piece of fabric used as a backing. These layers were then sewn together and used for bedding and worn around the shoulders for warmth.

During the time of American westward expansion, pioneer women would have been working on their patchwork while their covered wagons were following the Oregon, Chisholm, or Santa Fe trails, as a means of passing the time and preparing for their new homes. Over time, the patterns became more detailed, and the craft of "quilting" – stitching an attractive pattern through all three layers to anchor the pieces together and extend the life of the quilt – became traditional. All of this work would have been done by hand sewing! In more recent years, quilting has extended beyond its traditional uses to also become an art form, using specially designed fabrics and contemporary patterns, and using special machines to stitch the quilting, even to do very intense embroidery in the project. Today, you can go to a quilt show in any city or town and find pieces that replicate what great-grandmother may have done or pieces that should be hanging in some museum of modern art. You will also find more practical items, such as tote bags, purses, back packs, slipcovers, pillows, dresser scarves, placemats and coasters made from quilting fabrics, batting and backing together.

But let's clarify some vocabulary here. A "quilt" is the finished product, composed of a top, batting and backing. The top, which is decorative, has been "pieced" using fabric cut into various shapes like squares, rectangles, triangles, and circles and arcs. The filling is the "batting", and can be all polyester, a blend of polyester and cotton, all cotton, all wool, all silk or even bamboo. The batting provides the loft and warmth and controls the drape, or how the quilt hangs, smoothly or sharply. The "backing" completes the sandwich which becomes your quilt. It is then either "knotted" or "quilted" to bind the layers together and prevent them shifting. Knotting a quilt is done by tying knots through the three layers in the quilt with thread, yarn, embroidery floss, or ribbon. Quilting is the decorative stitching done either by hand or machine, which does a more complete job of securing the three layers together. The design can be either very simple, such as straight lines back and forth or up and down the quilt, or very intense, with patterns of feathers or shells or waves or pebbles or even animals, toys or tools. Virtually anything your mind can dream up can be stitched into your quilt.

Among the most memorable of the quilts I have made is the one that I call "Grandma's Quilt". My grandmother had given me a box of squares that she had stashed in a closet, which had been appliqued with the "Prairie Rose" pattern. Whether she or another member of her family had made the blocks, or if she had purchased them at an antique show, I do not know. I held onto them for some years and eventually decided to put them together in a quilt to give to Grandma for Christmas 1993. As we were living more than 700 miles from home, I didn't get to enjoy the moment when she opened her gift, but I understand that she was very pleased with it. Another favorite is the Christmas cardinal wall hanging that goes up right after Thanksgiving every year and comes down some time after Christmas. It shows a cardinal sitting on a tree branch in the center, surrounded by blocks in the Log Cabin pattern, a very old and traditional pattern. I am also quite proud of the quilts that I made for the veterans at my church. For each of these, I purchased a preprinted panel depicting a patriotic scene, stitched three sets of color coordinated strips around each panel, and then knotted in the panel field and "stitched in the ditch" (along the seam lines of the strips) to complete the quilts. I may not have cut my fabric into shapes that got patched together, but adding the colorful strips, and knotting and stitching in the ditch qualify these as quilts.

If you are interested in learning to do patchwork quilting, I recommend that you find a fabric store that specializes in quilting and is able to help you get started, or even gives classes. There are also a number of internet sites and programs on Public Television that are very helpful no matter your level of skill. There are many magazines and books that can also teach you this very rewarding craft, available in stores and possibly your public library. Choose a simple pattern and project to get started with, such as a Nine-Patch or Rail Fence pot holder or baby quilt. Limit yourself to no more than three fabrics that are pleasing to you, and purchase the best quality fabric that you can. At a quilt store, fabric will be about $12/yard and is normally worth the price. You can purchase fabric at discounted prices on many websites, and they are often the same fabric that you can purchase at the quilt shop. But if you are limited by budget, Wal-Mart, Hobby Lobby and JoAnn Fabrics carry perfectly acceptable options. There also may be a quilters' guild or club in your area that you can join to learn additional quilting techniques and skills. Since retiring to our farm, I have joined the Sew & Sews Quilt Guild in Franklin, WV and picked up quite a few tips and tricks of the trade.

There are three other rules to follow. Quilters all over will argue about which is the most important. You will find constant references to an "accurate ¼-inch seam allowance" in every project, and many will tell you this is the most important factor. However, I argue that being accurate in your cutting is the most important. If your patches are cut poorly, no "accurate ¼-inch seam" is going to save you! The carpenter's rule of "measure twice, cut once" applies equally to quilting. (Now if I would only learn that and remember it!) The third rule is to purchase the best equipment and supplies that you can. A good sewing machine will become your best friend. You don't need a fancy expensive machine to start with, but you may want to upgrade to a better one as you become more involved in this hobby. Also, buy twice as many pins and spools of thread as you think you will need!

    I could go on for many more pages about the art of patchwork quilting. There is so much to discover and learn. I hope I have piqued your interest in pursuing another aspect of the self-reliant lifestyle skills that we have chosen to preserve and promote. Please feel free to contact me if you have questions or would like an individual lesson. Also, if you will refer to our website, www.peeperpondfarm.com, you will find photos of many of my completed projects.

Post 119: Preparing Garden Soil - Back to the Basics

April 2, 2019

    Whenever you want to establish any type of garden or planting area, the first and most important issue is to determine if the soil and planting location will support whatever you want to plant in it. Several critical factors will affect your planting success—solar exposure, moisture levels, nutrient needs and pH levels. Solar exposure is the easiest and most obvious to decide and take into account. In many instances, it will be something you can't control, so you either need to select the type of plant you will grow based on the amount of direct sunlight your planting location receives or you will have to select a different planting location to satisfy the solar needs of the plant.

    Moisture levels will depend on drainage, seasonal rainfall patterns and water table levels If you dig into your soil and the hole fills with water, you have a high-water table. That may be a seasonal (periodic) issue or a year-round issue, which you will have to know from your experience or determine from historic records. If you want to put a planting bed in an area where sycamore, cedar, or willow trees grow, or you see wetland vegetation growing, you can expect the water table to be high most all of the time. Again, you will probably have to choose your plantings or garden location to fit the ambient water table levels. However, if your soil is occasionally dry, you may want to use commercial gel crystals when planting to help store the water you apply at planting so that the early roots will have access to the water they need to get started. If stormwater drainage is an issue, you may need to elevate your bed or dig an alternative drainage swale to protect your plants. At least you have some measure of control over that issue that you may lack with regard to the water table.

    Nutrient needs can be addressed through some form of fertilizer supplement (which are available at many stores) or through rotational plantings—in the case of a vegetable garden. Usually, the packages of the seeds you purchase will give you genera nutrient requirements for the plant. We have been rotating the crops we plant in our vegetable garden to allow the plants to regulate soil nutrient levels and minimize our fertilization costs. The roots of certain plants will increase nitrogen levels in the soil and others will diminish it. Learning how each plant impacts the soil will allow you to decide which plants to rotate from season to season to manage nutrient levels naturally. You can also use composted food waste to manage nutrient levels conveniently wherever you may decide (from your plant's health) that enrichment is needed.

Perhaps the most difficult soil preparation issue you need to consider is pH levels. Not only is it more difficult to measure, it is also very critical to your planting success. Soil can be highly acidic (with a very low pH level ranging from zero to six) or very alkaline or basic (with a very high pH level ranging from eight to fourteen). A pH level of seven is considered neutral. Many people collect soil samples and send them to a commercial lab to analyze soil pH levels. Once the analysis is completed, you will receive a bewildering report of soil data that is often hard to interpret or to understand what you need to do to correct it. However, we have learned a time-honored, simple, convenient and affordable way to analyze relative pH levels yourself using common household chemicals. We used this technique to determine how to amend our own vegetable garden soil to support the needs of the crops we plant. This is one of those times that our kitchen is called upon to serve as our Peeper Pond Farm laboratory. Please don't report us to the Health Department for doing this; they'll only have a conniption fit. If that doesn't cause you fear, here's how you do it.

First decide where you need to collect samples, depending on the size of your planting area. If you are planting a tree or bush, one sampling location may be all you need to test. If you are planting a garden, you may need to collect samples from several locations to ensure that each planting plot has the best relative pH level for the crop you intend to plant. For each location you wish to test, collect two samples of soil in separate cups (or divide one sample into two cups for testing). One of the samples will be used to test for acidic soil and the other will be used to test for alkaline soil.

The chemicals you will need to test soil pH levels are vinegar and baking soda, both of which are standard household cooking products. Vinegar is very acidic, so it will be used to determine if the soil is alkaline. Baking soda is very alkaline, so it will be used to determine if the soil is acidic. Many children have learned that mixing baking soda and vinegar will produce a strong reaction because they are on opposing ends of the pH scale. During my childhood, I used them as fuel for the simple (crude) pill bottle rockets I made.

However, before baking soda can be used to test your soil, it must be dissolved in water. Since water can be slightly acidic (depending on the source you use) you need to be sure that the water will not react with the baking soda you will use, or it will give you a false test result. Simply place a few tablespoons of baking soda in the water and watch for it to produce bubbles. If it does, the baking soda is reacting to acid in the water, which will contaminate your test. Whatever water you do use to test your soil for acidity must not react with baking soda.

When you have established that your water is not acidic, stir it well to dissolve the baking soda and pour the solution into one of your two soil sample cups. Make sure there is enough solution in the cup to make the soil thoroughly wet and stir it well to release any air that may be in the soil. Once it has been mixed, let it sit and watch for active bubbles to percolate through the wet soil and burst on the surface. Active bubbling in the sample indicates that the baking soda is reacting with acid in the soil, thereby indicating that the soil has a low pH level and is acidic. The relative ferocity of the reaction is an indication of how low the soil pH level is. A strong reaction means the soil is very acidic, where a light reaction means it is lightly acidic. This observation indicates relatively how much soil amendment you need to add to reduce the acidity to the levels you desire. If there is no reaction to the baking soda solution, your soil is either neutral or alkaline. You now need to test the second soil sample to determine which it is.

Take the second soil sample and add enough vinegar to it to thoroughly saturate the soil. As you did with the baking soda test, stir the sample well to completely saturate it, then let it sit. If the sample produces bubbles, it is evidence that the acidic vinegar is reacting to alkaline soil. Again, the relative ferocity of the reaction indicates whether the soil is highly or lightly alkaline. If there is little or no reaction to either the vinegar and baking soda, the soil is neutral with a pH of about seven.

Once you understand the relative pH level of your soil, you can amend it, which will help adjust the pH level to satisfy your planting needs. Our own Peeper Pond Farm garden soil tested slightly acidic, so we applied wood and pellet stove ashes to the garden plots where we will plant vegetables that need more neutral soil—such as carrots, beans and peas. This allowed us to make practical use of the ashes our cookstove and pellet stove produced throughout the winter. Otherwise, we would need to purchase some commercial lime to elevate the pH levels in those planting areas. You should be aware that soils tend to be more acidic east of the Rocky Mountains and less acidic to the west, but that is just a general observation.

If your test results show that your soil is too alkaline for your plants, then you will need to lower the relative pH level by applying an acidic amendment, such as coffee grounds (another typical household waste—especially in Seattle) or commercial sphagnum peat moss. Some commercial coffee shops will allow you to collect their used coffee grounds for this purpose. These are the most affordable amendments you can use to adjust the ambient soil pH levels of your planting sites.

These are the most simple and self-reliant techniques you can use to decide the best places to grow your plants or to adjust the conditions of your desired planting location to best suit your plant's needs. Old-time gardeners and farmers know and use these practices, as they are all based in common knowledge and "horse sense." We just wanted to share them with you as our way of preserving and promoting these traditional lifestyle skills.

Post 120: Making Goat Milk Soap

April 14, 2019

Saturday (April 13) brought us a beautiful, sunny spring day that encouraged us to open the windows throughout our house to air it out for the first time this year. Our high temperature topped out around 73 degrees and a light intermittent breeze made the air feel truly refreshing. The beauty of the day was made even more delightful by the return of Marina Barnett—the WHSV-TV reporter who filmed our dairy goat farming news segment in 2018—for her third visit to our farm. She was eager to learn how we make our goat milk soap, which we sell with our garden produce at the Farmers' Market. This time, she was accompanied by her fiancé, Johnny Oliver, who also works at the station as a reporter/videographer. Their wedding is planned for this November. We must admit, they make a very nice couple. We were also joined by Dale and Merrily Carroll, who operate a small goat farm at the entrance to Smoke Hole Canyon, about three miles south of our home. Our first goat kid, Essie, lives with them.

Our first couple of hours together were spent largely on our front porch enjoying lively conversation over a lunch of home-made barbecue sandwiches, coleslaw, chips, deviled eggs, and samples of our canned pickles and home-made goat cheese. Marina brought s'mores bars she had made for dessert. We traded stories and laughed heartily, losing all track of time. Finally, it was time to demonstrate the art of making our goat milk soap to Marina and Johnny. For this, we had to convert our kitchen back into the Peeper Pond Farm laboratory.

Goat milk soap is made using one of two basic techniques—a cold-process or a hot-process. We always use the cold-process. It is called a cold-process because it does not involve "cooking" the soap mixture beyond simply heating the various oils to liquefy them. We find the cold-process to be quicker to complete than the hot-process, although you have to allow the soap bars to cure over a long period of time (roughly three weeks) before they are ready to use. If you make soap using the hot-process, it can be ready to use as soon as it has cooled and hardened.

Soap involves three basic ingredients—a liquid (water or milk), lye, and a blend of oils, including a vegetable, olive, or canola oil, coconut oil, castor oil, palm oil and relatively small doses of scented or essential oils to give it the desired fragrance. Our soap is made with goat milk we had frozen from our prior dairy operation. Many natural soap consumers are very adamant that their soap contain essential oils. However, if you make it yourself, you quickly realize that the essential oils constitute such a small ingredient (by volume) that it makes little practical or noticeable difference in the quality of the soap. Its biggest impact is on the cost of making and buying the soap. Still, many people profess that the scent of essential oils has a much greater therapeutic effect than non-essential oils, so many soap makers defer to consumer choice. We have used both and have yet to be convinced of that belief in any material way. Perhaps it is because we don't patronize oxygen bars.

Lye, which is also a small ingredient by volume, is very potent and dangerous to use. Lye is very alkaline, which means it is caustic and can be harmful to touch or breath. Fortunately, we could use our open windows and the fresh, spring air to ventilate our kitchen while we were using it. We also use special containers that we use *only* for mixing soap to avoid any potential lye contamination or damage to our kitchen cooking utensils. Our first step is to mix the lye with water to dissolve it. It quickly generates heat and must be mixed thoroughly as it is added to water. We then let it sit aside to cool slowly (mixing it again occasionally to keep the lye from precipitating out) while we heat and mix the remaining oil ingredients.

We then mix our basic oils in the proper proportions in a separate pot and heat them on the stove. We divide our frozen goat milk and carefully mix (to avoid a potentially volatile reaction) some of it with the lye solution (to help cool it) and the rest with the heated oil mixture. The lye and oil solutions are mixed together when both have cooled to between 110 and 120 degrees. Since the lye solution can retain heat for long periods of time, we have found we often have to carefully set the lye solution container in an ice water bath, if the frozen goat milk is not enough to adequately reduce its temperature.

The combination is then mixed aggressively and steadily (we use an immersion blender for that purpose) as it begins to thicken into a combined soap mixture. This process is called saponification, which is the reaction between the lye and oil solution that gradually solidifies the mixture into soap. The mixture is blended long enough to reveal a "trace" when the mixer is removed. A "trace" is a raised residue of liquid on the surface of the mixture when the mixer is removed. That indicates that it is time to quickly add the fragrance oil and transfer the mixtures into molds for final curing into bars of soap.

This is the basic process used to make home-made soap. The earliest pioneers would even make their own home-made lye by placing fireplace or wood stove ashes in a large barrel, then adding water and letting it sit for several days. After it had set, they would carefully drain the lye solution out of the barrel for use in their soap. That process must be done with great care to avoid caustic burns that can occur when handling lye.

Unfortunately, our soap mixture hardened too quickly this time, perhaps due to a reaction that can occur with certain fragrance oils, and we were unable to place it in the molds. We will try to reheat and reduce it to a moldable solution at a later time. While soap-making can be a delicate process that can easily fail, we have found it can be occasionally salvaged with a little reheating. We were rushing the process a little and that may have contributed to the problem. However, our issues did not diminish the fun that everyone had. We also received a p easant side benefit. Our kitchen has retained a light honeysuckle fragrance from the scented oil Marina and Johnny chose. This is one of the pleasant benefits you can receive by undertaking the effort to make things for yourself—the traditional way. That is what we hope to teach everyone who visits us at Peeper Pond Farm. We wish Marina and Johnny a wonderful future together as they embark on their new life. We also hope they will want to carry on the traditions we value most and help them survive for another generation.

Post 121: A Glimmer of Hope
April 19, 2019

    Thursday, April 18 began with a cool morning and low, dense overcast skies that were swept away by strong southerly winds to reveal a sunny, balmy day with a high temperature of 80 degrees. It was the first time our daily high temperature had reached that lofty mark since October 8, 2018—more than six months earlier! The recent wave of spring warmth brought a number of our garden potato plants to the surface yesterday to join our early peas and onions. Our vegetable garden is certainly looking good thus far this season.

    April 18 was also the date for our long-anticipated meeting with Jennifer Greenlief, Assistant Commissioner for the Department of Agriculture and Andrew Yost, the Department's designated Dairy Specialist, to discuss their issues and concerns regarding our WV Farm Fresh Raw Milk Act bill. The bill was introduced to the legislature during the 2019 session, but did not advance out of committee. It was the first time since my initial September 18, 2017 meeting with Commissioner Kent Leonhardt (exactly nineteen months ago) that anyone from the Charleston central office had agreed to meet with me to discuss our bill. Throughout that time, I had researched the core issues, coordinated with concerned small dairy farmers across the state, drafted the bill and promoted the issue publicly. Even though I sent multiple drafts of the bill to the Department specifically requesting their constructive comments, all my efforts were met with silence from them—that is, until *after* our draft bill was introduced into the West Virginia legislature.

    Based on this history and my long unfilled requests for guidance and assistance, I did not know what I could expect from them. Many people and even a few elected officials had advised me that the Department of Agriculture was unlikely to be an ally in our efforts. The issue was simply too controversial within the modern dairy industry—dominated by large industrial farm operations and milk processing industries with lobbying money to back their specific interests—to make it comfortable for the Department to take a stand on our behalf. The small family dairy operations were largely dead for a reason, and I was bucking the entire system by trying to open the door to revive them. I always knew the reason for it, but that knowledge did not make it right.

    As Barb and I traveled to the Elkins Department of Natural Resources office for the scheduled meeting, I had to confide to her that I didn't know what to expect from the meeting. It certainly did not feel like the auspicious event I had wanted to believe it could be. Would it be a new opportunity or just another disappointing blow? It really didn't matter, as I was committed to the fight and could not simply leave the ring. My name is David, so I had to accept I would always be fighting Goliath.

Fortunately, the meeting went well. We talked openly for more than two hours. Jennifer and Andy were willing to listen and even acknowledge that our bill was a creative approach to the issue and contained some interesting provisions. They wanted to know what existing laws in other states our bill was based upon so that they could compare it to them and understand the source of its major provisions. I told them our approach to the bill was so different from other states that it would be hard to compare them, however the elements of the bill I designed to ensure that raw dairy farmers would be selling to informed consumers were loosely based on language in Vermont's law.

I noted that most other states (like Vermont) regulate and govern unprocessed milk quality based on periodic (perhaps two or four times per month) pathogen tests for milk samples that must be paid for by the farmer. However, as I explained, periodic pathogen tests do very little to ensure the safety of milk produced twice daily (roughly sixty milkings per month), and the standards different states use to limit pathogen levels are inconsistent, which suggests to me that there are no universally accepted standards. Why should financially-strapped, small dairy farmers bear the added cost of routine milk tests that provide little assurance to the buyer that their milk is safe to consume? In states that have no commercial testing labs (like West Virginia), a farmer might not be able to reliably receive the test results before the useful shelf life of the sampled raw milk he/she has to sell (which is inherently shorter than for pasteurized milk) has already expired. When the WV Health Department (which *is* a public in-state facility) tested Chris Keller's milk, he still hadn't received the results a full two months after he went out of business!

This situation creates an obvious hardship and incentive for a clever farmer to outwit periodic milk sample test requirements by freezing and storing more of their sampled milk than is necessary for a single test. That way, more of it can be submitted for later testing, after they have learned that it already passed laboratory testing. That's exactly what can occur when government regulations become too onerous, senseless and self-defeating to encourage or ensure compliance. It's a prime example of how government regulations become so unreasonable and oppressive that they create a greater incentive for people to circumvent them than to comply with them. If I had the money, I'd bet that's exactly what has been occurring in some states that do require periodic raw milk sample testing. I'd further bet the Department of Agriculture officials in those states, who have witnessed a wide range of clever strategies to circumvent overly restrictive and expensive farm regulations, wouldn't bet against me. All that should be required to understand the utter futility of periodic sample testing to ensure the consumption safety of raw milk is a little bit of critical reasoning.

Our approach was to require that farmers comply with a set of very specific best milking and milk handling standards that were carefully crafted to ensure that the natural quality of the milk is preserved as it was taken from the dairy animal and prepared for sale. If you do everything that a large Grade A dairy is required to do to limit external contamination of the milk, what more can be reasonably expected of a small farmer to do?

Our bill also requires that small milk producers offer tours of the dairy farm to every milk customer and specifically explain how the farmer's operation complies with all required best milking and milk handling requirements. This is just a good business practice to assure the customer that the farmer is doing what is required to maintain the natural quality and integrity of unprocessed milk. The farmer must further provide the customer with a list of guidelines explaining how to maintain the quality of the milk after purchase and minimize incidental contamination after the sale. This, in my view, is the best our law could do to ensure that every customer who purchases unprocessed milk is informed of what he or she is buying and that every producer understands that the penetrating eyes of the public are on them. Other laws I have read do not go to this extent to govern direct farm-to-consumer raw milk sales and ensure the quality of the product. These are the aspects of the West Virginia Farm Fresh Raw Milk Act that make it more innovative than those that have been adopted by the 31 other states that allow them. Our proposed bill has been carefully crafted to represent sensible, practical and affordable regulation from a West Virginia farmer's perspective, rather than a simple carbon copy of what other states do, regardless of the cost to the farmer.

While Jennifer and Andy acknowledged that these aspects of the bill were quite interesting and that the nature of the proposed legislation does not conflict with the Department's stated agricultural and regulatory policies, they advised a need for clearer administrative and registration requirements that are consistent with those required of other food products they oversee. I can't disagree with the logic, legitimacy and appropriateness of their request, but I certainly feel I could have done a much better job of that if the Department had responded to any of my earlier requests for comments on draft versions of the bill. I did, however, note that I would appreciate an opportunity to discuss with them the details of those additional procedural requirements to ensure that they are reasonable and affordable for small farm operators to comply with. There is no greater incentive for noncompliance with government-adopted rules and regulations than to make them difficult to understand, unclear and open to conflicting or shifting interpretations, unreasonably expensive to implement, gratuitously onerous, and/or potentially inconsistent with or contrary to generally accepted dairy farming practices—the potential consequences of which should be abundantly clear from my discussion of periodic sample testing requirements. Having talked extensively with them now, I honestly believe that Jennifer, Andy or the Department do not intend to request changes that would be patently unreasonable, but I always want to avoid as many unintended consequences as I can. Certainly, I have expressed those concerns and issues in many of my prior website posts.

Both Barb and I left the meeting with a strong feeling that we can work with the Department of Agriculture openly and cooperatively to address their stated concerns. Jennifer and Andy were very effective in helping us get beyond the suspicions and mistrust that arose from our initial communication failures and allow us to begin again with an affirmed spirit of trust and cooperation. We couldn't have asked for a better outcome, and I look forward to a forthright effort to improve the language of the bill and position it for reintroduction during the 2020 legislative session.

This coming Sunday will be Easter, and we will be joining our Dorcus Baptist Church family for their traditional sunrise service at the Sites Cemetery overlooking the community and Elkhorn Mountain. It is a time of rebirth and renewal that is very appropriate for the season. Spring always brings new hope and opportunities for the months to follow. After our meeting yesterday with Jennifer and Andy, we can now see a fresh glimmer of hope for the future adoption of our WV Farm Fresh Raw Milk Act bill. There are never any certainties when dealing with politics to change a law, even an oppressive one, but we are moving an important step closer to a better chance of success.

Whether we will eventually succeed or fail will depend as much on the support we receive from you—our loyal readers—as it will on anything I can do. Our sponsoring elected officials need to hear your voices to reinforce their advocacy for our effort. We hope you'll take the time necessary to express your vocal support for the changes we are striving to achieve. Please don't allow our opponents to control the agenda and crucify our cherished dairy farming traditions. If diversity is truly an important element of our lives, then preserving the cultural folkways that built our modern society and represent an important, defining aspect of our shared cultural heritage is every bit as important. We hope you won't sit silently on the sidelines only to lament the loss. We have to earn it if we wish to keep it. Remember, life is eternal, even if we are not. If we lose now, it will affect a lot of future generations.

Post 122: Whippoorwills

May 2, 2019

I opened the screen door at 5:15 AM this morning to let Calli outdoors. I followed her out onto the front porch and watched her trot down the stairs and disappear into the darkness. The sun is rising earlier these days, but some early morning clouds kept the pre-dawn glow at bay. The air was still and mild (our morning low was 53 degrees) and the subtle sounds of the night were still drifting softly across the featureless shadowed landscape. Suddenly, I became aware of the gentle, whistling call of a whippoorwill echoing somewhere in the distance. Its light and haunting call felt as reassuring as it did lonely—a solitary plaintive mating call drifting through the vast, visually-empty void.

No other bird call reminds me so strongly of my rural farm childhood in the Connecticut River Valley of New Hampshire. I remember hearing them frequently during my many night-time moonlit wanderings in the woods that surrounded our farm. Their calls were especially strong in the small hilltop cemetery across the road from our farm. As the designated daily keepers of the entrance gate, it was our duty to stroll up to the cemetery after sunset to make sure everyone had left before locking it for the night. It was there that I would often hear them welcome the descending nightfall. My adoptive grandmother would often say that whippoorwills could guide the spirits of the recently deceased into heaven—a thought that crossed my mind on many of those trips.

Being a resident of the deep woods, I never heard a whippoorwill in the outskirts of the few cities in which I eventually lived during my college years. By the time I returned to the rural areas of the Appalachian Mountains, their song had become rare. Often classified as a "nightjar," the whippoorwill is a seasonal resident of the eastern mountains where it returns each spring to reproduce. Although well camouflaged for the woods, they tend to build their nests on the ground, making them vulnerable to many intentional and unintentional threats—which is why they choose to nest in deep, uninhabited forests. Their night-time calls are an unmistakable hallmark of true rural wilderness areas, and their losses in my northern New England homeland are clear evidence of its transition away from its (and my own) rural heritage. I find it very reaffirming to routinely hear them again in our chosen retirement home here in West Virginia.

There are many sights and sounds that can send our minds on pleasant voyages into the distant past, but few of them to me are stronger than the call of whippoorwills floating in the night air. Their persistent calls probing the darkness for a response are one of the treasures I appreciate most about our life here at Peeper Pond Farm. I can think of no better guide for my own spirit, whether living or deceased. Once again, I realize I am home.

Post 123: Spring Rebirth in Smoke Hole

May 9, 2019

    The past three consecutive days (Monday, May 5 through Wednesday May 7) have given us perfect spring weather, with bright, sunny skies, low humidity and very pleasant temperatures. I usually classify days like them as, "one of the ten best days of the year." By the time the year is over, I've usually placed more than sixty days in that category. Monday was especially fine, and I dedicated four-and-a-half hours of that day to mowing our roughly two acres of yards. Although the beautiful weather made the job as pleasant as it can be, the struggles I have mowing the steepest and soggiest parts of our yards are a strong compensating factor. This was the fourth of an eventual fifteen-to-twenty lawn-mowings I must typically persevere each year. By early June, the grass in our remaining 3.5-acre field will have matured and reseeded the field, and I will mow it using our tractor, Ferguson and his mower deck. Ferguson and I will give that field a final mowing for the season sometime in August or early September to cut back the broom sage (before it is ready to drop its seeds), to keep it from gradually overtaking our field.

    As a special treat to salvage the rest of that initial beautiful day, Barb and I decided to take a mid-afternoon drive into Smoke Hole—our first of what I hope will be many in 2019. The majesty of that deep and winding canyon always makes me wonder why we don't spend even more time there. Once you enter Smoke Hole, nature closes in around you like a warm blanket on a cold day. Whatever problems or cares you may have had, instantly melt away as your attention is captured by the sights, sounds and scents of the wilderness that abound. I can only describe the sensation it gives me as a feeling of being truly immersed and baptized in nature. That's why I consider Smoke Hole canyon to be a "sacred place" for me.

    On this particular trip, the annual renewal of life that makes spring such a pleasant season had taken hold. We were dazzled by the beautiful, brilliant white and lavender colors of phlox lining the road along the banks of the South Branch River. The explosion of floral colors enticed us deeper into the canyon to enjoy the next view around each bend of the road. All the while, the sound of the thundering water rushing over every cataract in the river drowned out the sound of the car engine. We stopped only briefly to walk out on a concrete bridge crossing (which provides access to the former CCC park that was constructed along a shoe-string bottom along the river) and watched two fishermen patiently troll for trout in the placid waters of a large pool.

Eventually, we made our way to our favorite river beach area in Big Bend, the general location of the former Ketterman Post Office. I say eventually, because rushing your way through Smoke Hole would be an unforgivable sin. We parked our car and walked a quarter mile to the beach. The remains of a giant, old Sycamore tree that provided refreshing shade for our special beach site lay shattered along the shore, having been felled by the frequent floodwaters that we experienced last year. However, even it was showing signs of new life as a new sprig bearing fresh, green leaves was growing from the remaining tree stump. The water looked as inviting as it has every time we've visited over the past eight or more years. I was surprised to find the water temperature slightly warmer than I expected, even though it was still too cold for swimming.

Along our walk to and from the beach we encountered more signs of life. We managed to approach a rabbit to within ten feet before it darted into the woods. Also, as we made a pit stop at an outhouse along the path, we found a nest on the sill of a frosted window containing about five recently hatched baby birds. They were sleeping at the time we found them, but you could see them breathing comfortably in the nest. They were too young to identify what species of bird they were, and we were careful not to disturb them. Their mother had apparently left the structure through the roof vent to gather food for her offspring.

For me, our hour-long trip into mystical Smoke Hole Canyon was a perfect reward for the work I expended to mow our lawns on such a beautiful day. It's a reminder that the most rewarding aspects of our life are the little things we find in nature which remind us all that we are not alone, and we are not the most important thing in life. We often need experiences like that to humble us and keep our inflated human egos in check. I sincerely hope you can find and enjoy the humbling pleasure of those experiences in nature as you walk your own path in life.

Post 124: Our Son Becomes a Homeowner

May 14, 2019

This might seem like an odd subject for a farm website post, but if you will allow me to explain, I think I can help you understand the connection.

I have spoken of our son, Michael, in previous posts, primarily in *Bear Rocks* and *The Sinks of Gandy*. We raised him during our life in the modern, outside world, but the core values we tried to instill in him and teach him to live by were very traditional. To be sure, he passed through his rebellious teen years, where he labelled us as old-fashioned and sought to exert his own views on his life. His perspectives on life were not based on the adversities and struggles Barb and I experienced in our own childhoods, so he had little reason to accept our values as lessons for him to follow in his own life. We shielded him from most of the "hard realities" of life as we saw most of our modern society friends and neighbors do for their own children. It was what modern society accepted as proper. We thought we were giving him the life we never had, as if that was what all of us deserve. In the long run, I guess it just became a vain and misguided measure of how much we had "progressed" from our own childhoods. We mistakenly assumed that if we could give our son our idea of an idyllic childhood, it would automatically give him the better life we never had.

However, good intentions do not always beget good results. Mike eventually developed an expectation that life was easy and convenient. In his inexperienced mind, life *could* conform to his views and expectations. He wasn't eager to aggressively take charge of his own life, even as he demanded his freedom. He was making what I considered to be bad decisions—always seeking the easy way out of things rather than working hard to earn what he wanted from life. As long as we were paying the bills, hard work was simply unpleasant and unnecessary. We paid for his college education at Potomac State College in Keyser, so he didn't apply himself in class, resulting in very mediocre grades. Although he completed his two-year program of study, he never cared to complete the required internship, and he never received his diploma. Knowing how important that piece of paper was to his modern-society future, I couldn't justify in my mind the cost and investment of time required to complete the college program only to ignore and brush off the diploma.

When I saw these attitudes start to emerge while he was in junior high school, I tried to apply the brakes. That effort, though well intended, only made him resist and resent my guidance even more. I had become, in his young mind, the boogey man who wanted to control and manipulate his life against his better wishes. His rebellion only grew in response, and I could see the angry, combative relationship I had with my own adoptive father emerging all over again. It felt as though everything I had tried to do to guide him and give him a better life was failing miserably before my eyes. I guess we were both to blame for our deteriorating relationship. I told Barb we'd done a terrible job preparing him for the harsh realities of life, which I was sure would make the adversities he would soon have to face even harder to overcome. I have seen that shock in life turn many people into angry and resentful adults who become embittered by their disappointment that society never gave them the life they came to feel they deserved. Rather than learning to combat adversity, many of them became consumed by it—a frustration from which they never recover. My own younger biological brother is one of the best examples I know of those lost souls, but I have known many, many more. It seems to be even more prevalent among the youth of today. Does this perspective help explain the differences that have emerged between our respective generations?

However, I am pleased to learn that our son had internalized more of our traditional values than I first realized. He moved into his own Keyser apartment in September 2015 and, although he has only worked part-time (between twenty and thirty-five hours per week) for Wal-Mart, he has never missed a rent payment in the 3.5 years he has lived on his own. He also managed to avoid any long-term debt. He has learned how to fix small things (for his apartment and car) on his own. He has held onto a Wal-Mart job for nearly seven years, despite the adverse conditions he has worked under—especially the low wages and unsupportive (even envious at times) management. He is well known in the Keyser area for treating customers fairly and respectfully throughout his tenure. He has made sacrifices to maintain his financial solvency to avoid unnecessary debt. Most recently and to my complete surprise, he showed us he had internalized the traditional American value of wanting to own his own home.

When he first announced that he wanted to investigate buying a home this past November, I was not optimistic. Most young adults his age (27) have reportedly abandoned the dream of owning a home either because their finances are not sound enough to qualify for a mortgage or the cost of housing is so expensive in most urban markets that they can't begin to afford one. Average rental costs have increased greatly in recent years in response the realities of that captive market. Even Mike's rent has increased much faster than his income over the past few years, driving him to find alternative ways to manage his cost of living. For two years, he shared his one-bedroom apartment with a friend until his company became inconvenient. Having exhausted that strategy, he decided he needed to move into his own home, which would allow him to better control his long-term housing costs. Life was gradually and gently teaching him some valuable lessons that we were never able to impress upon him during his childhood. The growing maturity and responsibility I have seen him acquire in recent years has made me very proud of him.

Fortunately, the conservative values of self-reliance and fiscal solvency we did manage to teach him have served him well. When he approached mortgage lenders to prequalify for a loan, his credit report documented his timely payments of bills, credit cards and rent. Although his income was somewhat meager, his debt-to-income ratio was very low. As a result, his overall credit rating was just shy of 800—a truly remarkable score for such a young, part-time Wal-Mart employee! Even with his low-wage job (paying him just over $12/hour) and no college degree, he easily qualified for an $80,000 conventional mortgage—which placed him in reach of a small house in the West Virginia housing market. Our son had proved to himself that our fiscally conservative values eventually pay off. I believe many young people today would be more fiscally solvent if they would simply learn what we taught our son—the fundamental difference between a want and a need. That is a lesson I was taught early by my childhood farm upbringing, and this is the proof I can offer that those values *do* have relevance today. As you might expect, this is the reason why I chose to write a post about it for our farm website.

Mike did not have an easy house search. He chose to find a home in the state's fastest growing and most expensive housing market, the Eastern Panhandle counties of Morgan, Berkeley and Jefferson. Fortunately, a local benevolent benefactor created a grant program for first-time homeowners, known as HAP. It provides a forgivable grant that provides down-payment assistance of up to $14,500 to a qualified first-time homebuyer who agrees to complete a two-night household finance training course. The loan is forgiven at the rate of 20% per year, so that the entire loan is paid off after the owner has lived in the house for five years. Michael easily qualified for the grant and was approved for the full amount to buy the home he selected after viewing fifteen properties over a six-month period. In order to keep his housing costs as affordable as possible, he viewed many foreclosures. Unfortunately, the competitive nature of foreclosure sales left him at a bidding disadvantage with buyers moving to the area from more expensive suburban housing markets.

Mike finally settled on a two-bedroom, one-bath house adjacent to the town of Berkeley Springs (officially named Bath) in Morgan County. This is the town that's known around the world for its famous hot springs and bottled water. The house is modest, but contains a sturdy concrete block shed and some very fine knotty-pine kitchen cabinets. The rooms are more than large enough for his needs, and his estimated monthly mortgage costs are well below his current monthly rent. For the past month-and-a-half, he has worked through the process of inspections and reams of paperwork required to purchase the house. We have now completed that process to the point where we are very certain he can close on the house at the appointed rescheduled time of 2:00 PM on May 30. After five years of mortgage payments (when the HAP grant is fully extinguished), Mike's equity in the house will be at least one-third of its purchase value.

Mike is quite excited about the move and the prospects of living adjacent to the village of Berkeley Springs and its thriving arts community. With two prominent state parks and a large wildlife management area nearby, Berkeley Springs is a popular tourist community—a reputation it has maintained for over 200 years. With all the growth and job opportunities in the area, Mike has already found several new job opportunities that will pay him more and provide him with greater financial security than he had in Keyser. He also hopes he can find a market for some of the home craft projects he has been working to produce in his spare time.

While we will miss the closeness of Mike's Keyser life—his new home is twice as far from our home at Peeper Pond Farm – we are reassured by the knowledge that Mike will have a better life and future than he currently enjoys. Even more reassuring is the fact that our efforts to teach him the benefits of our traditional values have not been lost on him. I firmly believe they are the best defense his upbringing can give him against the harsh realities that even the most supportive government and society can never relieve. Mike's determination to take control of his own life has paid off. Adversity and sacrifice are not bad influences if we use those experiences to learn how to live our lives more successfully. That is the form of optimism I consider to be realistic and practical. I am *very proud* that our son has overcome an adversity that most people his age (and even many of today's wealthy politicians) only complain about, and he did it by living as self-reliantly as he could without a college degree or a full-time job. I wonder how many of the people complaining that our government is not doing enough for them have even tried to do it on their own—as our son did. Those people who feel that we should depend on our government to take care of all our basic needs ought to be more concerned about its long-term fiscal solvency than I am. After all, I learned how to live by my own means when I had to. This is the traditional living lesson that I hope all of you can find in Mike's homebuying experience.

Post 125: Crickets

June 4, 2019

We have been experiencing a truly delightful spring this year. We've had so many days I have classified as one of the ten best of the year that I have lost count. Oh, we've had a few early hot and humid spells to remind us that summer is knocking on the door, but they have been brief in duration and eventually replaced by dry and comfortable weather. Our highest temperature of the year thus far was 87 degrees on May 25 and 28, and we are now well into the first week of June without experiencing any highs of 90 or more.

I mowed our yards yesterday for the eighth time this season, and the air was so cool and crisp that, despite abundant sunshine, the high temperature never rose above 68 degrees. This morning, our low temperature bottomed out at 40 degrees, and I watched a foggy steam gently rise off our Peeper Pond, as I stood on the front porch reveling in the chill. Our last frost of the season this year occurred on May 15 after we had planted most of our garden vegetables. The low temperature on that morning had dipped to 35 degrees. Fortunately, our garden wasn't damaged, and our vegetables are again growing prolifically. Our local TV station, WHSV in Harrisonburg, had warned viewers in the coldest, low-elevation valleys of our area that patchy frosts were possible again this morning. Fortunately, we avoided that fate, which could have damaged a number of our more sensitive vegetable plants.

Despite the comfortable spring weather we are enjoying, nature is reminding us that we are rapidly approaching summer. The fireflies have returned to our farm in abundance, and their soft, yellow glow sparkles like flickering stars spread across our small hayfield. Our whippoorwills have ceased their nightly calls, but as I write this post in the soft morning glow, I can hear our resident mockingbird mimic their call as part of his raucous repertoire. He regales us with his singing talents daily from the top of the power pole along our driveway, occasionally leaping and fluttering his wings as he dances to his own music. His performance is a cheerful sight and sound to behold.

However, the early summer sign I appreciate most is the gleeful chirp of the crickets—a sound they make by rubbing their legs together. I know many people are annoyed by their incessant calls (especially when they invade the house at night), but I love to listen to them from our front porch. They remind me of lazy summer days during my childhood on the farm, when they could be heard chirping in great numbers in our dairy barn and the surrounding fields. Their calls assured me I was not alone when I made my nightly rounds to the cemetery above our farm to check for straggling visitors before locking the gate.

They also served as constant companions on my occasional wanderings through the woods that surrounded our farm.

Although many people are annoyed when a stray cricket gets into the house, such an invasion was considered a sign of good luck in days past. I even recall my adoptive father telling me that you could tell the temperature by listening to the crickets As the old weather legend goes, you can tell the temperature in your local area by counting the number of chirps a cricket makes in fourteen seconds, then adding 40. I don't know who spent the time necessary to figure that out, but I must admit, it does appear to work well.

Of all the bugs I have encountered, I find the cricket to be one of the most attractive. As children, we enjoyed trying to catch them as they leapt randomly to evade us. It always seemed as though they enjoyed playing with us. Since they don't bite or pinch, as many insects do, we always considered them to be excellent playmates. I have even enjoyed watching our cat, Calli, bounce playfully in our yard as she tries to catch an elusive cricket. Such are the simple joys of summer farm life here at Peeper Pond Farm. I hope you can find some spare time in your own life to enjoy and appreciate the crickets.

Post 126: Weeds

June 7, 2019

    I guess the most common definition of a weed is a plant growing where you don't want it to grow. We pull many of them from our vegetable garden with annoying regularity. However, we often forget to overlook the natural beauty of many so-called "weeds," as they brighten our landscape with vibrant colors and fill the fresh country air with their pleasing scents. That is why I consider spring to be the most fragrant season of the year. We also casually ignore their importance to the honeybees that dutifully pollinate the plants in our vegetable garden that we depend upon to survive. Our early ancestors learned the medicinal value of many common weeds from the Native Americans who preceded them. Some weeds can even help keep unwanted bugs away, many of which are also underappreciated and misunderstood. The truth of the matter is that we rely on all these tiny living things to keep our environment in balance and to make our lives more pleasant. After all, it's the flowering roadside weeds the Highway Department routinely mows that make a casual drive on our country roads such a pleasure to enjoy.

    Although we do remove competing plants from our garden, we try to appreciate the weeds that grow on our farm and work to give them a place of their own. We do this despite vociferous objections from one of our newest neighbors who feels our farm property detracts from his because we don't mow our lawns and hayfield to a manicured, regulation golf course height as he routinely does. I guess we just don't feel the need to maintain over four acres of manicured lawns merely for him to admire. We try to maintain a neat homestead farm environment, which is typical of our rural working landscape. We simply appreciate nature for what it is and try to work with it rather than transform it.

    It never ceases to amaze me to learn how former city people—who are attracted to life in the country because of its natural and scenic beauty—vainly seek to mold it into their own city-inspired model of suburban order and tidiness. Where they see only tall grass (weeds), we see a natural carpet in our hayfield, through which waves of soft summer breezes gently sweep during the day and that provides a nightly stage for tens of thousands of fireflies that twinkle softy like earthly stars throughout the night. Besides, they don't seem to realize that our hayfield contains a number of rock outcrops that would suddenly transform their zero-turn-radius riding lawnmower into a worthless pile of scrap metal. Just ask Scott Kimble, a local farmer, who harvested hay from our field for many years, how many times he had to repair his haying equipment from the damage those rocks caused.

As I've said many times before and still adamantly contend, it's the little things in life that we fail to appreciate that often make our lives more rewarding and that make nature function according to its design. Even with all their self-proclaimed education and sophistication, city people often don't seem to understand or value the true nature of rural areas. In my mind, many of them suffer from a multi-generational gap in their knowledge and understanding of the natural world. Having experienced life in both worlds (urban and rural), I feel that urban dwellers seek, by necessity, to adapt the natural world to serve their needs, while rural people work harder to adapt their living to fit the constraints of the natural environment that sustains them. While that is not a firm, mutually exclusive dividing line, it does reflect the different ways of thinking that distinguish between urban and rural values.

For us, weeds are not unsightly, useless, or undesirable intruders on our lives. They are simply part of the inspiring diversity of our natural world that enhances its beauty and teaches us how we should live within it. We enjoy all the delicate flowers and plants that abound on our farm and try to give them the space they need to exist. While we do try to control the invasive, non-native species that our modern, global economy has introduced and the plants that are poisonous to our dairy goats, we *manage* our property to maintain a proper balance between our essential living needs and theirs. I feel that is the best and proper way to live compatibly with nature, which is something more and more people today feel we should do. It is how I was taught to live by my childhood upbringing on a small, family dairy farm, and it remains a fundamental guiding principle of our homestead farming mission here at Peeper Pond Farm.

Post 127: Marketing Our Wares

June 23, 2019

    Our delightful spring began the transition to summer on Friday (June 21) with another refreshing breath of cool air. We have had virtually no hazy days this season, and the view we enjoy of our mountains and ridges has been sharp and clear nearly every morning. Although this bout of beautiful, pleasant weather will break sometime tomorrow afternoon, it has given us three days of relief from the heat. While we have not recorded our first high temperature of 90 degrees or more, we did top out at 89 degrees on Father's Day (June 16). We have now moved well beyond the day when we would typically expect to see our first 90-degree day, sometime around the first day of June. Not that we are complaining about it. After all, this spring was a welcomed change from last year when we struggled with excessive rain and long stretches of sultry, muggy days. This season is starting out with the coolest and driest weather we have seen since the summer of 2014, when we shivered through the fourth of July fireworks display at the Sugar Grove Naval Base. This morning's low was 46 degrees when I stood on our front porch and watched steam rise from our Peeper Pond, as it exhaled the warmth from its water into the calm, chilly air.

    In fact, we have had so much dry weather this June that we watered our garden with the sprinklers on June 17 for the first time in more than a year! This June will be the first month we've recorded less than average precipitation since the beginning of April 2018. Where we struggled against mold and rot in our garden last year, we are actually dealing with some early wilt this season. That is a good problem for us, since it is far easier for us to water our garden than it is to dry it out, even with a big hairdryer and a long extension cord. Even so, our garden is producing abundantly this year. We began setting up our booth at the Grant County Farmer's Market in Petersburg on June 15 this year as opposed to our June 30 first date last year. So far, we have sold nearly three five-gallon buckets full of sugar snap peas, where we had only managed to salvage about three meals' worth of peas (just for the two of us) all last season. We are eagerly anticipating a bumper crop of vegetables this season.

    We set up our booth for the second time yesterday morning and enjoyed some lively sales activity in the sunny, pleasant weather. Many of our regular customers and friends stopped by to visit with us at the market. We even sold nine of the ten bags of peas we harvested before we had finished setting up our canopy, nearly forty minutes before the farmer's market was scheduled to open! Although we didn't sell all the produce we brought with us, we had our third highest gross receipts we have received in a single day, since we began selling at the farmer's market in the 2017 season. With an afternoon high temperature of 77 degrees, it was just a beautiful day to be outdoors.

We hope to have a good farmer's market season this year. At least we are off to a good and early start. We are prepared for the typical hot and humid summer weather we know we will receive this year, but it was a real pleasure to enjoy our mild and fair spring weather. We hope you will join us during our Saturday morning appearances at the Grant County Farmer's Market. We'd love to chat with you and share the bounty from our farm. We wish each of you a very pleasant summer!

Post 128: They're Baaa-ck: Essie Comes Home

July 25, 2019

   Our long-dreaded bout of July summer heat and humidity came to an abrupt halt yesterday as the very pleasant and dry weather that so characterized this spring returned. July has given us our hottest high temperature of the year thus far (96 degrees on July 20), but we are somewhat relieved that we are now past the average hottest day of the year (around July 21). I welcomed the refreshing 52-degree chill of the morning air as Calli led me out onto our front porch to begin the new day. This day, above all others, I have anticipated for nearly two years. It not only swept away three weeks of oppressively torrid air, but it also marks the return of dairy goats to our farm. Our beloved original Oberhasli goat kid Essie—who we raised to be the foundation of our planned dairy goat herd—came home to Peeper Pond Farm today!

   I remember well the day we sent our dairy goats and all our dairy farming aspirations away. It was August 5, 2017. After having lost our other foundation goat kid, Gertie, to meningeal worm and loading our three adults into a trailer to be taken away to their new home in Pennsylvania, we were left with our lone goat kid, Essie. As soon as the adults left the barn, she began to panic, frantically racing from one end of the goat pen to the other, braying at the top of her lungs over her fear of being left alone for the first time in her life. I spent the next hour by her side, consoling her, as we made the final arrangements with our local goat colleagues, Merrily and Dale Carroll, to deliver her to their farm at the entrance of Smoke Hole. Essie leaned and rubbed against me the entire time pleading for my constant attention, until I finally loaded her into our truck. She simply couldn't comprehend what was happening to her. Having been removed from her mother at birth, we were the only parents she had ever known and the only familiar source of companionship she had left. She would spend the next 24 months at the Carroll's farm, as she struggled to establish her position amongst their large herd of Dwarf Nigerians. I returned home that dreaded day to a silent and lonely goat barn, having lost all seven of our animal companions—including our nearly fifteen-year-old cherished housecat, Ninny—within a span of three torturous weeks. I felt Essie's pain and loss as intimately and overwhelmingly as she did.

   The sudden silence of our farm was as disparaging to me as it was stunning, as I struggled to come to terms with the bitter, staggering loss. In fact, as Barb can attest, I would enter that somber barn no more than seven times after losing our goats—only as was necessary to close down our operation and to store and retrieve our tractor, which we sheltered there over the past two long, frigid winters. It was the only thing we had left to fill the empty void. However, throughout the past month, I have spent many rewarding hours working in that deserted barn to prepare it in anticipation of Essie's return.

I made every effort to visit Essie at least once each month of her long exile. I only failed to see her in one month during that two-year period, although I did visit her multiple times in several other months. It always amazed and reassured me to realize that she never forgot who we were and recognized us each time we returned. All I had to do was call for her in my special way, and she would respond as loudly and enthusiastically as she always did when she lived at our farm.

At least Essie managed to adjust to the change and find comfort with her new surroundings. I never did, and I was haunted by hindsight as I struggled with unrelenting regret. I had let her and the retirement dream I determinedly built for years with my own hands simply slip through my fingers. However, the sudden loss of our dairy goat operation motivated me to pursue changes to our state's abject prohibition on sales of unpasteurized milk and milk products. That excessively oppressive law and attitude is the dagger that ultimately determined the fate of our planned dairy goat operation. All the time, I held on to the fleeting hope that I could, someday, bring our Essie home. Today is the day that endlessly elusive hope became reality!

We arrived at the Carroll's farm shortly after 10:00 AM. Dale was just getting ready to feed their goats. Essie noticed that I was carrying a zip-lock bag of sliced McIntosh Apples (her favorite), and she approached us eagerly. Merrily also introduced us to a baby Dwarf Nigerian doe kid that they were also willing to part with so that Essie would have a companion. The kid was born on July 1 and will require bottle feeding for at least four to six more weeks. We have decided to name her Shadow because she follows loyally in Essie's shadow. Dale gave Essie her annual CDT vaccination (for Clostridium C and D and for tetanus), and after waiting to make sure she did not have a reaction to it, we loaded them into our truck and brought them home.

Essie appeared comfortable with her surroundings as we led her back to the goat barn where she was raised nearly two-and-a-half years ago. I find it hard to believe that she could remember it, but she showed no signs of confusion or fear regarding the environment. Shadow clearly acted nervous about her new home, but soon enjoyed a playful romp around the goat pen. We tried to feed her a small bottle of milk, but she wasn't very hungry. She did appear to learn quickly how to drink from the bottle. Still, it's quite a big adjustment for a juvenile goat to make in a single day, so we don't know if she'll make the adjustment well. Essie appears to accept her presence well, but I'm not sure how happy she is to have her follow behind constantly. We will have to work on earning Shadow's trust since she is naturally afraid of us, as all the new goat kids we've raised have been at first. We'll see how it goes. At least they have brought life back to our farm and renewed hope for the future restoration of our dairy operation.

To be sure, we are entering this era of renewal slowly and carefully. We will not resume milking our goats right away. Essie has not been bred, so she won't produce any milk for some time. Our new Dwarf Nigerian is too young to be bred. Besides, I would prefer to buy a second Oberhasli kid in the future to milk alternatively with Essie. I am most satisfied with the quality of the Oberhasli does we milked when we first established our dairy operation. We are taking our time to ramp up our operation so we can make sure we can manage the cost of keeping our goats. Once we prove we can do that affordably for a year or so, we will proceed cautiously and incrementally with our milking operation. At least we won't have to repurchase any of our milking equipment. I couldn't bring myself to sell or dispose of any of it, as it was all I had to validate my desperate hopes that I could restore our dairy operation. In the interim, I will use my time and energy to get our West Virginia Farm Fresh Raw Milk dairy bill adopted. I have all the time my life and health will give me to achieve my long-term dairy farming objectives.

I want to express my deepest and most sincere gratitude to Dale and Merrily Carroll, who kept our Essie and gave her their love over the past two years. I could never express in words just how deeply I appreciate their sacrifices. They freely offered to give us a second chance to pursue our dairy goat aspirations that we would never have without their gracious assistance. I have come to understand how much they came to love and appreciate Essie, so I also know how hard it is for them to part with her now. Because of that, it was a gift I just couldn't bring myself to ask of them but one that I will appreciate forever. I hope they will be able visit her periodically as we did during her absence from our farm. Perhaps, in the future, Essie will give us some offspring we can share with them. It is the least that Essie and I can do in appreciation for the unconditional love they gave to us both. Their generosity has given substance to our hopes and dreams—a rare and precious gift, indeed. At least we can now begin a new chapter at Peeper Pond Farm. Thank you, Dale and Merrily, for the support and sacrifice you have given us to help make that happen. I only wish there was more I could do to show how much it means to us. You have made our future as bright and promising as the refreshing change in weather that we are now experiencing.

Post 129: Catchin' Up

July 29, 2019

    Whew! It has been a hectic month for us, which is why I left such a gap in our regular website posts. Barb and I have been working on so many projects that we've barely been able to keep up with it all. As if the garden and our four Saturday farmer's market appearances in July weren't enough, we've spend time preparing for the return of our beloved goats, helping construct and paint a small cash er addition to the Lion's Club booth at the Tri-County Fairgrounds, preparing our home craft and garden exhibits for the fair (which we delivered to the fairgrounds on Saturday, July 27), mowing our yards, helping our son get settled into his new Berkeley Springs house, helping transport a local friend to cancer treatments at the Western Maryland Regional Medical Center in Cumberland, doing part-time planning work for the City of Cumberland, and treating our hayfield for milkweed—a plant that is hazardous to our goats. Our only major recreational activities over the past month were attending the Fourth of July festivities and fireworks in Petersburg and making a long-awaited July 9 day trip to visit and tour the Cumberland Gap National Historic Park at the common boundaries of Kentucky, Virginia and Tennessee. You will find pictures of our visit to the famous gap in the Cumberland Mountains on the "Dave's Pictures" page of our website.

    Helping our goats adjust to their home here at Peeper Pond Farm has been a big challenge for us. Essie went through a brief one-day melancholy period over the loss of all her companions for the past two years. She ultimately became the queen of the Carroll's Dwarf Nigerian herd, and her family was suddenly reduced to one new-born kid. It was difficult to motivate her to interact with us on Friday (the first day of her return), as she just stood resolutely in a corner of the barn trying to comprehend it all. Eventually, with repeated brushing and attention from us, she emerged from her somber shell and resumed eating, wandering around and seeking our attention. Now, two days later, she seems better adjusted and more engaging.

    Our new Dwarf Nigerian doe kid is another story. She had to make the biggest adjustment of all for a four-week-old baby. She was removed from her mother (from whom she was nursing), forced to accept bottle feeding, moved to an entirely new living environment and stripped of all her companions except for Essie. So far, we have not overcome her fear of us, and we must work hard to catch her for her feedings. We must wait several minutes after catching her for her to settle down and stop trembling in fear before attempting to feed her. We only managed to get her to drink about six ounces of milk on the first day and slightly more than that on Friday. I was concerned that she would not make the adjustment, and we'd have to return her to her mother before she dried off and stopped producing the mother's milk her baby needed to survive. However, we added a small bit of sugar to the milk we were feeding her, and it seemed to make all the difference. She drank a full twelve ounces of milk on Saturday and Sunday and seemed to be catching on to the idea that she could suckle milk from the bottle we were forcing her to drink from. She should be drinking more for her current age, but she is nibbling on hay and grass, so we feel more confident that she will eventually adjust.

    Yesterday afternoon, we encouraged Essie and the new kid out into our goat pen. They wandered around exploring and tasting many of the natural treats they discovered along the way. While our baby doe still isn't comfortable with us, she walked around us confidently and comfortably, which is a big improvement to her recent behavior. She is probably a little young for fresh grass, as her stomach (rumen) hasn't developed enough to properly digest such lush feed, but we let her at least enjoy a taste of it to help reinvigorate her desire to eat. We have seen her nibbling on hay quite a bit, which will help her rumen mature. Fortunately, Essie is developing a motherly attachment to the kid and is encouraging it to share the hay with her.

    I should also note that we recently decided to rename our new Dwarf Nigerian. She had not been given a name when she came to us, and we have discussed many potential options. On her first day at our farm, we initially called her "Shadow" because she clung so close to Essie that it seemed she was always in her shadow. You will see her referred to by that name in our first (July 25) website post announcing her arrival at our farm. However, I found that name difficult to remember. I struggle to remember names and often make one up that is as close to the true name as I can guess just to get it out of my system. In Shadow's case, all I could think of was "Snowball" because she looked to me like a tiny ball of snow.   Barb liked the name and agreed it was more appropriate and easier to remember. Consequently, we decided to change her name to Snowball and will add her to our website under that final name.

    It is a joy for us to spend time with our goats. It has been a long time since we last enjoyed their company, and I am filled with hope for our farming future. Although I was raised on a cow dairy farm, I adapted to dairy goats quickly and find I have a great affinity for them and the rich, sweet milk that they produce. They are very affectionate (after they become accustomed to people) and a pleasure to be around. We know that we can earn Snowball's trust eventually, just as we did with the baby buck (Billy The Kid) we raised and sold two years ago. We are truly privileged to have our Essie and Snowball, and we are again thankful to the Carrolls for sharing them with us.

Post 130: Another Fair Showing

August 4, 2019

    This year marked the 99th consecutive Tri-County Fair in Petersburg. Although it remains small, it is well attended and appreciated by local residents in Grant, Hardy and Pendleton Counties. Once again, we participated extensively in the fair, serving as the Pendleton County judge for the parade, working several meal shifts at the Lions Club food booth and exhibiting many of our farm products. We submitted a total of thirteen products for judging this year, as opposed to our eleven entries last year, and we actually received more ribbons. Where we had earned a total of eight ribbons in 2018, we garnered a total of eleven this year. Barb's Carpenter's Wheel lap quilt—made with goat-print fabric—not only received a second-place ribbon, it also won the People's Choice award—perhaps a strong reflection of the growing local interest in raising goats. Our exhibits earned a total of five blue (first place) ribbons, including Barb's quilted WVU table runner and our canned sweet and sour red cabbage, bell peppers, wax beans and carrots. All in all, it was another banner year for Peeper Pond Farm at the Tri-County Fair.

    I have wanted to bring our dairy goats to the fair for people to see, but we weren't able to do so in either 2017 or 2019, the two years that we have owned them during the fair season. We were busy trying to save Gertie from the Meningeal Worm infection that eventually killed her in 2017, and I am still working with our new kid goat, Snowball, to help her make the adjustment to our farm this year. We still struggle to earn her trust and to get her adjusted to a regular bottle-feeding schedule. She is still not eating as well as we would like to see her, but we are encouraged by the fact she gained one pound and twelve ounces of body weight during her first week in our care. She is still very small for her age, weighing in at only six pounds and fourteen ounces at one month old, but we are optimistic about her chances to do better in the coming months. Once we can get her weaned from kid formula, we can work on earning her trust. When we received her on July 25, she had never been in the immediate presence of humans, so she acts more like a wild goat than a domestic animal. This has been a source of our problems working with her in an unfamiliar environment separated from her mother.

    Overall, all of our friends appeared to enjoy the fair this year. I was impressed by the growing number of goat farms that have been represented at the goat judging competitions in recent years. Many local farmers are discovering that prices for market (meat) goats is growing and becoming strong in our area. Even one of our neighbors has expressed interest in buying some market goats to raise next year. Goat meat is a healthy choice for many people because it tends to be very lean. We were given some goat hamburger from a friend three years ago and discovered that we had to mix an egg in it when grilling goat burgers because the meat is so lean that they crumble easily without a binder to hold them together. When seasoned, goat burgers actually taste no different from regular cow meat hamburgers, even though they have lower overall fat levels.

While we enjoyed our participation in the 2019 Tri-County Fair, we are relieved that it is over. It is a challenge to manage our small farm when dedicating so many hours to the fair. Fortunately, we served many of our local friends and farmer's market patrons as they visited the Lions Club booth. It is good to see the friendly faces that make our community so enchanting to us. Perhaps, during the 100th anniversary fair next year, we can exhibit our Essie and Snowball to help introduce local farmers to dairy goats. However, for the time being, we are looking forward more immediately to the State Fair (which we plan to attend on August 14) and the Treasure Mountain Festival coming up on the third weekend in September. It's the festival time of the year, and we like to attend as many as we can. Hopefully, we'll see you at one of them or at our remaining farmer's market appearances. We hope you will enjoy the remaining summer weather. Please make the most of it outdoors in the fresh air.

Post 131: Our Mischievous Goats

August 7, 2019

    Although we do not yet have what I would consider to be extensive experience with goats, we have learned a lot about their behavior. Our dairy goats are generally easy to work with and very docile. However, they do have a very pronounced mischievous streak that they love to exercise and display occasionally. During our first goat-keeping experience two years ago, we were introduced to this behavior trait by Cara (one of our original milkers) and Dancing Lady (who was dry and not producing milk at that time). Cara was the escape artist. She had learned how to open a door with a round knob. She would clench her mouth around the door knob and twist her head to turn it. She had managed to escape from the goat barn using that talent and let all of our goats out into the yard. A strong gust of wind followed behind her and slammed the door shut, trapping them outside the barn and leaving us without a clue of how they had managed to escape. We only learned how she did it later, when her previous owner told me she had done it repeatedly on his farm. That forced me to purchase a child safety cap to place over the door knob. It wasn't always easy to use, but it kept Cara in the barn.

    Cara also had a rather frustrating habit of digging holes in the dirt floor of the goat barn. She was the only goat that did this, and we never really understood why. We were told by her previous owner that it was "just her way." I assumed it was a way of claiming a desired sleeping place or she liked to cool feeling of the dirt better than the soft straw we spread over the floor. Whatever the reason, she eventually dug so many holes in the dirt that our floor began to look more like the lunar surface than the nice, level barn floor I had carefully groomed. It certainly didn't make it easy to carry five-gallon buckets of water in the barn or to muck out the straw periodically. Fortunately, none of the other goats we kept picked up that trait.

    Dancing Lady was the "smooth operator." She spent most of her time nearest to the barn door that Cara first opened. I was milking two goats at the time (Cara and Emerald), and Lady knew my routine very well. Since my milking stand was stationed in our garage, I would always have to attach a leash to each goat and lead it from the goat barn to the garage—a distance of about twenty-five feet. I always milked Cara first, then returned her to the goat barn to place the leash on Emerald and lead her to the garage. Over time, Dancing Lady learned just where she could stand to squeeze through the barn door when I was returning with Cara or leading Emerald to the garage. Once through the door, she would make a mad dash to the garage so she could get to the milking stand first. She knew that the stand contained a feed bowl that I would fill with sweet goat feed for the goats to eat while I was milking them. By getting there ahead of me, she would gobble up as much of the grain as she could before I could catch up with her.

Now that Essie has returned to our farm as an adult and we have a new Dwarf Nigerian kid, Snowball, I am getting introduced to their own quirky behavior. Yesterday, I was working in the barn to attach a fine wire mesh screen to the fence panel of the kid pen to keep Snowball from getting into the hay I stored there. She is so small that she can squeeze through the six-by-six-inch gaps in the fence panel. Now that I have scaled back the number of goats we keep, I decided to use the small kid pen in the barn to store the hay bales we will feed them through the winter. I discovered recently that snowball was getting into the pen and pooping on the fresh hay. While I was working carefully to attach the wire mesh screen to the fence panel using zip ties, I was not keeping a close eye on Essie and Snowball. When I was struggling to fasten a zip tie in a tight corner of the fence, Essie managed to work the kid pen gate open with her nose and carefully crept into the pen behind me. When I finally looked up, she had climbed to the top of the stack of bales and was eating greedily from them.

I led her down from the haystack and out of the kid pen when I realized I didn't see Snowball in the barn. I turned to see if she had walked out into the goat yard, but she was nowhere in sight. For a moment, I was afraid she had escaped. However, as I re-entered the goat barn to search for her, I discovered that she had climbed into one of the hay racks mounted along the barn wall and was laying on the soft bed of feed hay I had put out for them that morning.

I can recall a few antics our dairy cows pulled when I was a growing up on our family dairy farm, but none of them was as eccentric as the capers I have witnessed during my first six months of goat-keeping. Goats are very clever and creative in exercising their personal quirks. They will test your skill and challenge your sense of humor. I guess I don't mind it too much. It's all part of life on a farm.

Post 132: Haying Season

September 4, 2019

I'm sorry for the long delay in my postings on our farm website, but we were experiencing technical difficulties in retrieving photos from our cell phone. It took us many trials and errors to convince our phone that it could do the job. None of the solutions we had learned from past experiences seemed to work. Our advanced technology simply refused to cooperate until we finally stumbled upon the source of the problem. We can only hope it will choose to be more cooperative in the future. I know, good luck with that!

The summer months are typically known to farmers as "haying season." It is the traditional time when fields of grass and alfalfa are processed into hay bales to feed livestock throughout the fall, winter and spring months. I remember well the hard, determined work required during my childhood years on our dairy farm to harvest the hay crop we needed to feed our herd of thirty cows. We mowed, raked and baled alfalfa hay at least twice (and even three times in some generous years) in four or five large (ten-fifteen acre) fields on our farm. To produce high quality, dry hay bales, a farmer needs at least three to five continuous days of dry, sunny weather. That means that all the work to cut, bale and load the hay must be done in the hot summer sun. By the time we had managed to load 100 or so bales of hay from one of our flat-bed trailers, we were drowning in sweat. However, the work wasn't done.

After the hay was loaded on the trailer, we delivered it to our barn where every bale was unloaded, placed on an electric elevator and restacked in the loft of our barn, which was even hotter to work in than was the open field where we first loaded it. Temperatures in the enclosed hay mow could easily top 105 degrees on a hot day, and there was little or no breeze to provide any relief from the intense heat. To further compound our misery, we had to choke on the dust and chaff that filled the stagnant air, as we tossed the bales around the hayloft and stacked them. By the time we emerged from the barn after stacking a load of hay, our bodies and clothes were coated with golden-brown hay dust and chaff that stuck to our sweat. Our only relief came from a large pitcher of ice-cold Kool-Aid (which any of us could empty in a few big gulps) or a quick swim in our pond.

Now that we have reacquired dairy goats at our farm, we rejoined that annual, desperate pursuit of hay to feed them. The excessive rains and periodic floods that occurred throughout 2018 resulted in a poor hay crop for most local farmers, so the competition for good feed hay this year is very tight. We knew we'd face either high prices or a very limited supply, so we talked to as many of our farm colleagues as we could to decide where to find the supply we need.

Our farm has a 3.5-acre hayfield, which could provide an adequate amount of hay for our needs, but we lack the equipment needed to harvest and bale it. Also, the grass in our field is better suited to livestock raised for meat than it is for the higher protein nutritional requirements of dairy goats. One of our neighbors has expressed an interest in harvesting the hay from our field to feed his intended market goats so it will not go to waste. We, on the other hand, have to obtain our hay from other sources.

Fortunately, one of our good friends has a small hayfield and the equipment necessary to produce small, rectangular hay bales from it. Because we don't have the ability to move and store the big, round bales that most farmers produce today, we need a supply of small, rectangular bales that we can handle by ourselves. Since our friend needed some help from us to pick up the hay he produces, we joined him on August 12 to help with the haying work. Wayne had already mowed the grass several days earlier and raked it into windrows (using a traditional, wheel-operated, side delivery rake) so that the gentle summer breeze could dry it thoroughly. He then attached his hay baler to the tractor and baled the windrows into rectangular bales, as Bonnie (his wife), Barb and I followed behind with trailers to load up the bales.

By the time we finished loading the hay bales, we had a total of 34 bales on our trailer and another 40 or so on Wayne's trailer. The bales on Wayne's trailer were delivered to his daughter's farm about three miles down the road, and we stacked the bales on our trailer to be loaded into our garage and goat barn. In total, we have now stored roughly 60 bales of hay that we hope will be adequate to feed our two small goats throughout the winter months. If not, we will need to buy more hay from another farmer or one of our local feed stores. For the time being, our goats are happy and so are we. Now that we are in September, the summer haying season is rapidly coming to a close. Our next big task will be to clean up our vegetable garden for the winter.

Post 133: Adversity

September 6, 2019

    Earlier this week, I was reminiscing with a good friend about all the things we routinely did for ourselves when we were growing up that very few people seem to do anymore. When we were young, it wasn't uncommon for people (even those living in small cities and towns) to plant a garden and grow their own fresh vegetables, cut and split firewood to heat their homes during the winter, change the oil in their own vehicles, and *push* a lawn mower to mow the lawn. Growing up on a farm, as both of us did, we did a lot of additional farm chores that non-farm kids never had to do.

    When I turned six years old, I began to assume simple farm and household chores, including feeding hay and grain to the cows that were to be milked, helping my father carry partially filled five-gallon stainless steel milk pails into the milk room to be emptied into our bulk tank, bringing wheelbarrow loads of sawdust into the barn and spreading them behind the stanchions to serve as bedding for the cows, and mixing and feeding our calves milk formula using a small nipple pail. I also stacked and retrieved firewood to feed the endless appetite of our kitchen wood cookstove, cleaned out the barn gutters, helped weed our nearly 12,000 square foot vegetable garden, and "various other chores as assigned." The list of farm and household chores I was responsible for doing increased over the years, as I became capable of more strenuous work. Fortunately for my overall workload, some of my earliest light chores were handed down like outgrown clothes to a younger sister, who was the only other child willing to do farm work. By the time I was starting high school, I was paid the enormous sum of $2.50 *per week* for all of my farm and household work responsibilities. It wasn't always fun to be the only boy in a family of five children.

    However, despite all the physical labor we had to do that modern conveniences and technological advances have since made easier or altogether unnecessary, we still found time to play, swim in our pond and enjoy the descending nightfall on a gentle summer day from a lawn chair in the back yard. By the time I was finishing my thirty-year professional planning career, I felt that my life seemed far less frantic and stressful when I had to do all my childhood farm chores. I also realized very early in my career that I had shoveled more manure working for local government officials in the public sector than I ever did working on a dairy farm, but that's fodder for a different story. My friend feels the same way I do about it all.

I left my childhood farm behind because my adoptive parents refused to pass the farm down to us. After all, they saw no future in dairy farming that could sustain us, and they needed to sell the land to pay for their retirement and my father's medical expenses. As I was told, all I needed to do was go on to college and get a cushy office job in the outside world that would give us a better standard of living and far less physical labor. It seemed simple in concept, but adjusting to the very different lifestyle of modern conveniences just never felt as easy as it sounded. After learning to live as self-reliantly as possible in order to avoid debt and make my life affordable, I found it very hard to spend my earnings to purchase all the trappings and technology that make modern society so convenient. For many years, I felt like I was doing something wrong because so many of our neighbors (who I knew earned no more income than my wife and I did) seemed to own many things we felt we could not afford, like bigger, fancier cars, back-yard swimming pools and all the other conspicuous trappings of wealth. I just thought they must have come from wealthier families than I did. Although I later learned that most of them were living "borrowed lives" by incurring debt that we refused to assume, I struggled to know how to reconcile my traditional core values with the reality of how the modern world that surrounded us worked. Traditional values of self-reliance just don't work well in modern society.

This observation reminded me of the third post I placed on our farm website nearly three years ago, entitled, "Why Would I Want to Do All of That Farm Work." In it, I recounted a discussion I had nearly five months before my retirement with a former professional colleague who never lived on a farm. He couldn't comprehend why I would want to do all that hard farm work in my retirement when I could become a private consultant and make more money without all that strenuous physical labor. While I agree that my professional work—which I often called "butt work" because that was the primary muscle I exercised by doing it—was far less laborious, I always found it to be much more stressful than farm work. While farm work may be exhausting, it never deprived me of a good night's sleep as did the stress of working in the politically-charged public sector.

Our technology- and money-driven modern society clearly bestows many lifestyle conveniences on us. As I've noted in this post, it has reduced the amount of physical labor we have to do in the conduct of our lives and, as a consequence, created new job opportunities for people to satisfy those needs. However, we also bear a cost for those conveniences. Fewer people today will become debt-free because they can't afford the rising labor and material costs of those conveniences. People are also becoming less healthy because their modern lifestyles leave them with less physical labor to do for themselves. Even the simple act of getting off a couch to change the channel on the TV has become an unnecessary expense of labor. All our modern conveniences have also made modern living more consumptive and wasteful, which only increases our impact on the natural environment, regardless of how "sustainable" we feel our self-proclaimed advances have made it. When you consider all of these unintended and unconsidered consequences (and others I have not specifically mentioned), it seems clear to me that our lives would be far less stressful, less impactful on the environment and less costly, if we exercised the traditional values of hard work and self-reliance rather than casually yielding to all the alluring conveniences of our modern society.

People always say that you can't go back to the way things were. That may be especially true of a society that increasingly views manual labor and hard work as unnecessary and inefficient. Why do all that hard work when our technology and modern conveniences make it unnecessary? Hard work and physical labor are just adversities that we have outgrown. We've found a better way that alleviates people from those responsibilities. After all, eliminating all of life's adversities is a good thing, right?

Well, if you choose to think that way, I have some unpleasant news for you. Adversity is *not* a good or bad thing. It is an unavoidable aspect of life in the real world that must be understood and overcome, not ignored. Even the most determined optimist cannot simply will it away. You may like to think that our modern conveniences are eliminating adversities, but they are only creating others our descendants will have to face down the road, from higher and more unaffordable health care costs, environmental stress and degradation, and the looming (growing) fiscal insolvency of our government and economy.

Life is naturally adverse for a reason. Farmers understand this better than most other people today. It is nature's way of winnowing out the weak from the strong. It drives the check and balance system necessary to sustain life in the closed environment of our planet. While we may avoid an adversity today, we may only end up creating a bigger and, perhaps, more complex one tomorrow. We all need to face our adversities today and conquer them to survive.

This is the lesson I have learned from my traditional, self-reliant upbringing that I feel many people today who suffer from low self-esteem would benefit from. Your self-esteem is not enhanced when life is handed to you on a silver platter. Those who have to work for it and overcome the adversities they fear in life will always be more self-confident. It is not whether or not you can overcome an adversity in life that truly defines your character; it is *how* you face it that does. That's the enduring value I believe you can gain by internalizing and practicing our traditional lifestyle values that we promote here at Peeper Pond Farm. If the potential consequences of our modern, convenience-driven lifestyle come to pass, you may eventually learn that you need to rely up them to survive an even greater future adversity. Welcome to Adversity University, the *original* school of hard knocks.

Post 134: Can-Do

September 13, 2019

    An important aspect of our can-do self-reliant lifestyle is preserving food from our garden for the winter months. Doing so extends the summer cost of living benefit we receive by eating the vegetables we grow in our garden rather than buying them from the store. Preserving food can be done in many ways. Virtually all early pioneers constructed "cold cellars" in which they stored foods that were not typically canned, such as fresh or dried fruits and potatoes. When I was a child, we stored our garden potatoes for the winter in a long wooden bin in the dirt cellar beneath our house. Some pioneers who didn't have a cold cellar would dig trenches and line them with straw, hay, or sawdust within which they could bury cabbages, fruits, or potatoes during the winter. However, doing so meant having to carefully dig through the snow, dirt, and/or frost in the cold winter months to retrieve them. Meat can be conveniently smoked or packed in salt to preserve it over the winter. One way or another, self-reliant families found creative ways to preserve their summer farm bounty to feed themselves over the long, cold, lifeless winter months.

    We don't produce meat at our farm, but we do occasionally repackage and freeze meat we buy in bulk from various local sources. What excess vegetables we obtain from our garden that we do not consume fresh or sell at the farmer's market we either can or freeze for the winter. Canning is a time-honored traditional folkway that we and many of our neighbors still practice. Some of the older families in our area (multi-generational natives) can huge volumes of vegetables even though there may only be two people living in the household. Most of their canning recipes were designed to serve big farm families with many children that have gradually shrunk in size over the generations because children in the modern society have become more of an additional expense to raise than an essential and necessary source of household labor. It is common for us to hear our older farmer's market customers talk about buying our vegetables to can thirty-or-more quart jars that would feed a small army of people because their canning recipes were originally designed to feed a household of six-or-more people rather than the two that are left behind today. We typically can and package most of our winter food in half-pint jars or single-meal freezer bags so that we only have to open (unseal) what we actually need for each two-person meal.

    I recall many late summer/early fall days during my childhood when my adoptive mother and grandmother would transform our large farmhouse kitchen into a food processing plant. In that era, our canning was done in canning jars that had glass lids with a rubber gasket to seal them. Those jars were typically sealed in a large pressure cooker to vacuum seal the lids. However, it ended up being a hit or miss preservation process, if the gasket didn't seal well or was reused from a prior season (as we often did to save money). I can remember being sent by my mother into the cellar to retrieve jars of canned vegetables stored on shelves lining the walls. In the latter part of the winter season, some of them became so discolored by a purple-shaded brine that I couldn't tell what they contained. This occurred because the seals on those jars had been compromised, resulting in contamination of the contents. That may explain why my adoptive mother overcooked so many of the vegetables we ate (as an effort to kill off any pathogens that might be growing in the canning jar). When you canned vegetables in glass jars with glass lids, you had no easy way to know how well they were sealed until you could see that their contents had spoiled. The more modern canning jars with metal lids and threaded outer rings have a button on the top that depresses when the jar is sealed, so you can always know which jars sealed properly and which didn't. When we can our food today, we immediately know which jars didn't seal properly before we store them. We simply put the occasional improperly sealed jars in our refrigerator so we can eat them first before they spoil.

Our canning process begins with a canning recipe. There are many such recipes, and it is a hit-or-miss proposition to find the one you like best. Some of our vegetables, like green beans, are simply cut up and packed in a jar with boiling water prior to sealing. No specific recipe is needed for that. However, other food products you may wish to can, such as pickles, jellies, catsup, sauerkraut, or relish, require advance food preparation and processing time before the canning work can be done. For this reason, you have to find a recipe that you like best to prepare your food for canning.

It is also important to understand that there are at least two main canning methods you can use, depending on the food you intend to preserve. Non-acidic foods, such as beans, carrots, beets, turnips and even meats are canned using a pressure cooker, which consists of a stainless-steel pot with a self-sealing lid and a built-in pressure valve and gauge that is used to regulate the amount of pressure that builds up within the pot. Water is placed within the pot to a specified level and the water is brought to boiling before the canning jars are placed inside and the cooker lid is attached to begin the pressure sealing process. Careful attention must be placed on the time that has elapsed and on the pressure gauge to hold it at a specified level, once it has been attained. When the proper sealing time has passed, the lid must be removed and the sealed jars extracted and set out to cool. As the jars cool, a popping sound can be heard as the button on the metal lid depresses, indicating that the jar is properly sealed. I always test the buttons on all the jars to make sure they have been sealed before tightening the canning rings. If any of the buttons are not depressed—as some lids may not seal properly—those jars must be resealed (with a new lid) or placed in the refrigerator for more immediate use. Never think that you can wash and reuse a metal canning lid, as the seals are not designed to last beyond the first canning use.

Acidic fruits and vegetables, like tomatoes, pickle relish, sauerkraut, peaches, apples and blackberries should be canned using a boiling water bath in an unpressurized pot, such as the large ceramic-lined pots that we use. These pots have a metal lid that rests loosely on the top of the pot and a metal rack that sits in the bottom of the pot to keep the jars from resting directly on the bottom of the pan. The pots are filled with water to a level that is roughly one inch above the top of the canning jars that will be placed in it and brought to boiling. Once the water is boiling, the jars can be placed into the pot (with the lid set on the top of the pot) and left to boil for a specified period of time. The time required to seal the jars using this method is usually longer than is required for a pressure cooker because no pressure is built up in the pot to force the jars to seal, but you don't have to focus on maintaining a constant pressure level. When the recommended boiling time has passed the jars can be removed to cool and seal in the same manner as for the pressure-cooking method.

We also preserve some of our garden vegetables, such as broccoli and potatoes, by direct freezing. We slice our potatoes into french fries and deep fry them lightly to put a light glaze on them, but not to a deep golden brown. This helps reduce moisture in the potatoes so that they will not become too mushy when they are defrosted. We then seal them in plastic bags with a portable vacuum sealer and load them in our chest freezer for long-term storage. Other vegetables like broccoli are blanched or par-boiled before they are sealed.

Corn is a different item to preserve, as it can be done in many ways. We have frozen some of our corn in kernel form and as creamed corn. We also have dried some of our corn and ground the kernels into corn meal that can be used as an ingredient to make cornbread or other foods. Many pioneers stored corn on the cob by hanging them from the husks in a shed. Beans and certain fruits also can be effectively stored by hanging them to dry. In pioneer days, beans that were strung and dried were often known as "leather breeches."

Preserving food for the winter, whatever method or recipe you use, is a fine way of extending the value you obtain by growing your own fresh vegetables and fruits in a garden. You'd be amazed at how much money can be saved by preserving your own home-grown food. During the early days of my childhood, we visited a grocery store less than twice per month on average, and most of those trips were to buy staples, such as flour, sugar, salt and yeast, that we typically used to make other foods but could not conveniently produce at home. Food preservation is one of the most essential and important skills to acquire for self-reliant living, and it is the most critical to know if our modern society should collapse. Being wholly dependent on grocery stores or restaurants for all your food needs is the best and quickest way to starve to death when they are no longer available. That's why we practice and promote our most essential and cherished traditional lifestyle skills here at Peeper Pond Farm.

Post 135: Fall In

September 25, 2019

 All I can say is, what a wonderfully delightful summer we've enjoyed in the Potomac Highlands of West Virginia! As autumn enters the stage, I can look back at the past spring and summer and appreciate all the pleasant weather we enjoyed this year. While our highest temperature reading for the year topped out at 96 degrees, and we had at least two-and-a-half cumulative weeks of typical hot and humid weather spread out through July and August, the vast majority of the other days were sunny and dry with crystal clear skies. We had very little of the milky haze that accompanies the most torrid summer weather and washes out our view of the mountains. Although we are experiencing very dry conditions in late August and September with little rainfall, the respite from all the excessive rain over the prior year-and-a-half can be appreciated. Hopefully, the dry conditions will end before the leaves on the trees dry up so that we will enjoy a brilliant fall foliage season. The initial glimpses of fall color we see at the highest elevations of our region certainly give us hope.

 I awoke this morning to a brilliant and colorful sunrise with gentle shades of red, yellow and aquamarine framed by bold strokes of con trails from early morning flights leaving Dulles Airport. Later in the morning, I drove across mighty Shenandoah Mountain to Harrisonburg, VA (our local "big city") to do some essential monthly shopping. Some items we need are hard to find in our rural region and others are more affordable where there is greater retail competition. As I ascended the Pendleton County flanks of the mountain, I was treated to a broad brushstroke of brilliant yellow foliage on the trees above a tall rock cliff from which the highway was once blasted out. The brilliance of the leaves was a welcome preview of the fall splendor we anticipate each autumn. Soon our mountain ridges will be dappled with a montage of bright red, yellow, orange, crimson and bronze colors that only nature's artist palette could create. The intense beauty of the fall season is nature's encore performance for the bountiful spring and summer season we have enjoyed. I certainly hope it will be joyful to behold.

 Summer gave us a very good return from our Grant County Farmer's Market appearances in Petersburg. We were able to make a record number of appearances this year and our net proceeds were strong. We also appreciate the return of dairy goats to our farm after a two-year absence. We were proud to see our son purchase his first home in Berkeley Springs, and we are making good progress on our proposed raw milk sales bill. However, we have experienced a significant setback on Friday, September 20, when Barb was admitted to Winchester Medical Center for emergency hernia surgery. She experienced a setback to her recovery two days later, when she received follow-up surgery to remove a subsequent hematoma. She is now in recovery, and we hope that she will be released at the end of the week.

Our next concern will be the financial impact from the surgery. Medical and health care costs are a heavy burden for rural farmers to bear. Internet statistics reveal that at least 200,000 Americans are forced into bankruptcy each year due to mounting medical expenses from which they can never recover. When I see data like that, I am forced to agree that our health care industry is one of the leading contributors to the persistent and growing epidemic of poverty in our country, as its costs have inflated faster than the public's ability to pay. It is certainly one of the most pervasive impediments to economic self-reliance for most rural citizens. Like many of those unfortunate people, we here at Peeper Pond Farm live on the margins of fiscal solvency, which leaves us with few resources to afford the enormous medical expenses we will likely incur.

This is where I feel the Hippocratic Oath that governs professional doctors becomes a "Hypocritical Oath." It is relatively easy to make decisions about how to save a person's life when your interpretation of Hippocrates' "Do No Harm" rule is limited to the immediate task of curing a patient's illness. However, if the doctor's work is successful, the patient must still be able to survive *after* the surgery, which is as much an economic necessity as it is a medical one. Would it be so easy for a doctor to decide how to "Do No Harm" if he/she had to consider the ongoing financial implications for the patient after surgery? The "compassion" that doctors and nurses claim to have for their patients is not restricted to what occurs within the hospital. However, it is much easier for them to just place blinders on "Do No Harm" and look the other way when the patient leaves. Unfortunately, the exceedingly boated charges for their services have become an unavoidable burden on all lower income people, like us, who live on the political and economic margins of society. It is a concern that our political leaders have failed to resolve and health care professionals casually and, as I have already encountered, callously dismiss when you appear before them for medical treatment.

Welcome again to Adversity University—which I ironically discussed in my prior September 6, 2019 website post. We now face a graduate degree in adversity that we may not ultimately be able to afford. Be careful, lest you become the next financial victim of our unaffordable, overpriced, dysfunctional and increasingly bureaucratic health care industry. There may be more room for you in our growing select club of impoverished Americans than you may think.

Post 136: How to Identify A Native West Virginian

October 6, 2019

    As you probably know (from many of my prior website postings), I was born and raised in New Hampshire. Although I'm not a native West Virginian, a true native West Virginian once confused me for being one because we shared so many similar rural farm experiences during our respective childhoods. I recounted that experience in my May 22, 2018 post entitled, *"Man, I Lived It, Too."* When you are raised on a small family farm in the Appalachian Mountains and taught to live self-reliantly, you learn the traditional values, experiences, folkways and mannerisms that are unique to—but shared by—all eastern rural mountaineers. This basic understanding and cultural familiarity allows me to understand native West Virginians and "fit in" better than most outsiders from other states. After all, our states have similar core values. The official motto of West Virginia is "Mountaineers are always free," while New Hampshire's is "Live free or die."

    Even so, I find many ways that native rural West Virginians are different from the rural people I knew in New Hampshire. One of the most basic ways is the special way that native West Virginians give directions. To most outsiders (or "come-here's," as they are commonly known), the cardinal directions of north, south, east and west are typically used as basic guides for travelling directions. All primary Federal and State highway routes bear those orienting words to help direct travelers because the routes are built to follow those bearings. However, West Virginia is so intensely mountainous that, even though the main highways are labeled by their "general" orientation, you may end up driving south, east and west on a northbound route as you wind through the mountains to get to its ultimate destination. Anyone with a compass in their car would get dizzy just trying to keep up with it. Also, it is often easier to wind around the mountains in order to reach your destination than it may be to take the shortest route over the steep terrain. In West Virginia, the shortest distance between any two points isn't the most convenient way to travel between them. This is why many natives will confidently tell you that West Virginia would be bigger than Texas, if you flattened it out.

    Fortunately, native West Virginians are far smarter than they are credited with being. They still use the same directions their ancestral pioneers used to understand how to travel across the rugged terrain. In those early days, there were no roads to follow—only Indian hunting trails and rivers. Therefore, if you ask a native West Virginian the best way to drive north from Franklin to Petersburg, he will likely tell you to go "down" U.S. Route 220. Since this road roughly follows the flow of the South Branch River, you drive downstream along the valley when you travel north from Franklin to Petersburg. The "downstream" nature of your journey was more important to know than the fact you will be heading north because you know it requires less effort to travel downhill. Likewise, to go from Petersburg to Franklin, a native will tell you to go "up" U.S. Route 220, because you must travel upstream through the valley. However, if you want to go west from Franklin to Elkins, the same native will tell you to go "over" to Elkins along U.S. Route 33. Although that highway is an east/west route, it winds up and "over" many steep mountains that require you to travel northeast and southwest at many points to circumnavigate the steep terrain. Also, if you ask how far it is to get to Elkins from Franklin, he will probably tell you how many hours it takes (roughly two hours by that highway), because you have to drive so slowly at many points that the distance doesn't bear any realistic relationship to how many miles you must drive to get there. These are very good ways to know you are talking to a native West Virginian.

Another way to identify a native West Virginian while driving along a road (especially a less travelled road) is to signal him by using the "West Virginia wave." A native West Virginian will not raise his hand to wave at you like a friendly driver in another state might do. The roads in West Virginia are far too narrow and windy to safely remove your hands from the steering wheel for any length of time. However, a native West Virginian will "wave" to a neighbor he passes on the road by raising his index finger from the steering wheel while keeping his hands on it. Of course, it only makes sense to do this with the index finger of the hand resting highest on the steering wheel at the time. Even native West Virginians standing or walking along the sides of the road will respond to this gesture from a friendly passing driver. Also, you would be wise to never confuse your index finger with your middle finger when "waving" to a native West Virginian, or you would likely provoke a very different reaction from the approaching driver. I wouldn't want you to say I didn't give you fair warning about that.

Over the years I have now lived in my adopted home of West Virginia, I have learned many other simple ways to distinguish true native West Virginians from "come-here's." Here are some of the best ways to distinguish between the two…

1. For native rural West Virginians, there is no difference between the terms "working hours" and "daylight hours."

2. You will never hear a native West Virginian ask, "Why do so many of your cows have only one teat?"

3. You will never hear a native West Virginian ask, "How much wood do I get in a cord?" (For those "come-here's" among you, a cord of cut, split and stacked firewood measures four feet high by four feet deep by eight feet long or about 128 cubic feet. Even a dumb New Hampshirite knows that.)

4. Native rural West Virginians do not have Labradoodles as pets. They much prefer a good Mountain Cur or a Bluetick Hound.

5. If you encounter a large, four-wheel drive pickup truck that has been modified to have a stacked exhaust pipe, you can rest assured that the driver is most likely a native rural West Virginian. (A truck must have a raised exhaust pipe to negotiate a ford across a creek or run, especially after a heavy storm).

6. No self-respecting native rural West Virginian would ever drive a Smart Car or a Yugo in public view (much less own one), unless it is 25 or more years old.

7. A true native West Virginian can tell you all you need to know about a person's general character in three words or less. As an important corollary to this rule, a native West Virginian will not accept you as a person he knows unless he knows your father's and/or mother's character.

8. A true native West Virginian knows that the word "Hollow" is properly pronounced "Holler" and "Kanawha" County or River is properly pronounced "Kannaw."

9. Native West Virginians prefer to drive an ATV on a wilderness trail to walking it on foot. (It's more exciting that way, and it takes less time.)

10. You will never hear a native West Virginian ask when hunting season begins and ends. Also, the answer most native West Virginians would give to that question, if asked, is that they don't recognize a beginning or ending to hunting season.

11. Only a native rural West Virginian would not be able to tell you the one cut of meat he/she prefers most from any game animal. They all know there are too many good cuts on any one animal to choose only one.

12. A native rural West Virginian will never be able to tell you where any land is available for sale, unless he knows your father or mother or it is his own.

13. Every true native West Virginian can tell you the state's motto, and official animal, tree, bird and song, and can even name at least six famous native West Virginians without having to stop and think about it.

14. All native West Virginians will look you in the eye when they talk to you. Also, if they know your mother or father, they will always ask you to come in and visit for a spell.

15. A native West Virginian knows that ramps are good to eat and when to harvest them. A "come-here probably won't even know what they are."

16. Native West Virginians know how to find their way out of the woods without a GPS. In fact, native West Virginians have no need for a GPS because they know there's no satellite service in the woods.

17. The most honest, forthright, unassuming and polite person in a casual group conversation is most often a native West Virginian. Likewise, the person in a group conversation most easily riled by the mention of a typical West Virginia stereotype is also a native West Virginian.

18. A native rural West Virginian will only go to a farmer's market to buy what didn't grow well in his/her own garden that season and will likely haggle over the price.

19. The only person in a room full of people who will know how to fix a piece of heavy equipment using some ingenuity and whatever is just lying around is either Angus MacGyver or a native rural West Virginian. By the way, Angus MacGyver is *not* a native West Virginian, although through his Scottish roots, he might well be related to one.

20. The only person you will ever meet who can be a dollar short and still make a good living without it is a native rural West Virginian.

While there may be some instances where a "come-here" could appear to be a native (assuming he or she has lived here long enough) or a native doesn't quite fit the pattern, any person who satisfies *all* of the above criteria is certain to be a native rural West Virginian. They are simply the best caliber of people I have had the privilege of getting to know. Perhaps I can't claim to have been born in my adopted home of West Virginia, but I consider that to be an accident of birth I simply couldn't control. At least I can say that I got here as soon as I could, and I have no compelling reason to ever leave. I hope you have enjoyed these little pearls of wisdom I can offer you from our experiences here at Peeper Pond Farm.

Post 137: Autumn Glory

October 21, 2019

Over the past month, I have been working hard to get everything ready for winter. Barb hasn't been able to help due to her recent surgery and hospitalization, although she has recovered significantly over the past two-plus weeks. Throughout that long work and recovery process, most of our time was spent either at the Winchester, VA hospital or at home. Now that the work is done and Barb is feeling much better, we decided to take a recreational ride to Blackwater Falls State Park and Canaan Valley on a sunny Saturday (October 19) to relax and enjoy the splendor of our fall foliage.

Most of the highest elevations in our area are past peak color, but Blackwater Falls was still strutting its foliage finery. We found the canyon walls lined with nature's pallet of brilliant red, orange, bronze and golden leaves that so epitomizes the season. The hard frost we experienced the night before had taken its toll on the foliage, but the colors remained bold. Our expectations of the season had been tempered greatly by the extended dry period we experience through August and September, so we were overjoyed that so much strong color remained. Many of the leaves in our own valley dried and withered before changing color leading us to believe that we would be disappointed in the display this season.

We competed with a large throng of tourists to find the few remaining parking spaces available at the major canyon overlooks. We had never before visited the park when such a large crowd was present. The foliage was obviously the biggest attraction. After spending more than an hour at the park, we drove through the tiny town of Davis to Canaan Valley hoping to enjoy more color. Regrettably, most of the foliage there was past its peak brilliance or had already dropped from the trees. Nevertheless, the breathtaking mountain vistas in Canaan Valley are always worth the trip, regardless of the season.

We are now waiting for the first snow of the season. Our vegetable garden is bare, except for one remaining row of yellow onions that I am hoping will mature a little more before we harvest them. They are very hardy plants, and the recent hard freeze didn't appear to faze them in the least. Now that the annual fall preparation chores are complete, we look forward to some long-deserved relaxation. It has been a busy year here at Peeper Pond Farm, and I hope we have earned some relief. Our winter supply of firewood and pellets is safely stored in our garage, and we cautiously hope we are prepared for whatever winter will throw at us. We wish all of our followers a pleasant and colorful fall.

Post 138: Apple Butter Season

November 3, 2019

We got a generous taste of early winter over the past few days. A strong storm front moved into our area on Halloween (Thursday, October 31) carried by strong, gusty winds that descended Cave Mountain and stripped away the remaining fall colors from the trees. The winds howled at more than 30 MPH at times throughout the long, dark night. It brought with it over an inch of rain, leaving us with a three-inch surplus of rainfall for the month of October. Whatever dry conditions we experienced in August and September were completely washed away in October. As the skies began to clear on Friday morning (November 1), I was surprised to notice a number of snowflakes drifting in on the intermittent gusts of wind that swept across our yard. The dry air that settled in behind the front treated us to the heaviest killing frost that we have seen this season, with a morning low of 23 degrees just before sunrise on November 2. All of this is a sudden change from the sunny, calm and mild autumn days that preceded it and blessed us with the most brilliant and glorious fall foliage we have seen in our area over the past five or six years. We will always remember the weather we experienced here in 2019 as one of the most pleasant and comfortable years we have enjoyed at Peeper Pond Farm.

Now that the harvest season has ended, we have turned our attention to helping our good friends, Jeff and Amanda Barger, make Apple Butter at their North Mill Creek Road homestead farm. We helped them harvest their wheat crop last year, and we were eager to work with them and their friends again this year to process seven bushels of apples into rich and creamy homemade apple butter. Processing apples into apple butter is just as labor and time intensive as processing wheat into flour; it's just done over a more concentrated period of time. The process began on Friday afternoon as we all gathered to peel and core all of the baskets of apples. We used both paring knives and hand-cranked apple peelers to accomplish the task, which required at least four hours of intensive work.

The work resumed early on Saturday morning (November 2), which was dedicated to boiling the apples down into a creamy butter. The boiling process was completed over a wood fire in a very large iron cauldron lined on the inside with copper. The sliced chunks of apples were gradually poured into the kettle along with water and a small amount of vinegar. The vinegar helps reduce the apples into applesauce, which will be later amended and thickened into apple butter. The apples must be stirred constantly to keep them from burning from the intense heat of the wood fire.

Stirring the boiling apples is the most time-intensive and laborious part of the process. We all took turns stirring the apples as they simmered using a traditional, handcrafted apple butter stirring paddle. This specialized device has a very long (at least four feet long) handle to which a wide, flat, slotted paddle is attached at the end, perpendicular to the handle like an overgrown hockey stick. The long handle is needed to allow the person stirring the butter to stand a safe distance from the intense heat of the fire. It also helps to do the work on a cool, fall day, like the one to which we were treated on the day we simmered the apples. Our biggest problem was having to "dance" around the kettle to remain upwind of the woodsmoke carried by the shifting gentle breeze. All the while, the deliciously sweet aroma that rose with the steam from the simmering apples lured us closer to the cauldron.

When boiling a large volume of apples, as we did, a long period of time is required to simmer the apples down into a smooth sauce, which thickens as the water content gradually boils away. At that point, seasoning can be added to taste. Jeff and Amanda prefer a mild, sweet apple butter, so they added a small amount of cinnamon and about thirty to forty pounds of sugar. Those people who prefer to make very spicy (hot) apple butter will add a larger amount of cinnamon and some ground cloves to the sauce. The best way to settle on a recipe that you prefer is to experiment until you produce the best results. There are many apple butter recipes to choose from and the process can be done in a stove-pot using a smaller and more manageable volume of apples.

We have yet to learn how many quarts of apple butter the batch produced. We had to leave early in the afternoon on Saturday, so we didn't have the opportunity to see how much apple butter was eventually canned. However, we did receive some left-over peeled and sliced apples, which Barb cooked into six half-pint jars of applesauce. She had already canned two quarts of apple pie filling earlier in the week to save for our upcoming Thanksgiving desert. Harvesting and preserving apples for the long, hard winter, no matter how it is done, is one of the traditional homesteading skills that we and many of our friends and neighbors continue to cherish and practice. We hope you will want to try it, too. It can be a lot of work, but I'm sure you will find the tasty reward to be well worth the effort.

Post 139: Allegheny Gnats

November 13, 2019

Winter weather has once again invited itself to our front door. On Monday afternoon (November 11), we were basking in 68-degree warmth. Later that night, a strong cold front swept through our area bringing a winter blast that caused the temperature to crash by more than forty degrees by the time I awoke around five AM the next morning. Tuesday was what I call an "upside down" day, climactically. Our high temperature for the day of 42 degrees occurred just after midnight and the temperature declined steadily throughout the day until we reached our low temperature for the day of 21 degrees just before midnight. The day also brought with it our third snowfall of the season.

The snow began to fall as I went to the barn to feed our goats around 6:30 AM. Although dawn was only beginning to break as a subtle glow over the mountains, I caught repeated glimpses of the first few tentative flakes of snow as they drifted before my face in the gusty breeze. This is the nature of the early snowfalls we experience in the Potomac Highlands region of West Virginia. My careful weather record-keeping over the past dozen years has taught me to expect about fifty days with snowfall over an average winter season. My records also clearly show that between one-third and one-half of those snowfall days will consist of light flurries that result in no measurable snow accumulation. That was the nature of the first two snowfalls we have experienced this month. Yesterday's snowfall resulted in only a dusting of snow on the ground even though it snowed almost continuously all day long and into the night. It only began to accumulate after the temperature dropped so far below freezing that the snow could persist on the grassy and elevated surfaces. Still, it was beautiful to watch from the warmth of our house.

Snow flurries in our area can be glorious to watch. I have actually watched flakes of snow drift down from the sky on a cloudless, sunny day. The high mountains to our west have the power to wring moisture from the clouds as they drift across their summits, causing the clouds to dissipate before they reach use. However, some of the snow those clouds deposit as they succumb to the tall mountain ridges is captured by the winds and blown into our valley. These wandering snowflakes can be carried for miles by the prevailing winds before they finally flutter down into our valley as a cloudless snowfall.

I enjoy seeing snowflakes drift aimlessly about in the wind from our front porch like tiny winter butterflies seeking a place to rest. However, I will also admit that these periodic snow flurries can be nuisance when I'm trying to do outdoor farm work because they seem intent to collect on my glasses, making it difficult for me to see what I'm doing. While the brim of the caps I wear are effective in keeping raindrops off my glasses, they are totally ineffective in protecting my glasses from snowflakes that wander about in the breeze. I guess it is this annoying tendency for snow flurries to attack your face when working outdoors that is the primary reason why natives of our region refer to them as "Allegheny Gnats." Our goat, Essie, and our cat, Calli, collect them on their fur whenever they get caught outdoors in a flurry. Unfortunately, I can't recommend a bug spray to keep them away, and you can't just brush them away with a swipe of your hand. At least they don't make highway traveling conditions dangerous.

Winters in our region can be long and confining. If heavy snow does not confine us to our homes, the fierce, biting winds will. At least we can enjoy the changing winter landscape as we generously feed our wood and pellet stoves and hibernate until the return of spring. We at Peeper Pond Farm wish you a happy Thanksgiving, a Merry Christmas, and a more prosperous New Year! If you do decide to brave the winter weather, just watch out for those pesky little Allegheny Gnats.

Post 140: The Denigration of Rural America

November 16, 2019

    If you have read most of the posts I have placed on our Peeper Pond Farm website over the past three years, you have observed my determined efforts to explain the perspectives of rural farmers and how they differ from the common misperceptions of many (but not all) urban residents in today's society. Having lived and worked in the shadows of modern urban society for most of my adult life, I have witnessed these common misperceptions in their varied forms. I have come to conclude, justifiably so, that many of them can be attributed to the lack of knowledge and experience an increasing number of urban residents have about rural lifestyles, the core values that frame them, and how they built and continue to support urban living. Today's urban youth are three-to-four generations removed from their ancestors who farmed and lived in rural areas. Over those generations, they have become progressively less knowledgeable about how the surrounding rural areas support their daily lives and the privileges they enjoy. Having been raised on a small, family dairy farm and made to feel ashamed of my heritage during my indoctrination into the outside modern world, my conscience has compelled me to educate urban society of the value our rural traditions and heritage serve to them, even today.

    Recognizing the importance and magnitude of this great educational challenge, I was deeply dismayed to learn about a November 5, 2019 social media tweet from a Harvard University-educated graduate Student Instructor at the University of California, Berkeley who boldly and arrogantly documented the level of ignorance to which urban attitudes about rural lifestyles have declined. In doing so, he has also documented quite clearly something I learned during my first semester as a University of California at Berkeley graduate student in the mid-1980s. Although I was raised and educated in my native New England by a rural community of farmers, considered by many outsiders to be close-minded conservatives, I discovered during my first UC studio class that there was such a thing as close-minded liberals—people who professed to be open-minded, but could not tolerate being challenged to rationalize or justify their views. How I came to learn it is another story that I have recounted many times in my past, but can't devote the time to explain in this post.

    Suffice it to say that I did not decide to attend the University of California entirely by my own volition. I was strongly encouraged to attend the university by one of my undergraduate school advisors who insisted that I needed to "broaden my horizons" by attending a graduate school widely recognized for being a bastion of open-minded thinking and "learning how people lived in a very different world from the one with which I was intimately familiar" (those being his exact words to me). My first choice of the five graduate schools to which I applied was McGill University, a small university and program in the big city of Montreal—the only home city of the graduate schools to which I applied (and was accepted to attend) that I had ever visited before. My strongest argument to attend McGill—that they agreed to give me a scholarship to attend—was defeated when UC, Berkeley awarded me with an out-of-state tuition waiver. Although I admit it was ultimately my choice to make, I was still transitioning into an outside world that I didn't fully understand or feel secure within, and I respectfully deferred, as usual, to the advice of the modern society experts who were kind enough to guide me. True, my attendance there gave me a piece of paper (my Master's Degree in City and Regional Planning) that was respected across the country and helped me secure jobs in my chosen career field. However, I have struggled over the years to accept (much less defend) the often-bizarre lines of thinking that have come from my graduate alma mater, but none more so than the recent "tweet" which I feel compelled to challenge. I have never felt so embarrassed to acknowledge that I spent two years of my life attending that institution. Fortunately, my life there was largely confined to the College of Environmental Design (I never lived on campus), and I never encountered someone so blissfully ignorant of rural issues and needs as the student of whom I am speaking.

I do not mention his name in this post because it is irrelevant to the core issues he raised. He is not the only person to feel the way he does about rural Americans. I do not care to attack him, because he has undermined his intellect enough by his own words that to do so would be a waste of my time simply to apply salt to his self-inflicted wound. If he doesn't feel any pain from stabbing himself, there's nothing I can say about him that would make him feel any sincere regret. I will confine my comments to his words, which is the knife he wielded publicly on social media. After all, he is not the only person I have known who has pontificated about rural issues and needs from an unenlightened urban-centric ideology and perspective.

"Mr. Urban" (as I will refer generically to him), was corresponding with someone on his Twitter account on the broader issue of affordable healthcare for rural Americans. This is an issue that I have mentioned in recent website posts over the past two months, as we struggle with the cost of my wife's recent emergency surgery for a strangulated hernia. As I, and other sources who have critiqued Mr. Urban's comments on the subject have noted and documented, the cost of healthcare has become one of the biggest contributors to rural poverty. On this point, Mr. Urban tweeted that, **"Rural healthcare *should* be**

expensive! And that expense should be borne by those who choose to live in rural America."

What he obviously did not understand is that is *exactly* what is already happening. Rural Americans (like us) who live on a fixed or limited farm income have so little access to affordable health insurance that we have struggled to afford it. My wife is currently compelled to have Medicare coverage and our required monthly co-payments for that coverage have made it too expensive for me (a fellow UC, Berkeley graduate school alumnus) to afford my own insurance coverage on our meager, fixed retirement income. Without insurance coverage, I can be freely billed (forced by law to pay) the full cost that any hospital and health care provider would choose to charge me, which is often highly inflated to make up for the money they would lose by accepting the lower payments that Medicare or other insurance providers will accept on their customers' behalf. Consequently, it is the people who have no insurance coverage (a large percentage of whom are rural Americans) who are forced to pay the full cost for their own healthcare, as well as the unpaid costs, whether legitimate or not, of those patients who *do* have insurance. That is, assuming they can even get convenient access to a hospital. Many rural hospitals have closed due to their inability to cover their operating costs.

However, Mr. Urban's offensive criticism of Rural Americans and their way of life did not stop there. He went on to pontificate, **"It should be uncomfortable to live in rural America. It should be uncomfortable not to move...I unironically embrace the bashing of rural Americans. They, as a group, are bad people who have made bad life decisions...Some, I assume are good people. But this nostalgia for some imagined pastoral way of life is stupid, and we should shame people who are not pro-city."** First of all, I would like to ask all self-proclaimed "Progressives" out there how his statements would sound to you if the words "rural Americans" in his rant were replaced by "African-Americans, or Jewish-Americans. As I have said repeatedly in previous posts, I have heard many self-anointed "Progressives" claim that they are "inclusive, enlightened, sensitive and tolerant," only to prove by their own words or actions that they are not. Mr. Urban is just the latest person from that body of intellectual elites who, by their own words, clearly demonstrate that they are not very smart. They can be just as capable of stereotyping a segment of people into a group so as to denigrate them with offensive labels as any other bigot they may despise. After all, a recent prominent "progressive" politician once relegated a body of rural people in my state to a "basket of deplorables." Is this any way to argue a point, whether you consider yourself conservative or liberal, Republican or Democrat? I'd like to refer Mr. Urban to my February 14, 2019 website post on the subject of "Shame." Hopefully, what I said in it will help make the image in his bathroom mirror a little clearer.

What many vocal critics of Mr. Urban's comments and beliefs have justly pointed out (including me in many prior website posts) is that he utterly fails to understand or appreciate where the food that supports his cherished urban lifestyle actually comes from. It is the rural Americans (like us) who grow the food that burgeoning urban populations depend upon to survive. It is also rural Americans and rural areas that produce or mine the essential natural resources that power our cities and serve as raw materials for the computer chips, transportation vehicles and medicines that make their lifestyle possible. It is the fiber from livestock raised in rural areas that provides material for his clothing and overpriced, athlete-endorsed sneakers. Rural America has made it possible for our cities to exist and grow. If every American had to grow or produce his or her own food and domestic products there would be no cities. There probably wouldn't even be enough arable land in this country to successfully house us all. This basic critical flaw in his thinking quickly undermines Mr. Urban's argument.

Although Mr. Urban eventually deleted his offensive comments and deactivated his Twitter account, he offered no express or sincere apology for his stated sentiments. He only said that he was **"pretty sure I did a bad tweet here,"** and noted that he wanted to **"reflect on it more later, but my tone is way crasser and meaner than I like to think I am."** I must agree with his sentiments about his self-image, but that's the problem I see with today's self-proclaimed Progressives. They so arrogantly and conceitedly believe they adhere to their idealistic values that they never consider how the things they say and do cross those lines. Is it any wonder why our society is politically divided?

I do remember one lesson I learned from my rural farm upbringing that I would like Mr. Urban and his fellow progressive urban elitists to learn. It was a rural pearl of wisdom I saw in the mid-1970s posted on the wall of a farm equipment dealer (R.N. Johnsons, Inc.) that we frequented on Charlestown Road in Claremont, NH. It simply said, **"Be sure your brain is in gear before engaging your mouth."** That store has long since closed. More's the pity. Since Mr. Urban is a student of philosophy, I consider that to be good food for his further "reflection." I guess this incident also explains why I say that our educational system should do a better job of teaching people *how* to think instead of *what* to think. What I'm trying to say is that the art of critical thinking has become lost in our desperate efforts to freely say and spread what we believe. If you would like me to elaborate on that statement, simply ask me to do yet another website post.

Post 141: Windstorm

November 30, 2019

    We hope everyone had a happy Thanksgiving. We enjoyed the day with our son, Michael, who was visiting from his new home in Berkeley Springs. Since moving there at the end of June, Mike has left his former Wal-Mart job to work at the Fairfax Coffee House in downtown Berkeley Springs, which is a fifteen-minute walk from his house. The shop is located across Fairfax Street from the famous Berkeley Springs State Park. We are very thankful for the change in vocation his recent move has given him because he can use the work experience he will gain by working at the coffee house to satisfy the internship requirement for his Potomac State College degree in Restaurant and Hotel Management. He has now completed the required number of work hours to satisfy that internship requirement, and we anticipate that the college will award his diploma some 7.5 years after he completed all of his coursework. If you will be visiting Berkeley Springs, WV, please feel free to stop by and say, "hello" for us.

    We are also thankful this year for surviving (with only minor damage) the Thanksgiving Eve windstorm that swept through our mountains. It is a storm that will be remembered for many years. It arrived as a "dry front" (a weather front that drops no rain or snow) late Thursday afternoon (November 27). By nightfall, the winds had built into strong, frequent gusts that roared almost constantly along the summits of the surrounding mountains. In our valley, some 1,426 feet below the summit of Cave Mountain, the ferocious gusts slammed into our house causing the walls and roofing to creak and pop under the strain throughout the long, dark night. Between the hours of 11:00 PM on November 27 and 4:00 AM on Thanksgiving Day the strongest gusts were almost constant, waking us up several times to the relentless force of the wind as it whistled through the tiniest cracks around the door and window frames. I could only imagine what damage was being caused by the periodic thuds, rattles and cracks I could hear somewhere out in the smothering gloom of night. I thought about our goats, Essie and Snowball, cowering together in a corner of their goat barn petrified with fear by the unseen ferocious night sounds just outside their walls.

    By 3:30 AM, I could lay in bed no longer. I knew I couldn't get back to sleep until I had satisfied my mind that our house or outbuildings weren't being torn apart. When I heard a brief lull in the fury, I got out of bed, put on my bathrobe and coat and went out on the front porch to see what was happening. The prevailing winds were blowing from the southwest and west. None of the furniture on our porch had been shifted, although I could hear one of the folding deck chairs I had collapsed and stacked against the wall for the winter season rattling in the intermittent gusts. That was one of the sounds I was hearing from our bedroom. I shifted it slightly, and it settled into a more stable position.

    I left the porch and walked away from the house far enough to see the slope of the roof. Our chimney pipe still stood resolutely, and I could discern from the shadowy outline of the roofline against the dimly lit starry sky that our roof remained intact. I strolled around three sides of the house to reassure myself that everything was okay and that the shed and garage doors had not been blown open. I watched the trees sway as they yielded to the brutal force of each wind gust, and I could hear loud creaking sounds from branches rubbing against one another in the woods along the ravine. I realized that might be another of the night sounds I had heard. I even stumbled once or twice as I struggled against the wind's fury. When I finally convinced myself that all was fine, I dashed into the house, leaning hard against the wind to close the door. Before I got it closed tightly, a large, dried oak leaf blew into the foyer and swept across the floor behind me. Somehow, I managed to get another hour of sleep before Calli leapt up on my side of the bed to announce that she was ready for her 5:00 AM breakfast.

    The winds began to die down shortly after dawn. By the time I had fed the goats (around 7:00 AM), they were willing to go outdoors. They seemed as curious to know how their world had been rearranged as I was. I surveyed everywhere around the house, shed, garage and goat barn. The only debris I found was some scattered limbs blown from our neighbor's dead black walnut tree. However, I did notice that our small tow-along trailer had been blown from its storage position at least ten feet back into the back corner of the garage causing several dents and scrapes in the metal siding. Although I had left the trailer ramp locked upright, the force of the wind was strong enough against the open mesh ramp to force it back. After moving it back to its original position, Barb and I chocked the tires in place with some rocks. Fortunately, the gouges left in the garage wall did not penetrate the metal siding. However, I realized that, if the trailer had not caught the back corner of the garage as it did, it might have rolled all the way down into the wooded ravine behind the barnyard (a distance of more than thirty additional feet), leaving us with a difficult task to retrieve it. Any trees in the view from our house that had retained their dead fall leaves were stripped completely bare by the windstorm.

    The windstorm also caused a recent wildfire to spread out of control in Smoke Hole Canyon (on the back side of Cave Mountain from our farm). As of today (November 30), the Dry Hollow wildfire, as it has been named, has burned

720 acres on both sides of the South Branch River. The strong winds caused many dormant and dead trees along the precipitous canyon slopes to fall adding fuel to the fire. The fire produced so much smoke that it spread throughout our valley during the afternoon on November 29 creating a smoky haze that obscured our view of the mountains beyond the nearest hills. The last such major wildfire in Smoke Hole Canyon occurred during October and November of 2013.

According to weather observations across our region, the peak wind gust we received from the storm topped 60 MPH. Official observations from the Cumberland airport to our north in Wiley Ford, WV recorded a maximum gust of 62 MPH, while the nearby Petersburg Airport recorded a peak gust of 64 MPH and Snowshoe Resort on the summit of Cheat Mountain (to our south) registered a maximum wind speed of 67 MPH. Although these peak gusts are comparable to a previous windstorm that I described in an earlier website post, entitled "The Lion Roars" (March 2, 2018), the average wind speed was much stronger during this Thanksgiving Eve storm because all of the strongest gusts we heard were longer in duration and occurred with greater frequency.

Windstorms of this nature can be relatively common occurrences in the Appalachian Mountains during the winter season (and into late fall and early spring). It is during the winter months that the northern jet stream, which is the track that drives most storms, settles along the Appalachian Mountain chain. The rugged topography of the eastern mountains compresses the winds as they flow over the folded ridgelines causing the downslope windspeed to increase as they descend into the adjoining valleys. This effect helps explain why the summit of Mount Washington (at 6,288 feet above sea level), in my native state of New Hampshire, has some of the most ferocious winds in the world.

Although our Allegheny Mountains are not known to be a "high" mountain range, they represent the first mountains of any consequence that eastward flowing winds encounter after descending from the Rocky Mountains. This is just another aspect of how the Allegheny Mountains distinguish the special natural character of our Potomac Highlands region from all surrounding areas. If you choose to experience it for yourself, expect weather conditions to be very different here. Be sure to hold onto your hat.

Post 142: Our Raw Milk Dairy Bill – Round 2

December 21, 2019

 Once again, we face the end of another year and the beginning of a new session of the West Virginia Legislature. After working closely and cooperatively with the WV Department of Agriculture's designated Dairy Specialist (Andrew Yost) over a five-month technical review period, I have revised our proposed West Virginia Farm-Fresh Raw Milk Act bill. A copy of the current bill can be found in the Appendix of this book. Although I am continuing my efforts to coordinate with the Department's attorney on their legal review, the time to submit the bill to our legislative sponsors has run short, and I felt obligated to pass it along to them to ensure re-introduction of the revised bill in the impending 2020 legislative session. I am pleased to report that Senator Dave Sypolt and Delegate Isaac Sponaugle have expressed to me their willingness to introduce our bill in their respective legislative chambers. This means we are now entering Round 2 (the second attempt) of the adoption process for our bill.

 This is good news for our ongoing efforts to open sales of farm-fresh raw milk directly between dairy farmers and informed consumers. The coming year is an election year, and many elected officials will be seeking support for their re-elections, which gives us an opportunity to build support that might not be as forthcoming in a non-election year. My prior work experience in public policy tells me that elected officials are more willing to listen and seriously consider their positions on proposed legislation when they face a re-election campaign, because their opponents might choose to make the issues and needs the incumbent rejects part of their opposition campaign. If that situation does not work to our advantage in the current election season, it may bode well for us in the legislative session following the election, if the incumbents who oppose us lose or abandon their re-election bids. This is the subtle process by which our political system evolves, and it explains why those issues with determined and dedicated advocates often prevail over time.

 While our cause faces considerable opposition from politically entrenched and well-funded lobbies, it is important to understand that we only seek to be included within the Department of Agriculture's long-standing policy of support for small family farms. As I have noted previously in my posts on our farm website, the rugged topography and limited arable land across our state makes modern, large-scale industrial farming practices very difficult if not impractical. Our heritage and land resources are far more conducive to traditional small-scale family-owned and operated farms and homestead operations, which our initiative seeks to support. It seems incomprehensible to us that any program to encourage small and diverse family farms in today's economically marginal agricultural market environment that casually ignores dairy operations could be effective. Yet, West Virginia remains one of the remaining nineteen states that still officially prohibits open consumer sales of raw milk products. More's the pity.

    We continue to care for our two dairy goats that we have raised. Esmeralda, who we raised to be one of the foundation goats of our small dairy herd, has returned to our farm. She has grown to be a very respectable milking prospect, but she spends her days wandering solemnly around her barn and goat pens. I would love to bring her into production, but absent any prospect for unprocessed milk sales, there is little justification for the cost of breeding her. We wish to encourage your support for our efforts to remove this unjustifiable sales prohibition. Please contact us if you would be willing to submit a letter documenting your support. We have done all we can to get our bill introduced. There is nothing more we can do to influence its adoption, if we can't generate meaningful public support from the consumers who will ultimately benefit. Our fate is now in *your* hands. Thanks for your continued support of our farming adventure. From all of us here at Peeper Pond Farm, we wish all of our loyal followers a heartfelt Merry Christmas and a Happy New Year.

Post 143: Christmas Frost

December 26, 2019

 Two years ago, Christmas Day 2017, we had the first official "white Christmas" of our retirement here at Peeper Pond Farm. This year, with a forecast high in the mid-50s, we weren't optimistic about our chances for a repeat, but we actually received a morning surprise that was every bit as special.

 I awoke on Christmas day uncharacteristically late (around 5:30 AM), so I was rushing about the house as quietly as I could to complete my morning routine. After feeding Calli and letting her outdoors, I quickly checked our e-mails, the weather forecast and the local news on the computer before preparing to take care of our goats, Essie and Snowball. By the time I had prepared the goats' morning apple treat, it was about 6:40 AM, and an early morning daybreak glow was beginning to emerge on the eastern horizon. As I exited the house into our barnyard, I noticed the bright sliver of a crescent moon rising just above Middle Mountain. The chilly air (the temperature was only 24 degrees) was clear at the time, and I could see the full disk of the shadowed moon glowing dimly by the sunlight reflected back to it from the Earth. The view was stunning, and I froze briefly in my tracks to appreciate the twinkling glow of the brightest stars sprinkled across the dark, cloudless sky above me.

 Realizing that I needed to get my morning chores completed before Barb and our visiting son Mike awoke, I refocused my attention on the task at hand and fed the goats their apple slices and sweet grain, cleaned up their scattered poops from the barn floor, replenished their supply of water and turned them out of the barn to enjoy the day. By the time I had finished my morning barn routine, the sky had brightened enough for me to see the landscape clearly.

 At first, I noticed a few wispy cirrus clouds above the eastern horizon basking in a faint orange glow that deepened as the sunrise evolved. The air temperature had bottomed out so close to the dew point that I noticed an ethereal foggy haze building low in Brushy Run Hollow. The ground and trees were blanketed in a heavy coat of frost that tinted every blade of grass and every tree branch in a hoary glaze of silver that basked in the morning glow. When I approached the cedar tree in our yard for a closer inspection, I noticed how each bough and twig was decorated with delicate crystalline tendrils of frosty ice that glinted brightly as they melted in the rays of sunlight, once the sun broke above the horizon.

I also noticed how quiet it was, as a gentle hush settled out of the still morning air. I watched as Essie and Snowball were standing quietly in their pen contemplating the stunning landscape with me. Perhaps even the typically boisterous animals and birds that surround our farm were awed to silence by the scene. Every breath I exhaled was revealed by a small puff of fog that hung briefly before me, then quickly dispersed into the frigid air. I stood in appreciation of the entire peaceful wintry scene completely captivated by its subtle beauty.

Christmas is a special day on which we celebrate the eternal biblical gift of spiritual life. It is a day of reflection and appreciation that, in our rush to conduct our traditional holiday rituals with family and friends, we occasionally forget to fully appreciate the bountiful beauty of the natural world that sustains us, regardless of whether it snows or not. Although my yearly hopes for a traditional white Christmas were dashed this year, I was reminded to appreciate the distinct beauty of the day we were given. After completing the rest of my morning chores, but before the sun broke over the mountains, I went out into the yard and took some pictures of the early morning scene. You can find them on the "Dave's Pictures" page of our Peeper Pond Farm website.

We hope all of you who read this post had a wonderful Christmas and that you were able to take the time to fully appreciate the natural beauty and wonder of the world around us. For that is the only way we can truly celebrate the life we enjoy. We all need to find some quiet time to reflect upon the full bounty of life, for no matter how long any of us may live, it is fleetingly short.

Author's Note: Although our homestead farming adventures will continue into 2020—and hopefully, far beyond—"Christmas Frost" is the final post from our Peeper Pond Farm website that I will incorporate into this book. Throughout the past three years of posts, I have tried to entertain you with mildly amusing incidents we have experienced, teach you the value and practice of living self-reliantly, explain the typical farmer's perspective and the core values that frame it and give you a better appreciation of the rural environment and lifestyle. I hope that they have taught you to better understand and appreciate farmers and their way of life, even if they might not convince you to live as we do. I also hope that you can find elements of self-reliant living that you can adopt to make your lifestyle in the modern world less consumptive and wasteful. That is the *first* and most critical step to make modern urban living more sustainable and affordable, if not more sensible. We appreciate all of our farm website followers and patrons, and we will continue our aggressive outreach and training efforts to preserve our small farm heritage and the traditions of self-reliant living. For those of you who reject them or can't accept my repeated assertions that they *do* have relevance to life in this new century, all I can say to you is good luck with that.

Epilogue

A Brief History of Farming

THROUGHOUT MY LIFE, I have heard many jokes about the "world's oldest profession," but I believe that farming (agriculture) is the first true profession. Why? Before humans developed the skills necessary to plant crops and domesticate wild animals to provide a reliable source of milk and meat, the only way their basic food needs could be satisfied was through hunting (including fishing) and gathering. While a hunting and gathering lifestyle can sustain a small collective (perhaps limited to an extended family or a very small tribe of related people), it is inherently inferior to an agricultural lifestyle. Hunting and gathering demands much more mobility to follow the wandering herds or to forage certain foods during times of the year when and where they would grow plentifully. It is dangerous work, as many hunters were injured or killed in the pursuit of wild game. Successful hunting also requires a team of individuals to track and kill the animal and to transport the meat back to the community. The discovery of agriculture some 10,000 years ago made it possible for humans to safely and reliably produce all the food they needed where they lived. Producing a reliable source of food where the people lived made it possible to support larger communities of people, which, in turn, led to the establishment of the earliest permanent towns and cities.

The rise of agriculture also made it easier for some community members to specialize in different pursuits. Here's the point in time where all other "professions" began to emerge. Agriculture made it possible to produce more food in far less time and with less labor than it took to hunt and gather, which gave people more time and work flexibility to learn new skills and specialize in them. Farming freed more people to pursue other lines of work that may have been better suited to their personal interests, talents and skills. In essence, farming provided the time and labor flexibility necessary for other trades (professions) to emerge. That is why I believe that farming has to be the world's first and most essential profession. Is it any wonder why it developed independently in so many areas of the world and spread so rapidly?

Once farming was established, human growth and cultural/technological development became totally dependent on it. Over time, new farming tools and methods emerged to help increase productivity to support further growth. In turn, these advances freed even more people to pursue other lines of work. Throughout much of our early history, human populations have grown and declined in direct proportion to the food supply and the climactic or societal factors (weather, wars, trade relations, etc.) that influence it. It is not a stretch of reasoning to say that the fundamental success of our society is directly influenced by agriculture and our ability to farm successfully. Yet, how much attention, understanding and importance does the average city-dweller give to the most basic farm issues and needs? How much basic respect and concern does the average farmer receive from the people whose lives and lifestyles he/she ultimately supports?

"Mr. Urban," who I introduced to you in Post 140: *The Denigration of Rural Americans*, brashly asserted that all rural Americans should be shamed for not abandoning rural areas to live in cities. Unfortunately, he is not the only person today who casually and irrationally feels that way. Although farming may be the world's first profession, it also may have become one of its least valued or appreciated. Would you or Mr. Urban really have the freedom and wealth to enjoy your non-farm lifestyle if not for farmers? Over the past century, farmers have humbly vanished into the unventured distant shadows of our increasingly modern society.

When I consider the questions I just asked, I am forced to realize that the rapidly expanding non-farming lifestyle freedoms so many people enjoy today are a relatively recent phenomenon. If you look back carefully in time, most of the early settlers of our country were engaged in some level of self-reliant agriculture until late in the nineteenth and early twentieth centuries. Our earliest founding fathers were farmers. Both George Washington and Thomas Jefferson maintained detailed records of their farming operations, and they devised many farming innovations even though they are remembered and revered almost exclusively for their work outside of their farms. Many people alive today are only two to three generations removed from ancestors who farmed. I am amazed how conveniently short our memories have become.

Even people living in relatively large cities raised vegetable gardens well into the twentieth century. Remember all the World War II Victory Gardens? Although commercial scale farming was not viable on small city or town lots, many people raised a cow or a couple of goats to provide fresh milk, a small brood of chickens for fresh eggs and meat, or maybe even a hog to butcher. Perhaps the best single example of these practices I can point to is the Great Chicago Fire of 1871. How many Americans have never heard the story of that fire being caused by Mrs. O'Leary's cow? Whether her cow actually started the fire or not is irrelevant. The fact she kept one in a barn on her property within the City of Chicago is irrefutable evidence that even city residents were practicing some basic farming activities in a predominantly urban setting. She was not alone. These simple farming practices may not have served the household's total food needs, but they supplemented it and made city living inherently more affordable.

According to the U.S. Census, the country's population did not become predominantly urban (more than 50% of the total population residing in urban areas) until sometime between the 1910 and 1920 Censuses. In 1910, the Census reported that 45.6% of the U.S. population lived in areas defined as urban. By 1920, that percentage had increased across the break-even mark to 51.2%. That urban population percentage has increased steadily ever since—even during the 1970s when there was a brief "back to the land" movement away from major cities. The most recent Census in 2010 recorded that 80.7% of the U.S. population lived in urban areas. Land development patterns over that span of time in the U.S. would show an even greater rate of conversion of farmland to developed land as well as from farmland to suburban land. World Bank population projections suggest that the world's population may have become predominantly urban during the first decade of the 21st century, or will become so by 2020.

In West Virginia, the gradual decline in rural population is not being driven as much by population growth in the state's cities (although some of them, like Morgantown and Martinsburg are growing), as it is by a comparatively faster population decline in our rural areas. As the traditional rural industries (not just coal mining) decline and employ fewer workers, rural residents (young and old) have moved away to other states in search of jobs or essential services. This rural industrial decline is a consequence of our national policies to promote global trade. It has accelerated over time, as businesses shifted their low-wage operations to former third-world and developing nations to reduce their labor and operating costs.

The gradual loss or relocation of these traditionally rural businesses and the jobs they provided actually hurt small farmers who were struggling to make a living from their farm operations, due to rising operation costs (especially for farm equipment and supplies) and unstable or anemic market prices for their products. The most determined small farmers turned to local businesses and industries to find off-the-farm, part-time jobs to subsidize the escalating costs of their farm operations. Even my own father sought a part-time sales job to earn extra income during the Arab Oil Embargo of the early 1970s.

Despite common public perceptions of rural areas, these farmers became an important source of affordable part-time labor for many rural industries as well as a stimulus for rural cottage industries, such as machine welding shops, garage repair shops and small lumber mills. A 2001 survey of urban/suburban views of rural areas commissioned by the W. K. Kellogg Foundation, entitled, <u>Perceptions</u>

of Rural America, revealed that respondents generally perceived rural America as being based almost completely on an agricultural economy even though direct farm employment only constituted, on average, about seven percent of all rural employment. When related support jobs are added, the farm-related employment total increased to slightly less than twelve percent. Isn't it ironic? As I explained at the beginning of this Epilogue, the invention of agriculture made it possible for people to create other lines of work and non-farm businesses. Yet, by the late twentieth century, the farm economy became so unprofitable that small farmers ultimately became dependent on outside non-farm employment to make ends meet. What does this evolutionary trend say about rural needs and the future of farming?

Only significant advances in agricultural technology and productivity, including a fundamental world-wide transformation to industrial-scale farming (which has been occurring in the U.S. for decades), could support and sustain our urban growth trends, *if* they are or can ever be truly sustainable. As farming becomes increasingly industrial in scale and further confined to the most productive lands, our essential food security will become increasingly threatened. Isolated weather disasters and even terrorism can become an increasing threat to farm productivity and food availability, and consequently, the price of food. Such potential threats to food supplies and price stability (not to mention increasing public health concerns over genetically modified foods) will encourage more people to desire fresh, locally-grown foods or pursue homestead farming practices, even if on a small scale. This public response has already occurred and is gaining in popularity across the country. Recognizing these recent trends, the West Virginia Department of Agriculture has espoused and promoted the economic potential for small, diverse farm operations throughout the state as a fundamental economic development strategy for a predominantly rural state. According to the 2010 Census, 51.3% of West Virginia's total population lives in rural areas, but that percentage continues to decline slowly. I hope that our effort to reopen direct farm-to-consumer sales of farm fresh raw milk will be appropriately embraced by Department of Agriculture officials as part of that platform. If you can agree, we need your support to convince them.

Our rural Potomac Highlands region continues to have one of the lowest average population densities in the state (especially in Pendleton and Pocahontas Counties) for three fundamental reasons. First, much of the region's land is publicly owned, falling within the purchase boundaries of the Monongahela and George Washington National Forests, and a significant percentage of the remaining private lands remains dedicated to farming. The extensive steep slopes throughout the region also limit more intensive development opportunities. These essential land characteristics are what attracted us to retire in Pendleton County and establish our Peeper Pond Farm there. As I have told everyone I know, the working, mountain landscape of the Potomac Highlands region reminds me of the rural, New Hampshire farming community in which I was raised during the time I grew up there.

While farming remains a significant element of the local economy, it has transformed significantly over time. Dairy farming, specifically, was once a much larger component of the local agricultural economy, but has since virtually disappeared. Having been raised on a dairy farm, I can usually identify former dairy farm operations in my travels around the region from the basic shape, style and design of the old, abandoned barns and silos that still stand. They are particularly prevalent or concentrated in the South Branch Valley, which possesses the largest tracts of flat land in the region. One of my greatest personal joys has been to ride around the region, admire and point out these historic dairy landmarks to my wife. She has even learned how to recognize them. Unfortunately, their demise also inspires a deep sense of loss and pain. Many of these farms have since been converted to poultry farms or market steer operations (feeder farms) with only enough cows to help maintain the herd. Several of our neighbors are raising small market steer herds because the market price for beef has been relatively strong lately. That allows me to stand on my porch, close my eyes and hear the distant lowing of the cows that was so familiar and reassuring to me throughout my childhood. These simple experiences reinforce my determination to live out the rest of my life in my adopted home of Pendleton County.

What It All Means to Us

Although our Peeper Pond Farm website posts cover a wide range of topics, the pride and respect I feel for farmers, farming and self-reliant living underscores them all. Our basic farming mission was to practice, explain and promote traditional self-reliant lifestyle skills, and our website posts provide an ideal forum to communicate those values. Through it all, I have encouraged people to understand how our unique natural features and resources inspired legends that help reinforce and strengthen those basic core values. In doing so they also foster a strong sense of community and identity among the generations of families who have lived and still live here. Their roots have grown deeper than any of the plants we grow in our garden. They are a people intimately tied and attached to the land that supports them.

For nearly forty years of my adult life, I lived within and tried to adapt to life in the shadows of the urban, modernized, outside world that surrounds and hems in our little slice of rural heaven. Our more recent past experiences living in the Washington, DC metropolitan area—a burgeoning, rapidly growing, urbanized area that was unfamiliar to both of us—eventually led me to regret leaving the more rural areas I had served throughout my early career. Barb and I both found it difficult to adapt to the intensely suburban environment we had suddenly moved into. The noise and traffic we experienced on a daily basis was overwhelming and unsettling. People drove so fast on the Capital Beltway that I often felt as though I was driving backwards.

We also quickly realized that urban society had become very different from the more rural communities we came to know in the early years of our marriage. The almost compulsive obsession with material wealth and vanity that we saw flaunted conspicuously throughout the Greater Washington society was as pretentious and suffocating as it was appalling. The inflated cost of living quickly consumed most of the pay we received. Many of the people I met seemed obsessively focused on a specific cause, almost to the point that they struggled to find any other meaningful purpose in life. Regardless of whether their political allegiances leaned to the extreme left or right of the spectrum, they become so entrenched in their own beliefs and positions that they simply could not give any meaningful consideration to alternative views. It often seemed that any political compromise they might be asked to consider could only be achieved at the expense of their close-minded egos and beliefs. I feel fortunate to realize that I haven't enough experience to say if these attitudes are more prevalent in our nation's capital than they are in other large cities. However, from my perspective, they help explain why politics today are so hopelessly divided and mean-spirited that no controversial issue can be effectively resolved.

I also became increasingly bored with the routine and repetitive nature of my planning work and disillusioned by the evolution of the profession in a more politically-biased and urban design-oriented direction. The different essential needs and issues of the rural areas I had served for so much of my career had become increasingly lost to an urban-focused profession that imposes a self-serving paternal attitude towards outlying rural areas and people. I struggled to reconcile the realities of how the modern business world actually worked with the traditional, rural core values that I internalized through my upbringing and could now more comfortably accept and appreciate. We had spent so much time living close to relatively isolated rural areas and small cities that we weren't adequately prepared for all the lifestyle changes we would encounter or the demands they would place on us. Over time, I began to feel as though I was a victim of my own education and experiences. After only three-and-a-half years, we desperately needed some relief from it all.

In the final analysis, it didn't matter that I had learned how to work effectively near, and plan for, urban areas. It didn't matter that I could truly appreciate a few aspects of urban life. It also didn't matter that I was driven into the outside world by the persistent cajoling of my adoptive parents and the frustrations and insecurities I harbored from my troubled family environment. I eventually came to the inevitable conclusion that I was naturally inclined to live in the rural mountain environment I grew to know from my childhood *despite* all the negative feelings and frustrations I internalized from my family. I guess Water Cronkite said it best, "That's the way it is." Just because a cat loves to eat fish does not necessarily mean it can learn to live more happily, comfortably, or successfully in the ocean. I needed a lifestyle and environment that satisfied *most* of my basic needs—not just a few. Some urban dwellers truly appreciate a rural setting and enjoy vacationing there, even though they would never desire to give up their cherished urban lifestyle conveniences to live in it. I came to the conclusion that I was inherently the opposite kind of person—and always would be.

That served as my motivation to create our own retirement homestead farm here in Pendleton County, WV. It also instilled in me a greater respect for the traditional, self-reliant lifestyle I lived during my early childhood and awakened my need to promote it as a valid and meaningful lifestyle choice. Without all the farms that feed our expanding urban population, you might find it difficult to place such high value on the latest overpriced, athlete-endorsed pair of sneakers or the newest high-tech device. I hope that my ramblings in the website posts I compiled for this book help you appreciate the sacrifices and hard work that our remaining farmers do to support the larger urban lifestyle that so many people enjoy and extoll. I hope some of you will realize the inherent value and benefits of traditional self-reliant living. I also hope that my writings will inspire you to support our ongoing efforts to reform laws that frustrate and ultimately strangle those cherished lifestyle folkways. But, most of all, I hope you will want to learn and practice these time-honored skills for yourself, for that is the best and most meaningful way to respect and preserve them for future generations who may ultimately need them for their survival.

These are my aspirations for this book, our ongoing efforts to revive our fledgling farm and my determined hope for our future. My writings represent a reverence for things that many people, especially Mr. Urban, all too casually dismiss as quaint, outdated and irrelevant. Traditional virtues, values and ways of living do not become less valuable or relevant to society simply because some people considered them to be old or outdated. Judging from the decline in civility and personal integrity inherent in today's urban society, I would suggest they have become *more* valuable, like a fine, functional antique. Having read my book, what do you think about them? Can you view them from a different perspective now? Can you appreciate them more today? If so, then you have paid me the greatest honor possible for all the work I put into this book. For that, you have earned my eternal gratitude and respect. I now hope you will help me pay it forward.

I hope you have been enticed to follow our ongoing life journey here at Peeper Pond Farm. Please feel free to visit our home. I'll gladly show you the grandeur of the view from our front porch. Then, I'll ask you to close your eyes and *listen* to the view. Every time I do that, I see a smile emerge on our visitor's face. That's when I know someone truly understands.

Appendix

WEST VIRGINIA FARM FRESH RAW MILK ACT

DRAFT – OCTOBER 10, 2019

SUBMITTED FOR LEGISLATIVE INTRODUCTION

DECEMBER 21, 2019

THE WEST VIRGINIA FARM FRESH RAW MILK ACT

October 10, 2019 DRAFT

AN ACT to amend the Code of West Virginia, 1931, as amended, by adding a new Article 38 to Chapter 19 relating to Agriculture; creating the West Virginia Farm Fresh Raw Milk Act; exempting certain sales from licensure and certification; providing definitions; providing conforming amendments; and providing for an effective date.

Be It Enacted by the Legislature of West Virginia:

> That the Code of West Virginia, 1931, as amended, be amended by adding thereto a new Article designated Chapter 19, Article 38, Sections 1 through 8, to read as follows:

CHAPTER 19   AGRICULTURE

ARTICLE 38   WEST VIRGINIA FARM FRESH RAW MILK ACT

§19-38-1. Short title.

This article is known and may be cited as the "West Virginia Farm Fresh Raw Milk Act."

§19-38-2. Definitions.

As used in this article:

> (a) "Delivery" means the transfer of a product resulting from a transaction between a producer and an informed end consumer. The delivery may occur by the producer's designated agent at a farm, ranch, farmer's market, home, office or any location agreed to between the producer and the informed end consumer;
>
> (b) "Farmer's market" means as defined in §19-35-2(c);
>
> (c) "Home consumption" means milk or milk products consumed within a private home by family members, employees or nonpaying guests;

(d) "Homemade" means food that is prepared in a private home or farm kitchen for eventual sale to a consumer;

(e) "Informed end consumer" means a person who is the last person to purchase any raw milk or raw milk product, who does not resell the product, and who has been informed that the product is not pasteurized;

(f) "Producer" means any person who milks a dairy animal (cow, goat, or sheep) to obtain milk for direct sale or processing into a milk-based product that is intended for human consumption as food or drink;

(g) "Raw Milk" means FLUID milk sold for consumption in its natural state at the time of milking and that has not been pasteurized or homogenized.

(h) "Raw Milk Products" means any food product prepared from Raw Milk for human consumption including, but not necessarily limited to skim milk, cream, buttermilk, whey, butter, cheese, ice cream, and yogurt.

(i) 'Transaction" means the exchange of buying and selling.

§19-38-3. West Virginia Farm Fresh Raw Milk Act; purpose; exemptions; assumption of risk.

(a) The purpose of the West Virginia Farm Fresh Raw Milk Act is to allow for the sale and consumption of homemade and farm fresh raw milk and raw milk products and to encourage the expansion of raw milk dairy sales by small farm producers and accessibility of their products to informed end consumers by:

(1) Permitting the limited purchase and consumption of farm fresh raw milk and dairy products made from raw milk;

(2) Expanding the agricultural economy and opening competitive markets for small dairy farms;

(3) Providing informed West Virginia consumers with unimpeded and convenient access to farm fresh raw milk and raw milk products from known sources, and

(4) Empowering the West Virginia Department of Agriculture to administer the West Virginia Farm Fresh Raw Milk Act and to

register and inspect participating small dairy farms for compliance with the Act.

(b) Notwithstanding any other provisions of law or specific requirements of the West Virginia Farm Fresh Raw Milk Act, there shall be no licensure, permitting, or certification required by any agency of any political subdivision of the state which pertains to the preparation, serving, use, consumption or storage of raw milk or raw milk products under the West Virginia Farm Fresh Raw Milk Act. Nothing in this article shall preclude an agency from providing assistance, consultation or inspection, with the consent of the producer.

(c) Transactions under this section shall:

(1) Be directly and exclusively between the producer and the informed end consumer. No consumer resale of farm fresh raw milk or raw milk products purchased under this Act shall be permitted;

(2) Only be for home consumption by the informed end consumer;

(3) Occur only in West Virginia;

(4) Not involve interstate commerce.

(d) Nothing in this article shall be construed to impede the West Virginia Department of Agriculture and/or Department of Health and Human Resources in any investigation and/or prosecution of a food borne illness that has been determined by a qualified physician to have been caused by a food-borne pathogen ingested from a food product sold under this article.

(e) Nothing in this article shall be construed to change the requirements for animal health inspections and/or any applicable vaccination requirements.

(f) Producers selling farm fresh foods in full compliance with the West Virginia Farm Fresh Raw Milk Act shall not be held liable for any consumer illness that may result from improper handling, storage, contamination, or use of the food product by the customer that occurs after the sale.

§19-38-4. Best Sanitary Milking and Milk Handling Practices.

All of the following milking and dairy herd practices shall be followed in the production of raw milk sold or processed into dairy products for human consumption in accordance with the West Virginia Farm Fresh Raw Milk Act;

(a) All dairy animals shall be milked in a fully enclosed structure or room with a concrete floor that is separated from indoor animal housing pens by a wall. Any animal waste and/or spilled animal feed or soiled bedding debris, as may incidentally result from the milking operation, shall be swept or washed from the concrete flooring of the animal milking area or parlor as soon as practicable after each milking. For small animal milking herds (goats and/or sheep), the milking area may be housed in a fully enclosed room or accessory structure (such as, but not necessarily limited to a shed or garage) having a concrete or alternative durable, washable, and impervious, flooring surface, such as but not limited to tile or vinyl, as long as its integrity is properly maintained against routine animal traffic wear and tear.

(b) Prior to milking, each udder and teat of the dairy animal shall be cleaned using a sanitary wash or wipe.

(c) Prior to milking, a strip test of milk from each teat shall be performed to check for possible milk infections. If the strip test results indicate that the animal's milk is clotted and/or bloody, no milk from that animal shall be sold or processed until the animal has been determined to be healthy and subsequently produces a clean strip test.

(d) Each dairy animal shall be milked using a fully sealed and self-contained mechanical or hand-operated vacuum system that conveys all milk directly from the teat via hoses to a glass, FDA approved food grade plastic, or stainless-steel receiving vessel.

(e) After a dairy animal has been milked, a sanitary teat wash or dip shall be applied to each teat before the animal is released from the milking stand, stanchion, or parlor.

(f) All milk collected in a self-contained milking system shall be subsequently strained (using a sanitary strainer material) when transferred to a sanitized container for eventual consumer sale and stored in a cooling device that will effectively reduce the temperature of the milk to forty (40) degrees Fahrenheit or less within two (2) hours after milking is complete.

(g) All milk handling components shall be thoroughly cleaned and sanitized as soon as practicable after each milking.

(h) Any and all raw milk intended for sale under the West Virginia Fresh Food Freedom Act shall be stored in a refrigeration device or system that will maintain the temperature of the milk between thirty-five (35) and forty (40) degrees Fahrenheit until the date of sale.

(i) Any dairy animal determined to be ill with a disease or infection that could be contagious to the rest of the herd and/or would materially impair the natural quality of the milk produced shall be housed in a separate holding pen or facility (such as a designated quarantine or recovery pen) from the rest of the herd and not milked until the illness has been treated and the animal has fully recovered. No milk incidentally or accidentally produced from any such ill dairy animal shall be processed or sold from the farm.

(j) All dairy animals shall be fed water from a clean, potable water source. All hay shall be stored in a dry location, and all pelletized feed shall be stored in a dry location and in a storage container that effectively restricts pest infestation.

§19-38-5. Registration and required permits.

(a) All producers wishing to sell raw milk and/or raw milk products shall first register with the West Virginia Department of Agriculture, providing the name of the farm, the name of the proprietor or primary operator, the mailing/physical address of the farm, a daytime contact telephone number, and the e-mail, website, and/or Facebook address of the farm, the specific milk products to be sold, and the type and number of milking animals in the producing herd. The producer shall be responsible for updating the registration information with the Department of Agriculture within ten (10) days of any changes to the required information.

(b) Prior to selling any raw milk or producing any authorized raw milk product for consumer sale, every producer shall request an inspection by the Department of Agriculture to establish the producer's compliance with all applicable requirements of the WV Farm Fresh Raw Milk Act, to ensure producer understanding of the applicable administration and penalty provisions, and to work with the inspector to identify and evaluate potential sanitary and health safety concerns regarding the producer's proposed milk handling and processing operation. The Inspector may make a written or e-mail note of his/her concerns to which the producer must respond in writing or by e-mail with proposed measures to address the Inspector's concerns, prior to authorization by the Department of Agriculture to commence sales of the intended raw milk or raw milk products. In the event that the sanitary or health safety concerns affect only one discrete element of the producer's operation, the Department of Agriculture may authorize commencement of the producer's operation limited exclusively to those elements of the operation not affected by the unremedied sanitary and/or health safety concerns, until such time as the producer has submitted an acceptable measure to address or an acceptable response to refute the applicable concerns.

(c) Prior to preparing and/or selling any authorized raw milk products, each producer shall obtain a valid WV Food Handlers card from the WV Department of Health and Human Resources. The Department of Agriculture shall inspect the raw milk production facilities as part of the initial inspection prior to the processing and sale of raw milk products, as required by §19-38-5 (b).

§19-38-6. Administration, violations, and penalties.

(a) The West Virginia Department of Agriculture shall conduct annual pre-scheduled inspections of a raw milk dairy farm operation to ensure compliance with all required Best Sanitary Milking and Milk Handling Practices or other applicable provisions of the West Virginia Farm Fresh Raw Milk Act. Such inspections may be conducted during the producer's standard milking times to ensure compliance with all applicable milking and milk handling requirements. The West Virginia Department of Agriculture also may conduct more frequent pre-scheduled follow-up inspections as may be deemed necessary [in accordance with §19-38-6 (b) and/or (c) below] to address any violations of the aforementioned requirements and provisions or until full compliance has been determined.

(b) If, during the course of a farm inspection, an inspector has determined that a producer has violated one or more of the Best Sanitary Milking and Milk Handling requirements specified in §19-38-4 of this act, the Department of Agriculture may, at its discretion and based on the severity of the violation, require the producer to comply with any or all of the following corrective measures:

(1) For a first violation,

(a). Attend a routine or special compliance training class to be scheduled and conducted by the Department of Agriculture for a reasonable training fee to be established by the Department,

(b). Suspend all sales of raw milk and milk products by the producer for not more than three (3) consecutive weeks or until the violation has been corrected as determined by a follow-up inspection (whichever is less). Any follow-up inspection(s) conducted by the Department of Agriculture to confirm a violation has been remedied shall be conducted on or before expiration of the raw milk sales suspension,

(c). Compel the producer to submit to and pass not more than four (4) additional periodic inspections within one (1) year of the date that the violation first occurred.

(2) For repeat violations,

(a). Any or all corrective measures specified in §19-38-6 (b) (1) above,

(b). Pay a fine of fifty dollars ($50) for each documented inspection violation of the act, but not more than five hundred dollars ($500) for all documented violations in any single inspection,

(c). If livestock illness is a suspected concern, the producer may be required to hire a veterinarian to certify the health condition of the milking herd.

(c) If an investigation by the Department of Health or the Department of Agriculture determines that a producer's milk or milk product has caused a food-borne pathogen illness to occur, or that a producer has falsified required registration information or materially interfered with any food-borne pathogen investigation, the following corrective measures and penalties may be imposed by the Commissioner of Agriculture on the producer,

(1) For a suspected, but not confirmed customer illness caused by the producer's milk, the Commissioner of Agriculture may, at his/her discretion, temporarily suspend all sales of raw milk and milk products by the producer until the source of the

contamination has been determined, not to exceed thirty (30) consecutive days. Any follow-up inspection(s) conducted by the Department of Agriculture to confirm the violation has been remedied shall be conducted on or before expiration of the raw milk sales suspension,

(2) If a food-borne pathogen illness is confirmed to have been caused by a producers milk or milk products, or a producer has falsified information or testimony or otherwise obstructed or interfered with an investigation of a food-borne pathogen incident, the violations shall be prosecuted and penalties assigned to the producer in accordance with the procedures specified in §19-11e-10 through §19-11e-15, inclusive. As an element of required remedial actions, the Commissioner of Agriculture may require the producer to submit to the WV Department of Agriculture two (2) samples of blended, unpasteurized raw milk from the producer's active milking herd for testing at his/her own expense. The required samples must be obtained on different days taken prior to authorized resumption of raw milk sales and/or raw milk products for sale. Said blended milk samples shall be determined by the WV Department of Agriculture to comply with the bacterial, somatic cell, and coliform counts/levels required by the Grade A Pasteurized Milk Ordinance, as amended, for raw milk that is to be pasteurized.

§19-38-7. Product sales requirements and standards.

The sale of raw milk and raw milk products shall be permitted where all of the following sale requirements are satisfied by each producer:

(a) Raw milk sales shall not exceed eighty (80) gallons per day,

(b) Sales of raw milk products (encompassing, but not limited to, butter, cheese, ice cream, and yogurt) shall not exceed forty (40) pounds per day,

(c) All milk sold shall be produced in full compliance with the Best Sanitary Milking and Milk Handling Practices specified in Section 19-38-4 of this article.

(d) All fluid raw milk shall be sold to a consumer within three (3) days from the date of milking. The processing of any raw milk product intended for sale under this Act shall commence within three (3) days from the milking date of the fluid raw milk.

(e) All milk products sold shall be labeled, in a form required by U.S. Food and Drug Administration guidelines, to identify the producer, provide a physical address and contact information, state the date upon which the milk (or milk product) was produced, net quantity of contents (in both U.S. and metric measures), the common name of the hooved animal producing the milk or milk product, and clearly state that the milk contained has been prepared in compliance with all Best Sanitary Milking and Milk Handling Practices, but is not processed, licensed, or certified by any State or Federal Agency. For all processed products prepared with raw milk, the labeling shall also list all ingredients in order from most to least by weight and list any potential allergens that the product may contain.

(f) All producers shall make available and offer each customer specific written Safe Raw Milk Handling and Use guidelines stating, at a minimum, that raw milk should always be kept in a pre-sanitized container and refrigerated at a temperature between thirty-five (35) and forty (40) degrees; not left to sit unrefrigerated for periods of time longer than may be necessary for immediate use; should be consumed or used not more than seven (7) days from the date of purchase, and should be disposed and not used or consumed if incidentally or accidentally contaminated by the consumer. The guidelines shall also include a statement that pregnant women and customers with weakened immune systems should consult a qualified physician prior to consuming raw milk or milk products. The producer may add any further handling and use guidelines that may be deemed necessary, in consultation with his/her insurance provider, to address specific liability concerns. The guidelines may further state that the producer assumes no liability for illness that is caused by improper handling and use by the customer.

(g) The producer shall offer and afford any potential customer an opportunity to schedule a tour/inspection of the producer's farm, animal housing, milking operation, and/or milk processing operation prior to purchase of any raw milk or milk product under this Act. The producer shall, as a minimum requirement of each tour, specifically explain and demonstrate how his/her operation complies with each of the required Best Sanitary Milking and Milk Handling Practices outlined in Section 19-38-4 of this Act and either provide a printed copy of those requirements or permanently post a printed copy of those requirements in the milking area/room, which shall be replaced as may be necessary to ensure legibility against fading, wear, and tear.

(h) Any formal agreement or contract for raw milk or milk product sales between a producer and customer shall include and state (affirm) the producer's compliance with the Best Sanitary Milking and Milk Handling Practices outlined in Section 19-38-4 of this Act.

§19-38-8. Effective date.

This act is effective immediately upon completion of all acts necessary for a bill to become law as provided by the West Virginia Constitution.

(END)

Made in the USA
Columbia, SC
11 February 2021